The Free *

Patrick County Virginia in the Civil War

By Thomas D. Perry

Copyright 2011 Laurel Hill Publishing LLC

ISBN-13: 978-1460928257
ISBN-10: 1460928253
Library of Congress Control Number: 2008934024

Cover photo by Elizabeth Ann Guynn Markwith in 1990 at the first Civil War Encampment at the Laurel Hill Farm of cavalry reenactors fighting at J. E. B. Stuart's Birthplace in Ararat, Virginia.

Title Page Photo by Thomas D. Perry of Confederate Veterans Statue at Patrick County Courthouse in Stuart, Virginia. Plaque on base is of James Ewell Brown Stuart. Statue is Confederate Infantryman placed on courthouse grounds in 1936.

Third Edition Copyright 2011 by Thomas David Perry

All rights reserved.

Laurel Hill Publishing
4443 Ararat Highway
P. O. Box 11
Ararat, VA 24053
freestateofpatrick@yahoo.com
www.freestateofpatrick.com

For my father Erie Meredith Perry

"One can never understand what the United States is
until one understands what the Civil War was."
-- James I. Robertson , Jr.

January 26, 2019

For Aaron,

Hope you enjoy!

M Perry

DEAR BOBBY

SOMETIMES YOU GET LUCKY AND STUMBLE ACROSS HISTORY. THE LUCKIEST MAN ALIVE IS ONE WHO HAS FRIENDS SUCH AS YOU.

AARON
1-31-2019

Also by Thomas D. Perry

Ascent To Glory:
The Genealogy of J. E. B. Stuart

The Free State of Patrick:
Patrick County Virginia In The Civil War

J. E. B. Stuart's Birthplace:
History, Genealogy, and Guide

Images of Patrick County Virginia

Images of Martinsville Virginia

Mount Airy, North Carolina

Notes From The Free State Of Patrick:
Reflections On Patrick County, Virginia, and Regional History

Patrick County Oral History Project: A Guide

J. E. B. Stuart Birthplace: A Guide

Visit www.freestateofpatrick.com for more information

Table of Contents

Foreword	7
Chapter One Patrick County During the War	9
Chapter Two Patrick County's Confederate Soldiers	27
Chapter Three Rufus Woolwine and the Fifty-First Virginia Infantry	35
Chapter Four Company K, 50th Virginia Infantry Regiment	53
Chapter Five Company H, 42nd Virginia Infantry Regiment	111
Chapter Six James Ewell Brown Stuart and Patrick County	137
Chapter Seven George Stoneman's 1865 Raid	157
Chapter Eight Civil War Letters 1861-1865	171
Chapter Nine Regimental Histories of Patrick County Units	235
Roster of Confederate Soldiers	247
Roster of Union Soldiers	323
Pension Applications	324
Disability Applications	330
Patrick County, Virginia and Confederate Officials	332
Southern Claims Commission Applications	334

Robert E. Lee Home Applications	335
United Daughters of the Confederacy Applications	336
Patrick County Patrol Rosters	337
Free Negros and Slave Requisitions	339
Acknowledgements	342
Bibliography	346
Index	353

Foreword
"The Undiscovered Country"

"War, war, war," Vivien Leigh says as Scarlett O'Hara at the beginning of the movie Gone With The Wind foretelling our country's obsession with the cataclysm that nearly split our nation asunder. Between 1861 and 1865, this nation fought a war that still leaves its mark on us today. Whether it is states' rights or civil rights, the war resonates through our national epoch as the single most important historical event along with our most popular movie.

The Lincoln Administration called it the "War of the Rebellion," viewing the Southerners as traitors. Calling it the "War Between the States" is popular in the South to mark the importance of states' rights in the conflict. Most historians, the public at large and even participants such as Nathan Bedford Forrest refer to it as a "Civil War." For the people of Patrick County it was the "War for Southern Independence" reflecting an inheritance from the American Revolution and the independent nature of those inhabiting the "Free State of Patrick."

The "Free State of Patrick" is more a state of mind than a historical fact. The term "Free State" has two different meanings with relation to the Civil War. The residents of Lunenburg County, Virginia, refer to it as "The Old Free State." Lunenburg, representing the pro-Confederate viewpoint, threatened to secede from the "Old Dominion" if Virginia did not secede from the United States. Patrick County came from land once part of Lunenburg in 1791. Jones County, Mississippi, represented the pro-Union viewpoint during the war calling itself the "Free State of Jones" and acting as an independent country within the home state of the President of the Confederate States of America Jefferson F. Davis.

War is a hard lesson for a nation and harder still on the people involved. This book relies on facts divulged from primary sources and the contributions of countless others. These writings try to show the many aspects of life including the struggles and contributions of those famous and infamous, both black and white, of Patrick County involved in a war over one hundred and forty years ago and the cost they paid for it. For those of African descent, the war made Virginia a "Free State" in name, but another hundred years would pass before it was a reality. The people of Patrick County were among the first Americans to lose a war. It left some bitter, but most moved on making a future for their families. Some of the actions depicted reflect well on those involved and some do not. These people lived in a time not our own. We should remember their sacrifice and their role in shaping our nation's history not judge or deny them empathy because they do not reflect our present view of the world.

This book began in 1990 as articles commemorating the bicentennial of Patrick County for the local newspapers. The ideas to combine those articles on J. E. B. Stuart, Rufus Woolwine, Stoneman's Raid and enhance the research of the late Ophus Eugene Pilson in the History of Patrick County on Confederate soldiers and their unit histories came in late 2002.

Anyone reading is encouraged to share photos, letters, or any other information relating to the many subjects touched on by this book for future additions. All mistakes are mine and corrections are welcome.

Robert E. Lee said, "It is history that teaches us to hope." History can shed light on our past and project hope for our future. The Civil War reunited a nation, which saved the world from fascism and communism in the twentieth century. This nation continues to be a beacon to those who strive for freedom and democracy. Shakespeare called the future the "Undiscovered Country." If we as people can delve into our past and divine inspiration from it, the future will be bright for the United States of America. After all, as Scarlett stated so aptly, "Tomorrow is another day."

Patrick County Notes, courtesy of Gerald Via printed by Sterling, Campbell and Albright of Greensboro, North Carolina and served as currency during the war.

Chapter One
"The Free State of Patrick"
Patrick County During The Civil War

Patrick County's population, according to the 1860 Census of the United States, was just over 9,300 people. Of these, twenty-two percent were slaves and one percent were free persons of color. There were two hundred fewer people in the county than in 1850 and less than three hundred people lived in the county seat of Taylorsville, but better known as Patrick Court House. Agriculture continued as the main source of livelihood with 655,454 pounds of tobacco, 185,202 bushels of corn and 19,571 bushels of wheat produced in 1860.

The presidential election in November 1860 changed the course of American history for generations to come. Patrick native Lieutenant J. E. B. Stuart of the First United States Cavalry, then building Fort Wise in the present-day state of Colorado, favored John Bell of the Constitutional Union Party. Bell won Patrick County by two votes and carried Virginia over former U. S. Vice-President and future Confederate General John Breckinridge who represented the Southern Democrats. The other two candidates, both from Illinois, were Stephen Douglas of the Northern Democrats and Abraham Lincoln of the Republican Party. Lincoln, the winner and sixteenth President of the United States, did not appear on the ballot in Virginia.

Events moved rapidly after the election. South Carolina seceded on December 20, 1860. Governor John Letcher, a Democrat and cousin of the Stuart family, called the General Assembly of Virginia into special session in January 1861. A special election held on February 4, 1861, sat delegates for a convention to consider Virginia's secession. That same day delegates from the seven seceded states (South Carolina, Mississippi, Florida, Alabama, Georgia, Louisiana and Texas) met in Montgomery, Alabama, to form the Confederate States of America.

Samuel G. Staples, representing Patrick County, joined 151 other delegates in the Virginia Convention that began meeting on February 13. The United States inaugurated Abraham Lincoln as president on March 4. On April 4, Staples voted against secession. Lincoln called for 75,000 troops to put down the "rebellion" after the firing on Fort Sumter on April 12. In response, the Virginia convention voted 85 to 55 on April 17 to submit secession to the people for a vote. On May 23, 1861, Virginia's citizens ratified secession from the United States of America and joined the Confederate States of America. Patrick County voters (white male landowners) went 699 to 161 for secession. The Confederates moved the Southern capital from Montgomery, Alabama to Virginia's Capitol, Richmond, where it remained for the next four years.

A group of "Gentleman Justices" elected by the voters met once a month at the county seat of Taylorsville to govern Patrick County as the Board of Supervisors does today. The county recorded the actions of these men in Order Books 8 and 9, which form the basis for much of this chapter. A roster of those who served is included in this book.

Patrick County appropriated $10,000 to equip local troops for the "defense of the state." Other than the hiring of contractors to head off a possible "derangement" of the mail service, life continued in the "Free State of Patrick" with no notice of the impending crisis. County records show the murder of John Vaughn, a break-in at the "stillhouse" of John Anglin, expenditures of $400 to complete the Christiansburg/Floyd Turnpike, and a charge of "basterdy" against another man.

As early as May 1861, the county showed concern for the "Indigent Soldiers," those lacking the necessities of life due to poverty, and their families. The justices chose one of their own from each geographic section they represented "to wait upon the families of the volunteers." As the war progressed, material and food became harder to obtain and taking care of these people continued to be a major source of discussion, expense, and concern for county officials. A month later, the county approved $600 for the families of the volunteers and a bond issue of $20,000 for equipping the volunteer soldiers with thirty dollars going to each man. The justices appointed Beverly A. Davis, Thomas J. Penn, and Hardin W. Reynolds as agents to issue the bonds.

County officials included Commonwealth Attorney John W. Shelton at an annual salary of $150.00. Clerk of Court Henry Tuggle received an annual salary of $75.00. Sheriff Murray Turner collected pay as jailor for a total of $100.00. The Surveyor of the Road, James Soyars (Sawyers), received $2.50 in May 1861. J. W. Hatcher received $3.00 for patrol duty. Captain J. Thomas Clark took home $4.09 for patrol duty. The firm of Joyce and Fain received $10.00 for an inquest. John Cruise collected $1.50 for conducting an election. Asa Wood received $36.00 for twelve days work as a Justice. An expenditure of $300.00 for building a fence around the courthouse made the total expenditures in June 1861 $2,847.76. Patrick County reported 343 births and 207 deaths in 1861.

The life of free blacks and slaves in Patrick County during the war included tight control and forced service to the South. A law passed in 1793 required all "Free Negroes" to register at their local courthouse every three years and purchase a certificate at a cost of twenty-five cents. The law required them to give their name, age, color (mulatto or black), status, to report what court had emancipated them and made it illegal to employ a free person without the above certificate. In June 1861, four free black women--Hannah Going, Ruth Going, Jennie Johnson and Rachel Johnson--registered at Taylorsville.

Five hundred thousand "free people of color" lived in the entire nation in 1860, and a quarter million lived in the South. Virginia's free black population reached nearly sixty thousand. One hundred and thirty-one called Patrick County home in 1860. Between 1820 and 1860, never more than 140 "free people of color" lived in Patrick County. As blacksmiths, wagoners, wheelwrights, farmers and laborers, these "free people" made up a productive part of the population, though only five owned real estate. Always suspected of being runaway slaves, they lived under a harsh set of rules that forbade them entry into certain professions and even prevented selling agricultural products without a license.

The Virginia General Assembly passed a law on February 12, 1863, calling for the "enrollment and employment of free Negroes" in the war effort. On September 29, 1863, Confederate authorities conscripted James or Jarvus Beaver, Alis Fenly, Josephus Givny, Soloman Johnson, Edward Loggin, Jackson Loggin, Samuel Nelson, Governor Phillips, Peter Rickman, Harrison Steward, Henry Steward, Salie Stuart, Granville Stuart, William H. Travis and John Vaughan into service. This service was for laborers, not soldiers.

Records exist relating to several of these people. Governor Phillips stood five foot ten inches tall with black eyes, black hair, and black complexion. On July 1, 1864, he reported to Lieutenant Poole under the direction of the Confederate Quartermaster Department commanded by I. H. Lacy at New Bern in Pulaski County, Virginia. Granville Stewart, Josephus Goins, William Harris, James M. Hickman, Soloman Johnson and Jacob Lac reported to New Bern also. These men enrolled from several counties, but all were born in Patrick County.

The rise of Union General Ulysses S. Grant, coinciding with the fall of Forts Henry and Donelson in Tennessee in early 1862, sent Southern hopes spiraling downward. Men from Patrick County fought and died along the Tennessee and Cumberland Rivers. The county granted James B. Smart administration of the estate of his dead son, William S. Smart of the 51st Virginia Infantry Regiment, who had died at Fort Donelson.

Problems closer to home made life in Patrick County harder for those left behind on the home front. Inflation, transportation problems, labor shortages, and the seizure of food and livestock were among the hardships Patrick County residents endured.

On March 8, 1862, Virginia's General Assembly confirmed a contract for 4,000 bushels of salt. In May, the county appropriated $13,000 to purchase salt. The "white gold" served as the main preservative for meat and fish before the days of refrigeration. Reverend Beverly A. Davis acted as agent for the county. Distributors throughout the county included Henry B. Terry, James Rangeley, George Hylton, Nathaniel S. Moore, Charles Ross and William H. Corn. No one received more than twenty pounds of salt. The county purchased the salt from Stuart, Buchanan and Company of Saltville managed by William Alexander Stuart, Patrick native and brother of J. E. B. Stuart.

Not everyone experienced shortages of salt and other primary goods. Abram David Reynolds, oldest son of Hardin and Nancy Cox Reynolds, recounts in his memoirs (written fifty years after the war) many interesting stories relating to life in Patrick County during the war. Born in 1847 at the Reynolds Homestead, Rock Spring Plantation, Abram Reynolds, was too young at the beginning of the war for active service, but his persistence soon got him into the fray.

In the fall of 1862, Hardin Reynolds sent his fifteen-year-old son to West Virginia with a four-horse team and one slave to purchase salt for the family. Young Reynolds traveled with a Mr. Patterson of Franklin County, who also had a team and brought one slave along for the journey. Together they came up with a scheme to make their trip a success. One day Reynolds rode ahead on Patterson's horse and collected corn and feed for the teams. The next day Reynolds stayed with the wagons while Patterson traveled ahead. The country they entered was desolate and many people traveled before them. Reynolds wrote, "Before we could reach Charleston we were ordered to turn back and everything was being rushed at such a rate the Salt wagons had to leave a part of their load which we bought at nearly the same price they paid. So very soon we had all the Salt we could pull with our corn which was not half yet fed." Reynolds "peddled" tobacco to pay for expenses along the way, and his father "rejoiced" at his return with 4,000 pounds of salt that they sold at their store until the end of the war.

Another person living at the Reynolds Homestead was Kittie Reynolds, the slave whom tradition says saved the life of her owner, Hardin Reynolds, when she distracted a raging bull long enough for him to escape it. Perhaps her children should be more famous. On November 29, 1877, two of her sons, Burwell, age 19, and Lee, age 17, got into a fight with the white brothers Green and Aaron Shelton. The cause of the altercation was verbal harassment by the Shelton boys directed at a school for former slaves. The site today overlooks Campbell's Branch near the maintenance garage of the local school system. The resulting fight ended with the death of Aaron Shelton and murder charges against the Reynolds brothers. The case known as Ex Parte Virginia reached the Supreme Court of the United States, which agreed that the Reynolds did not receive equal protection under the law violating the Civil Rights Act of 1875 and the Fourteenth Amendment.

The Virginia General Assembly passed laws in March and May 1862 for banks to issue notes for less than five dollars and greater than one dollar in towns of 2,000 or more in population. The "Gentlemen Justices" of Patrick County approved the printing of $12,000 in money in

June of 1862. The county distributed and redeemed this money, better known as the "Patrick County Notes," in one-third increments in January 1863, 1864, and 1865 respectively. The county authorized $500 in five-cent notes, $2,000 in ten-cent notes, $4,000 in fifty-cent notes and $2,500 in seventy-five cent notes in June 1862. In September 1862, the county authorized $100 in five cent notes, $200 in twelve and one-half cent notes, and $12,000 in one dollar notes. In November, the county ordered $2,500 in one dollar notes. Inflation and economic pressure made the larger denomination more convenient. Abram Staples extended the "Patrick County Notes" in small denominations valued at $5,000 with 1,000 in fifty-cent notes and the remainder in one-dollar amounts during July 1863. Sterling, Campbell and Albright of Greensboro, North Carolina printed the Patrick County monies. The shortage of paper resulted in printing the 1863 notes on the back of bank notes from the Farmers Bank of North Carolina, in red, green and black ink. (Two large collections of these finely scripted notes still exist.)

The excess of available printed money such as the "Patrick County Notes" along with concerns about the real value of currency, no regulation of money, no internal taxation, and the lack of circulation within Federally controlled areas resulted in inflation that plagued the Confederacy during its short existence. Inflation curtailed credit and the South's ability to supply and wage war. Two years after the firing on Fort Sumter, domestic goods cost six and one-fourth times more, and were eleven times higher a year later. In January 1865, the $1 that in April 1861 was worth $1 in gold was worth $53. One dollar's worth of flower in 1861 cost $43 four years later. Bacon cost $67 in 1865. Coffee worth $1.30 at the beginning cost $196 at the end of the war.

The Confederate States of America implemented the first draft in American history in April 1862. All white men ages 18 to 35 were "subject to the military service of the Confederate States." Authorities took action one month before the twelve-month enlistments of the 148 regiments ran out.

The hiring of substitutes became a controversial part of the system with fraud becoming prevalent. The law permitted one substitute per month per company. Early in the war, payment for a substitute ranged from $1,500 to $3,000. The law exempted many professions from the draft such as government clerks, mail carriers, college professors, and plantation overseers. An extension of the upper age range for conscription from 35 to 45 occurred in September 1862. Another law passed in February 1864 expanded the range to fall between 17 and 50 years of age.

In the summer of 1862, the C. S. S. Virginia fought the U. S. S. Monitor in the first battle of ironclads. Confederates had built the Virginia on the hull of the Union vessel Merrimac. Tradition states that

Confederate authorities considered the quality of the iron ore in Patrick County so "superior" that some of the finished iron plates protected the Virginia. No written documentation exists on the connection between the Patrick County iron and the ironclad.

The major industrial complex in Patrick County during the war was Samuel Hairston's furnace and forge along the Smith River. George Hairston II, son of George Hairston and Elizabeth Perkins Letcher Hairston began iron operations and mining on Goblintown Creek after 1836. Samuel W. Hairston inherited the property in 1851 and continued operation until 1862 when John P. Barksdale, Jonathan B. Stovall, and Elisha Barksdale of Halifax County purchased the "Iron Works and Union Furnace" of 4,840 acres for $150,000. Much of this area, later known as Fayerdale, lies beneath the waters of Fairy Stone State Park today.

Another interesting sidelight to the war effort involved Major William Werth. He served early in the war in the 45th Virginia Infantry and after the war owned the Patrick Springs. Werth, a chemist, made steel from iron ore through a blistering process at Barksdale, Stovall and Company. The process involved placing ore underneath boxes of iron bars with chemicals placed in the space between the ore and the iron bars. This created blistered steel when fired. Stoneman's raiders destroyed the forges near the end of the war.

As the summer of 1862 progressed, Robert E. Lee led the Army of Northern Virginia into legend with victories in the Seven Days and at Second Manassas until checked along the banks of Antietam Creek near Sharpsburg, Maryland. (Confederates named battles after local towns or landmarks while Union forces named the same battle after a nearby body of water or geographic landmarks.) Patrick County native James Ewell Brown "Jeb" Stuart emerged as a cavalry leader during 1862 with multiple rides around enemy armies that provided solid reconnaissance for Lee.

In 1860, nearly four of the nine million people living in the states of the Confederate States of America were slaves. Virginia's slave population was nearly five hundred thousand. The 1860 Census of Patrick County listed 2,070 slaves with 318 owners. Taxes on slaves made up about eight percent of the county revenue. Samuel Wilson owned the largest number of slaves with ninety-nine, but over half the slave owners held five or less.

At the beginning of the war, the county appropriated 4,000 dollars for equipping patrols to "police for the county." Patrols for the six districts had the following captains: Penn's Store, J. Thomas Clark; Court House, D. L. Hanby; The Hollow, Madison Carter; Mountain, R. A. Terry; Elamsville, Charles Ross; Hancock's, Peter Corn. These patrols looked for runaway slaves, broke up slave gatherings, searched for deserters, and kept the peace in general throughout the county during the war. Patrols continued with the following captains in December 1862: District #1, Richard Ziglar; District #2, D. S. Hanby; District #3, H. J. Moore; District #4, M. L. Lawson; District #5, S. H. Turner; District #6, S. G. Joyce. This book contains a roster of the men who served.

Near the end of 1862, Patrick's justices received a request from Governor John Letcher for non-combatant slaves "to labour on fortifications and other works necessary for the public defence." The county appointed a committee including Barnes Carter, Asa Wood, G. H. Ashworth, J. W. Brammer, Reuben Ziglar, and Richard Wood to procure slaves in each of their districts. Sheriff Turner received 63 slaves on December 30, 1862. The use of slaves as teamsters, cooks, personal servants to officers, and laborers to dig trenches and build earthworks enhanced the Confederate war effort and made up for the disparities in numbers between Union and Confederate forces. September 1863 brought another requisition of forty-eight slaves for delivery on October 12, 1863.

In 1862, Abraham Lincoln took the opportunity of Lee's strategic loss at Sharpsburg to announce the Emancipation Proclamation. The document freed slaves only in those states in "Rebellion" against the Federal authorities and took effect on January 1, 1863. Lincoln exempted the slave states Delaware, Kentucky and Missouri, keeping their slaves in bondage.

Meanwhile, emboldened by his son's success with the salt, Hardin Reynolds sent Abram from Patrick County to North Carolina cotton mills to purchase "spun cotton" for resale to loom operators. Ignoring the warning signs of a smallpox outbreak, Reynolds returned to Patrick County with the cotton only to have his father censure him severely. Hardin immediately vaccinated all his children against the disease. The three youngest children died in late October 1862. Within two months, Hardin wrote to the Virginia Military Institute requesting an appointment for his oldest son.

Patrick County parents saw many of their children die of disease during the war due to smallpox and fevers. In two years beginning in 1862, the death register reports 145 children dying of diphtheria alone.

The condition of the jail plagued county officials throughout the war. The war produced larger numbers of prisoners and the facility in Patrick could not safely hold them. Early in the war, Floyd County held prisoners for Patrick, and Henry County did the same in 1863. In October 1862, the "Gentleman Justices" voted to build a new jail for the county and appointed a committee to look into construction. Commissioners Crawford Turner and Silas Carter advertised to build a jail in July 1864, but they received no bid within the limits. In 1862, the county charged the Confederate government $10.30 and Virginia $23.40 for jailing deserters. By October 1865, the Order Book stated that using the jail was not possible.

The Danville Appeal reported "considerable excitement" in Patrick County when, on October 10, 1862, Jack Bryant fired a pistol at a recruiting officer named Jones, who returned fire and mortally wounded the offender. The paper also reported that same day that an officer named Hatcher was escorting two prisoners, Moore and Rorrer, to Danville. Near Bull Mountain, someone ambushed the party, wounding Rorrer. Hatcher fled on foot after the ambushers shot his horse. The paper noted that the county was "thoroughly aroused."

The year 1863 witnessed the "Confederate High Tide" with victories in the eastern theater and the march into Pennsylvania. Victory in the western theater at Chickamauga in northern Georgia cost the lives of men from the "Free State" as did the Battle of Gettysburg. Patrick County's own "Jeb" Stuart had his greatest day as a soldier when he took command for the wounded "Stonewall" Jackson in May at Chancellorsville. Stuart reached his zenith in June when commanding nearly 10,000 men in the largest cavalry battle of the war at Brandy Station.

In April, the county court convicted Henry, a slave of Thomas J. Penn valued at $1800, for breaking in and stealing property from his owner including $1,300 in currency, $13,000 in bonds, clothing, a horse, bridle, and a saddle worth $700. In addition, Henry broke into the workshop of a free black man named James Travis on the Penn's property, stealing clothing and cash. The judge sentenced Henry to hang on June 26, 1863.

Patrick County became increasingly concerned about the plight of its "indigent soldiers" and their families and $4,000 approved in 1863 for them. In May, the county appointed Nathaniel S. Moore to travel to Georgia to buy corn for the "relief of the people of this county" and have it shipped back to Patrick County via High Point or Greensboro, North Carolina. The county suffered through a drought in the summer of 1862 and a very harsh winter into 1863. Patrick County appointed Murray Turner commissioner and authorized him to borrow $15,000 for the indigent soldiers and their families in October 1863.

The county made payments to officials such as $200 to John Shelton as Commonwealth Attorney, $100 to Abram Staples as acting Clerk of Court, $75 to Sheriff Turner, $20 to L. G. Rucker as Jailor, $100 to James Nowlin as Keeper of the Court House and $21 to Banes Carter for seven days service as Justice of the Peace.

As Lee's army fought at Gettysburg in July 1863, the justices instructed James Moir to act as agent to procure salt for the county. Moir asked 8,000 dollars to purchase two "Negro men" for assistance with the salt works in Saltville. Benjamin Campbell distributed 200 bushels of corn among the poor women and children of the county. The following month John Staples, representing Patrick County in the General Assembly of Virginia, requested an exemption on the grain tax due to a shortage in the county and asked that the county's indigent soldiers, widows and children receive the money.

A letter written to officials in Richmond from Henry County in August 1863 reports a growing concern about the morale of the people and the problem of desertion in Patrick and surrounding counties. "The people seem completely demoralized, and this state of things exists to a great extent among the best citizens. They think and say we are whipped and are bound to be overrun and subjugated. The impression has very extensively obtained that our Army is dispirited and is deserting by hundreds; that whole regiments have left at a time; and the upper counties of North Carolina are much worse than those that I have mentioned, so I learn. A good many deserters are passing the various roads daily, and greatly increase the demoralization. These deserters almost invariably have their guns and accouterments with them, and when halted and asked for their furloughs or their authority to be absent from their commands, they just pat their guns and defiantly say, 'This is my furlough' and even enrolling officers turn away as peaceably as possible, evidently intimidated by their defiant manner." Confederate President Jefferson Davis offered pardon to all deserters that month, if the men would return within twenty days. The General Assembly passed a law in October making local officials responsible for organizing "Home Guards" to arrest deserters.

On September 22, the General Assembly of Virginia passed an act to "suppress the further issuance of small notes to be used as currency." Patrick County printed the last group of "Patrick County Notes" on October 1. With the shortage of paper Sterling, Campbell and Albright of Greensboro, North Carolina, printed the money on the back of notes from the Farmer's Bank of North Carolina.

In December 1863, Governor John Letcher pardoned a Patrick County man, ending the strange case of Notley Price Adams. The case began in April 1859, when officials accused Notley P. Adams of burning the vacant home of Jefferson T. Lawson near the Patrick and Floyd County lines along the Dan River and the Laurel Fork. The evidence consisted of a strange horseshoe track and a broken twig off a bush from near the burnt home. Two months earlier, the records of the Patrick County courts listed five cases involving Notley including perjury, assault, and battery.

Born the illegitimate son of William Price in 1801, Notley was not an Adams. The court records state that trouble between Notley and William Price began in 1832 and local tradition claims he changed his name to his stepfather's in defiance of his father. Notley married Celia Akers in 1823. Their union produced nine children.

Local tradition says Notley P. Adams stood before a judge in 1859. Asked to state his name, "Not Adams" he replied. The aggravated judge said, "Well, then who are you?" which he heard again, "Not Adams." The exasperated judge stated, "Well, if you are not Adams, who are you?"

Over the next four years, Adams had four trials. The first, in April 1860, resulted in a hung jury. The next, in July, resulted in a guilty verdict. The presiding judge overturned it. In September 1862, another trial held in Henry County resulted in another hung jury and a year later another guilty verdict. Adams spent nearly three years in prison and his health suffered.

Gabriel Bowling, who married Adams's daughter, led the campaign to pardon his father-in-law. Lawyers deposed many prominent citizens of Patrick County about the case. Others expressed an opinion on the pardon in private communication to the Governor. Among those in favor of the pardon was William Burwell, and against it was Rufus Woolwine.

Trouble continued to follow Adams after the Civil War. He declared bankruptcy in 1868. Notley Adams died of a "deranged mind" on November 15, 1882. Jefferson Lawson served as Captain of Company K, 50th Virginia Infantry during the war and was a state senator afterwards. The Library of Virginia holds Adams's pardon papers in the Executive Papers of Governor John Letcher.

William "Extra Billy" Smith assumed the Governorship of Virginia in 1864. In Patrick County, human needs continued to rise in prominence for the county government with 840 indigent soldiers dependent for support and 2,520 bushels of grain needed to feed them. Commissioners Banes Carter, R. J. Wood, and S. J. Adams distributed corn to these people. Gabriel Critz, A. A. Moir, Nathaniel S. Moore, Henry B. Terry, and W. H. Moir distributed salt.

Abram D. Reynolds began seven months at the Virginia Military Institute in Lexington, Virginia in the summer of 1863, but appeared unannounced at home in March 1864 saying he had been dismissed. Reynolds, now 17, qualified for service in the ever-expanding age ranges for Confederate soldiers. He rode to Taylorsville, gave a rousing speech and in an election as company captain defeated a John Stovall, who campaigned with a ten-gallon jug of apple brandy. Reynolds entered Company I, Fifth Battalion Virginia Reserves. By September, Reynolds (recently promoted to major) commanded 66 men.

Benjamin Campbell, the county agent to the Confederate States of America, asked permission for 2,500 bushels of corn and wheat and petitioned the authorities in Richmond for another 2,000 bushels as there was a surplus of government grain in the county. The county authorized $10,000 and appointed James M. Tatum as agent for the county to purchase cotton yarn, raw cotton, and cards of cotton and wool.

In April 1864, the county appointed another committee to "procure corn" for indigent persons. Hardin W. Reynolds, Abram Staples, Nathaniel S. Moore, Thomas J. Penn, Charles Ross, and John Anglin as members were to purchase iron from Barksdale, Stovall and Company, carry it to Georgia and swap it for corn. The county asked the Confederate secretary of war, James Seddon, to supply transportation.

Other signs of the pressure citizens dealt with included 1864 when Barksdale, Stovall and Company refused to release a list of slaves for possible requisition by the government. Delinquent property taxes grew to an alarming level. Even those charged with keeping the law were under stress. Officials charged Sheriff Turner along with William F. Tatum with mutual assault and battery.
By April, the corn procured from the sale of the iron in Georgia was in Augusta waiting for rail transportation to North Carolina. James C. Moir, salt agent for the county, reported that the salt stored at Christiansburg was "exposed to loss from various ways." He felt that personal attendance of an agent would prevent loss.

Elections held on May 26 gave David A. Robertson a four-year term as Commonwealth Attorney beginning on July 1, 1864. L. G. Rucker won a six-year term as Clerk of Court, while Austin J. Cabell and M. S. Robertson won two-year terms as Commissioners of the Revenue. Voters reelected Sheriff Turner to another two-year term, as did Joseph Clark and Sander Rogers as Constables. William Martin, John W. Hancock, James A. Ingram, and Thomas Lawless became overseers of the poor for four of the six districts. Officials reported that 1,587 persons needed support and 1,500 bushels of grain were necessary. Total expenditures reported in May 1864 were $4999.

John Staples and Beverly A. Davis acted as agents to visit hospitals and examine the condition of "our sick and wounded Soldiers" and to aid when necessary. The county authorized $3000 in Patrick County Notes, $10,000 for salt and $19,000 to purchase corn for indigent families along with $18,000 to meet the debt of county bonds. In September, the county authorized Joseph H. Clark to impress or seize grain from private citizens.

In August, the county asked the Confederate States of America to suspend conscription of 45 to 50 year old men due to an insufficiency of labor. This sentiment continued in October when the county asked Confederate authorities to allow C. C. Nowlin, a tanner, to remain home, as there was no one else to complete his work. The county asked consideration for another tanner, John Tuggle, to return home along with various mechanics.

The situation worsened in November. Delegate John Staples asked Confederate authorities for grains "on behalf of our suffering poor" as the county could not purchase or impress any. According to the Order Books, crimes did not stop. William Tudor stole two pigs and someone murdered A. J. Foley.

In 1864, other signs of growing security needs in Patrick County reflected in the appointment of deputies, Nanance Harbor and J. Thomas Clark, and the election of Isaac W. Underwood as constable in District #4 in July. The county held a "Special Court" at Elamsville on April 11, 1864 "to patrol and make search for deserters and other delinquents lurking and passing through the county." The court appointed a patrol squad of Grenville R. Conner, John Hooker, James Taylor, Isaac Adams, Wellington Thomas, and Lee Ross to search for deserters. The General Assembly passed another law in early 1864 making it illegal to assist deserters.

Confederate Secretary of War James A. Seddon wrote to President Jefferson Davis on November 8, 1864, reporting on his detectives in southwest Virginia. He noted an "infestation" of a group called the "Heroes of America" in Floyd, Montgomery, Giles and surrounding counties including the conscripts working at Saltville. Seddon called for a suspension of the writ of habeas corpus and asked that martial law govern Southwest Virginia. He feared there was a movement to form "a new State of Southwest Virginia."

The pacifist Quakers and Moravians of piedmont North Carolina started the "Heroes of America" in opposition to the Confederacy and the war. By 1864, they held sway over the piedmont counties around present day Winston-Salem and the already mentioned areas of southwest Virginia along with eastern Tennessee. Confederate authorities believed members of the 54th, 63rd and 22nd Virginia Infantry Regiments held a strong attachment to the group. Clandestine groups with secret codes, signs, counter signs, and handshakes networked together to assist escaping deserters or those still loyal to the United States. They recognized each other by the wearing of red strings on their lapels. These groups supplied information to Federal officials and military in the area.

If a soldier deserted after hearing from home of starvation, disease or other deprivations, local officials might persecute his family, causing more bad feeling and creating a vicious circle that led to more desertion. Capture of a deserter and a resulting execution or punishment led to more disloyalty with an ever-growing base for pro-Union feeling. Deserters stayed out of sight in the rugged areas of the mountains, choosing to visit their homes under the cover of night. Often, bands of deserters formed guerrilla units and began raiding the area. The lack of local workers crippled efforts of the Home Guard to protect the populace.

In 1861, over eighteen percent of Patrick County's voters went against secession. Loyalty to the Union continued throughout the war. The records of the Southern Claims Commission show several questions dealing with those a claimant knew remained loyal to the United States. Several names including W. W. Stoops, John L. Anglin, David and John Scott, James Branch, Mark A. Stovall, Paul Howell, Thomas D. Rorrer, John Hughes, George Rogers and Thomas Hopkins show up repeatedly in these documents.

W. W. Stoops claimed a loss of $185.00 including a horse, saddle and saddlebags. William O. Creasey claimed a loss of $445.00 including two horses, two mules and some corn. Both losses occurred at the hands of Union troops under George Stoneman. The United States rejected these and nine other claims for various reasons such as the fact that the claimant had voted for secession.

James Light and Thomas Shelton received compensation for proving they were loyal to the Union in 1878. Each claimant answered eighty interrogatories or questions about their actions. Light said, "I never did or said anything against the cause of the Union...gave food and protection to those who deserted from that (rebel) cause." Light listed local citizens such as Charles DeHart who had threatened him with hanging for his actions. He lost a son, James M. Light, conscripted into Company E of the 6th Virginia Infantry. The U. S. Government paid Light $150.00 for a horse taken by Stoneman's troops on April 8, 1865.

Shelton received $190.00 including $100.00 for a sorrel mare, $60.00 for 300 pounds of bacon, $25.00 for 25 bushels of corn, and $5.00 for 500 pounds of fodder taken by Stoneman's troops on April 8, 1865. The United States rejected his claims for 25 fowls, a rifle, two silver watches, and other claims for a grand total of $245.00. Shelton's sons Josiah, William, James, Charles and Peter fought for the Confederacy. He claimed two of them fought for the Union. Patrick County's grand jury indicted Shelton for disloyalty to the Confederacy, but the end of the war precluded any action. (This book includes a list of those who made claims.)

The natural class distinctions between the predominantly English descendants of the piedmont and the Scots-Irish and German descendants in the mountains played roles in the "civil war within the Civil War." Geographically being half piedmont and half mountain, Patrick County was a natural target for deserters and those wanting to encourage anti-Confederate behavior. Located between two of the major areas of operations for these groups, the county certainly felt the influence of such organizations. The location and small population allowed deserters of both sides to operate in the rugged areas along the northern section of the county. Union deserters came from the mountain counties to the west. Confederates leaving the scene of the siege around Richmond and

Petersburg saw the untouched land of Patrick County as a place for survival and looting. The extraordinary efforts of officials of Patrick County in caring for the families of the soldiers protected the people from the troubles of surrounding counties. In contrast, Carroll County officials allowed vigilante behavior by its Home Guard that led to the killing of many deserters.

Deserters and lawless bands, not necessarily from Patrick County, continued to be a persistent problem as the war ended. Near the end of 1864, Sabrina Frashure, widow of James W. Frashure of Company C, Fourth Virginia Infantry, requested her dead husband's pay, bounty, and allowances. A deserter killed him after he joined a local patrol while home recovering from his own battle wound.

During January 1865, the county received the third request for slaves from the Confederate government. Local officials allocated nineteen persons to appear at the courthouse on April 17 and reported 214 able-bodied male slaves in Patrick County. As the war in Virginia ended on April 9, 1865, it is doubtful that these seventeen people ever saw service for the South. The total number of slaves requisitioned for Confederate service throughout the war totaled 130 souls. (This book contains a list of the slave owners and the number of their slaves requisitioned into service.)

Robert E. Lee commented in early 1865, "We must decide whether slavery shall be extinguished by our enemies…or use them ourselves." The Confederate Congress approved "the authority to recruit, muster and organize Negro troops" on March 13, 1865. The War Department instructed Dr. P. J. Hale to recruit in Franklin, Henry, and Patrick Counties. No information exists about the results of this effort.

Slavery ended with the ratification of the Thirteenth Amendment to the U. S. Constitution in December 1865. The Fourteenth Amendment ratified in 1868 guaranteed citizenship, equal protection and due process for the former slaves. The Fifteenth Amendment in 1870 protected voting rights, but it would be another hundred years before the descendants of Patrick County's "free people of color" and slaves fully realized these rights. For additional material, the reader should see Gertrude Becker's master's degree thesis "Patrick County in the Civil War" at Virginia Tech, which gives an excellent view of the many social aspects of life in Patrick County during the war.

Abram Staples, agent of the county for grain "could not obtain grain" and appealed to the Confederate authorities through delegate John Staples in early 1865. There were 1600 indigent persons needing 4800 bushels of grain to survive through August 1865, according to the Order Books.

On the night of March 27, 1865, Abram Reynolds assisted William T. Akers, former Major of the 51st Virginia Infantry, in handling some "very dangerous characters" on Shooting Creek near the border with Franklin County. Reynolds approached the home of the suspects with Samuel A. Penn, formerly of the 42nd Virginia Infantry, and Thompson Washburn, formerly of the 51st Virginia Infantry. Reynolds and Washburn entered the home in front with Penn directly behind. At that moment Sheriff Turner, not recognizing them, encountered the party attempting to take the same prisoners and ordered them to halt. When Reynolds and Penn raised their arms, Turner mistakenly fired at the party wounding Reynolds in the shoulder. "Poor Sam Penn" took the entire load of buckshot in the chest and yelled "Oh Lord, I am killed by one of my friends." Reynolds lost the use of his right arm for many years.

After the close of the war, officials in Richmond appointed Sheriff Turner as Provost Marshall. Turner organized two companies under command of Reynolds and Penn with "authority to organize a military court to try these marauders and execute or imprison them." The county ordered the sheriff to organize militia "for the purpose of suppressing the lawless outrages now being committed. The county stipulated, however, that this militia was "not intended to interfere in any manner with the authority of the United States or any other legitimate state of Federal Government."

Abram Reynolds gathered men to break up the camp of "Major" Scott and 300 men at Martha Brown's home. Scott had raided the home of Mrs. George Hylton, who had just delivered twins. Reynolds's memoir states: "One of my neighbors Joe King called to see me and said Mrs. George Helton had given birth to twins and some of Scott's men had come and robbed her crib and commenced to take her bed clothes. She said 'Men, I consider myself a widow. My husband was killed or captured soon after he was at home about nine months ago and I have not complained at your taking horses and feed, but do spare me my bedding.' One man a neighbor who had joined Scott's command drew his pistol and said 'if you open your mouth I will blow your brains out.' ... I jumped to my feet and said if I have surrendered to a government who will tolerate such treatment as that I will sell my life as dear as I can and die. I got on my horse and rode for three days making up a company of men to arrest Major Scott and his 300 men mostly Confederate deserters."

Reynolds scouted the camp and visited Henry County, recruiting fifty men for the attack. He found another fifty men waiting at Mrs. Hylton's and prepared to attack Scott's camp at sunrise. He divided his men to attack on all sides. He wrote, "When we got in sight of the camp we saw the U. S. flag hoisted and over half of our men were on parole and we hesitated to fire on troops under the U. S. flag." Reynolds and John E. Penn decided to approach the camp under a flag of truce and demand surrender. Just as they began to confer with an officer, the other part of Reynolds's men attacked the camp wounding the other officer. The camp was a treasure for the destitute former Confederates with horses, cattle, clothes, corn, bacon, leather and all kinds of produce, all of it stolen from the local populace.

Sarah Catherine "Kate" Penn Hylton gave birth to twins, Barbara Ann "Annie" and Clark Penn Hylton on April 16, 1865, a week after Stoneman left the area. Mrs. Hylton died of causes unknown on May 15, over a month after the raid. Clark P. Hylton died on June 6, 1866. Kate's husband, George Wade Hylton had enlisted on September 5, 1861 in Company H, 58th Virginia Infantry. He operated a remount station for the horses used by Confederate forces during the war. Hylton returned to service in October 1864 as a private in Company D, 10th Virginia Cavalry. Captured at the Battle of Five Forks, Hylton was a prisoner of war at Point Lookout, Maryland until June 14, 1865. He came home to Patrick County and lived until 1898. Family tradition reports that he believed the deserters were from both sides.

Colonel Peter Hairston of the 24th Virginia Infantry years later recalled after the war that Scott was a member of Stoneman's command, but information on the deserter leader is sketchy at best. General James A. Walker reportedly killed Scott in Pulaski County for creating a similar band of ruffians there.

After the war, Abram D. Reynolds, like many other returning soldiers, made his mark on the world in the tobacco business. His son started the Reynolds Metals Company, makers of products such as Reynolds Wrap. Reynolds had left Rock Spring under the stigma of possibly causing the death of three of his siblings in October 1862 when he brought home cotton tainted with smallpox. He did not know what kind of reception he would receive upon arriving in Patrick County. He wrote years later: "My father was a fine disciplinarian and always kept me at a distance and I never knew he loved me until then when he saw me he ran to meet me and threw his arms around me and said 'My Son the Yankees have been here and torn up every thing and my Negro men have all gone with them but since you have come back alive and well it is all right. We can rebuild our lost fortune.' I was glad my father made this demonstration it made a better man of me. Love is the greatest gift that was bestowed on man. It has brought back many wayward children. Parents should never give up on a wayward child."

On January 26, 1870, the United States of America welcomed back the "wayward child" of Virginia during Reconstruction. Patrick County nearly missed seeing any soldiers on its soil from the United States, but the county suffered mightily, the price of war reflected in its dead, the loss of a slave labor force, and the plight of its hungry people. The county showed great compassion in the care of its soldiers and their families during the war. Today, the "Free State of Patrick" remains a memory in the minds of her people and in their independent spirit.

Rufus James Woolwine of the 51st Virginia Infantry wrote a memoir of his experiences during the war. *Courtesy of the Virginia Historical Society.*

George Wade Hylton served in the 58th Virginia Infantry and the 10th Virginia Cavalry. *Courtesy of Barbara Baughan.*

Chapter Two
"One of the hardest trials of my life"
Patrick County's Confederate Soldiers

Today the statue of a lone Confederate veteran shown on the cover of this book stands atop a large base erected in 1936 in front of the Patrick County Court House. Many people confuse this infantryman with the county's most famous soldier, James Ewell Brown "Jeb" Stuart, but Stuart's image adorns a plaque on the front of the base where you will read that he was born "near" the town that bears his name. In 1907, Richmond placed an equestrian statue of Stuart on Monument Avenue and the base of it states that he was "Born in Patrick County, Virginia." He faces north, still symbolically keeping an eye out for invaders, protecting the city he gave his life defending.

The largest contribution of Patrick County to the war effort was the men serving in the armed forces of the Confederate States of America. Patrick men fought in all of the major engagements in Virginia, Maryland, Pennsylvania, Tennessee, Kentucky, and North Carolina. The majority of these men enlisted from Elamsville or Ararat at opposite ends of the county.

In April of 1861, two militia companies, the 18th and the 156th, provided some military training to Patrick's men. In the 1860 Census, 1617 men between the ages of 15 and 50 lived in Patrick County. Eighty-seven percent served in the war. These soldiers faced daunting odds in their service for the South. Seventeen percent became prisoners. Union soldiers wounded nine percent. Most horrifying for their families, twenty-seven percent made the ultimate sacrifice for Southern independence. There were at least 152 men from Patrick in the 42nd Virginia Infantry and only 6 at Appomattox. Of the 334 Patrick County residents who lost their lives in 1862, 102 died due to the war.

Patrick County men served in fifty different regiments of artillery, cavalry and infantry during the war. Twenty-five percent of them served in the 51st Virginia Infantry Regiment. The 50th, 24th and 42nd Virginia Infantry Regiments contained the next largest numbers. Seven percent of Patrick Countians served in the cavalry and three percent in artillery units. Others served in diverse organizations such as the 5th Battalion Virginia Reserves, 6th Virginia Infantry, 58th Virginia Infantry, the Orange Artillery, and the 21st Virginia Cavalry. Many served in North Carolina units such as the 53rd Infantry Regiment or 2nd Cavalry Regiment.

The hardships endured in the army took a heavy toll on Patrick County's soldiers. Living in a somewhat secluded environment, they quickly contracted diseases such as measles, mumps and smallpox, which many times proved fatal. Unsanitary living conditions caused many of them to come down with typhoid fever which, combined with pneumonia, was the most common cause of death.

Families sometimes came to the camps and took their loved one's body home for burial. Born on the Smith River in Patrick County, Jefferson Turner lived at the crest of the Blue Ridge Mountain in Floyd County before the war. He served in Captain Sparrell Griffith's Company H, 54th Virginia Infantry. Turner died of disease at Abingdon in May 1862. Family tradition states his wife, Susan Short Turner, traveled by wagon to Abingdon, brought his body back, and buried him at the head of Shooting Creek, a journey of almost 300 miles.

The records indicate that half of all Patrick County soldiers went "Absent Without Leave" (AWOL) one or more times during the war. Officials listed large percentages as deserters. Some went home to help with family problems. With most men away in the army, often no one at home could plant or harvest the crops. When wives and children got sick, fathers came home to see about them. In many cases, the soldiers returned to their units later. Many of the records are incorrect because of poor record keeping and the inability of company clerks to keep up with the men due to hospitalization, capture, or transfer. If a man was not present at roll call and the clerk did not know his whereabouts he was listed "Absent Without Leave." Some companies did not attempt to keep records near the end of the conflict. Toward the end of the war, some Patrick County soldiers took the Oath of Allegiance to the U.S. Government and "went North" with some joining the U. S. Army.

A company of infantry commanded by a captain and two lieutenants consisted of 100 men. On paper, a regiment contained ten companies with one thousand men commanded by a colonel. Ideally, a regiment had a lieutenant colonel, major, adjutant, quartermaster, surgeon, assistant surgeon, sergeant major, quartermaster sergeant, commissary sergeant, hospital stewards and sometimes a band of musicians. While some companies and regiments started with the ideal numbers, very few maintained those numbers for very long. Desertions, illness, wounds, and deaths played havoc with manpower. Seldom did replacements fill all of the vacancies. For instance, at Antietam Lee's regiments average 170 men. Most units ended the war with only a fraction of full strength.

A regiment served in a brigade with three other regiments usually from the same state commanded by a brigadier general. A brigade served as the basic tactical formation in battle and usually went by the name of its commander such as the "Stonewall" Brigade. Two brigades made a division commanded by a major general. At least two divisions made up a corps commanded by a lieutenant general. An army made up of corps commanded by a general was the top unit in the Confederate hierarchy.

The chain of command for a Confederate private worked along these lines. In March 1865, Private George M. Agee served in Captain Rufus Woolwine's Company D, 51st Virginia Regiment of Infantry. Major William T. Akers commanded the 51st Virginia. The regiment was part of Wharton's Brigade commanded by Major Peter J. Otey in Wharton's Division commanded by Brigadier General Gabriel C. Wharton. They belonged to the Second Corps led by Major General John B. Gordon in the Army of the Valley commanded by Lieutenant General Jubal A. Early, who reported to Secretary of War John C. Breckinridge, who served in the cabinet of Jefferson Davis, President of the Confederate States of America.

All of those who left Patrick in 1861 were volunteers. Enthusiastic speakers, often militia officers, organized meetings in several sections of the county. They made stirring speeches that resulted in hundreds of young men eagerly volunteering their services for repelling any invasion of the hated Yankee armies.

One of the first units organized in Patrick County was a company from the Spoon Creek area near Critz, which began enlisting men on May 22, 1861 and become Company H of the 42nd Virginia Infantry. This unit was led by Captain John Edmund Penn. Military tradition was strong in some families. Captain Penn descended from Colonel Abram Penn, commander of the area troops in the Battle of Guilford Courthouse during the American Revolution.

The first men from the "Free State of Patrick" to leave for war were ninety-eight men of Company I, 24th Virginia Infantry, under Captain A. M. Lybrook. Andrew Lybrook, an attorney, organized the unit at Patrick Court House. This company enlisted men on May 31, 1861.

On the north side of Bull Mountain, Captain David Lee Ross organized and trained a company on his farm near Elamsville. On June 14, 1861, he inducted a large number of volunteers that later became Company D, 51st Virginia Infantry Regiment. Captain Greenville (Granville) Conner organized a company on Smith River near the present Jack's Creek Covered Bridge. This company became Company H, 51st Regiment of Infantry. More Patrick County men served in these two companies of this regiment than in any other outfit in the Army during the war.

In the far western section of the county, men joined a Carroll County company organized at Fancy Gap. Captain Alexander Haynes, a Patrick County native, commanded this unit that became Company E of the 29th Virginia Infantry.

In July 1861, Jefferson T. Lawson organized a company near Taylorsville that became Company K, 50th Virginia Infantry. At Patrick Court House on July 6, 1861, George H. Booker, a graduate of

Randolph-Macon College and an Episcopal minister, organized and enlisted for one year and commanded the "Patrick County Grays," Company H, 58th Virginia Infantry Regiment.

A new reference book, Civil War High Commands, contains a section on the birthplaces of Confederate generals. The book credits Patrick County with J. E. B. Stuart, Alfred Cleon Moore, and Alexander Watkins Terrell.

Alfred Cleon Moore, born in Patrick County on December 12, 1805, moved to North Carolina as a boy. A physician and legislator in the "Old North State" at the outbreak of the Civil War, Moore returned to Virginia and from April 17 until June 8, 1861 served as a brigadier general in the Provisional Army of Virginia. In November, he ranked as colonel of the 29th Virginia Infantry Regiment.

The 29th fought in Southwest Virginia and Kentucky, where in 1862 they fought future United States President James A. Garfield in the Battle of Middle Creek. The regiment transferred to Petersburg as Robert E. Lee's Army of Northern Virginia moved north into Maryland. Moore held the position of colonel until his resignation on April 8, 1863, due to "advanced age and failing health." He served in the reserves in Wythe County and after the war continued as a physician. Moore's mortal remains reside in the McGavoc Cemetery near Fort Chiswell, Virginia.

Born in Patrick County on November 3, 1827, Alexander Watkins Terrell at the age of five moved to Missouri. He attended the University of Missouri and moved to Texas in 1852 where he became a judge. Like his friend Sam Houston, Terrell opposed secession. In 1862, Terrell found himself a Captain in the First Texas Cavalry. He rose in rank to colonel by June 1863 in Terrell's Texas Cavalry Battalion.

The regiment fought in the Battle of Mansfield, Louisiana, along the Red River in April 1864. In September, he commanded a brigade of three Texas cavalry regiments for seven months. On May 16, 1865, Edmund Kirby Smith promoted Terrell to brigadier general in the Trans-Mississippi Department, but the Confederate Senate did not confirm his appointment. Two days before his promotion Terrell disbanded his regiment. In July, he fled to Mexico and became a colonel in the Mexican army for four months. He received a pardon from the United States in November 1865.

After the Civil War Terrell practiced law and served in the Texas legislature with a stint under President Grover Cleveland as United States Minister to Turkey from 1893 until 1897. Due to his work in the legislature on education, many consider him the "Father of University of Texas." He wrote two books, one published in 1933 entitled From Texas to Mexico and the Court of Maximilian, and the second he co-edited in 1874 entitled Cases Argued and Decided in the Supreme Court of the State of Texas. He ran unsuccessfully for the United States Senate from

Texas and served as president of the Texas Historical Association. Alexander Terrell died in Mineral Wells, Texas, on September 9, 1912, and rests today in the state cemetery in Austin, Texas.

Many average Patrick Countians were, as Civil War soldier and Chief Justice of the U. S. Supreme Court Oliver W. Holmes said, "Touched by fire" during the war. The following are some of their stories.

James Gabriel Penn, born in 1845 at Penn's Store, served in the Corps of Keydets from the Virginia Military Institute at New Market in May 1864. He became a banker in Danville and a founder of the American Tobacco Company.

First Lieutenant Peter Washington Dalton of Company H, 42nd Virginia Infantry found himself a member of "The Immortal 600" in September 1864. A prisoner of the United States of America at Morris Island, South Carolina, Dalton lived under the fire of the Confederate guns at Charleston as a reaction to Union prisoners treated similarly. While still a teenager in May 1861, Dalton enlisted from Ararat. Wounded at Kernstown in March 1862, hospitalized in July 1862 at Charlottesville with small pox and a year later in Richmond with fever and captured at Spotsylvania Court House in May 1864, Dalton went to Fort Delaware for imprisonment. On August 20, 1864, Union officials transferred him to South Carolina, where they held him under fire as an "Immortal" from September 7 until October 21, 1864. Imprisoned at Fort Pulaski, Georgia, until November 21 then transferred to Hilton Head. Dalton returned to Fort Delaware on March 21, 1865.

For many the war was a very negative experience that left them bitter. Isaac Underwood enlisted in March 1862 in Company D, 12th Virginia Infantry and proceeded to see just about every Confederate hospital including Petersburg, Williamsburg, Charlottesville, Richmond and Lynchburg. He suffered from diseases such as typhoid, pneumonia and smallpox, but survived to desert in 1864 and lived to write his memoir: "I was forced to go into the War in sixty two.... I stayed in the War until it closed, or rather, I stayed in the army and other places until it closed. I went North and stayed ten months in the winding up of the rebellion for I was no war man anyway, and it was slaves that the issue was about, and I had none of these to fight for, and I thought it was wrong for me to fight for other people's property unless they paid me for it. This was one of the hardest trials of my life. To leave my wife and baby exposed to all the elements of danger at home, and myself plunged in the midst of cannons and swords and bullets, and all kinds of weather and camping out on the ground. Being very weakly, I soon became unable to do any service in camp at all, and was nearly always in the hospital. I there had typhoid fever, pneumonia, smallpox, and scrafulus [scrofulous], and was a burden to the hospital and myself, and a constant distress to my wife, fearing that I could never return home anymore."

Joshua Branch served in Company D, 51st Virginia Infantry and Company K of the 140th Indiana Infantry. Born in Patrick County, Branch's enlistment papers describe him as a farmer, five foot nine inches in height at twenty-two years of age, with blue eyes, brown hair and a dark complexion. He joined the Union army on October 6, 1864, and spent time at Murfreesboro, Tennessee, and then in the campaign to take Fort Fisher in North Carolina. He mustered out at Greensboro, North Carolina, in July 1865 and lived until 1907. Joshua Branch lies in the Pedigo Cemetery adjoining the J. E. B. Stuart's birthplace, Laurel Hill, in Ararat.

Others came to Patrick County after the war such as James A. Grogan of Company D, 10th Alabama Infantry. His regiment organized in Montgomery in June 1861 and fought at Dranesville with J. E. B. Stuart in December. The unit joined the Army of Northern Virginia in 1862, serving in Cadimus Wilcox's Brigade of Longstreet's then A. P. Hill's Corps until surrender at Appomattox.

A headstone in the Hunter's Chapel Church Cemetery in Ararat lists James T. W. Clements of Pittsylvania County, 6th Virginia Cavalry. Sheridan's cavalry captured Clements along with sixty men making a last stand at Yellow Tavern the day "Jeb" Stuart received his mortal wound on May 11, 1864. Present in Harrisonburg, Virginia on June 6, 1862, Clements' company carried the dead Turner Ashby from the field. Clements served time in a Yankee prison before returning home to Virginia.

Andrew Jackson Stedman of Gates County, North Carolina, enlisted as a sergeant in Company B, 49th North Carolina Infantry, and received a wound at Malvern Hill in July 1862. He became a first lieutenant in the Signal Corps. He married Susan K. Staples of Patrick County after the war, practiced law in Stokes County, North Carolina, and edited the first newspaper in Patrick County, The Voice of the People, in 1876.

Finally, there is Samuel Granville Staples, the man from Patrick who voted on April 17, 1861, for secession at the state convention. The son of Abram Staples, he was born in Patrick County in 1821 and educated at Randolph-Macon, the University of Virginia and the College of William and Mary. Staples practiced law, served as Clerk of Circuit Court from 1844 to 1852 and as a member of the House of Delegates from 1852 to 1854. For two months during the war, he served as a volunteer aide-de-camp to General J. E. B. Stuart in 1862 until discharged because of physical disabilities. Post-war, Staples served as a judge in the county for ten years and worked for the Department of the Interior in Washington, D. C. He lived until 1895.

With the exception of a raid by General Stoneman's Federal troops near the end of the war, no Union forces entered Patrick County. Despite that fact, no war in history had so much effect on the lives of the people as did the Civil War. As early as 1863, Virginia had passed a law for "Relief of Indigent Soldiers and Sailors," where each county would provide money and services. After the war in 1867, Virginia passed a law for artificial limbs. Virginia passed pension acts in 1888, 1900 and 1902 and noted in this book along with disability claims.

The aftermath of war had many effects on the women and children left behind. Survival became the main problem and many applied for pensions. In 1915, Virginia covered funeral expenses for veterans and paid pensions from 1888, 1900 and 1902 once a year. Pensions varied from $180 for blindness and $78 for the loss of limb to $43.20 for disability from disease. Matrons in Confederate hospitals received $48 and widow's pensions ranged from $30 to $48 depending time of death. Sarah Guynn began receiving $30.00 a year beginning in 1888 for her husband Levi of Company E, 29th Virginia Infantry. Family tradition states that the Carroll County Home Guard killed Levi, but Sarah's pension application states he died from fever after he returned home in September 1863.

The pool of men of marriageable age forced many women to marry much older men such as Edward Noah Martin, who was forty-eight years older than his bride, Naomi Caroline Moran. She kept a sense of humor, stating that, "I'd rather be an old man's darling than a young man's slave."

Many children grew up never knowing their father such as Susan Emma Moss, born after the death of her father Jesse Moss of Company G, 51st Virginia Infantry. Moss died of measles and rests today ten miles north of New Market in a cemetery near Mount Jackson. His wife's pension application is the only record of his service in the Confederate Army.

Descendants of the veterans formed the Wharton-Stuart Camp of the Sons of Confederate Veterans on April 14, 1906, with George T. Munford as commandant, Samuel M. Lybrook as first lieutenant commandant, R. H. Dunkley as Second Lieutenant Commandant, R. E. Woolwine as Adjutant, L. C. Dickerson as surgeon, John A. Adams as quartermaster, John W. Wimbush as chaplain, along with a treasurer, color sergeant, historian and over seventy-six members.

Families discover parts of their past to this day. Mentoria Dehart Weaver lost her husband Jesse Dehart during the war. She married Daniel Weaver and one of their children Walter G. Weaver designed Patrick County's two surviving wooden bridges, the Bob White and

Jack's Creek in Woolwine. Jesse Dehart fought in Company A, 24th Virginia Infantry. As part of Pickett's Charge at Gettysburg in Kemper's Brigade, Dehart received a wound and faced capture and imprisonment. Exchanged in 1864, Jesse Dehart lost his life at Chafin's Farm near Petersburg. His recently discovered marked grave lies near George Pickett in Richmond's Hollywood Cemetery.

Patrick County's Civil War soldiers are all gone. They rest in graves from northern Georgia and Fort Donelson, Tennessee to Finns Point, New Jersey, and Elmira, New York. The last veteran of the War, Joseph Henry Brown, served in Company G of the 24th Virginia Infantry. Born in 1843, he survived the war after capture at Five Forks in April 1865, as Robert E. Lee's lines were broken around Richmond forcing the retreat that ended in surrender at Appomattox. Brown died in 1940 at the age of 96, ending the last human link to the war.

David Lee Ross commanded a company from Patrick County in the 51st Virginia Infantry. *Courtesy of Paul Ross.*

Chapter Three
"A Journey of Four Years"
Rufus Woolwine and the 51st Virginia Infantry Regiment

In studying the Civil War, focusing on battles or leaders and forgetting about the ordinary infantry soldier is commonplace. In Patrick County, the same is true for James Ewell Brown "Jeb" Stuart. You see his name and image everywhere, but there were many infantry soldiers who fought in the war and deserve recognition.

Rufus James Woolwine of the 51st Virginia Infantry Regiment saw many important places and events throughout the war. Not only did he live to tell about it, he kept notes during his time in the army. Immediately after the war, he compiled these notes (and probably hindsight) into a three-part diary. Mrs. Mabel Barksdale Norris, Woolwine's granddaughter, presented his papers to the Virginia Historical Society in 1962. During spring cleaning, she discovered the journal in a glass jar buried in an abandoned well. Louis H. Manarin edited and published the diary in the Virginia Magazine of History and Biography in October 1963.

The Patrick County community of Woolwine gets its name from Rufus's father, the first postmaster, Thomas Woolwine. Sarah Adams Woolwine, his mother, was the daughter of Notley P. Adams. Rufus James Woolwine, born October 20, 1840, attended the common schools and went to work with his father as a saddler. He enlisted on June 14, 1861 as a private and mustered in as a fourth corporal on July 26.

According to all available records at least 391 men from the county served in this unit. More Patrick Countians served in the 51st Regiment of Virginia Infantry than in any other regiment. The companies from Patrick County formed in June 1861. One group became Company C under David Lee Ross. Ninety-seven men drilled on his farm on present-day Highway 57 near the intersection with Pole Bridge Road. Captain Ross served as an officer in the county militia before the war. Other officers included William Tyler Akers, Abner J. Harbour, and Charles F. Ross serving as lieutenants in Company C. After a few months, this company became Company D.

Another group called the "Blackhawk" company organized under Granville P. Conner at Davis Shop on the Smith River. This unit, originally designated as Company F, became Company H with William G. Price, John M. Cruise, and Nathan B. Terry as lieutenants. Both companies drilled until July 24, 1861, then marched to Christiansburg where they boarded a train on the Virginia and Tennessee Railroad for Wytheville. Augustus Forsberg wrote of them at this time, "It was interesting to notice the personnel of the volunteer-like mountaineers, they were courageous, fine physical development, and could compare with any troops on earth...Some in uniforms they had made at home, some with squirrel rifles, some with flint locks and bowie knifes. Some had never seen a railroad. Once the sound of a locomotive was heard and the men acted like being shocked, one called out 'She's a coming', down went all guns and like a flock of sheep, ran down the hill to see the Iron Horse."

Born in Sweden in 1832, Forsberg served as a Swedish Army Engineer before coming to America in the 1850s. He rose in rank to Colonel and command of the 51st Virginia Infantry Regiment in 1863.

Young men going off to war inspired Captain Ross' black servant, Britt, to poetry. Born in 1822 as a slave, Britt and a twin brother, Jordan, reportedly could not read or write.

"The twenty fourth of July, may long remember be,
The volunteers from Patrick the men to march away,
The patriotic spirit induces them to go,
To meet the Northern plunders and keep them from the shore.
A true hearted soldier he stands at his post,
In danger he's never found out of his course
He's willing to fight if it's five to their ten
Lord aid Captain Ross and all his brave men.
Lord aid our captain while we are in camp,
Grant every man to have oil in his lamp,
and be ready if called on with a load to depart,
with a beautiful beed on a northern man's heart.
Here's health to the poet that did make the song,
his life to be merry, his day's to be long,
good luck to all our soldier's that live under the sun,
success to Captain Ross and all his brave Patrick men."

After having dinner at Gabriel DeHart's home on Rock Castle Creek at the foot of Tuggle's Gap, Rufus Woolwine wrote in his diary on July 24, "The scene of parting is a day that can never be described, never be forgotten. Twas then we bid farewell to home, friends, and connections and took up the lines of march to meet the serried ranks of a strong but dastard foe. Twas then many of us looked upon our native soil as we thought for the last time." Upon arriving at Christiansburg, their accommodations caused Woolwine to write, "Landed there about one o'clock in the night and I do assure you that our feathers fell when they lighted us to our stall... What we were furnished with there over night discouraged several so they laid in an excuse and plead for a discharge."

At Camp Jackson in Wytheville, they joined seven companies of the 51st Regiment of Virginia Infantry under the command of an 1847 graduate of the Virginia Military Institute and civil engineer, Gabriel C.

Wharton. Men from all over southwest Virginia joined the regiment under "Old Gabe." Companies C and F from Patrick County joined their fellow Virginians such as the "Wharton Grays," Company B from Wythe County under David P. Graham.

Other companies in the regiment included Company K, the "Bland Tigers," under Samuel Newberry, Company G, the "Floyd Gamecocks," under James W. Henley, and Companies A and D from Grayson County under Stephen M. Dickey and Ezekiel Young. Company B, the "Nelson County Rifles," under John T. Dillard and Company E, the "Wythe Rifles," under William H. Cook, Company I contained men from Washington County under John P. Wolfe.

The last unit to join, Company L, hailed from Tazewell County. The men listened to its eleven-piece regimental band. Burton Highley watched over the spiritual health of the men as minister of the regiment and James Estill performed the duties of regimental surgeon. The eleven companies came together due to Brigadier General John B. Floyd's need for troops in the Kanawha Valley, in present-day West Virginia.

The men learned the hard lessons of war quickly. During their initial training, the troops received three days' rations. They ate all the rations at once and went hungry for two days. During the first year of the war, Woolwine "messed" or ate with N. C. Akers, J. F. Via, his brother D. G. Via, J. J. Vaughn, Tiller Thomas, and William Dennis Via until the reorganization of the regiment in 1862.

In August 1861, the regiment took the train to Bonsack Depot, just east of present-day Roanoke, and camped from August 5 until September 19. The regiment moved to the Kanawha Valley in present-day West Virginia in early September leaving the two Patrick companies behind. The men from Patrick rejoined the regiment after about three weeks. An epidemic of measles broke out in the two Patrick companies. Two men, James Ross and Robert Hodges, from Company D died from measles.

The 51st joined the 3rd Brigade in the Army of the Kanawha, taking part in Sewell Mountain Campaign. Robert E. Lee arrived on September 21 to take command. Rufus Woolwine and John T. Washburn heard Reverend G. S. Tuggle preach and they slept in the pulpit the same night. Woolwine celebrated his birthday on October 20 at Raleigh Court House noting, "I enjoy our social activities, the association with ladies and gentlemen of like background, and the many warm friendships that have resulted, both locally, and all over the south." Lee failed to meet his chief objective: preventing the Union forces from organizing these western counties into a new state. The Confederates lost control of the Kanawha Valley and retreated into the mountains. Disease, terrible weather, impassable roads, and lack of supplies including weapons, food, and shelter caused terrible hardships for the new troops resulting in death and desertion.

Woolwine traveled home to Patrick for one of his many visits during the war. On his return, the 51st transferred to take part in the defense of Fort Donelson, Tennessee, in 1862. The regiment traveled to Bowling Green, Kentucky to assist General Albert Sidney Johnston in his unsuccessful attempt to stop General Ulysses S. Grant. General John B. Floyd, a former governor of Virginia, commanded a division including the 51st.

The trip to the "Bluegrass State" took eight days for the regiment. The men traveled via five railroads to Bristol, Knoxville, Chattanooga, Nashville, and Bowling Green. During the stay in Kentucky, Woolwine reported the death of General Felix Zollicoffer at the Battle of Mill Springs on January 17, 1862, and his first pay: "Here we drew the first money we ever drew from the time we come into the service." James I. Robertson quotes General Floyd on the 51st in 1862 saying, "They have not a single dollar to purchase the least little comfort, even for the sick."

U. S. Grant earned the moniker "Unconditional Surrender" when he forced the capitulation of Fort Henry and Fort Donelson. The 51st Virginia under the command of another VMI graduate, Colonel James W. Massie, fought in the thick at Fort Donelson in February 1862. This battle was a rugged baptism into the rigors of war for the young Patrick Countians.

Rufus Woolwine wrote of the battle, "There we took a boat for Fort Donelson. Got there that night. On Wednesday the Twelfth of February we was marched out for fight. Worked all night throwing up breastworks. On the thirteenth, we lay in our ditches all day and such heavy cannonading was never heard before. That night it rained and we just had to lay in our ditches. Fourteenth, skirmishing along the line. Lay in our ditches that night. Fifteenth, just as day began to dawn upon the silvery waters of the Cumberland we engaged the enemy and drove him from his camp. When we succeeded in ascending the first hill such a sight my eyes never before beheld. Twas there I beheld the mangled dead and dying, laying in all imaginable forms. Yes, there several hundred miles from our native homes, and from those that was bound to us by the strongest ties of affection. I am happy to say that thanks to God Virginians done their duty as becomes true men and patriots. Though distantly situated, they thought of their happy homes far away that they was fighting for. With them as with all of Jeff's boys, they done all men could do."

On February 15, Wharton's Brigade attacked the Federal right and opened an escape route at the cost of 9 killed, 43 wounded and 5 missing. The sniping generals, Floyd and Pillow, failed to follow up the success of the breakout. The next day Floyd's command escaped before the surrender of the fort. The men made their way to Nashville, Chattanooga, and finally to Abingdon. Going into winter camp at Glade Spring, the wounded recuperated in the hospital at Emory and Henry College.

The 51st continued in Wharton's Brigade in the Army of the Kanawha and remained in the Department of Southwestern Virginia through the rest of 1862. Captain David Lee Ross resigned from the company and returned to his farm at Elamsville. He assumed command of the county militia with the title of Lieutenant Colonel. Later in the war, authorities inducted all militiamen into service. Ross then joined the 21st Virginia Cavalry Regiment.

At the beginning of the war, soldiers elected their own officers. When the 51st reorganized in 1862, William Tyler Akers became captain of Company D. Woolwine received promotion to Second Lieutenant. He went to work as adjutant, purchasing supplies and salt, and recruiting in the counties of Scott, Tazewell and Patrick. Special duties including that of recruitment brought him home to Patrick County many times. During one of these visits, he arrested two "bushwhackers." Other duties included arresting men for making and selling liquor in Giles County in July 1862. He visited Patrick County in 1862 on May 5 through May 25, November 21 through December 12, and December 21 through the 28.

One of the principal objectives of the Union forces involved capturing the salt mines at Saltville and the lead mines in Wythe County. These threats required the Confederate government to keep forces in southwest Virginia to protect these sources. The mines were essential to the Confederate armies as the largest sources of both salt and lead were in southwest Virginia. In the spring of 1862, the 51st went to meet a Federal force that had captured Princeton. The regiment succeeded in driving the Federal forces from the nearly destroyed town.

A unit of the 51st under Captain William T. Akers traveled to White Sulphur Springs and lost to a stronger Federal force. Captain Akers and his troops escaped by burning a bridge behind them. In June 1862, the 51st returned to Giles County. Later that month, it encamped at Peterstown, now in West Virginia. On July 3, the unit assisted in defeating a Federal force at Mercer Courthouse. For the next several weeks, members of the 51st remained in camp near Narrows in Giles County.

In August 1862, General W. W. Loring assumed command of the Department of Southwestern Virginia. Wharton's Brigade (including the 51st and 50th Regiments and 23rd Battalion of Infantry along with Stamp's Artillery) moved into Monroe County and at Lewisburg on August 28 routed a Federal force led by future president Colonel Rutherford B. Hayes.

Threatened by a much larger Union army, Wharton returned to

Narrows. The 51st Regiment, now under command of Lieutenant Colonel Augustus Forsberg, moved to Grey Sulphur Springs where it drilled for several weeks and served on picket duty. In early September 1862, the brigade moved back into present day West Virginia and defeated a Federal force at Montgomery Ferry on the Kanawha River. It captured a large quantity of supplies including food, clothing, and arms.

The Confederates again occupied Charleston, driving the Federal forces toward the Ohio River. They camped for several weeks, enjoying the luxury of the captured supplies. Loring decided to move from Charleston back to the Greenbrier River. General Lee replaced him with General John Echols and ordered the unit back to Charleston, but a large Federal army already occupied the city. The brigade returned to Narrows, Virginia, where it remained for the winter of 1862-1863.

In March 1863, Colonel Wharton received orders from General Samuel Jones, commanding the Department of Western Virginia, to place his brigade where it could defend the lead mines, the salt wells, and the Virginia and Tennessee Railroad in southwest Virginia. He established headquarters at Glade Springs, Virginia. His command of 1,154 men included the 51st and 50th Virginia Regiments, the 30th Virginia Battalion of Infantry, and Stamp's Artillery.

Desertions became a serious problem and recruitment of replacements became necessary. Lieutenant Woolwine headed a recruitment team that had some success getting sixteen men and found those making and selling whiskey and returned six deserters from Company A in Russell and Wise counties.

In June 1863, the 51st moved into Tennessee to support General Buckner's forces near Chattanooga where an expected attack did not appear. After two weeks, the regiment returned to Glade Springs. On June 27, Confederate cavalry drove away a Federal force at Saltville. Colonel Wharton reported that the 51st had 972 men.

After taking the train to Staunton, the troops marched to Woodstock and joined the Army of Northern Virginia under General Robert E. Lee on his march away from Gettysburg. On July 8, Wharton received promotion to Brigadier General and Forsberg to Colonel of the 51st.

Early in August, General Lee ordered Wharton's Brigade to Warm Springs to block Federal General Averell's advance. Averell backed off and returned to West Virginia. During the summer of 1863, the 51st marched from Staunton to Glade Springs via Winchester, Orange Courthouse, Warm Springs, Dublin Depot, Abingdon, and Jonesboro, Tennessee.

Near the end of August, the brigade returned to southwest Virginia as the Federals made a determined effort to destroy the salt works, the lead mines, and the railroad. They captured Bristol and burned the town. The Confederates gathered all the forces they could get to oppose the Federals. At the last minute the Union forces under General Burnside gave up the effort and returned to Knoxville. The Confederates pursued as far as Jonesboro, Tennessee.

General Robert Ransom assumed command of the Department of Western Virginia and Eastern Tennessee. He moved Wharton's Brigade to Blountville, Tennessee to support General Longstreet who was trying to recapture Knoxville. All during the autumn of 1863, the 51st marched and counter-marched in the Rogersville-Bean Station area of Tennessee between the Holston River and the Clinch Mountains, expecting contact with the enemy at all times but seeing little fighting.

In January 1864, the 51st marched in General Longstreet's failed attempt to trap a Federal force near Dandridge, Tennessee. Many of the men had no shoes, and their bleeding feet left red marks in the snow. The men spent much time foraging during the bitterly cold winter, for in addition to food, they lacked good clothing and shelter. The harsh winter took the lives of a number of soldiers. In one month, the strength of Wharton's Brigade (including the 51st and 45th Regiments and 30th Battalion of Infantry) dropped from 915 to 725 men.

The brigade, barely at the strength of a regiment, moved to Bull's Gap to protect the headquarters of the Department of East Tennessee in February. They repaired roads and performed picket duty. They had not seen battle in over a year.

Woolwine witnessed the execution of deserters in Tennessee. By February, he was back in Patrick County attending a "Frollick at Widow Celah Hubbard." He continued a myriad of duties from commanding the company in April to acting as adjutant to Lieutenant Colonel John Wolfe.

In April 1864, the regiment marched to Abingdon in terrible weather over the muddiest possible roads. Woolwine presided over the execution of a deserter, writing, "the regiment being formed in two battalions to march out to the execution of John H. Jones of 30th Battalion Sharp Shooters of Grayson County for desertion. He was executed at two o'clock p.m."

Early in May 1864, General Lee reorganized the Army of Southwest Virginia and placed General John C. Breckinridge, a former vice president of the United States, in charge. The 51st, stationed at Narrows, Virginia, transferred north to the Valley of Virginia on May 6, 1864, riding the train to Staunton and marching north, down the valley, to meet the oncoming Federals. Wharton pushed the brigade of 1557 men (including 30th Virginia Infantry, the 62nd Mounted Infantry, and Company A of the 1st Missouri Cavalry along with the 51st) an amazing 187 miles in 8 days.

On May 13, Wharton's Brigade as part of Breckinridge's Division in the Army of Northern Virginia halted two miles south of

New Market. The cadets from Virginia Military Institute joined the brigade there. At the famous Battle of New Market, the 51st was on the front line in the thick of the fight under command of Lieutenant Colonel John P. Wolfe using the Keydets as reserves to drive the Federals from the field.

On May 15, Woolwine wrote, "at one o'clock company moved out for New Market in the county of Shenandoah. Day very inclement. Threw up rail works some two or three miles from New Market. Enemy did not advance. Marched forward and attacked the town at 9 am. Whipped and drove the enemy across the North Fork of the Shenandoah River. They burnt the bridge. We captured many prisoners, five pieces of artillery, wagons, and small arms."

After New Market, General Lee ordered General Breckinridge's troops to proceed to Hanover County to aid in the defense of Richmond. The entire regiment now numbered 588 men. They defended the junction of the Virginia Central Railroad with the Richmond, Fredericksburg, and Potomac lines. The 51st successfully prevented the destruction of the bridge over the South Anna River and repelled a Federal attack near Henry Clay's birthplace on May 28. Companies A and D, led by Major William T. Akers, skirmished with Federal troops and lost four men.

Fighting continued throughout the area after the Battle of the Wilderness as General Grant engaged in his relentless campaign to wear down Lee's troops and capture Richmond. In the battles of Mechanicsville, Cold Harbor , and Frayser's Farm, the 51st suffered heavy losses.

Woolwine reported they took a train, the "General Stuart," and went to Hanover Junction. The 51st joined the Army of Northern Virginia. Woolwine wrote, "heavy skirmishing along the entire. Enemy moved last night. Great many troops coming in. Saw General R. E. Lee...Passed Ashland and camped near where Henry Clay was born." A few days later he writes," Twenty ninth, Fortified. Thirtieth, some skirmishing...Thirty-first, Had to fall back under a galling fire. Joseph Rose killed. Heavy firing from artillery. During the day sharpshooters kept very busy. June first, drove them from their rifle pits...That night we were relieved and marched to Mechanicsville. Slept a few hours and day dawned. Second, To Chickahominy. At Gaines Farm drove their sharpshooters from their pits and fortified. Third, at dawn of day enemy attacked General Echols. They were handsomely repulsed with great slaughter to them." This battle took its name from a local tavern named Cold Harbor.

On June 7, General Lee ordered Breckinridge's forces back to the Shenandoah Valley to block the advance of the Federals under General David Hunter. Born in the Shenandoah Valley, Hunter, a militant abolitionist, seemed to relish punishing the Southerners. He burned much of Staunton and Buchanan, captured Lexington, and burned the Virginia Military Institute along with most of the town. His forces captured Liberty, now Bedford, and fully expected to capture Lynchburg, which served as the junction of the railroads on which their armies depended for arms and food; its capture would have been a serious blow to the Confederates.

General Wharton assumed temporary command of the division as Breckinridge recovered from wounds received at Cold Harbor, and the brigade took the train to Lynchburg. By June 16, the 51st built breastworks near Thomas Jefferson's Poplar Forest and, by various ruses such as marching and counter-marching for the next two days, outwitted General Hunter. After severe fighting, Hunter retreated from the city back toward Liberty. Confederate forces followed and engaged Hunter at Hanging Rock near Salem defeating him.

In a period of a month, the 51st assisted in repelling three superior armies at New Market, Cold Harbor, and Lynchburg. On June 16, Woolwine wrote, "Left an hour early and marched for Lynchburg, distant 13 miles. Passed through city to camp west of fair grounds. I went back to town and had quite a nice time."

The 51st, now a part of Franklin County native Jubal Early's command, serving in Wharton's Brigade, Echols' Division, chased Hunter into West Virginia. The regiment fought for Early in the Shenandoah Valley Campaign of 1864. They marched almost constantly for three months and Woolwine rose in rank from first lieutenant to captain.

Late in June 1864, the army started down the Shenandoah Valley and reached Winchester in early July. It captured large quantities of food and other supplies abandoned by the retreating Federal forces. After a day's rest, plenty of food, and some new clothes, the 51st marched to Martinsburg where it chased away a Federal force under General Franz Sigel. After crossing the Potomac River and routing several more Federal forces, it proceeded toward Washington. On July 8, the regiment repelled an attack at Middletown as fighting occurred at the Battle of Monocacy.

Woolwine reports on July 9, 1864, "On to Frederick City. Layed in line of battle all day. Gordon's division whipped the enemy. We crossed Monocosy (Monocacy) River, camped for the night." On the Eleventh, he wrote "Went within 5 miles of city Washington." Echols Division guarded the trains, and although ordered up it never engaged in the fighting. A few days later Rufus wrote, "Heard sermon from third chapter 18th verse James by Rev Brillheart on the bank of the Opequon." The verse ironically reads, "And the fruit of righteousness is sown in peace of them that make peace."

On July 10, the army camped only five miles from Washington. The regiment remained there two days within sight of the Federal

Capitol. General Early thought it too risky due to the large Federal forces on its way to protect the city. He crossed the Potomac into Virginia where he encountered and defeated several small Federal forces. Temporarily, all Federal forces were out of the Shenandoah Valley. Shortly thereafter, General Early's cavalry crossed back over the Potomac and burned the town of Chambersburg, Pennsylvania in retaliation for the burning of Staunton, Lexington, and Buchanan by General Hunter. The 51st stayed near Sharpsburg, Maryland, while McCausland burned Chambersburg. Early's men returned to Virginia and camped in the Winchester area.

In August 1864, General Philip Sheridan assumed command of the Federal forces and launched an offensive against Early in the Shenandoah Valley. He began a relentless campaign that resulted in the complete destruction of the Valley. In a series of battles, General Early's troops retreated south up the Valley.

Woolwine wrote on August 12, "Left before day. Moved on in direction of Strasburg, passing Middletown. Formed line of Battle on Hupp's Hill near Strasburg. Some skirmishing. Remained all day. At night to Fisher's Hill. Formed our command on right of road. Thirteenth through the seventeenth threw up some works. Some skirmishing. Seventieth, the enemy had gone. Pursued and fought at Winchester. Took the fort. Lost of 51st was 3 killed, 28 wounded. Ladies met us on the field."

On August 22, while Early advanced up to the Maryland line, Woolwine wrote, "stopped our brigade at an old church known as Trinity church, built during the reign of Ann Queen of England. In rear of the crumbling structure and dilapidated walls is a grave with the following inscription: 'Sacred to the memory of John Baker who departed this life May 30, 1798, aged 67 years.' I went to town and saw the identical spot where justice overtook John Brown." He witnessed the twenty-second execution of a fellow Confederate for desertion.

On August 25 he wrote, "Moved out at sunrise, crossed fields and old road. Struck pike at Leetown. We passed beyond church. Loaded. Sent 51st forward as skirmishers. Engaged the enemy and drove them a piece. Enemy flanked us and we had to fall back. Our loss in killed, wounded and captured was 102. Lt Col Wolfe and Lt John Akers were among the slain." The next day he wrote, "We moved back by the old battleground, passed the usual horrors of war, over Col. (John P.) Wolfe's grave and went to church and camped for the night."

Picket duty occupied the 51st from September 15 until the nineteenth at Stephenson's Depot near Winchester. Heavy fighting occurred with heavy losses. Members of the 51st scattered several times, and a number fell into enemy hands. During the fighting around Winchester, William Tyler Akers received promotion to major and for a time commanded the 51st Regiment. R. J. Woolwine replaced him as captain of Company D. The Confederates won some skirmishes, but could not hold out against Sheridan's relentless pressure from far superior numbers.

During September, Woolwine and the 51st fought at Fisher's Hill on September 22 with Wharton's Brigade (including the 45th Virginia and the 30th Battalion of Infantry). The regiment was the size of a company and the brigade had only 417 men. Woolwine wrote on the nineteenth, "enemy attacked flanks of Thirtieth Virginia Battalion. We fell back and formed our line nearer town and repulsed them several times ordered to Winchester, then move to rear and repulsed enemy. Our line was giving way, but we fell back in good order to our works. From there we got out in great confusion. Loss heavy. Continued the retreat...sent to Strasburg to stop stragglers. During engagement enemy rode over me and I captured a horse and came out on it. The same was stolen from me at Strasburg. Loss was five kelled fifty five wounded and seventy four captured." On the twenty-second he wrote of the Battle of Fisher's Hill, "I received the order announcing my promotion to the Captaincy of Co D. We stampeded." Three of the 51st died and 28 were wounded.

Reinforcements joined the brigade while it waited for a chance to go on the offensive. On October 13, 1864, the Confederates reentered the Valley and marched toward Winchester where they encountered Sheridan's army at Cedar Creek.

At first, General Early's troops drove back the Federals. The 51st, led by Major W. T. Akers, charged a Federal entrenchment and succeeded in driving the Federals away, but superior strength prevailed and Major Akers' forces fell back. The Union Sixth Corps and cavalry wrecked the 51st. The retreat soon turned into confusion that resulted in a rout. General Early retreated up the Valley to New Market. Woolwine wrote of the Battle of Cedar Creek on October 19, "Moved out at one o'clock a. m. Some of the army flanked. We moved in front and drove enemy out of their camp on the hill at Cedar Creek. But at 4:30 p.m. the tide of battle turned and we fled the field back to Fisher's Hill."

Later that month Woolwine wrote, "Took train for Richmond, Visited soldier's home and Camp Lee." During November and December he reported, "Snowed and Hailed...On working detail. Had the misfortune to get one man killed. Private Henry Lindsey Co. I, 50th Regiment, Carroll County Va. 45th Virginia Regiment refused to drill 51st went to arrest those that refused to drill, my Company took possession of their arms...I took command of the 45 Regiment."

The 51st moved to New Market and into winter quarters. On December 16, Wharton's men, the only Confederates left in the Shenandoah Valley, moved to Fishersville in Augusta County. Since

June 1864, the 51st had marched 1,670 miles and participated in 75 battles or skirmishes.

In January at Fishersville Woolwine wrote, "Where oh where shall I be twelve months hence? Perhaps in vast eternity. All are now taking their sweet repose. Lt. Cheely and myself are enjoying ourselves eating fine apples. Have just completed my pay rolls." He returned to Patrick County for almost a month in January and February 1865 continuing to attend "Frollicks." His uncle, Notley P. Adams, sent General Early $250 in Confederate money.

The Battle of Waynesboro on March 2, 1865 began with sleet and snow falling as the regiment prepared to cross the North Fork of the Shenandoah River. Wharton reported that his division (including the 45th, 50th, and 51st Virginia Regiments and 30th Battalion Virginia Infantry) had 800 men against 7500 "splendidly equipped" Federal cavalry under the immediate command of George Custer and overall command of Phillip Sheridan. Colonel Forsberg commanded the brigade with Major Akers commanding the 51st on its last battlefield. The cavalry surrounded them, and most of the regiment surrendered. Woolwine wrote, "There we was all captured."

While the following list may not be complete, the men listed from Patrick County were captured at Waynesboro and spent the remainder of the war in Federal prisons: George M. Agee, William Tyler Akers, Carr Allen, John V. Anthony, John W. Bowling, Thomas J. Burroughs, Stephen M. Cannaday, John R. Clark, John Conner, John M. Cruise, Samuel W. Davis, Pleasant DeHart, Thomas J. DeHart, Thomas T. DeHart, Peyton Foley, James Franklin Hall, Thomas R. Hall, John T. Hancock, Peter Handy, William T. Harris, Eden T. Hatcher, Elkanah Hatcher, Harvey D. Hopkins, James M. Hopkins, Caleb Howell, Jonathan W. Hubbard, Thomas M. Hubbard, William J. Jefferson, Naamon W. Knowles, James M. Lawson, David H. Martin, Edward N. Martin, T. J. Martin, Green McGee, James Tyler Morrison, John Tatum Morrison, Robert Moss, Charles M. Nolen, Valentine Hamson Pendleton, Paul C. Pigg, Thomas C. Pigg, Richard R. Rakes, George W. Reynolds, William A. Reynolds, Landon Roberson, John W. Rorrer, William T. Ross, John Salmons, John W. Scott, Samuel Scott, Lewis T. Thomas, James R. Turner, Tazewell A. Turner, Elijah DeHart Via, J. Williams and Rufus James Woolwine.

Rufus Woolwine's career as a soldier for the Confederate States of America was over. He served from the very beginning in 1861 and fought to within one month of the end. He saw twenty-two men executed for desertion. His duties included recruiting, chasing deserters, catching whiskey makers, acting as messenger, and fighting beside his men as an infantryman.

General Wharton and the rest of the 51st Virginia joined the

Army of Northern Virginia and served under General John B. Gordon. Forces of the United States captured most of those left along with their battle flag on March 25 at Fort Stedman. Wharton went to Lynchburg to defend the city and was at Christiansburg on April 10 when he heard of Lee's surrender. The 51st Virginia Infantry Regiment disbanded that day.

After the war, Wharton lived and married in Radford, Virginia. He served two terms in the Virginia Senate, where he was involved in the creation of Virginia Tech. When he died in 1906, his family wrapped him in the battle flag of the 51st Virginia Infantry Regiment.

A replica of the battle flag of the 51st Virginia Infantry buried with Gabriel Wharton.

The prisoners from Waynesboro marched to Staunton, Winchester, and Harper's Ferry and then to prisons at Elmira, New York and Fort Delaware. Captain Woolwine and most of his company went to Fort Delaware. On March 9, he wrote of leaving Harper's Ferry, traveling to Baltimore and staying in prison at Fort McHenry, the site of Francis Scott Key's immortal poem that is today our national anthem.

Fort Delaware, completed in 1859 after ten years of construction, is today a state park on Pea Patch Island in the Delaware River outside present day Wilmington. The river is ten miles wide at the site half way between New Jersey and Delaware. Brigadier General Alban F. Schoepf commanded the prison when the members of the 51st Virginia Infantry arrived on March 11, 1865. Schoepf, born in Poland in 1822 and educated in Vienna, served in the Austrian army until he joined a failed Hungarian revolt. He escaped to Syria and made his way to North America in 1851. After working in the U. S. Patent Office and War Department, he fought early in the war in Kentucky.

Prison life at Fort Delaware involved living in a T-shaped barracks divided for officers and enlisted men. Described as lice-infested in the summer and bitterly cold in the winter, the quarters consisted of bunks stacked four high. Food for a day consisted of, "one small loaf of bread and one small piece of meat, together with a half pint or sometimes a pint of weak vegetable juice soup." The following is a stanza of a song rendered by the prisoners at Fort Delaware.

"Now white folks here's a moral; dars nothing true below
For life is but a tater patch, the debil has to hoe
Ebery one has his troubles here, tho's he go near and far,
But the most unlucky debil, is the prisoner of war."

During Woolwine's imprisonment, he continued writing: "March 24th, drawn one pair of drawers. 25th, drawn one pair socks. April third, Drawn one blanket, 1 pair drawers, heard of the fall of Richmond. Fourth salute fired." On the twentieth he wrote, "Where will Lt (John M.) Cemise and myself be one month hence? At home well and hearty I fondly hope." On the twenty-sixth he wrote, "Oh what a lovely day. How much I wish I was in old Patrick this beautiful evening. At _____ with Miss _____, yes the beautiful accomplished _____. The sole subject of all my earthly affection. Oh what a proud consolation it would be to know that she is well and still thinks of her absent, as well as unchanging friend, Rufus." He read books in prison including The New Testament, The Wild West Scenes, Tempest and Sunshine and volume one of The Conquest of Mexico.

Religion continued to be a strong theme in his writing. On Sunday the 30th he wrote, "Glad would I be to quit the life of a prisoner of war and return to my quiet home in the mountains of Patrick. There to rest from the cares and troubles of a four years hard campaigning. I'll trust a merciful god. Myself and Captain Dobyns expects to be at home to day one month hence." On Sunday, May 14, Woolwine wrote of the Charity meeting, "Oh how much I wish I was there. To mingle with old friends that I love so much. I truly hope to be there at the next meeting." The next day he wrote, "My motto is Trust to Luck. Would like to exchange my present abode for my home in old Patrick. Just had a pleasant nap. I was far far away from here in my dreams." The following Sunday he wrote, "Today is Jack Creek meeting. Wish I was there to mingle with friends and relatives, but alas! I see no prospects of a speedy release from this place. Well! I await patiently the action of the government...From this time forward I shall earnestly endeavor to quit the habit of using tobacco in any way whatever." Sprinkled among his writings were quotes in Latin such as "Whilst I Breathe I Hope" and "Never Despair."

Dr. James A. Davis, President of Shenandoah University, wrote in *51st Virginia Infantry Regiment* that these men came home to "no cheering crowds or clanging bands," but to "broken fences and fields of weeds." They fought the "forgotten war." Seldom were they with Lee and the Army of Northern Virginia, but they were protecting the salt works and railroads of southwestern Virginia. They experienced everything imaginable including death, disease, desertion, harsh weather and fighting without supplies and the full strength of manpower. In battle, they cleared an escape route from Fort Donelson, saw victory at New Market and marched to within five miles of Washington D. C. with Jubal Early. These men did not fail in their cause because of a lack of courage or skill as fighters. Those who survived moved on with the remainder of their lives.

Woolwine took the Oath of Allegiance on June 17, 1865, and began his return to Patrick County two days later on the steamer "Richard Willing." He arrived home on the June 27 after a trip that took him from Baltimore via water to Newport News and Richmond, where he saw Washington's statue on the Capitol grounds "draped in mourning." As he traveled by railroad toward Lynchburg, he had to get off at Burke's Station and walk, then catch another train to Farmville. He rode the last five miles to Lynchburg on the James River and Kanawha Canal, then caught a train to Elliston and walked home from there. Woolwine ended his journal with these thoughts: "Thus ends a journey of four years through the most eventful campaign known in the history of men or nations. Now that peace once more smiles upon our land and country, let us look to the wise disposer of all human events and implore Him in His infinite wisdom and mercy to smile upon and bless us, a subjugated people. God grant that our course may be such as to meet with the hearty approval of those in authority, both on earth and in heaven. Oh! That we may yield placid obedience to the laws of our land and the laws of god, so that we may again place our dear old state in her original high standing. And when we shall have done this and have finished our pilgrimage here below, may we all join that celestial host of angels in bright glory to sing praises forever more, to the great Jehovah."

Woolwine settled on Russell Creek in Patrick County, where he manufactured tobacco and sold dry goods. In 1866, he became deputy sheriff of Patrick County. He married Sarah R. Brown in 1868. She received attention from R. J. Reynolds, but chose Woolwine because he had visited her in college. They had four children: Sallie, who married M. V. Stedman; Ada, who married H. S. McKinley; Mabel, who married J. C. Barksdale; and Rufus E. Woolwine, who served as commonwealth attorney of Patrick County for twenty years.

Former Captain Woolwine moved to Stuart and served as sheriff from 1891 until 1904. He lived in retirement until his death on December 4, 1908. The old soldier rests today in the Stuart cemetery near his messmate William Dennis Via. For thirty years Woolwine served as secretary of the Sunday school at Stuart Methodist Church, where his favorite hymn was "A Charge To Keep I Have." Rufus James Woolwine lived as a good citizen, obeying and even enforcing the laws. He put the war behind him, but left his thoughts and feelings to give us insight into an important time in our history.

On December 6, 1900, an aging man from Sweden rose to speak

to the Garland Rodes Camp of the United Confederate Veterans in Lynchburg. Augustus Forsberg said, "Many years have passed since the events I have just narrated, and, like similar details of warfare, not of such importance as to merit a place in history, they will soon be forgotten. But the participants in the struggle of those 'days that tried men's souls' cannot readily forget the trials and perils to which they were exposed."

In July 1913, President Woodrow Wilson presided over the fiftieth anniversary of the Battle of Gettysburg. As a young boy, Wilson, a native Virginian, saw Jefferson Davis brought through Augusta, Georgia, after the Confederate President's capture. This memory was still strong when Wilson spoke at this historic moment saying, "We are made by these tragic, epic things to know what it costs to make a nation—the blood and sacrifice of multitudes of unknown men lifted to a great stature in the view of all generations by knowing no limit to their manly willingness to serve." One veteran from the North and the South represented each side on the platform near Wilson. In a symbolic gesture of reunification, the President grasped the hand of both men simultaneously. Photographs show Dr. William Dennis Via of Patrick County, the Southern soldier holding a Second National Flag of the Confederacy that is on display in the Patrick County Historical Museum.

Born on September 8, 1838, Via enlisted in the Ross Company of the 51st Virginia Infantry in June 1861 serving with Rufus Woolwine. After the war, he married Minnie Via and had five children: Daisy, James, Marcie, Mary and Posie. Dr. Via, a dentist, served as one of the first Trustees of the town of Stuart and possibly mayor in 1884. Less than a year before his own death, the old soldier still attended reunions, the last one in Jacksonville, Florida. As the last survivor of his mess, his time as Corporal, Company D, 51st Virginia Infantry dominated his thoughts. Dr. Via died on March 6, 1915, and lies today in Stuart town Cemetery near his friend, Rufus James Woolwine. On February 20, 1914, reflecting upon the death of his friend Via wrote the following poem and sent it to Woolwine's daughter.

President Thomas Woodrow Wilson and William Dennis Via of Patrick County and the 51st Virginia Infantry at the Gettysburg Reunion in 1913.

"Oh! Death thou has taken him away,
  And his suffering was so great.
I stayed with him all I could,
  For he was my last 'messmate'!

My 'mess' have all left me now,
  And I am left here alone.
Captain Woolwine, the last to leave me,
  Our friendship was truly known!

We traveled over mountains and valleys,
  Where crystal streams ran down.
Now all their travelings are over,
  Not one of them can be found!

The Lord has done right with them
  I hope they are all at rest.
Though I am left here alone,
  I hope they are with the blest!

If they are with their Saviour,
  Though I cannot long here remain.
My 'mess' has gone and left me,
  Though true happiness I hope to gain!

We loved and respected each other,
  While we together roamed.
But they have all left me now,
  And I will seek a heavenly home!

Now I hope to meet them all,
  In the sweet bye and bye.
And walk the golden streets of heaven,
  Where we will never, never

The 1903 Confederate Reunion in Stuart, Virginia. Rufus Woolwine is on the far left second from the end wearing the bowler hat.

Chapter Four
"The Patrick Boys"
Company K, 50th Virginia Infantry Regiment

From 1862 through 1864 fighting from Fort Donelson in Tennessee to Spotsylvania Court House in May 1864, few men saw fiercer combat than the 50th Virginia Infantry Regiment. From the first festive exciting days at the start of the war to the somber end four years later, men from Patrick County served with the regiment in a company that initially named themselves "The Patrick Boys," but later became Company K. Rather than trying to tell their stories solely through the history of the regiment, this chapter allows them to speak for themselves through their letters in sometimes humorous, often in poignant and too many times tragic ways.

Cheley B. Rakes
50th Virginia Infantry.

Courtesy of Lisa Smith.

Highland Forest, Kentucky, January 30, 1861
Dear Uncle,
    What a grand thing the art of printing is, over where understood in its humblest forms; and what a grand thing is the U. S. Postal system. By the aid of these agents we are able to communicate with each other, though hundreds and thousands of miles should intervene. Should we, in our humble capacity be able to achieve so important a result as to conversed with each other whilst residing in different states, is it any

wonder that such great things should be brought about by these means then placed in hands competent to use them. But this is not my intent.

    The allusion above to the U. S. Postal system brings to mind the humiliating fact that in all probability we shall shortly have no U. S. Postal system, together with the convincing on my part, that if the arguments, held out by many of our leading men be valid, we shall shortly have no Union, nor never have had according to the view I take of the matter. If the Doctrine of the Right of States to secede from the Union at pleasure be orthodox, we emphatically never had had any Union, but a mere association of States which could be dissolved at any moment that the caprice of disaffected members might dictate. I make bold to say that the Constitution, in spite of the praise which heaped upon it, has proven itself to be a weak and inefficient instrument and I will sustain my position by logical argument. But before I arraign the Constitution let me say a word concerning secession. I am sure that no one can show, by argument or other wise, that secession is contemplated in the Spirit of the Constitution. I also think that none of the States primarily recognize secession, but that it is an original dogma, sprung to aid in carrying out the designs of ultra-politicians. Considering the nature of the Federal Compact, it is absurd in the extreme to regard secession as any other than revolution, for we all know that an agreement, when signed by all parties concerned, because a law; for what would be the use of entering into a compact if it were not expected that all parties should be bound by it. During all our previous national troubles, no State ever contemplated secession except South Carolina, and then the entire power of remaining States discountenanced it upon the grounds that it was revolutionary. If secession was revolutionary in 1833 it is none other now, and it is my opinion that a revolution under the present circumstances would be highly dangerous. But to return to the Constitution was formed for the purpose of consolidating our strength and interests so as to enable us to protect our right in all our relations as an independent nationality. Its spirit is strictly federative. It was expected to retain full scope of power, unimpaired by the legislation of separate members. This any one may see who will read it. How very absurd then to argue that a State has the right to join the compact, partake of benefits, be protected in its relations and then withdraw at pleasure. Suppose for instance that the Government should be involved in foreign difficulty and some of the States, as was the case in both the War of '12 and that with Mexico, should be violently opposed to the policy of the Government, they may if we recognize the right of secession, with draw from the Union, withhold their support and precipitate the Confederacy into the danger of falling a prey to foreign invasion, and aggression generally.

    No sir, the States ratified the Constitution with no such views, but with the understanding that they bound by it as a supreme law governing their actions, to which they were to conform forever. The framers of the Constitution entered such sentiments. The object of their labor was to form a united Government and to render that Government permanent. And is there any permanence in a compact, which may be broken at the will of any party or parties. No, such an idea is at war with reason. These are the outline of my views concerning the legality of secession. I have no time to show why I think that as a policy it would be ruinous to the very parties who would avail themselves of it as a means of redress of grievance.

I have said the Constitution was inefficient. This inefficiency consists in it's neglecting to provide for the executions of its provisions. It is true it makes the President its executive but has left him without any very effective means of performing this duty. He is told to execute the laws. This is very easily done where there is little or no resistance, but when the resistance becomes so great as to require forcible measures, he is compelled to desist for fear of violating some other important principle of the Constitution. It should have provided for the immediate and consistent execution of its purposes, under any and every circumstance. But it is oblivious, as I have always patriotic and willing to make individual concessions for the public weal. That our fathers should have made such a mistake, considering their foresight and acquaintance with human nature, seems rather singular. To a people, enlightened, patriotic and perfect this form of Government would do. But to take a vast people, possessing a full quota of the passions and prejudices of imperfect humanity, and I fear that our eminently Republican Government is a little too Republican.

Do not infer from my remarks that I regard the actual secession of some of the States, and contemplated secession of others, as being the first violation of the Constitution. Had the nullification of the Fugitive Slave Law and the passage of Personal Liberty Bills never taken place we would not now have been upon the brink of ruin. If the Constitution had given the President the power, or having the power, had he promptly proceeded against those Northern violators of the Constitution all would now be well.

As matters now stand, I am unable to say what it will come to. If there exists a secession, the mere election of Lincoln is no excuse for seceding and I think that such men as Tombs and company who boldly got up in the Halls of Congress and declared themselves rebels against the government, before they had any cause, their proclivities. Upon the multitudinous, other questions pertaining to this subject I shall say nothing, for there is no use of spinning my views out to a volume when there is no probability of their being respected where they will do any good.

Kentucky agrees with me finely. I have never been in better

health than at present. I have flattened up until my coat, which used to be abundantly large, will not meet on me by about four inches. In fact, I have become so fleshy that I have a double, dry, snow alternating so rapidly that I can't say which we have had the most of. Money matters are hard in the extreme. Every thing down and hardly a dime extant. This immediate section of this country don't suit me. If a person owns a farm and will half week it, he can live very easily. I haven't a farm and shan't locate here permanently, for at present at least. As soon as I can raise a few dollars, I am going down to the Ohio River, and down it a piece to see the country. You need not write until you hear from me again. You won't know where to direct. Let them all read this. Give my best respects to all. Oh! I must say that I can survey land and plot it accurately. I have invented a plan and instrument to measure the distance to an object without going to it. It is entirely new and so plain that I wonder that it is not in my books. The rule is invariable; no doubt about that. I intend writing to Davies to learn if it be entirely original. If it is, it must have the credit of the discovery. I will explain it to you when I see you. I have made the instrument myself. The Post Office is so unhandy is the reason I don't write to everybody in your country. Tell them that if the Union don't burst they my look may look forever so many letters before long.
         Powell Benton Reynolds

  In the spring of 1861, Captain Alexander W. Reynolds of the United States Army Quartermaster Department found himself stationed at San Antonio, Texas, under the immediate command of General David E. Twiggs. Texas secessionists appointed Reynolds the state's chief quartermaster after he and Twiggs turned over to them U. S. property including $30,000 in gold and silver. Reynolds never resigned and eventually the United States Army dropped him from its rolls. Born in Virginia in 1816, Reynolds graduated from the United States Military Academy in 1838. He fought in the Seminole War the next year and served two stints in the Quartermaster Department from 1847-1855 and 1858-1861. Reynolds became the first commander of the 50th Virginia Infantry Regiment.
  One of the largest groups of soldiers from Patrick County served in Company K of the 50th Virginia Infantry. The "Patrick Boys" organized under the direction of Captain Jefferson Thompson Lawson at his father's home. Another group organized at Bartlett Smith's home and another at Patrick Court House in May 1861. The Company officers in addition to Captain Lawson were First Lieutenant Martin Staples, Second Lieutenant Walter T. Noel, and Third Lieutenant Benjamin F. Cloud.
  In Ararat, family traditions speak of the Bowman and Puckett families along with their neighbors holding a party before their young men went off to war. Reed Puckett and his brothers Robert, Doctor

Floyd, Elijah, Ephram, and John, joined Company K of the 50th Virginia Infantry. Other brothers Hosea and Riley joined other Confederate units. The oldest brother, Lewis, who had moved to Ohio in 1850, fought for the Union in the 175th Ohio Infantry. In total, then, nine men from the family of Jacob and Sarah Marshall Puckett fought in the war.

Other young men from Patrick County joined the regiment. At five feet and nine inches, with blonde hair and blue eyes, Jehu Barnard set out for war. His brothers James W., Thomas A., Richard Joseph, Charles, and his brother-in-law Thomas Smith eventually joined him in the biggest event of their lives.

On June 22, the men enlisted at Patrick Court House for one year. Two men with different fates enlisted that day. Samuel Harden Dunkley rose to the rank of sergeant of Company K. G. Boston Scott rose in rank to commissary sergeant. Five days later, the men traveled at the personal expense ($25) of Captain Lawson to Christiansburg.

Camp Jackson, Wytheville, July 10, 1861

We arrived here night before last and are all in good health and spirits. We have a plenty of everything. Fare is excellent and water very good for limestone. General Floyd says we have the finest company in camp. We expected to parade in Wytheville today and anticipate great applause, especially from the ladies. Our journey to this place has been one general ovation. The people collected in great crowds along the road huzzahing and showering the bouquets upon us. I received at least a dozen bouquets. One lady handed me one with a paper attached, on which was written some poetry and signed, El Wade. We came from Christiansburg to this place after night. The ride was a fast one and delighted some of our boys exciting…We have messed out. Henry Webb, Asa Scott, L. D. Reynolds, G. B. Scott, Floyd Dickerson, John Boswell, Jack Reynolds and F. M. "Buck" Spangler constitute "Mess Davis." Henry Webb is "Head of Mess." We expect to stay here about 3 weeks. England says the blockade shall be open again the end of September, peace or no peace. It is the impression that peace will be made before we leave camp.

             G. Boston Scott

Patrick County, Virginia, July 14, 1861
Dear Brothers,

I have seated myself to drop you a few lines. We are all as well as common with the exception of Mother. She is complaining some today and was sick yesterday too, but she says she thinks she will get well in a few days. I hope this will find you both well. We received your kind letters the 13th and was glad to hear from you and also we got your pictures too and was glad to get them, but they looked so much like you and we could not see you. It made us all feel mighty bad. Mother said she thought they was the prettiest things she ever saw in her life and I thought so too. We showed them to several people and I showed them to Wilch and Hence Bowman and they both burst out crying and could not hardly look at them. And me and Liza and Texanna got the presents you sent us and was glad to get them, but I was sorry you spent your money for them, but we will keep them as long as we live and remember you. Dan was not able to send us anything to remember him, but we will remember him. Also, I wish I had a present to send you both, but I haven't anything to send. Liza said she would write to you, but she said she could not.

To William Smith,
    We will try to save you clover and grain if we can. Some of us. Mother has sent word to Uncle Jehue to come and cut your grain, but I don't know whether he will get the word or not. Dad, he is gone over to Mr. Arrington to buy him a cow so he can't send you any word, but he is getting along tolerable well with his work. Bill, you are excusable for not writing no more to me. Those girls is getting along fine only they are lonesome, but they ain't as lonesome as I am. So, I will quit. I will write more the next time. Excuse all bad spelling. I remain your loving Sister till death

To Daniel Smith
    Daniel, I was glad to see you thought enough of us to write to us. I am sorry to tell you the trouble that Adaline Terry has… See, her Mother has had her leg cut off and they say there is no hope of her living if she is alive now and you know she sees trouble. You must write me and her a letter and cheer her up. Don't think you can't. So, I must quit. Dan, don't you and Bill forget me. I know I won't forget you and the fun we have seen together, but I am afeared we not see no more fun nor satisfaction.
Mary Smith

Camp Jackson, Wytheville, Virginia, July 28, 1861
Dear Sir (Tirea Barnard),
    I take my pen in hand to write you a few lines to let you know that I have had the measles, but I am improving very fast. I hope these few lines may find you and all well. I have not wrote to you yet by reason of my inabilities but you must excuse me for it. There are about 75 of the Captain Lawson Company sick with the measles, but they are mending very fast. Mrs. Barnard, I shall recollect you for the kindness of presenting me that blanket for it has been a great friend to me in this

exposed camp. I yet give you my best thanks for it. There was the greatest battle fought at Manassas Gap last Sunday that ever was fought in America.

    We lost in killed 200 and in wounded 1000. The Yankees lost killed 5000 and in wounded 12000, besides several other battles which have been fought lately and we took about 1500 prisoners and are bringing them yet. We got 1500 stand of arms and 60 cannon all old except 2 pieces. I want to see you all very bad and I would be glad if you would write to me as soon as possible and tell me how all the neighbors is getting along and how the crops is in that country. So, no more but remain your affectionate friend until death.   Henry A. Hefflefinger

    At Camp Jackson in Wytheville, "The Patrick Boys" became Company K upon joining the 50th Regiment of Virginia Volunteers under the command of Colonel Alexander W. Reynolds, Lieutenant Colonel William W. Finney, an 1848 VMI graduate and Major Charles E. Thorburn, an 1853 graduate of the U. S. Naval Academy.

    Camp Jackson was the assembly point of numerous companies selected by former Virginia Governor and recent United States Secretary of War, John B. Floyd to be part of a brigade that President Jefferson Davis had asked him to recruit. The newly formed brigade consisting of the 45th Virginia Infantry, 51st Virginia Infantry, 23rd Battalion Virginia Infantry, 8th Virginia Cavalry, and the 50th Virginia Infantry. On July 25, the 50th Virginia departed Wytheville, en route to active operations in western Virginia. However, "The Patrick Boys," whose 4 officers and 102 men had been riddled with disease, were left behind until August 12. The letters from the men of Company K at this time reflect the challenges, disappointments, frustrations, as well as some of the pleasures, of this first phase of their war. They rejoined the regiment to fight at Cross Lanes, now in West Virginia, on August 26, 1861, claiming they would "drink good Brandy and kill as many Yankees as we please." The 50th Infantry Regiment, in addition to Company K, consisted of: Company A, the "Lee Rifles," of Lee County, commanded by Captain Jonathan Richmond; Company B, from Lee County, commanded by Captain Alexander S. Vandeventer; Company C, from Tazewell County, commanded by Capt. Francis W. Kelly; Company D, the "Wilson Rifles," from Grayson County, commanded by Captain Lynville Perkins; Company E, the "Smyth Grays," from Smyth County, commanded by Captain Columbus F. McDonald; Company F, the "Pedlar Mills Guard," from Amherst County, commanded by Captain Robert W. Snead; Company G, the "Floyd Blues," of Washington County, commanded by Captain David D. Dunn Company G (2nd), of Lee County, commanded by Captain William S. Hannah, organized in March 1862; Company H, the "Wise Yankee Catchers," of Wise County, commanded by Captain Logan H. N. Salyer; Company I, of Pulaski

County, commanded by Captain Thomas Poage; Company L, of Smyth County, commanded by Captain Patrick C. Buchanan, which became Company E, 23rd Battalion Virginia Infantry. Three cavalry companies initially were also part of the 50th Virginia: Company A, the "Smyth Dragoons," commanded by Captain John H. Thompson; later became part of the 8th Virginia Cavalry Regiment; Company B, the "Lee Grays," commanded by Captain Daniel S. Dickinson, and was mustered out of service in September 1861; Company C, the "Nelson Rangers," commanded by Captain Thomas P. Fitzpatrick; later became part of the 8th Virginia Cavalry Regiment.

Wytheville, Virginia, August 2, 1861
Dear Folks (Tirea and Eliza Barnard),

    I take the present opportunity to inform you that I am getting better, hoping these few lines may find you enjoying the same. I came over in town day before yesterday and Davy Harrell came to wait on us. I would be very glad to see you all, but it is not worth my while to write any news for you know more than I do. Everything is dull here. Everybody is sick, but they are getting better. The other regiment is going to start a Monday. You must do the best you can. Everyone give my love to Litha Martha and Mary. So, I must come to a close by saying goodbye to you all. Excuse my bad writing, but still remain your loving son.

    I have received your letter this evening. Thomas Lambert was right. I was sick then was taken the measles. I was taken with a pain my head and back and hurting in my joints. I was taken on Thursday and broke out Sunday night. It will be a week day after tomorrow since I broke out. If you all get the measles, you must boil plenty of Sheep Tea for them about the time they break out. I have not got the sense to write now and you must excuse me for I have to site on my bed and lay it on my knee.

    I don't care whether you come out or not for it will not do me any good. So, nothing more.

Jehu Barnard

    As the men of Company K recuperated and waited their time to deploy, they wrote home about their health, their reactions to some of their officers, and gave advice to family about joining the army. The absence from Patrick County of the men from Company K created challenges to those left behind. There was farm work to do and crops to harvest.

Wytheville, Virginia, August 5, 1861
Dear Father (Tirea and Eliza Barnard),

I take the present opportunity to inform you that I am still on the mend hoping these few lines may find you enjoying the same. I am tolerable weak and have moderate appetite. You know how anyone feels after having the measles by experience. Our Captain was appointed Colonel the Fourth Regiment and Martin Staples has gone to the Manassas Gap to get a bigger office and Tim Noel is our present Captain. They are all in confusion about it. I, myself, am always contented. Some swear they will go home if Martin Staples is our Captain.

Tell Richard and Isham that if they go volunteer to come and go with me for I would not be satisfied for them to go with anybody else and not go with me. Tell Uncle Will to come and go with me if he is going to volunteer. Tell him that he must not volunteer until he is compelled to volunteer or be drafted. Tell Him that he must not volunteer till he is compelled to for he lacks a good deal of being able to stand the fatigue.

I sent my likeness by Henry Dutherage and I want to know whether you ever got it or not. Jim you must write to me to let me know many rye stacks you mowed. How many the reed field made about all about it.

Jim, you wrote to me to come home next Saturday but I shall not try to come for I don't care about coming until the war is over and then if God spares our lives we will see one another again.

Give my best respects to all that wish any good for me and still more for them that hates me. You will please excuse my bad writing and awkward dictating. Keep in good spirits for I can hardly have time to think of you there in so much fuss going on here, let alone to think to write to you. So, I must come to a close by saying good-bye to you all.
Jehu Barnard

Wytheville, Virginia, August 9, 1861
Dear Brother (Isham and Richard Barnard),

I seat myself to let you know that I am well hoping these few lines may find you enjoying the same. We are going to leave today. Joel and Cloyd is getting better. They act gaily as ever. They was when they was going a fox hunting. Joel says that you must come and join our company if you join any and we will drink good Brandy and kill as many Yankees as we please. So, nothing more.
Jehu Barnard

The Confederates under John B. Floyd routed the heavily outnumbered 7th Ohio, and the letters from Company K reflected the ease of the victory. Writing several months after the battle, Asa Scott's letter described the Union defeat. Closer in time to the battle, the letters of the men in the unit not only reflected the ease of the victory, but also the sobering realization by some in the company that they might not survive the war. John Boswell's letter gave several men a chance to express these feelings.

Camp Gauley, Nicholas County, Virginia, August 29, 1861
Dear Father and Mother,
     An opportunity has offered itself at last for me to write to you. I can inform you that I am not well at present. I have been sick for several days but I have not been dangerously bad. I can say to you that I have been in more battle of course. We came out victorious. I suppose there was about Seven Hundred Yankees and about Eighteen hundred of our men. We killed about Sixty-five or Seventy and wounded about forty and taken a hundred prisoner. We sent the prisoners to Richmond yesterday. They never killed but four or five of our men and wounded some five or six...There was not a single one of us touched, but the balls whistled all around us. I said I was in the battle and so I was, but I never shot at anybody from the fact that they was so fast in retreating that not half of us could find them at all we all found several guns and pistols and several other things too tedious to mention and I will like to forgot we took several wagons and carriages and a horse or two prisoners too. That is about all of the most important things. We are expecting a battle every day but perhaps we will not fight anymore for a month or two. P. S. As Fleming wants to write some I will not write anymore at present but at some more convenient time. I will write a long letter. I still remain your affectionate,
     John W. Boswell

John Boswell
50th Virginia Infantry.

Courtesy of Vera Y. Stanley

Sis,

    I have acted badly in not writing to you but I have not had the chance. You must take good care of your self until I come back if I ever do come back well if I do not you must remember me. Remember me tis all I ask I could not wish for than more there to be cherished by a heart so tender and so pure. Tell Caroline to write me and not to forget me

                        Fleming M. Spangler

Well Tighey,

I can inform you that I am not dead yet and has not forgot you all and I want soon I wish to be remembered to all of the family. We have been in a fight none of our company was hurt but I shall say no more it about it. I want you to remember me until dead or return and take good care of my likeness I have not much to write at present. I will come to a close by saying remember your true George W. Yeatts

Camp Joseph Johnston,
Near Bonsacks, Botetourt, Virginia, August 30, 1861
To Those At Home,

    I take this opportunity to write to you to let you know where I am at. I am staying at a house sick, about one mile from camp. Jehu Barnard, W. R. Underwood and Gabe Richardson are with me. We are attended on very well by three widows. I was getting nearly well of the measles when I left Wytheville, I came down here on the cars partly after night it rained and I took cold, and have been laid up ever since I have been here. I feel a little better this morning and hope I am getting well. The siege I had has been very painful and tiresome. Jack George, Sam'l Hall and Green Harris are at a house about two miles from here very sick. Jack has the fever. Doctor Pucket and Bob came down from Wytheville a few days ago. They was unable to march and I got a free ticket for them to go back to Wytheville until they got well. I rode in the omnibus down to the depot day before yesterday evening and saw them and Virgil Gates leave for Wytheville. I have not heard from them since. They are six or eight of our boys at Wytheville. Yet, about a week ago I saw Asa Tilghman and Jack Shoulder their guns and knapsacks and start for Lewisburg 84 miles from here. I am a little uneasy about Asa Tilghman and Jack. They were tolerable weak, not having fairly recovered from the measles yet and to march 84 miles and carry a gun and knapsack will mighty near trot them through. I reckon though if they break down they will take up at some place. Buck is as well as he ever was. You ought to see me since I have been sick. I have fell away about 35 pounds. I have had my hair cut off close and look for all the word like a skeleton. I am very well satisfied, and if I was well, I wouldn't want anything else just now.

    The people are mighty kind in this neighborhood more so than they were at Wytheville. The Colonel said yesterday that there were over 200 sick men here and nearly all of them are in the neighborhood at private houses.

Tell J. Green Lenny that I received his letter while I was a Camp Jackson, and will answer it as soon as I strike any news to write. Tell C. M. R. that I received his letter about midnight on the cars at Christiansburg Depot and will answer it soon. He must write every chance.

Tell Nancy that I received her letter and was just making preparation to answer it, but Tyler Boling got in before me. If you write to me direct your letter to Bonsacks, Botetourt County, Virginia. Write very soon for I shall leave here soon as I get able to march.

General Floyd's Brigade I understand is about three miles the other side of Lewisburg. Two runners came here at 2 o'clock last night from General Floyd, but I don't know for what purpose. It is rumored in camp that we will go to Missouri. Tell Dick to write.

Enclosed I send a letter that I received from J. L. Mabry. It contains a good many particulars of the great battle of Manassas.

G. Boston Scott

Camp Joseph Johnston,
Near Bonsacks, Roanoke County, Virginia, August 30, 1861
Greene,

I take this opportunity to inform you that I am very unwell, and have been so ever since I saw you. As I came down from Wytheville, I took a severe cold, which has settled on my lungs. I have a very good place to stay at but the water does not suit me. If I do not get better shortly, I shall come home.

I have not heard from Asa since he left here which was a few days after we arrived at this place, though I saw a wagoner who saw you company come up with the brigade, but he couldn't tell me anything about Asa because he didn't know him.

When our company marched, they left nine or ten men here. Since that time some have went on after the company, some went to Wytheville, and some went home. So there is none but me here now. I am staying with three widows who are mighty kind but they talk to me entirely too much. I can't stand the jabber of old women especially when I don't feel well. If I come home I shall come by Wytheville. I want to see about those fellows that are there. Doctor and Bob Puckett, Jack Lewis, J. G. West etc. were at Wytheville, which I last heard from them.

You will notice that I am so nervous that I can scarcely write, I don't know what the reason though I have been so ever since I had the measles. I wrote home some time ago and told them to direct their letters to Bonsacks, Botetourt County when I ought to have said Roanoke

County. The cause of the mistake was that I am staying in Botetourt County, but the post office is in Roanoke County.

One of the widows that I am staying with is a second cousin to General Washington. This is undoubtedly a fact though she does not boast on it herself. I read a chapter or two of the bible for her every night.

I need not write any general news for you can read the papers well as I can.

G. Boston Scott

Company K fought for the first time in present-day West Virginia in the Sewell Mountain Campaign on August 26, 1861. One Patrick native, Asa Scott, said of his first battle that it "didn't last but 15 minutes." The regiment with the 51st Virginia fought in the center of the line against Union General William S. Rosecrans at Carnifex Ferry on September 10. Floyd hastily retreated after victory, causing another Patrick native, Jehu Barnard, to say, "the Yankees got everything except my blanket."

The 50th Virginia, like Robert E. Lee, found itself between two former Virginia Governors and rivals: Floyd and Henry S. Wise in present-day West Virginia. Lee arrived on September 24 and organized the Army of the Kanawha into three brigades. The First Brigade under command of Colonel Henry Heth included the 45th, 51st and 50th Virginia infantry regiments. Floyd consolidated the 50th into the 51st regiment for one month due to low numbers present.

Greenbrier County, Virginia, September 20, 1861
Dear folks (Tirea Barnard Family),

I take the present opportunity to inform you that I am in tolerable good health hoping these few lines may find you well. I have some news for you this time more than I will have time to write. On the ninth there was a fight taken place between Floyd and the Yankees and there was 9 thousand of the Yankees in the fight and twenty two hundred of Floyd men and it was told by the Yankees that we killed two thousand of them and they killed 4 thousand of us. They took two of our men prisoner and put them in a smoke house and they said that the Yankees buried all next day and they only got about half of them buried and the next night they got out and swam Gauley River and come to the army. Floyd never got nary man killed. He got seven wounded and they fought 4 hours and a half and me and Joe and Cloyd was sick in a barn and Joel could not walk and our captain sent us word that if we could not walk we would have to stay there and we happened to get a horse for Joel to ride or the Yankees would have taken us and we was not able to tote our knapsacks and we had to leave our knapsacks and the Yankees has got everything except my blanket and I have nothing but the clothes I have on but we are having some made. I was not in the fight but the bombs fell thick all around me. The doctor sent all the sick across the river. It is supposed that John Boswell is taken by the Yankees. He was left behind with the fever and we haven't heard from him since. I have not got a letter from you since I left Camp Jackson and I wrote four letters you must write as soon as possible.

    Direct your letters to Lewisburg, Greenbrier County, Virginia, Floyd's Brigade in care of Captain J. T. Lawson. You must write how you came out with the measles and how everything is getting along there. We have tolerable hard times here and you guess at the balance. Write how much rye you made on the… field whether you have got it threshed or not.

    Jim, write how the girls is getting along and I will write how I get along with gals in this country. All the gals in western Virginia seems to take a liking to me and sometimes I have a good deal of fun with Dutch gals.

    I had a good supply of paper and envelopes laid in and the Yankees got all. So, that is the cause that I didn't write soon after the battle. So nothing more.

                  Jehu Barnard

    After retreating from Carnifex Ferry, General Floyd fell back to Meadow Bluff. There on September 24, Floyd reorganized his Army of the Kanawha into three brigades. The First Brigade under command of Colonel Henry Heth included the 45th, 51st and 50th Virginia infantry regiments. Moving to reinforce General Lee at Sewell Mountain, Floyd arrived there with his army on October 1. Having consolidated the 50th into the 51st Virginia regiment due to low numbers of men in the 50th, Floyd departed Sewell Mountain on October 12 with a mission to attack Union forces at Gauley Bridge, where the New River and the Gauley River joined to form the Kanawha River. Driving Union forces from Raleigh Court House (now Beckley), Floyd passed through Fayetteville and arrived near Gauley Bridge on October 21. In sharp contrast to high morale at the front were the low feelings of the numerous sick from Company K who remained hospitalized and unpaid at various locations, including Greenbrier White Sulphur Springs.

White Sulphur Springs, Greenbrier County, Virginia,
October 1861
Dear Father, Mother, Brothers and Sister,
    I take this opportunity of writing you a few lines to inform you that I landed here yesterday from the Meadow Bluff and I think that I feel some better this morning and I think I will be well in a short time. They is thirty of our company here not that is sick. Some of them is very

bad. Now I will give you the names of some of them, Fell Spangler, Scott, Perkins, McPeak, Samuel Smith, William Smith, Dick Fry and so many more that I can't tell you their names this time. These is the ones that is the worst off. I wrote to you for some things when I was very sick and I have forgotten what I wrote. I want one pair of pants and drawers and one short tailed shirt. Tell Charlie that I let you…for five dollars. So give my best respects to all the connection and friends. So no more, but shall remain your true affectionate son until death. I heard yesterday that General Jackson at Cheat Mountain whip the Yankees. The report is that he killed 25 hundred of them and the Yankees retreated from Big Sandy Mountain.

James Barnard

Greenbrier White Sulphur Springs, October 16, 1861
Dear Father (Tirea Barnard),

    I seat myself to inform you that I am not well greatly hoping these few lines may find you all well. I have had the fever and am just getting so I can go about. I write a letter every two or three days and you don't write about getting them and I have ten or twelve. It was a while that I couldn't hear from you, but I hear from you every day or two now. I got John's chestnuts and was very glad to get to eat something that had come from home and more than that I was gladder to eat that John had sent me than all the balance. I got the pair of socks that…fetched and they sure came in good time for I'd just wore out the last pair. Tell grandfather that I have wrote something to him nearly every time I wrote, but I suppose you have got none of them. Tell Uncle Bartlett's folks that Bill is sick with the fever and has been very low but he is on the mend now and will soon be well if he get no backset.

    Dan is well and hearty. Buck Spangler has the fever. He is getting better and several that I won't mention their names all in the same house.

    Tell all my brothers, sisters and friends to write. The letters I sent to you are about hard times, but its not worth while to commence writing about that for we have nothing else but hard time here. We haven't drawed any money yet and I have spent all but five dollars that I got for the Tennessee bill and am spending that now.

    There's some of the boys that has been out of money for a long time and they have suffered a great deal it ain't only a few but nearly all. Tell Polly and Sally that I lost the gloves they sent me and I am very sorry when I thought of their being gone. I have got a pants now. James sent that was sent to John Hatcher and he was dead and bought them and gave two dollars and 25 cents for them. They were very good jeans and were lined through out with factory cloth. He was owing me some and thought I had better take the pants. I want you to send me my brown jeans jacket, one towel and tell Isham to prepare leather to make me a good pair of boots against big snows come.

      You wrote to know whether I was coming home at Christmas or not. If I am able and can get an honorable furlough I am coming home and not without. I would be very glad to see you all but I would rather not see you than to have the name of running away. Sam Hooker and Will Holt ran away the other morning because they could not draw no money. John, you and Jim must pick up me some chestnuts and dry them and keep them till I come back and I will you a mug a piece that cost 37 cents a piece. If Hub will haul them. So nothing more.

                                      Jehu Barnard

Camp near Hawks Nest, Fayette County, Virginia, October 23, 1861
To Those At Home,
      I take this occasion to write you a few lines to let you know where I am at etc. We have been marching for a week or two. We left Sewell Mountain about two weeks ago, came around by Raleigh and Fayette courthouses and arrived here 1 ½ miles from the Hawk's Nest day before yesterday we had some fighting with the Yankees across the river 5 or 6 of our men were wounded. The numbers of the enemies killed and wounded is not known. We have a force of 5,000 under Floyd. General Lee and Loring are supposed to be crossing down on the other side of the river. We have possession of Cotton Hill. Our guns command three ferries and the Kanawha Road, which effectively cuts off the enemy's supplies except by the Summerville Road, which will soon be impassable. The Yankees have been at Raleigh Court House and Fayetteville, robbed the stores, burned the houses, broke into the clerks offices, the streets are literally strewn with pieces of law books and county records. Asa and Buck Spangler are at the Greenbrier White Sulphur Springs.

      I am well satisfied and in high spirits waiting to get a pop at a Yankee. Write and direct to Company K, 50th Regiment, Floyd's Brigade, care of Sergeant Lawson.

                                      G. Boston Scott

      The 50th spent November fighting at the confluence of the New and Kanawha rivers near the Gauley Bridge on Cotton Hill in present day West Virginia. It was an isolated spot. The lack of mail seemed to bother some more than Union bullets. By the end of the month, the men thought they would winter at Peterstown, but then transferred to Newbern in Pulaski County. On December 16, Jefferson Davis ordered Floyd's men to Kentucky to assist General Albert Sidney Johnston.

Camp Dickinson, Fayette County, Virginia, November 7, 1861

    I take this occasion to write again although I think it almost useless as I don't believe letters ever get from here home, or at least, I know they never get from home here. I have received but one letter since I left Wytheville and that was while I was a Bonsacks. I have wrote four of five letters home, one to Uncle Thomas, one to Uncle Wolford, three or four to N.... Together with miscellaneous letters to other persons since I left Bonsacks and have not received a single answer.

    I have been tolerable well since I have been with the Army, having been on the sick list only once. Asa is at the White Sulphur Springs and has been sick but is improving very fast. Buck Spangler is at the same place and was very sick the last I heard from him. Jeff Lawson and Jack Reynolds are at Raleigh Court House sick, but not dangerous. Bob Pucket, Tilghman, and Henry Webb are here and well. James Monday, Jehu Barnard, Bill and Dan Smith are at the White Sulphur. Our company here numbers about 40. The Yankees are encamped at Gauley Bridge and along up and below on the river, about 3 or 4 miles from here. We have to go out every day or two on picket. There has been a regular cannonading kept up between the two armies for a week. The first two days of the fight we were sent down on the river with our rifles to pick off the officers. The musket balls, pieces of shell, and that flew near us. The cannonading is still kept up. I don't know how it will terminate. General Floyd I suppose intends to take up winter quarters at this place. If he does we will undoubtedly freeze out. This is a mountainous, cold, uninhabited, unfriendly portion of the country.

    There was rather a sad accident happened yesterday morning within twenty steps of our tent. A gun went off killing one man instantly and wounding another so that he died within fifteen minutes. Yesterday was the election. The day was so unpleasant that few of us voted, in fact, we took but very little interest in the election. We have something else out here to think about. I am very well satisfied. Bullets, shell etc. are small matters, being shot at has become so common that nobody cares for it. I experience more uneasiness about my health than I do about being shot in battle. You must all write whenever it is convenient and direct your letters to Company K, 50th Regiment, Floyd's Brigade.

                                                       G. Boston Scott

White Sulphur Springs, Greenbrier County, Virginia
November 19, 1861
Dear Uncle (Tirea and Eliza Barnard),

    I avail myself of the present opportunity to drop you a few lines to let you know that I am well at this time and hope that when this comes to hand it will find you all well. I received a letter today from T. D. Scott, which says there is a heap of tales going about them clothes that Isham

Barnard brought out to me at Wytheville, so I thought I would state to you how it was as near as a I could for your satisfaction. Now, I had the measles when Isham came in and handed me the clothes and I understood him to say that these were some clothes for me and Robert Puckett tied up in a handkerchief and that one vest was mine and the rest was Roberts. Well, I set them by in a stall where John J. Reynolds lay sick with the measles and Jack took off the handkerchief to spread over his face to keep of the flies so when I handed Robert his clothes there was two pair of socks and one shirt missing. I suppose they were stolen out of our stall for there were several things stolen from there. I hope this will satisfy you all that I do not blame Isham about it. Jehu left here about two weeks ago. He has gone to the army and was well when he left. James J. Monday, Joel and Cloyd Mankins, Joseph and Samuel Smith, Abraham Pendleton and Abram Mays left here this morning for the army. I should have went with them, if I had not been appointed nurse of the sick that is left here from our company. Give my love to all your family and tell them to write to me every opportunity as I would be glad to hear from them at all times and be sure to write yourself, as I should have written sooner, but for the want of paper I must come to a close. Your affectionate Nephew, Asa Scott

White Sulphur Springs, Greenbrier County, Virginia, November 30, 1861 Dear Grandpa (Thomas Scott),

This is the first opportunity I have had to drop you a few lines. This leaves me well and I hope it will find you well and doing well. I have no news to write at this time of interest. I will give you a short account of the battles I have been in. The battle of the... which was the first battle didn't last but 15 minutes. We had three regiments engaged in the fight. The enemy only had one. We aimed to surround them. The 45th Regiment engaged the enemy in front the 50th, which I was flanked on the right and the 36th on the left the firing rifles and muskets was very sharp for a time, but the Yankees did not stand long they retreated in great confusion leaving their weapons and baggage behind. We pursued them for five miles. Our loss was 4 killed and 17 wounded. The enemy loss was about 200 in killed, wounded and prisoners. After this fight was over, we fell back about 2 miles and fortified ourselves in the bend of the Gauley River. After being here about two weeks General Floyd's pickets came in and reported that General Rosencrans was advancing and already within 2 miles. In two hours, they appeared before our works and the fight was commenced and lasted 4 hours. We repulsed them in all directions, but after night we fell back across the Gauley River and burned the bridge. This was a severe fight. Several balls struck in a few inches of me. Our loss was 6 or 7 wounded. The enemy lost 5 or 6 hundred. I believe though their loss is not known yet but I am certain it is considerable. After this fight, General Floyd fell back to Meadow Bluff where I taken the fever and was sent to the hospital here at White Sulphur Springs where I have been ever since and I can't tell when I shall leave here for the Doctor has appointed me mess of the sick. There is not any of my cousins here except James J. Mundy. He is well at this time. I have not heard from James for two months. He was with the army then and was well. Some persons think that the Yankees are preparing to attack Wise's Legion, which is quartered 25 miles from here at Meadow Bluff. If this is true, I can't get a furlough to come home soon.

        Goodbye, Asa Scott

50th Regiment, Floyd's Brigade, December 1861
Dear Father (Tirea Barnard),
  I seat myself to inform you that I am well greatly hoping that these few lines may find you enjoying the same blessing. No news. We are fixing to take up winter quarters near Peterstown. You can direct your mail in care of Captain J. G. Lawson, Floyd's Brigade, 50th Virginia Regiment, Peterstown.
  Jim, I sent you $50. I want you to buy some corn with it to winter mine and your hogs on it and let Charles have $5 for that Tennessee bill and the balance you can use as you please and if you have no idea for all of it. If I get sick you can come to see me.
  Jim, I sent you and John a ring apiece by Stephen Bolt and want you to write whether you got it or not. I got all the things you sent me and they come in a good time and I was very much pleased with them. If I don't get to come home about Christmas, I want you or Richard to come out if all are well.

        Yours forever, Jehu Barnard

Pulaski County, Virginia, December 26, 1861
Dear folks (Tirea Barnard Family),
  I seat myself to inform you that I am well generally hoping these few lines finds you well and enjoying the same Christmas is about over here and it has been a tolerable jolly time. We bought a big turkey gobbler all ready to cook and a dozen of us had a big dinner. All of it cost us…and we had a bit to spare. The 51st Virginia Regiment started this morning to Bowling Green then…and we have orders to start in the morning. I will send you my old shoes and uniform coat by Mr. Thomas or DeHart one. He will leave them at William Lawsons. I am afraid some of you will start out and I will be gone west. I must bring this to a close for I have to cook two days rations.

        Yours forever and ever,
        Jehu Barnard

The stay at Peterstown was not long. In response to orders from Richmond, General Floyd moved his army on December 5 to Newbern, in Pulaski County, where he was near the Virginia and Tennessee Railroad. On December 16, Floyd received orders to move his army as soon as it was fit for active service at Bowling Green, Kentucky, to reinforce Confederate forces there. Floyd's army began moving on December 24. Company K and the 50th Virginia were among the last to board the train.

Riding five railroads in eight days and nights to get to Bowling Green, the 50th Virginia found itself not immediately required to perform service in the field. During the lull, the men of Company K contemplated reenlisting.

Bowling Green, Kentucky, January 18, 1862
Dear Father,
I seat myself to inform you that I am well greatly hoping these few lines may find you enjoying the same blessing. I have no news to write to you we have plenty to eat such as beef and sugar and coffee wheat bread and rice and sometimes we get green beans and potatoes and pork. I found out James Monday had Jim's knife and took it away from him. It done most as much good to get his knife as it would to have seen him. I was well pleased just to see his knife. Jim, you and Isham and Richard and Charles must hold on and not volunteer unless you are going to be drafted for there will be a draft made as soon as our time is out and then we all can go together. They tried to get us to volunteer again, but they never got nary one. They offered for two more years and that is what makes me think there will be draft made for the volunteers will all want to go home.
Your forever, Jehu Barnard

On February 6, 1862, Ulysses S. Grant forced the surrender of Fort Henry on the Tennessee River and moved to Fort Donelson on the Cumberland River. The 50th, which arrived at Fort Donelson on February 13, fought in the breakout from the fort in McCausland's Brigade on February 15. The regiment lost at least 19 killed and 30 wounded, with some estimates of casualties ranging up to one hundred. The next day the 50th escaped before the fort's surrender with the bulk of General Floyd's brigade. Escape, however, meant that while some men in the regiment road steamboats to Murfreesboro, many others in the regiment trekked 140 miles overland to that city. A week after the battle, the 50th's strength at Murfreesboro was 285 men and officers.

Camp at Murfreesboro, Tennessee, February 25, 1862
Dear Pa,

    I write you a few lines at present. I am well satisfied. I just landed here on retreat from Fort Donelson yesterday evening. All of the company have not yet come up although safely landed on the opposite side of the river to the enemy on the morning the retreat commenced. They are on their way no doubt. Our stay at Fort Donelson though only a few days was fought with remarkable as well as serious consequences. The two first days after getting to the Fort we were held as a reserved placed in rear of the entrenchment in a very exposed place; in fact so much that four of our company got wounded with shell on the morning of the first day. No regular engagement was had with the enemy until Saturday morning when we sallied out from our entrenchment and gave them a regular "Field fight" or "Woods fight" if you please. I saw our plan of attack formed as we were, to proceed to the engagement, in an old field on our entrance left. Some of our boys didn't know what was up. It wasn't so with me I know we'd soon have a battle and what was more I was willing to engage as it as our prospect for success appeared very flattering, considering our long lines of infantry and cavalry that were drawn up nicely and with so much system. As soon as everything was in readiness, we pitched off in the direction of the enemy. Soon the fight commenced here I will cease trying to describe the offered and give as near as possible the result of the fight. The killed on either side was considerable. The loss on our side in killed and wounded has been reckoned at 2,000 men, that of the enemy 5,000. I am knowing to the just that the enemy lost considerably more men than we did. Our company lost three men killed and about 8 wounded. Our regiment took nearly a hundred killed and wounded.

    O the fight lasted from daylight in the morning until 5 o'clock in the evening. I was in the thickest of the fight all of the time. I never got a scratch. Our success in the fight must be attributed to the Floyd Brigade; in fact, nearly the whole fight was made by it. I picked up a Yankee cap, which I have on my head now. I also got me a sword and a shirt. I could have gotten a great many things if I had taken them.

    This is Yankee paper on which I now writing. I also got a number of Yankee letters which afforded me some amusement in their perusal by this means I could arrive at the strength of the war spent enemy

    My company fought with marked energy in the battle. In fact, all Virginians fought well. So much for my account of the fight, I shall not say anything about the disgraceful surrender made that very night after we had whipped them in a field fight. I don't understand the cause of this surrendering. Anything further you wish to know apply to M. T. Sawyer.
                  Yours truly, T. D. Reynolds

P. S. Oh I had look to have forgotten. I saw John C. Breckinridge yesterday. I haven't heard anything from Burton at all.

From Murfreesboro, Floyd marched his army overland 120 miles to Chattanooga, with advance elements arriving on March 6. Floyd was relieved of command on March 11. The brigade moved to Knoxville on March 18 where men who had re-enlisted were furloughed and ordered to reassemble beginning May 1. Companies from the 50th began to arrive at Camp Jackson, Wytheville, soon after that date. On May 10, two companies of the 50th participated in a skirmish at Giles Court House. On May 12, 1862, the companies of the 50th completed their reorganizations. In Company K, Captain Jefferson was re-elected. First Lieutenant Martin Staples lost and Second Lieutenant Walter T. Noell replaced him. The men elected Sergeant Asa B. Scott to Second Lieutenant. Third Lieutenant Benjamin F. Cloud lost election to Sergeant James H. Rangeley. Five days later, several companies of the 50th, including Company K, fought near Princeton in present day West Virginia. That battle, matters of health and home, the company reorganization, and speculation about the election of officers to command the 50th occupied the minds of men in the company. Like other units, they suffered the difficulties of hard winters, inadequate food, and insufficient clothing. Tilghman D. Reynolds of Company C, 50th Virginia Infantry, died on April 30, 1862, of diphtheria.

Left, Tilghman Reynolds and I. B. Shelor, right, of the 50th Virginia Infantry both lost their lives during the war not of wounds, but of disease. *Courtesy of Catheryn S. Vaughn.*

Hospital at Emory and Henry College, May 22, 1862
Dear Wife,

      I cannot refrain from writing you a few lines this evening to inform you how I am and where, do not let the name of the hospital afright you for I am a great deal better than I was when I wrote you before. The cause of my coming to the Hospital was this, the Commandant of the Post at Camp Jackson, ordered that all who were not able for service, must be sent to the Hospital. I came over here on the cars last evening, and to my surprise I found a very clean in every respect comfortable place. Although there is a good many sick men here, the room we are staying in is nice and clean. They don't even allow men to spit on the floor, this room, one of A. J. Cassell's son, one is from Wythe, the other from Lee County. They are all so they can go about, none of them has the fever, I mention this so you will not be thinking I am shut up in a room with it. Our fare is as good as I could wish. We have fried ham, biscuits and coffee for breakfast; Boiled meat with beans, biscuits and water for dinner; Boiled meat, biscuits and tea for supper. Oh my Dear, you cannot imagine how unhappy I felt when the Doctor said I must go to the hospital. I knew it would grieve you so much. When you heard it, but there was no way to help it for the Doctor give special orders not to let any to private houses, so you see there was no other chance, for I was not able for duty. Oh and I fear I never will be, though I don't see any chance to get off. I mean a discharge.

      This is Friday morning, May 23rd. through the kind mercies of God I am still blessed, with increasing strength. I think I shall be as well as I ever am in a few days. Oh my Dear, you don't know how bad I hated to leave Camp Jackson the evening the letter came Henry was to send it on to me, so I expected it here last night, but to my sorrow it did not come. Oh if I only can't, so I will try as Paul said, "to learn to be contented in whatever situation I am placed." Susan wrote in her letter of the 8th that Willie had cut his foot I have been uneasy about him ever since, though you have doubtless wrote to me before this letter reaches you, givening me all the particulars about it. If you have not I want you to and tell me how he has got. Write to me how all the children, God bless their little lives, are getting along, how Mary Agnes is coming along with her lambs and how John Floyd is coming on with his young claves and how Lee is getting on with his walking. The Bell is ringing for breakfast I must go. I can inform you I have had the pleasure of attending preaching twice since I left home. The first time was at Wytheville, the first Sunday after I got to camp. The profession was Episcopalian. The preacher was dressed in a long black robe and when he prayed he would repeat a few verses and the members of the church would all respond by repeating a few verses. They had a great deal of unnecessary formality about it. Though they had a most beautiful singing and music. Then they had preaching here yesterday at 4 o'clock, the preacher was a missionary he done right smart, it was source of great pleasure to me to attend worship after being in camp and seeing the wickedness and confusion and gambling, drinking, cursing and immorality of men and officers generally. I can assure you it brought home and friends most vividly to my mind, it made me almost look around involuntarily for you and the children but alas, you are fare, fare away.

    You have all heard of the fight near Princeton, Mercer County, before this will reach you. I believe our Company was in the fight, but none of them was hurt so far as I can learn. We killed about 200 Yankees and lost nine killed and 17 wounded. Colonel Moore was in the fight but never lost a man. I don't know whether Bob is with the Company or not. You can tell Benton, Captain Elliot was killed in the fight. Tell Pa and Mother I saw John Thompson at Camp Jackson. He said Uncle William and Aunt Polly was well as common though they are breaking very fast. Henry Thompson is here. He has been very sick, but is getting well.

    Cousin William Shelor, Uncle Jacob's son, is here. He has had the fever, but is getting nearly well. There is about two hundred and seventy-five here at this time, though a great many of them is convalescent. The building I stay in has one hundred and twenty rooms in it and as many windows. I write this because it will amuse the children. I can't tell you how long I will stay here. The men that is here and has been here sometime, says when a man get in here once, it is a hard matter to get away. I have been here two days and the Doctors have not examined me yet. Though I believe from what I can learn, if my Captain would interest himself a little I could get exempt. I think the chief Doctors at this place are very intelligent wise men.

    I understand our Company is coming back to Camp Jackson. I do not know how long they will stay there. If I was able I had rather be with the Company. Our Regiment is not organized yet. Captain Lawson and Captain Page is candidates of Colonel. I hope Jeff will get the office if he does Tim Nowell will be our Captain which would be very expectable to us all for we would have the Captain and Colonel both of our choice, though it matters not with me for I never expect to be able to render any service as a soldier.

    Major William Shelor is Lieutenant Colonel, now you can tell the relations. He is very popular in his Regiment. I have no news of any importance to write you a public character. It is the general talk that the war can't last long or may terminate in our Independence. There is some talk of France interfering in our behalf though I have no confidence in the report.

    I expect the Yankees are making attempts at this time to take Richmond. If they get it, I know not where we will go to. We have not received our bounties yet and I know not when we will. I have spent four dollars since I left home. Money will not buy hardly anything now. We have to pay two dollars per quire or 8 cents per sheet for the smallest sized paper. You had better send and get you some paper before it gets so high you can't get it. For if, I could not get a letter from you I could not stand it. I believe I would run away and try to come home. If I was hindered from writing for two thousand dollars, no not for the world, I feel like I wanted to write you every day but you know my money would not hold out to do so. I have wrote three letters and sent by mail since I have been from home and one to your father. I payed the postage on all the letters I have sent, but I shall quit it for fear you don't get them. Tell Susan that Henry is at Camp Jackson. He is complaining with the bounties. Now my Dear, you must not neglect writing to me very week if you can. I know you have a bad chance but that is all the pleasure I see, don't fail to write because any of you are sick, for when you don't I think that is the cause. So I rather you would write anyhow. Tell all the family howdy for me, I must try to close this letter for want of space. If you don't hear from me before you write direct your letter to this place and if I am gone it will be sent to me. I will take leave of you and the children by praying the Lord may restore me to you all again.

        I. B. Shelor

Rocky Gap, Bland County, Virginia, May 31, 1862
Dear Brother (James W. Barnard),
  I seat myself to inform you that I am well greatly hoping these few lines may find you enjoying the same. I am well now and have been ever since I left home. Richard is well more than he is complaining of a bowel complaint. I recon you heard that we had a little fight out at Princeton. We went out Princeton one day and they was a regiment came in behind us and we prepared for them and soon made them take to their heels and I never seen so many canteens, haversacks, cups, cartridge and overcoats and everything else stowed along the road. So, I must come to a close for I have to start out on picket at two o'clock. James, I received your letter.

       Yours, Jehu Barnard

Camp Narrows, July 17, 1862
Dear Father Mother Brothers and Sisters,
  I seat myself to answer your kind letter, which I received this morning it was dated the 14th. It gave me much pleasure to hear you was on the mend. I am well as to health, but I have got another large bile on my ankle, which hurt me right smart and hope when this comes to hand it may find you all well. I have no particular news to write. I will tell you of a thing that takened place last Saturday night. Joseph Brown struck G.

W. Spangler on the head with his gun and almost killed him and he is very bad yet. I don't believe he will get over it anymore and they have got Brown in the guard house with his hands tied behind him and his feet tied together and they don't give hardly anything to eat that will use him very rough if not take his life. Mary, that little piece you wrote with a pencil was rather hard to understand I received from a girl this morning. Tell George I received from him night before last and all so tell that his regiment is here and I think that we will stay together all the time I am sorry I can't write him a letter, but this will do for you all I never sent my letters. Direct your letters to Dublin.

         Yours respectfully,
         Daniel Smith

  The 50th Virginia moved to Rocky Gap in May. There on the twenty-fifth the regiment completed its reorganization, electing Captain Thomas Poage, Company I, colonel, Captain Alexander S. Vandeventer, Company B, lieutenant colonel, and Captain Logan H. N. Salyer, Company H, major. A Special Order during this times gives the reader an idea of the expectations for the newly elected officers when it states that, "Officers will be examined upon tactics, ordinary branches of an English education and the examining board will also report upon their general efficiency and 'perfect sobriety'." The regiment spent the month of June in camp or picketing at Rocky Gap. In July, it moved east to Narrows on the New River.

  At Narrows in late August 1862, the 50th became part of General John Echols Brigade with the 63rd Virginia Infantry, 23rd Battalion Virginia Infantry, Chapman's Artillery and some cavalry. Echols' brigade was part of the General W. W. Loring's Department of Southwestern Virginia, containing the counties of present day Virginia west of Roanoke. On September 6, Loring moved his army from Narrows on a campaign to capture Charleston. He accomplished that on September 13. A week later, the events of the capture were such old news that letters from Company K hardly mentioned the action.

  Loring kept his army at Charleston, refusing to cooperate or assist other Confederate forces in the region. Ordered to Richmond, Loring moved his entire force from Charleston on a 60-mile march before being relieved of command. The 50th Virginia with the rest of his army retraced its route to Charleston, arriving there in late October after a 120-mile effort that accomplished nothing except to tire and exasperate the men. On October 28, the Confederates began a retreat from Charleston, during which the 50th endured 30-mile daily forced marches over several days. On November 4, the regiment arrived at Narrows.

Near Charleston, Virginia, September 21, 1862
Dear Father and Mother (Tirea and Eliza Barnard),

I seat myself to drop you a few lines to let you know I am well hoping these few lines may find you all well. Richard and Thomas Smith and Joel Mankins is well. We received your letter yesterday which gave much satisfaction to hear that you was well. I started a letter last week stating about our travels and fights. I reckon it is not worth while for me to write anymore about that. I wrote a letter when I was at the Narrows and wrote that you need not send my coat to me for I had got me a round about coat and I gave the letter to old Billy Bowman and a ring for Ruth. I want you to write whether you got the letter or not for I was offered four dollars for the ring and I sent ten dollars in Richards money and I want you to write whether you got the letter of not. Your affectionate son until death.

A few lines to James Barnard. Jim, I want you to keep as still as possible and keep from coming as long as possible. Jim, you must give my best respects to all the pretty girls in that country and sing Skeetam Dink when you see Dump Bolt or Mary Jane Dickerson. So, I must close.
Jehu Barnard

On November 11, 1862, General John S. Williams replaced Echols as commander of the brigade. On December 16, the 50th Virginia moved east through Richmond to near Petersburg. On December 20, the 50th, with 29 officers and 821 men, joined the 29th Virginia Infantry, 54th Virginia Infantry, 63rd Virginia Infantry and the 27th Battalion Virginia Cavalry in Raleigh E. Colston's Brigade.

Camp Narrows, Giles County, Virginia, November 5, 1862
Dear Father and Mother,

It is with pleasure that I have once more taken the opportunity of writing you lines to let you know that I am well hoping for these few lines to reach you enjoying good health. We have taken camp near our old camp and I expect we will stay here two or three weeks. We have had a terrible hard march and not enough to eat none of the time. Reed Boyd got here last night and said that he left Tom and James at Newbern and Isham and Hubbard Bolt had left them and was going by King's salt work.

Tom and Jake landed here last night and Jake started to the 45th this morning and he will get there this evening. Pap, I want you to send my overcoat to me as soon as possible that is as soon as you have a chance. I got two pairs of socks and one pair of pants, one shirt and one pair of drawers and one pair of socks and one shirt was Jim's. I started two letters to you when I was at Charleston and when I started back they come to me and I just tore them up. From your son, Jehu Barnard

Camp near Petersburg, December 30, 1862
Dear Father and Mother,
    I seat myself this evening to drop you a few lines to let you know that I am well more than there is a little hard knot in my throat, yet that bothers me a little of a morning though I am with the Regiment hoping for these few lines to reach you enjoying the best of health. I had the diphtheria though I have not been very bad. There is nothing new in this country. We can't hear of no fighting nowhere. Since the Fredericksburg fight, James Monday has got back to our company. Our Regiment and their Battalion got close together and Sergeant Rangley went out and got him back. So, I must close. Yours forever, Jehu Barnard

    Jehu has been writing and just quit for he said that I might finish his paper. I am pleased to inform you that myself and Thomas A. Barnard and Daniel is all well. Jehu is a little complaining, but I do not think he is anyways dangerous. Joseph Barnard is complaining he has got yellow jaundice. I hope these few lines will find you all enjoying the best of health. I haven't any news particular to write you. There is some talk today that we will go back to Dublin in a few days. That would please me very much for I do not like this country though I am quite healthy so far. I hardly know to write to you all. When I commence writing, for I have saw so many curiosities since I left home and it takes so much writing to explain it to you. I can't get time to write it and paper is so hard to get we can't write everything we want to tell. Grandpa, I forgotten him. Tell him I have saw that great place, Richmond, that I have heard him talk about so much. I have also saw Petersburg and that is a great place too. Give my best respects to old grandfather and mother Barnard I have been trying to find out where Willy and Sanders is ever since I have been here but cannot. I want to know where they was when they wrote home last. Also tell Isham, Richard, James and John Ingram and all my old friends I haven't forgotten none of them, but cannot write to all, but would like to receive a letter from any of them and they must write because they have a better chance to write than we have. I would like very much to come home now and tell you all about my travels, but I do not know when that will be but I think if we go back to Dublin I can get to come home a little while, but that is uncertain. You will please tell Polly to see this so she can see that I am well. I do not expect to write to her this week. I have written two letters to her since I have been here and want to hear from her very bad. I will stop. Thomas A. Barnard wishes to say a few words, write soon.
                        Thomas Smith

    Dear Father and Mother, Brothers and Sisters, I once more have the opportunity of writing you a few lines to inform you that I am well much hoping when these lines reach you all may find you enjoying good health. I am in good spirits, yet but the smallpox is raging very bad. I remain your friend.

Thomas A. Barnard

In January 1863, the 50th found itself in General Roger A. Pryor's Brigade with the 63rd Virginia along the Blackwater River in Southampton County in southeastern Virginia. On January 30, at the end of an extended foraging operation, the Confederates were surprised in their nighttime encampment by Union forces. In the resulting engagement at Kelly's Store, Colonel Poage, commanding the regiment, bled to death from wounds. The men in Company K did not conceal their loss in the battle. Despite the hard marching to get there, some men of were pleased with their new location.

Camp near Franklin Depot, Virginia, January 13, 1863
Dear Folks (Tirea and Eliza Barnard),
    I seat myself this morning to drop you a few liens to let you know that we are all well at this time, but we are terrible tired at this time. We have marched 60 miles in two days and part of one night and we are very near broke down for we have got so much to tote. I got the box you sent me and everything came in very good time. I got some apples and flour and balls of butter and a bucket of lard and a bucket of sausage and my overcoat and comforter and union we are all camped about eight miles below Franklin Depot. You must direct your letters to Franklin Depot, Virginia 50th Virginia Volunteers.

Yours, Jehu Barnard

    Jehu ask me to date his letter and sign his name and I put it on the wrong side in a hurry.

Thomas Smith

    Jim, I received your…in which much to read, but was sorry to hear that you was not able to manage the girls in that country for I know that you must be bad off when you get so you can't manage the girls or else they got mighty…since I left. Jim, if I come home anytime this winter or spring I want you to ask grandpaw if he thinks I could lodge at the Travelers Rest and if he thinks I would I'd prepare myself for the fuss without he thinks I could find better at the…Jim, I went to Jerusalem yesterday and it was such a bad looking place that I concluded it was the not the Jerusalem that the scriptures tells about and on them terms I left and I think I will not go back there anymore. So nothing more at present.
Jehu Barnard

February 10, 1863
Dear Father and Mother (Tirea and Eliza Barnard),

    I seat myself this evening to drop you a few lines to inform you that I am well greatly wishing for these few lines to reach you all well. I received your kind letter was very glad to hear that Richard was on the mend. I hear that James and Isham has to go into service. You wrote for me to write what I got when Asa came down. I got my overcoat some butter and bucket of lard and a bucket of sausage and my comfort and some apples. W. P. Barnard was shot in the foot and had his left cut off and he is bad there is not much prospect of his getting well. Tell Mom, I want her to make me a coat and pants and send to me by Lieutenant James W. Rangley. If you can spare the cloth, Mom, I want you to have my coat made cut frock fashion long tale so I won't wear out the seat so quick get cotton cloth and line my pants for they last as long again. Ruben Terry was supposed to be killed in that fight.

                              Yours, Jehu Barnard

February 11, 1863

    I will finish this paper. Tell Richard I would like to be at home and talk with him and sit around his warm fireside and enjoy the pleasures of life, but here I will remain. I suppose till peace is made or as long as I live, but I still have a hope to see peace once more. We will have to start toward Suffolk tomorrow or next day. Tell Caroline she must do the best she can. Tell her I tried to get a furlough and the General wouldn't approve it. If they start tomorrow, I can't go with them. So no more only remaining your affectionate son till death.

                              Thomas A. Barnard

Dear Father and Mother, (Tirea and Eliza Barnard)

    I again have the opportunity of writing you a few lines to inform you that I am not very well at this time, but I am still doing duty much hoping that when these lines reach you may find you all enjoying good health. We have hard times here, but I stand it with good heart for I thin they are the best prospect of peace that ever has been. Tell Isham and James they had better join the cavalry for I think it not as hard on men and they fare better. Tell Isham to not let no one see the letter I sent him. I can't come to tend to that suit of Green Pucketts. I never expect to come home till peace is made and if I live to survive the war I will quickly return to my sweet home where I can spend the balance of days in quietness and peace. The report is we are going to march on Suffolk in a few days. Tell my brothers and sisters I send my love and best respects to them all and I hope to be remembered by them all. R. P. Terry, I have no doubt but what is killed. I don't think Pat will ever get well. He is very low. I hope we won't have to stay here next summer for I don't think I can stand if here. My bowels is in very bad order now and if I have to stay here I am afraid I will be sick all the time. So, I must close give my respects to all my connections and friends and all inquiring friends. Ever your affectionate son till death.

Jehu Barnard

A few lines from Joel. To Brother and friends, This leaves me well and fairly hoping this finds you all well and doing well as for news I haven't much more than there is talk of peace and I fear there is more talk peace, though I hope not. It is a very hard time here for to face. We had a fine pot of peas for dinner and a big one of corn bread. Isham, I can't advise you what to do for the service is service it makes no odds where you go. I can't write anything that will interest you so write often and give me the news and I will do better next time.

Joel Mankins

  The 50th remained in the Blackwater River area near Franklin until March 13 when it began a move that would take it back to southwest Virginia. It arrived at Dublin Depot on March 19 and most of the men received a furlough, with orders to return on April 5. Colonel Alexander W. Vandeventer took command in Major General Samuel Jones' Department of Western Virginia.
  A call for reinforcements for Lee's Army of Northern Virginia soon had the 50th en route east again. On April 9, the 50th arrived in Lee's army where it joined John M. "Rum" Jones Brigade (21st, 25th, 42nd, 44th and 48th Virginia Infantry Regiments). As part of the division of Raleigh E. Colston, the 50th camped in the Moss Neck area near Fredericksburg on the Confederate right flank along the Rappahannock River. The thoughts of impending battle brought a premonition to one member of Company K, as well as a desire to find a way out of the service.

April 5, 1863
Dear Father and Mother (Tirea and Eliza Barnard),
  It is with great pleasure I take this opportunity to drop you a few lines to let you know that I and Jehu is both tolerable well hoping when this reaches you it will find you both in good health…is more than I ever saw in the same length of time and it is very disagreeable anyway they is generally…at this time R. J. Barnard is well and Daniel Smith is well. Pap, we want you to send C. D. Dearthridge bond back as we have received pay from him he said that he bought a ticket for you which cost $11 and we have paid him for it and you need not pay anybody else and write whether moss…has called on you for the debt yet or not now you need not put yourself to any trouble to pay it and you can destroy that

order I gave you on Austin Bowman for he has paid it since he came back to the company. I heard yesterday that Uncle William Barnard had his arm shot off by the…give Uncle William my best love and respect and tell him to write to us. Now, no more at this time your ever loving son until death. You must excuse my bad writing for it is getting dark and we have to get supper and Mr. Newman is going to start early.
        J. W. Barnard
        Jehu Barnard

Camp Eight Miles below Fredericksburg, Caroline County, Virginia,
April 16, 1863
Dear Father and Mother (Tirea and Eliza Barnard),
  This morning permits me to write you a few lines to let you know that I am well at this time greatly hoping to hear you are all enjoying the same God's blessing. I have no news to write you at this time. We are in about three miles of the Yankees. It is reported they are a making plans for a move up the river. Some thinks we will have a fight here in a few days. If we have a fight here, it will be one of the biggest fights that ever has been. We can see the Yankee's Battalions every day. There are a heap of troops there and we can't but nothing we have to eat bread and we are all starved for something to eat. We are on half rations. My dear Father and Mother, I am sorry to say it but seems to me that I am low in spirit. It just seems to me that I will never live to see you all again. Although I am in good health, if I never seen you both anymore I want you to know that I have not forgotten you yet nor never shall till my remains is moved to eternity. So I must close by saying I remain your affectionate son.
        Thomas Barnard

Camp near Fredericksburg, Caroline County, Virginia,
April 16, 1863
Dear Brothers (Isham and Richard),
  I take the present opportunity of writing you a few lines to let you know that I am well and gaily it would be to me to hear that you and your families was enjoying the same God's blessing. I have no news to interest you at this time. The sorrowful news came to me that old grandmother Barnard is dead. I consider that we have lost a good friend and if I was as sure that I would go to rest as I am that she is there I would be more hopeful than I am. Jim is well, so is Thomas Smith and so is Burrell. Thomas Smith says he would write this week. Direct your letters to Guinea's Depot, Virginia, Company K, 50th Virginia Regiment. Tell Caroline that James Puckett told me to be sure and tell he was well. I was glad to hear from her Isham Brice Duncan has got a boy. I think you could get for me a substitute, if you and Richard will get him

I think I can put him in and keep it still and do all you can for me. Give him any price you think I can pay. Try him soon as you can. Tell Caroline to try to remember me as a friend. Give my respects to Grandpa and receive some for yourselves.

Thomas Barnard

Montgomery Springs, April 30, 1863
Dear Father and Mother (Tirea and Eliza Barnard),

    I have the opportunity of writing you a few lines this morning to let you know how I am getting along. I can say to you that I am mending very fast. I have got so I can set up some and I have got so I can eat right smart greatly hoping this may find you well and doing well. I have been looking for some of you to come after me all this week. I think if you all could come, I could get a furlough to go home with you. I think if I mend on as fast as I have been I could ride home on a horse by next Monday and if you can come a horse back or get a carriage. You do as you think best about bringing a carriage for it will be uncertain about getting a furlough. I expect and I think by the time you can get here I can ride on a horse and if you can't start a Monday. I don't think there is any use to come with the expectation of me getting to come home with you. If you come fetch me a roasted chicken or two and bring me some of your twist tobacco. I have nothing new to write to you so will close. I forever remain yours truly.

Jehu Barnard

    Uncle Tirea if you come bring me some of your tobacco, if you have it to spare and I will oblige.

Your friend, George Smith

    At Chancellorsville, Colston's men marched in "Stonewall" Jackson's famous flank march and joined the attack on May 2, 1863. In the resulting confusion following that assault, the 50th found itself separated from its brigade on the night of May 2. It formed on the left of James H. Lane's brigade of North Carolinians and was there when Lane's soldiers fired the volley that mortally wounded General Jackson. The next day Patrick County men served under J. E. B. Stuart as he took command of the Second Corps and reunited with Lee in victory. The 50th suffered 31 killed, 64 wounded and 3 captured during the battle. No letters from Company K tell about the battle directly. However, letters from Patrick County provide some insight into the company at this time.

May 12, 1863
Dear Brothers,
    This evening affords me the pleasure of dropping you a few lines

rather to show that I have not forgotten you for I have no news of importance to write. I am well and hoping for this to reach you in good health and spirits. Tom, I hear Captain Lawson says that he means to send you and R. P. Terry back to your old company and Caroline's mother ask him about it and he said that he wasn't agoing to send you back, but didn't intend to keep them from taking you anymore for every time they was anything said about their taking you back you always run to him for protection and them went on to say something about your voting against Mat some two or three years… Jeff has bought Rubes home and says that Anna will be without a home in twelve months from now. Tom, I went out to Bucky's to get your fine colt to bring home and when we went to catch it, it turned its heels for to charge us and Buck run out of the stables and I had to halter it by myself. As soon as I let it…a little I got up on it and rode it some and you just ought to have been here to of seen it rare and pitch, but I stuck to it and now it is nearly gentle enough for Billy to ride and the finest filly I ever saw. Jim, I want you to send Dump Bolt a…for the clash she has about you to Claib Lawson.

May 18, 1863
    I were expecting to send this letter by Jase, but he has not got able to start back yet our connections is all well at this time and I still hope these few lines may reach you enjoying the best of health. We have heard of the Battle that you have been in the hard times that you have been seeing and was sorry to hear of it and was sorry to hear that Thomas Smith had been wounded and Jims being sick and so badly exposed.
    Thomas Smith, we hear that you are badly wounded and I want you to get a transfer to the Mountgomery Sulphur Springs for you would better attend to and try to get a furlough and if nobody else won't come after you I will come myself. So I must close
    Most Respectfully yours, John Ingram

Jim, I am here yet though I may get to you before this letter will.
    Jehu Barnard

Camp near Fredericksburg, Virginia, May 24, 1863
Dear Friends (Tirea and Eliza Barnard),
    I take this opportunity of dropping you a few lines to let you know that I am well at the present greatly hoping these few lines may find you all doing well haven't any news of any importance to write this time more than there is a strong talk of us crossing the river and if we do cross I expect that we will see hard times though we will do the best we can for ourselves and you must do the same. There was talk awhile of us going back to the west, but that is…in the head. You must write as soon

as this comes to hand and give me the news that is a…Give all my friends my best respects and tell them they must write and I will do the same. Yours, H. A. Hefflefinger

To John M. and James W. Barnard
    John, you must plant a heap of potatoes, pumpkins and me and Henry will…help eat them. We might have us a little brown jug of brandy a setting under the bed and you might have your old shang high roster fat by the time we come and me and Henry and Tom will ring his neck for him, but you must have his great old he comb cut off for if we was to see his old he comb we could not eat him and you must have us a big patch of turnip salad and we will come home and help you put them in holes.
    Yours, H. A. Hefflefinger

    Robert E. Lee took the Army of Northern Virginia north in June 1863. The 50th crossed the Potomac and camped near the old battlefield on Antietam Creek on June 17 as part of Major General Edward "Allegheny" Johnson's Division. On June 22, Lieutenant Colonel Salyer commanded the regiment. Three days later, the 50th was in Chambersburg, Pennsylvania and on June 29 near Carlisle.
    On July 1, the 50th marched 25 miles arriving in the afternoon at the sleepy college town of Gettysburg. The regiment saw heavy action on July 2 as part of the attack on Culp's Hill by Richard S. Ewell's Corps. The regiment sustained losses of 22 killed, 48 wounded and 13 captured. Retreating from Gettysburg, the regiment crossed the Potomac coming south on July 14. On August 1 the 50th began a month long encampment near James Madison's home Montpelier in Orange County, Virginia.

Hanover Junction, Virginia, June 9, 1863
Dear Father,
    I this lonesome Sunday evening take the opportunity of dropping you a few lines to let you know that I am not well at this time greatly hoping these few lines may find you all well and hearty. I can inform you that there is another fight expected there and Jase is alone with the army by his self. Thomas has left and I am in the hospital and Jase is…by his self and if he gets wounded there is nobody to care for him. The troops is passing every day going to reinforce General Hill and they say that this will be the biggest fight that has been fought yet. The army was moving night before last at two o'clock and haven't heard from them since. I don't know what they are doing now. I expect that they are marching some said they are again to cross the river. I don't know what they are going to do myself. Me and Abraham Pendleton is and Abe is mighty good to me. The other day we was down on the river on picket and Abe

was the Corporal of the guard and I was sick and he excused me and made me lay in a house out of the weather and Pap, I want you to tell old W. Pendleton about how good Abe was to me so he can see that when anybody does me a favor that I don't forget it right straight. Also G Boston Scott when I had the mumps it seems that I would died there if it had not been for him, he and Abe, Mose went and got me a tent and Mose give the old doctor a good talking about the way that he had done me and said that he would report them to the General. Tell…folks that he is right sick and tell them that he said he would not write this time so I will stop for my stomach hurts me so bad that I can't write at all. You need to write to me till you hear from me for I don't know where I will be sent. Please excuse my bad writing.

        James W. Barnard

Lynchburg, Virginia, June 15, 1863
Dear People,
  I this beautiful lonesome Sunday evening have taken my pen in hand to inform you where I am and have been. I am at Lynchburg hospital sick and I am right sick and I believe if I can't get home or to some other hospital I shall just famish to death for this reason that the cooks is so nasty that I can just find the flies in the coffee and we just have coffee and this old hornets nest little bread and I can't eat that. My money is about to give out and when that gives out I don't know what I shall do I have just got five dollars and I will be out in a short time. I would write for you to send me some if there was not so many rogues that want to rob the letters and take the money and I mean that you had better not send me none for I don't know what hour I may leave here. I have been sick for about ten days and I just had to lay out all the time till night before last in all the rain and all and then I got to Lynchburg and then I got in the tent and I am so weak that I can hardly walk and nothing that I can eat at all. I wish I could get transferred to the Montgomery White, but there will be no chance you must write. Direct your letter to Owen Hospital, Lynchburg, Virginia in care of Doctor Murray and if I am not here the doctor will send them on. I reckon you had best not send me any money for I don't have any thought that I would get it for I don't get half the letters that you send. I sometimes have a notion of going home till I get well. A. C. Pendleton is with me and he would come along with me if I was to start. The doctors don't give any medicine to the sick at all though we are always down at town they would not know that I was gone for a week. There is no guard at all. I am outside the town in some woods. Will quit for am a tired. Write soon as this comes.

  Thomas A. Barnard

Washington County, Maryland, June 19, 1863
Dear Father and Mother (Tirea and Eliza Barnard),

  This evening I seat myself to drop you a few lines to inform you that I am well greatly hoping these few lines to reach you enjoying the best of health. We have a very hard march since we left Fredericksburg and had a heavy fight at Winchester though our Brigade was not in the fight more that we was under the fire of their cannon. Early's Division done the most of the fighting and captured some four thousand prisoners and all their commissary stores. So much I can't mention it all on a sheet of paper and took all their artillery, some fifteen or twenty pieces. We are lying in camp today though we are ordered to be ready to march a moments warning. So we don't know what time we will have to start or what time we may get into a fight for we are in the midst of the Yankee army. Some things we will attack them at Harper's Ferry though we don't know what we will do.

  Jim was sent down to Culpepper and came to use there and he was mending, but Doctor Breton said he was not in a condition to go with the rest and sent him back though I don't know where he went. I think he was mending very fast though he was in a bad fix, his stomach was swollen and had been…I heard that Thomas Smith had gone home and if he is there give him my love and respect and to stay there till he gets well if he has to stay under the shade of a big pine for this is not the place for a man that is not able for service. Tell my brothers and sisters that I may never see them anymore in this world though I hope that we may be prepared to meet each other in heaven. We draw bountiful to eat since the fight we have flour beef beans sugar and coffee tobacco cigars and smoking tobacco and them that don't use tobacco gets candy. So, I must close. I got the letter you sent by Joe. That's all we got since I left.

  From your ever loving son, Jehu Barnard

Camp near Orange Court House, August 7, 1863
Dear Mother,

  I received yours of the 26th of July yesterday morning it having been about a week on the road. I also received one from you while we were at Hagerstown in Maryland, dated the 18th of June. So first and last, I suppose I have gotten all the letters you have written. It seems that you have all the writing to do for I get no letters from any of the rest, nor can I hear of them writing any. I suppose I shall have to excuse them up to this time since they have all been sick, but I give them fair warning that if they do not get to writing pretty shortly now, I shall get after them. I do not know what there can be to prevent Pap, Elam, Hortense or Columbia from writing me a letter almost every week, I cannot imagine. Probably I should consider that I have been somewhat slow about writing myself, and therefore have no right to complain. It is true, I have not written since I wrote the one of the 10th of June of which you spoke but you must consider the circumstances under which I have been placed.

I suppose that the first thing you wish to hear about is the state of my health. I have had about as a hard a time of it as I ever had in my life, but have managed to keep up so far. I stood the march. But from the time, we crossed the Potomac going to Maryland I could feel a perceptible difference every day until it seemed almost impossible for me to get along at all. I kept along until the day before the fight at Gettysburg, when I was so broken down that I had to get a seat in an ambulance, for the first time since I have been in the army. Before going into the fight, I left my knapsack and all my clothes I have in the world are on my back. I kept up with the regiment while it was supporting our batteries but when it started upon the charge I found that I could not keep up with it. I caught up with the company shortly after the charge was over, a little after dark, and was with it through all the fighting the next day. I was not with Dozier when he was wounded, nor did not see him afterwards. When we started to fall back from that place, I was compelled to throw away my gun in order to keep up. Since that time I have been able to march part of the time and a part of the time have had to be hauled. We have been resting four or five days now and I feel a little better than I have. I have fallen off until I can span my arms anywhere. I weighted 177 lbs when I left Dublin, but suppose I would weigh 135 now. But do not let this render you uneasy, for I think if I can get some rest I will recruit up again.

I would like to be able to give you all a full account of our Pennsylvania Campaign, but it would require too much time and room for this place. I must content myself with a brief sketch now and defer giving the details until I get home or get more leisure.

You have heard before this time of the part we took in the Battle of Winchester. We moved directly forward by way of Charlestown, to the Potomac, which we crossed at Shepherdstown, ten miles above Harper's Ferry. We stayed several days near Sharpsburg in Maryland, lying in line of battle three or four days and nights. We could plainly see the "Stars and Stripes" floating over the enemy's works in Maryland Heights some ten miles distance. We went across Maryland by way of Hagerstown, and entered Pennsylvania at Middleburg. We took the road for Harrisburg, passing through Greencastle, Chambersburg, Shippensburg and numerous other small towns. We proceeded as far as Carlisle, supposing all the while that we were going to attack Harrisburg, where we learned that the militia were assembling. But we about faced at Carlisle, and shortly took the road for Gettysburg, crossing the Blue Ridge. We met up with the enemy at the town of Gettysburg, and fought the greatest battle of the war, the particulars of which you have heard before now. I will just remark here that it is given up by good Judges that such cannonading has never taken place before in the world.

We retired from before the enemy's works on the night of the third of July, and spent the fourth lying in an open field exposed to the rain, about two miles from the town. During the night of the fourth, we again commenced falling back, and continued our retreat through rain and mud until we arrived at Hagerstown. We there took a position and fortified it strongly to keep the enemy in check until the Potomac got fordable. We recrossed the river ten miles above Shepherdstown; at Williamsport, Maryland on the morning of the 12th of July. We had it to wade, it taking us up to the armpits. We came back to Winchester by the way of Martinsburg. We came on to Front Royal aiming, as I suppose, to recross the Blue Ridge at Manassas Gap the way we went into the valley, but we found the Yankees there. So we went some 25 miles further up the Shenandoah and crossed near Luray. We then came by way of Madison Court House to this place.

We have been here four or five days, expecting to move every minute. We may stay here several days yet and we may leave in half an hour. I have no idea where we will go. That is wholly dependant upon the movements of the enemy.

We are faring some better here than we have been. We have a much better chance to cook our rations, and have been getting a little fruit to eat with out meat and beans. We have been getting some corn meal and bacon, which goes much better than fresh lean beef, sour at that if it has been cooked any length of time. We have been able to wash up our clothes too, and consequently we feel and look much better. I wore my shirt without having it washed from the 15th of June until the 3rd of August. It could not be helped. We are all pretty ragged and a great many of us are barefooted. I have shoes now, but was entirely barefooted three days since we came back to Virginia. One day I had to march. So and being sick and tender footed both at once, I suffered more that day than I ever suffered in one day in my life.

The soldiers are all in bad spirits and are deserting in gangs. If matters look as dark in the country as they do in the army these is dark times indeed. Our Pennsylvania Campaign had done more to dispirit and demoralize this army than anything that has occurred since the war. I knew it could only serve to discourage our soldiers and unite the enemy before it was made. But I am really sorry that so many are deserting. If there is not a stop put to it, it will ruin both the army and country are full of runaways. It is too disgraceful! Some are too ready to give up. It is a gloomy time, but there has been darker times, and light yet come. I do not doubt our ultimate success, and will hang on to the best.

I was really sorry to hear that you all were having so hard a time with sickness, and am really glad to hear that you all have gotten through safely. I am glad to hear that you all have a pretty fair crop, for what you do not produce you will have to do without. You fairly made my mouth water speaking of your vegetables in yours of the 18th of June. I am afraid though that I shall not be there to help eat them. Tell my little brothers that I am glad to hear they are industrious, and I hope they will behave well. Nearly all I think about of late is getting back home and having a good peaceable time studying and working with them. Tell Pap that I have been keeping 50 dollars for him and Grandpa a long time but have had no chance to send it. Tell Grandpa that I hope to get to talk over these war matters with him in peace one of these days yet. Give my respects to the girls and tell them to write to me. Clum and Hortense and Columbia must write. I wrote to Pyrrhus the other day and sent my respects to Oliver. Uncle Henry is well. I would like to know if Dozier has gotten home yet.

      Your Affectionate Son
      Powell Benton Reynolds

  In September 1863, the 50th Virginia moved into camps along the Rapidan River, first at Morton's and later at Germanna fords. The men served in the Bristoe Station Campaign in October and the Mine Run Campaign the next month. Lieutenant Colonel Logan Salyer commanded the regiment during the battle at Payne's Farm on November 27, an action in which the regiment lost 2 killed, 4 wounded and two captured. Following the battle, the regiment took position at Morton's Ford.

  The 50th as part of John M. Jones Brigade in Johnson's Division went into winter quarters on December 22 east of Orange Court House at Mount Pisgah Church, which is located in Orange County near Clark's Mountain. For the next several months, the regiment's main duty was periodically picketing the Rapidan at Morton's and other fords along that river. The most significant action occurred when Union forces attempted to cross the river at Morton's Ford on February 6, 1864. Although it is hard to tell from the following letter, the 50th Virginia was not involved in the action.

  A Union cavalry raid rousted the 50th Virginia from winter quarters on March 2 in an attempt to block the path of the raiders. The march did not result in anything more disturbing than the regiment spending a night on March 4 camped on the old Chancellorsville battlefield.

  Upon return to winter quarters, the men of Company K expressed views on a range of topics, but getting home on furlough was on everyone's mind. On January 1, 1864, general orders for the Army of Northern Virginia authorized furloughs granted at the rate of 12 for every arms bearing man. In March 1864, the Jones' Brigade reported 24 officers and 371 men. On March 23, the authorization changed to permit just one for every one hundred arms bearing men and one furlough for every company having 50 or more arms bearing men present for duty. In selecting men for the indulgence of a furlough, commanders considered gallantry, good conduct, and the necessities of the soldiers' families.

Morton's Ford, Orange County, December 7, 1863
Teet and Richard,

When I was in Lynchburg about The 21st of November, I wrote a letter to you stating how I disposed of my horse etc. and enclosed a box of caps. After leaving Lynchburg, I went to Hamilton's Crossings and got four boxes of clothing for the regiment. I then got up to the army 25th after about twelve days on the road from home to the army. When I arrived, the army was in line of battle and on the 27th, we had a considerable fight. I was four or five miles in the rear and had the satisfaction of hearing the fight without being in danger. <u>You See I Am In The Music Department Now.</u>

Jack Robertson, James Campbell, Ned Moore and Oliver Marshall of Carroll and myself are musicians and mess together. Jim Campbell got a box from home last night with mince pies (moldy), sweet cakes, onions, butter, apples, pepper and molasses in it. We are living fine now.

We are in camp near Morton's Ford about fifteen miles below Orange Court House. There is some talk of us moving our camp nearer Orange Court House and then we will go into winter quarters. The Yankees are reported to have fallen back as far as Manassas. There is no money in the army. The "sutlers," a sort of army storekeepers, have got it all. They sell apples at four dollars per dozen and will give you three ginger cakes for a dollar. I am…two dollars… coffee, one dollar per quart, and strange to say despite their enormous prices they sell fast as they can bring them. Soldiers will pay any price for an article they want. They are more to blame for the depreciation of our currency than any one else.

Jack Reynolds, Benton, Henry Webb, Jehu and Jim Barnard and Asa are well. Asa brought Wilson West a pair of socks when he came from home. Dick Yeatts' brother was missing in our last fight, is supposed to be a prisoner. Nobody was hurt in the company.

                                                      G. Boston Scott

Camp near Franklin Virginia, February 7, 1864
Dear Brothers and Sisters

I thought as Jehu was going to write I would write a few lines. I have wrote so often and ain't heard from you. I am almost out of heart of hearing from you anymore. I am as well as heart could wish though I am just about barefooted and half…and know prospect of being any better. I hope this may find you all well and family well. We have had another fight with the Yankees. I am bound to say they whip us this time for our men left the field in time of the fight. Patterson Barnard was shot in the foot with a shell and the doctor says the foot will have to be cut off. He was sent to Jerusalem. Joseph Barnard went with him. There is two others missing. Rueben Terry and Berry Epperson. Nobody can't get any account of them. Colonel Page was killed the second shot that was shot. Amos was slightly wounded in the arm. I can't list the particulars for I wasn't in it. I was on picket and had to stand six days. Some of the boys will give you a more accurate account though I think from the best account there ain't any of them can tell much about it. So, I will say no more of the fight at this time. You must all write to me as soon as this comes to hand for I am very anxious to hear from you all. From your affectionate brother,

Joel Mankins

Camp near Orange Court House, Virginia, February 7, 1864
Dear Father and Mother (Tirea and Eliza Barnard),

With the greatest pleasure I have taken my pen to drop you a few lines to let you know that we are about well at this time greatly hoping these few lines will find you both well and hearty. As for news, I have none that would interest you at the present more than we had a little fight yesterday, but none of the our regiment was hit. The Yankees crossed the river and captured about twenty of our men, but we got as many of them as they got of us. I am disturbed that I can't think of nothing to write. I have just heard of Isham and Richard a being taken. I just know that them two love life rogues had a hand in it. I wish they was right at the…now. I reckon you all know who I am talking about for there ain't any rogues in that country, but two at the present, but let it. There will be a day of freedom sometime and I will be as free as anybody. I just thought that they was caught for I dreamed that I got rattlesnake bit a few nights ago. I will quit for tonight as Joseph is again to start in the morning. Nothing more. Write soon and tell us if you please if we didn't guess right about who took them be sure and write soon this time.

Your affectionate sons,
James W. and Jehu Barnard

Orange County, Virginia, February 23, 1864
Dear Friends (Tirea Barnard and family),

I appreciate the opportunity of writing you a few lines to let you know that I am well as common hoping when these few lines comes to hand they will find you and family well and hearty. I will say to you that times about like they was when you was here. I wanted to have talked with you more when you was here, but you know how times was when you was here so I will say to you that I consider my life in a bad condition for I hain't got no father nor mother to see to me in now way to even write to me if I had some connection I would feel better satisfied if I had some connection in this country. I have left a weekly woman to mourn my absence, but I still live in hopes that I will survive these wars. I have to…against my brothers, but I don't fell condemned in the sight of my god is so doing for we read in the scriptures that the devil must have his way. I will say to you that I hain't had my trial yet, but I think it will come off in a few days, but I don't think they will hurt me much. Tire, you know that I never… and I want you to help Margaret all you can in her trading for she will have to sell out her property I expect. I would be glad to come home, but I never expect to see that place anymore, but it ain't my fault. I will send you this letter and one to Margaret. Tell Ruth that I want her to take it to her if she can. It looks like it will almost take my life to stay from home, but I have these things to bare. I want you to write to me and let me know how you got home and about the times in that country. So must come to a close by saying farewell till we meet again.

Reed Boyd

Camp 50th Virginia Regiment, March 6, 1864
Dear Sir:

    As Uncle Henry starts home tomorrow I will send you a few lines. I am as well as common. Times have been a little exciting for the last five or six days but things appear quiet now. Uncle Henry can tell you all that I could write you about this matter. I hope that the Yankees will not run us out of our comfortable winter quarters at this inclement season of the year. Some of the most disagreeable weather of the season for being out of doors is yet. We have been housed up so long that to start out now would be almost like starting in to the war afresh. We have had very fine weather the greater part of the winter, only a short day or two of right cold weather during the whole time. I hear there has been a spell of very cold weather up in your country this year.

    I was surprised to learn that Lieutenant Rice had sent my money. I am sorry that he would not have sent it while it was worth something. But I suppose that I can lose it without subjecting me to any great inconvenience. I probably ought to give that much towards our currency. For my part, I would not care if the Government repudiated the last cent of the Confederate money in circulation. I believe that it would be best for the country. The currency bill is a roundabout road to repudiation, and I would not care if it was a direct one. If I can get out of this war with my life and my independence I shall be perfectly satisfied, without grumbling because I have lost a few paltry Confederate dollars, I have no patience at all with those who are continually complaining of pecuniary losses. They make a much louder lamentation over the loss of a little property or money than they do over the loss of the demoralization of our country. The rich should be content.

I should like to see Lieutenant Rice's letter and know is said anything about the balance of the 5th Kentucky Regiment. Did he intend to do or where he belonged? How did he get out of Chuse? I am a little interested in knowing the whereabouts of Kentucky troops, for I sometimes think that when I have to leave this position I will get a transfer to some part of the Kentucky cavalry. I do not want to have to take it afoot through another campaign.

Silas Dodson is near here. He belongs to Cook's North Carolina Brigade. He is Brigade Commissary Sergeant. I wrote him a few lines by Allison Chuly sometime ago but have not yet received a reply. Silas is married.

Jack Robertson's brother George was down here not long since. He is Orderly Sergeant of a cavalry company in William L. Jackson's command. He said that Dallas belonged to a company in his regiment. They were encamped near Warm Springs, Bath County.

My prospect of getting a furlough is rather slim. There are so many who want to go home, and they contend so strongly that only those bearing arms in the Company shall have furlough that I may not get one. However, if they continue to grant furloughs until late in the Spring I may get around Lieutenant Noel and get one. If I do not I can stand it very well. I would like very well to come home, but there is no use of being childish about it. I have not thought about it, so if I get one it will be that much clear, and if I do not it will be no disappointment. Give my respects to all and write. Yours truly, Powell Benton Reynolds

Camp near Orange Court House, Virginia, March 7, 1864
Dear Father and Mother,

With the greatest pleasure I have once more taken my pen to drop you a few lines to let you know that I and Jehu are both well at this time greatly hoping these lines will reach you in haste and find you in good health. The last letter that we sent you we was under marching orders. We started that morning and was in the march for three days, but didn't have any fight, but I will tell you that we had some hard marching. We lay on the battlefield of Chancellorsville and it is a horrible looking place. The men's bones has been buried and the men was laying with their heads stuck up on their hands or on sticks. Nothing more at present.
      Yours,
      James W. Barnard

Dear Father and Mother,

I seat myself to write you a few lines to inform you that I am well hoping these few lines reach you enjoying the best of health. Pap, I will send you fifty dollars by Thery Webb and my pistol too. I never paid you that sixteen dollars that I paid out of your money for my jacket. You can pay yourself out of this. I will send you all of my bonds by Thery Webb. I will give you the amount of the bonds and who they are on. C. T. Lawson, 45 dollars, Asa Scott, 67 dollars, G. B. Scott, 250, Daniel Smith 17 dollars and fifty cents. Tell Isham and Richard that I was glad to hear of their great generalship after being taken. Tell them to write to me and James. I haven't got any letter from them since Christmas. So I will close.

Jehu Barnard

Camp near Orange Court House, Virginia, March 11, 1864
Dear Father and Mother,

    With great pleasure we have taken out pen to drop you a few lines to let you know that we are both well at this time greatly hoping these lines will reach you both well and hearty. There is no news that is worth writing about more than that they boys is all well and in good spirits. They all will get to come home this spring g and maybe I will get to come home for a while. Asa Scott will start home in the morning and I thought that I would write you a letter as I thought you would be sure to get it.

    A few words to Isham and Richard. I can tell you that every man said he was for you for staying at home. They say that you was done mean and they would do just like you if they was in your place. Richard, you must carry your flint and keep them away till I come and then I will reinforce you with a heavy piece of artillery and Isham you…

James W. Barnard

Dear Father and Mother,

    This foggy day I seat myself to drop you a few lines to inform you that I am well hoping for these few lines to reach you enjoying the best of health. I have no news worth writing to you. They is several to get furloughs before I get to come though I think I will get to come sometime this spring and Jim will get to come to if they keep on furloughing though it is uncertain whether anyone gets to come or not. I hope we will both get to come together. I hope this summer campaign will end the war. I have nothing to write its nearly as dark as night and I can't see. Me and Jim sends Ruth $2 worth of stamps by Asa Scott and some paper if he will take it.

Yours,
Jehu Barnard

Camp near Orange Court House, Virginia, March 25, 1864
Dear Brothers (Isham and Richard Barnard),

    I have taken my pen to drop you a few lines to let you know that we are both well at this time. We received yours of the seventh instant which gave us great satisfaction to hear from you and to hear that you was at home yet and was all well. We haven't any news that would be of interest to you at this time. We would not be surprised at any time to have a big fight down here. They have begun to fix for it now. General Grant has taken some of the Yankee forces down here and said that he is going to make a move on Richmond in a few days, but if he comes up in front of our works he will get mighty whipped for I reckon there never was any works that is equal to these.

    Richard, I wish I could be there with you and Isham and be there in peace. You must do the best you can and I will try to do the same. It is a very bad rainy day and I can't write much this time. I want you to write if there is any snow on the ground in Patrick. I can't think of anything more to write.

                        Your loving brothers till death,
                        James W. Barnard
                        Jehu Barnard

Camp near Orange Court House, Virginia, March 27, 1864
Dear Father and Mother,

    With the greatest pleasure I have once more taken my pen to drop you a few lines to let you know that I and Jehu are both well at this time greatly hoping these lines will reach you in haste and find you in good health. The last letter that we sent you we was under marching orders. We started that morning and was in the march for three days, but didn't have any fight, but I will tell you that we had some hard marching. We lay on the battlefield of Chancellorsville and it is a horrible looking place. The men's bones has been buried and the men was laying with their heads stuck up on their hands or on sticks. Nothing more at present.

                        Yours,
                        James W. Barnard

March 27, 1864
Dear Father and Mother (Tirea and Eliza Barnard),

    With great pleasure I have taken my seat to drop you a few lines to let you know that me and Joel is both well at this time hoping for these lines will reach you enjoying good health. I haven't any news that is worth your attention. It has been very bad weather for the last week down here. There is no snow right at this place, but I can look over on the Blue Ridge and see plenty of snow. It has been there for a week or two. Pap, I must tell you of a circumstance which happened down here one day when they was a now on the ground. General Rodes brought his division over and cornered snow balling the first brigade in our division. They whipped them very badly and the Brigadier General of the brigade. They whipped of our division sent a dispatch to old General Johnson and…soon as old Blucher received the dispatch he came…and went around to all of the brigades and had the long roll beat and they advanced on General Rodes and gave him a whipping and ran him through his camp and as our men came back through Rodes' men's camp they captured all the rations and they have had work to keep them from taking a right kind of a fit. I have nothing more that I can write. Write soon.

James W. Barnard
Jehu Barnard

Camp 50th Virginia Regiment, April 13, 1864
Dear Sir:

    I will jot down a few items for your perusal this morning. I am tolerably well. I have just gotten over a very severe cold and hoarseness', which weakened me considerably. For three weeks, I was unable to speak, expect in a whisper. I have nearly fully recovered my voice now.

    We have had more wet weather since the first of April than I ever saw in the same length of time in my life. I would like to know what kind of weather you have had up there on the mountain. I can see the Blue Ridge white with snow yet although it is tolerably warm now.

    Preparations are being rapidly made to open this spring Campaign. This army will enter upon active operations very soon. Everything is being placed in marching trim. All the wagons and harness have been repaired and inspected, and the quartermasters have been ordered to keep seven days rations on hand and their teams ready to move at any time. All extra baggage must be ordered to stay closely with their men. All sick men are being sent off, and all visitors to the army have been ordered to leave. This looks very much like squally times are expected soon. As soon as the weather will permit, the ball will open. If Lee does not advance upon Grant, Grant will advance upon him. Grant is with the Yankee army down here, busily engaged in reviewing his troops and laying his plans. I have not the least idea what the program of either party will be, but I am sure that a great Providence interposes to prevent it. It is generally believed that if we can be successful in the coming campaign we will have passed the crisis and our success is certain. All seem to be tolerably good spirits and to repose the utmost confidence in General Lee. Although he has to contend against the ablest one of the Yankee Generals, all think that he will be more than a match for him.

    I hear nothing much from other parts of the Confederacy, but I presume that the campaign will open soon on all sides. It is reported today that Longstreet is on his return to this army. I do hope it may be true for when Grant advances of we advance on him, I want to have men enough to fight him a good battle.

Governor Vance of North Carolina has been on a visit to the army, and addressed all the troops from that State. I saw him review part of Rodes' Division and heard him make a speech. He spoke well, and I think his speeches had a very good effect upon the Carolinians. He declared that North Carolina would stick to the Confederacy until the last, notwithstanding a great deal had been said about the disloyalty of her citizens.

I would like to know if Tom Clark is running against Abe Staples. If he is not I have a great mind to oppose him myself. Write to me and tell me what you think of it. I think I could get a very respectable vote if my friends would interest themselves and stir around a little. Give my respects to all. Write often.

        Yours truly,
        Powell Benton Reynolds

P. S. I am compelled to frank my letters for I cannot get postage stamps.

Camp near Orange Court House, Virginia, April 13, 1864
Dear Father and Mother, Brother and Sisters,

We are again allowed the pleasure of dropping you a few lines to let you know that we are as well as common much hoping that when these lines reaches your distant land they will find you all well. I haven't any news to write you more than we are yet expecting an attack with the enemy. They are reinforcing every day at Culpepper Court House and they have ordered every citizen that is any ways near the line between us to move to the rear and ordered that all of our own men that is not fit for field service to be sent to the hospital. J. J. Reynolds was sent off yesterday and R. J. Boyd will be sent today. I think he will be sure of a furlough. You can tell his wife he has got the quinsy the worst I ever saw it, has fell in his legs. I will close for this time.

        James W. Barnard

Pap, there is nothing to write that would interest. They is some big move up someway. I don't know what it is. They are drafting new wagons and ambulance and ordered the commissary to have seven days rations on hand and to send all our surplus baggage to Richmond and to be ready to move at any time and I thought well be as soon as the ground dries. We can't get any letters from you. Some have I don't know what if the cause of it. I wish me and Jim could be at home to help you fix up your farm for it was getting in bad condition last spring. I want to be at home as soon as spring of the year comes for a man should never be away from home at this time of year. I feel like I want to be making something to support, but we are here and here we have to stay till cruel war is over for lifetime one or other we don't move and we can't write any that week. I will quit for this time. I am your loving son.

Jehu Barnard

Camp 50th Virginia Regiment, Orange Court House,
April 25, 1864
Gran,

    Asa and me are well. I believe I have nothing new to write, as we haven't commenced moving yet. Yes, I forgot, I have some news, when we were on picket a few days ago 13 of our regiment went over to the Yankees, most all of them from the Pulaski Company. Asa is writing a letter today. I see at the top Miss Mary. I guess it's going to either Mary Shriver of Mary Morton.

    I have wrote several, several letters home lately but have not heard them. I also sent a bundle of paper home that you all might have no excuse for not writing. If that won't do. I'll send pen, ink and postage and then, if <u>THAT</u> won't do, why I'll furnish you some already wrote.

    I heard you was planting a large crop of potatoes. I expect to help harvest them. When you write direct like I have directed on the other side.

G. Boston Scott

    On April 17, the 50th Virginia moved with Jones' Brigade from winter quarters at Mount Pisgah Church to Morton's Ford for a week of picket duty. During that stint of picket duty, some fifty men from the brigade, including fourteen from the 50th Virginia, deserted to the Union forces across the Rapidan. None of the deserters were from Company K.

    The 50th took part in the Battle of the Wilderness on May 5 along the Orange Turnpike in Jones Brigade (25th, 21st, and 48th, Virginia Infantry Regiments). Private John N. Opel of the 7th Indiana Regiment captured the battle flag of the 50th earning a Congressional Medal of Honor. General Jones lost his life trying to rally his men.

    The following day Union forces captured fifteen men of the regiment including Sam Dunkley and Richard Joseph Barnard. Transferred to the federal prison at Point Lookout, Maryland, on May 17, Dunkley remained there until August 14, 1864, and then moved to Elmira Prison. He was released on June 23, 1865, after taking the Oath of Allegiance to the United States of America. Richard Joseph Barnard died of typhoid fever at the prison at Elmira, New York on September 22, 1864. He lies today in Grave #487 at Woodlawn National Cemetery.

    On May 9, the 50th, commanded by Colonel William A. Witcher and then Colonel John C. Higginbotham, moved to the "Mule Shoe" salient along Lee's lines near Spotsylvania Court House. The next day Higginbotham lost his life as Union General Emory Upton's Corps penetrated the western face of the salient. Colonel Robert H. Dungan of the 48th Virginia assumed command of the brigade.

As "Jeb" Stuart lay dying in Richmond, the 50th continued fighting in the "Mule Shoe" on May 12. The latter, described as the "hardest fought battle of the war" against the United States Second Corps, resulted in ten killed, twelve wounded, and 211 captured from the Brigade. Jehu Barnard and his brother James were among those taken prisoner.

On May 15, the 50th along with the 21st, 25th, 42nd, 44th, and 48th Regiments became part of the Georgian John B. Gordon's Division. The 50th lost 39 killed, 67 wounded, 270 captured and 8 missing from May 5 thru 20, 1864. On May 20, General William Terry commanded the few men remaining of the regiment.

Spotsylvania Court House, May 19, 1864
Dear Sir:

You have doubtless heard many rumors concerning the big fight here, and I suppose that you are all anxious to hear the straight of the matter. I will give you a few items concerning our company and regiment. Our regiment was first engaged on the fifth instant. Company K lost three killed and several wounded and captured on that day. Andrew Cockram, Sam Howell and Bob Newman lost their lives on the battlefield. Jack Lewis, Reed Puckett, Abe Mays, Davy Harrell, and some others received wounds. Taken prisoners were Lieutenant Rangley, Sam Dunkley, Colonel Hanby and some others. General Jones of our Brigade was killed. There was a heavy fight on the sixth instance, but our Brigade was not engaged.

The fight of the fifth and sixth was near Chancellorsville. The army then moved down the river to this place. There was some fighting, more or less, every day. On the morning of the 12th, the Yankees made their grand assault upon our lines. Under the cover of the fog, which was very thick, they charged in solid columns upon our lines. Their main attack was upon our Division. They charged over our works, and after bayoneting many of our men, took nearly the whole Division prisoners. Floyd Dickerson was the only one of Company K that escaped. The rest were all captured. Some forty or fifty of the regiment made their escape. Counting all the drummers, detailed men, nurses and sick, there is but eighty of the 50th left. It started into the fight with 490 men. Our Division has been entirely broken up. General Johnson himself was captured. We lost every Brigadier General in the Division. Generals Jones and Stafford were killed. General Walker was wounded and General G. H. Stewart captured. The remnant of the Division has been attached for the present to Early's Division. What was left of Stafford's

Brigade of Louisianans has been attached to Hay's Brigade of Early's command. The two North Carolina Regiments is Stuart's Brigade have been put in Ramseur's Brigade of Rodes' Division. The six Virginia regiments in our Brigade and the five Virginia regiments in the "Stonewall" Brigade and the three Virginia regiments in Stuart's Brigade have all been thrown together and make one brigade.

This has been by far the hardest fought battle of the war. The Yankees fought with more desperation than they ever did before. They charged our works seven and eight times a day with solid columns five and six line deeps. But it did no good. They were always repulsed with immense slaughter. General Grant issued his men rations of whiskey to make them fight. The Yankees that fell into our hands were partly intoxicated and had whiskey in their canteens.

The enemy again assaulted our lines at sunrise yesterday morning, but were repulsed with artillery. The Yankee officers did their best to get their men to charge, but it was no go. They fell back in spite of them. It is believed that Grant will go back across the river. His loss has been immense since the fight began.

Our loss has been very heavy, especially in the way of officers. Our Division has suffered more than all the rest of the army put together. We have lost many officers killed and General Longstreet dangerously wounded. General J. E. B. Stuart has been killed.

The news is cheering from all quarters, but I cannot tell how it may turn out yet. I cannot learn whether any of our company was wounded or killed on the morning of the 12th or not, but I think that none of them were hurt. Tell Aunt Elizabeth and Aunt Suzy not to grieve for Hal and Dozier for they will have a long rest now, and I expect will see a finer time than the rest of us.

I will write again if anything of interest turns up and there is any chance to send of letters. It is thought that when this fight is over our Brigade will be sent back somewhere on provost only to recruit. I hope it may.

Yours truly, P. B. Reynolds

Letters like that from Peyton B. Reynolds were one way that the people in Patrick County learned of the loss of family and friends. Casualty lists printed in newspapers were another. On June 4, the *Lynchburg Daily Virginian* published the names of men in the 50th who had been lost in the terrible ordeal of the Wilderness and Spotsylvania. The news it carried was nearly 30 days old, incomplete and inaccurate in some respects. Nevertheless, it spoke to the price that the men of the 50th had paid in May. For those who searched for information about "The Patrick Boys" the list also said that no company in the regiment had suffered a greater loss than Company K.

Grant continued to push Lee south to the North Anna River by late May and to the vicinity of Cold Harbor. On June 2, General John B. Gordon's division, with the 50th Virginia, launched a successful attack near Bethesda Church that routed a portion of the Union Fifth Corps. The victory brought the division accolades in the Richmond press. During the fight, a cannon ball inflicted a "Perforating wound" in the groin of G. Boston Scott that led to the amputation of his left leg at Shady Grove in Hanover County, Virginia. Union forces captured Scott and admitted him on June 5 to the hospital at White House landing on the Pamunkey River. On June 12, he came to the Armory Square Hospital in Washington, D. C.

Armory Hospital Ward F Number Eleven, Washington D. C.,
June 16, 1864
Dear Mother,

On the 2nd June, I was severely wounded in the groin and fell into the hands of the Union troops. I was then taken to the White House landing to the field hospital where I remained several days. I suffered a great deal, so warm and so crowded with wounded. I must not omit to express my gratitude to the Sanitary Committee, a society for the relief of the wounded, from which I received a great many nourishments such as pickles, teas, chocolate, soups, lemonade, and etc. I was brought to this hospital four or five days ago. I am quite helpless, have to lay on my back all the time. This is a beautiful hospital and I receive very good attention, much better than I could expect from a people that I have been fighting against, but after all I have but very little hope of ever getting well. My wound is of such a nature and in such a condition, that I think it is impossible. I will try and get some lady to contrive this through the lines so that you can know what became of me. I am dear mother, your very affectionate son, G. Boston Scott

Scott died on June 19, 1864. He asked the hospital officials to send his effects to his mother including a locket, set of earrings, breast pin, pocket book and diary. Ignoring his wishes, Union officials auctioned off his belongings on May 2, 1865, for $2.15. The diary was not among these items and its whereabouts is unknown. Eight months after his death, Mary Pointer wrote G. Boston Scott's mother the following letter.

Lexington, Rockbridge County, Virginia, February 2, 1865
Mrs. Spangler, My Dear Madam,

I hope you will pardon the liberty I take in addressing you, but being an old friend of your son's (Mr. G. B. Scott) and being anxious to hear from him, I feel justified in addressing you. I have not seen your son for two years, and have not heard anything of him for a year and a half. I knew him very well when I was living in Wytheville. The 50th Regiment was then at Camp Jackson. He left Wytheville in the spring of 1863, spent the summer in Rockbridge County, and then went to Richmond. I received a letter from your son written in August 1863. I replied to it, but never received any answer. I do not know whether he ever received it. I suppose you hear from him. Please let him know that you received a letter from me, and send my kindest regards to him. I shall be under many obligations to you if you will answer this letter and let me know when you heard from him. Please let me know to what command he belongs. His company, regiment, etc. I feel almost as if I knew you, as I heard your son speak of you often.

          I remain most respectfully yours,
            Mary E. V. Pointer

   The 50th Virginia Infantry continued to fight and by June 18, 1864, the men were with General Early at Lynchburg. On July 5, they again crossed the Potomac River into Maryland, fought at Monocacy on July 9 and skirmished in front of the defenses of Washington, D.C. on July 12. Falling back into Virginia, the 50th fought at Kernstown on July 24 with Terry's Brigade, which included the 21st, 25th, 42nd, 44th, and 48th Virginia Infantry Regiments. The regiment spent August in frequent skirmishing and hard marching. Major Lynville Perkins, exchanged following his capture on May 10, took command of the regiment by August 30. On September 19, the 50th fought a major battle at Winchester, suffering two killed, five wounded and five captured. That same day, the regiment transferred to General Gabriel Wharton's Brigade, commanded by Colonel Augustus Forsberg. Whether the transfer took place before September 22, when the 50th shared in the rout of Early's Confederates at Fisher's Hill is not known. However, by October 5, the 50th, with but 42 men, had joined Forsberg's Brigade, which also included the 45th, 51st Virginia Infantry Regiments and the 30th Battalion Virginia Sharpshooters. The 50th fought at Cedar Creek on October 19, and then retreated to New Market. Near there, on October 28, Perkins reported his unit's strength as 2 other officers and 53 men present. The men lacked many things, especially clothes and 78 percent of the men were deficient in shoes. Campaigning continued through November and into December. Not until Christmas day did the men of Forsberg's Brigade begin to build winter quarters at Fishersville in Augusta County.

   As part of the 50th settled into winter quarters, others from the regiment endured privations as prisoners of war. James and Jehu Barnard were among the men of Company K captured at Spotsylvania Court House in May. They arrived at Point Lookout, Maryland, on May 18. Sometime before July 30, 1864, when Union authorities sent them to

Elmira, New York, they found a way to send a letter to their family.

Prison, Point Lookout, Maryland, Date Unknown
Dear Father and Mother,
     Me and Jim is both here and well and doing as well as you could expect. All of our company is here except one or two that was wounded. Pap, send us some of the names and post office of your connection in the North that I may write to them. Our company seems gaily and well and hearty. I have nothing that I can write. They is thirty six of our company here that was taken in the fight and three that was here when we came. You must write small letters. I hope this will find both of you well. Direct your letters to Point Lookout in Maryland, Company F, Second Division.
                                        James and Jehu Barnard

Elmira, New York, November 29, 1864
Dear Father and Mother,
     This evening affords me the pleasure of writing you a few lines. I am well and all the rest of the company except J. B. Shelor. He has been right sick, but is getting better. Jim left here on parole on the 12th of October and I have not heard of him since. I hope he is at home. Pap, I got a letter from Davis Burch and they was all well and in his letter he sent me ten dollars, which came in a very good time. H. A. Hefflefinger is well. I have no news to write. R. J. Barnard is dead as is J. T. Hatcher and several more that you have heard of. Pap, I want you to send me some tobacco, if you han't started none send about 20 or 30 pounds, if Jim nor William Soyar has not started me none. John Shelor and H. D. Richardson is well. S. H. Dunkley and D. S. Handy is well. I am your loving son.
                                        Jehu Barnard

     James W. Barnard saw Union prisons first at Point Lookout, Maryland in May through July 1864, then Elmira, New York, from August until mid-October, and finally back to Point Lookout the rest of the month before being exchanged at Venus Point, Savannah River, Georgia on November 15, 1864. He returned to Patrick County by March 2, 1865 and then rejoined the army at Dublin eight days later.
     In February 1865, the regiment reported 74 men and officers present for duty in Forsberg's Brigade of 699 men. Indiandozier Boganshield Shelor of Company K died in prison at Elmira, New York on February 15.
     At the end of January 1865, the 50th Virginia, in winter quarters at Fishersville, reported 74 men and officers present for duty in Forsberg's Brigade, which numbered 699 men. On February 27, the

regiment moved to Waynesboro to meet the threat of George Custer and Thomas Devin's ten thousand Union Cavalry. The Battle of Waynesboro ended the career of many men from Patrick County in the 50th and 51st regiments with capture on March 2, 1865. Casualties in the regiment that day totaled one killed, one wounded and 63 captured. The remainder of the regiment traveled to Dublin in Pulaski County. James W. Barnard of Company K arrived there on March 10 and found nine members of his company. They disbanded on April 11, 1865, in Christiansburg, Virginia.

Dublin Depot, Virginia, March 12, 1865
Dear Father and Mother (Tirea and Eliza Barnard),
    This morning affords me the pleasure of dropping you a few lines to let you know that I am well at this time much hoping these few lines finds you both well and hearty. I haven't any news of much interest more than that the Yankees is in 16 miles of Lynchburg a trying to burn that long bridge. They was skirmishing last evening in eight miles of Lynchburg is the report this morning. I expect to be in a big fight in a few days we will get to Lynchburg tonight or tomorrow. We landed last evening and stayed all night with Mrs. Ames that married Mrs. Boswell's daughter and they treated me with great kindness. They are very fine folks. Pap, they say here all of the prisoners have come from Elmira and I think that Jehu will be at home in a few days if he ain't there now. I will have to close as I have to write a few lines to Mrs. Boswell. You must write soon to me.
                                        Yours forever,
                                        James W. Barnard

Mrs. Boswell,
    This morning affords me the pleasure of writing you a few lines, but I have to say that when I reached Dublin I went to Mr. Ames very eagerly to hear from H. P. Boswell and met you daughter at the door and enquired for Press and she said that he was dead and you can't think how I felt, but she said that he professed a hope. The train comes and I did not have time to write more.
                                        Yours,
                                        James W. Barnard

    Eventually, General John Echols assembled an army at Dublin numbering some 5,000. Echols moved from there on March 26 in an effort to block George Stoneman's Union cavalry raid. Echols attempted to join Robert E. Lee's army at Lynchburg. On April 9, when Lee surrendered, Echols' army was camped near Christiansburg. There on April 11 Echols disbanded his force. Six men of the 50th Virginia were among those who remained in the ranks at the end. Three of those men James W. Barnard, David K. Harrell and Daniel Smith were from "The Patrick Boys."

During four years of war, the regiment lost 523 prisoners with 125 dying at such places as Elmira, New York. Sixteen men took the Oath of Allegiance. Thirty-three joined the Union army. Nine became part of the "Immortal 600" placed under fire of Confederate guns in Charleston harbor in South Carolina in 1864. Of the 1,734 serving, 290 received wounds and 426 died of wounds, disease or other causes. At least 188 men from Patrick County served in this regiment.

The 50th Virginia contained the second highest number of men from Patrick County to fight in an infantry regiment for the Confederate States of America behind the only the two companies of the 51st Virginia Infantry Regiment. The "Patrick Boys" of the 50th saw the most and toughest action of the war. From Lee's failed campaign in present day West Virginia through Fort Donelson, the glory of Chancellorsville and the frustration of Gettysburg and the horrendous bloodlettings of the Wilderness and Spotsylvania, these men showed courage and sacrifice defending their native state.

Colonel Alexander W. Reynolds was in Egypt by 1870 fighting as a Brigadier General. When he died there in 1876, the United States celebrated its centennial. Of those writing letters in this chapter, most survived the war. Daniel Smith died in 1907, John W. Boswell died in 1881, Fleming Spangler in 1902, Powell B. Reynolds in 1914, Henry A. Hefflefinger and George W. Yeatts in 1922. Sam Dunkley returned to Patrick and married in 1866. He enjoyed a long and successful political career holding offices such as sheriff and treasurer of the county for 40 years. He had 11 children. He died on March 1, 1932, at the age of 91, the last of the 50th Virginia Infantry Regiment from Patrick County.

Powell Benton Reynolds served as President of West Virginia University from 1893 until 1895. In 1894, he set fourth a vision of a "new university," arguing that the school was "entering upon a new era" that could enable it to "rank with the best state universities in the country." Reynolds' plan for reorganization would make it "necessary to renew all the courses, and to readjust the work and the functions and relation of the Faculty, so as to secure co-ordination, harmony, and efficiency, and bring the University up abreast of the times."

After the war, James W. Barnard married Susan and lived along the Dan River in Kibler Valley. He died on April 23, 1923. Thomas A. Barnard moved to Tazewell County, Virginia in 1869, to Searcey County, Arkansas by 1871, and to Pueblo County, Colorado by 1877, where his family still flourishes.

Jehu Barnard returned to the "Free State" after being released from the Federal prison at Point Lookout, Maryland. He married twice

(Adeline Wood and Virginia Orander) and had twelve children. He served as county surveyor for eight years, taught school and was the first postmaster at a place called Mayberry in 1872. When his father, Tirea, died in 1877, he moved his family in with his mother Eliza and took care of her. Jehu died at age 90 on March 14, 1933. His daughter, Lois Barnard Harris, transcribed their family letters from the war and taught school at Blue Ridge High School inspiring many of her students with a love of history.

    Writing in 1862, John Dudley Greever of the 50th Virginia about Fort Donelson spoke for the entire experience of the war he witnessed. "Oh it was a scene I never want to witness again, but the brave Virginian boys won a name…that will live when their graves will have grown over with the green grass of the valley."

Jehu Barnard of the 50th Virginia Infantry with his daughter Lois Barnard Harris, who preserved his letters. *Courtesy of Helen Frazier and Mr. and Mrs. Blaine Barnard.*

Chapter Five
"Patrick Henry Volunteers"
Company H, 42nd Virginia Infantry Regiment

One of the earliest volunteer companies organized in Patrick County originated near Critz on Spoon Creek under the leadership of Captain John Edmund Penn. Company members officially enlisted on May 22, 1861 as the Patrick Henry Volunteers. John Edmund Penn was born in 1837, educated at Randolph Macon College and the University of Virginia. In 1860, the census listed him as a 22-year-old lawyer living in Ararat. Other members of the Penn family fought in the regiment. This chapter will intertwine their story with the regiment through their letters and service records.

Among the men of Company H, the Patrick Henry Volunteers, of the 42nd Virginia Infantry Regiment were the Penn brothers. The children of Mary Christian Kennerly (1803-1885) and Thomas Penn (1781-1858) wrote home often. The family descended from Revolutionary War hero, Abram Penn, who was instrumental in the formation and early days of Patrick County. Lieutenant Joseph Green Penn was born on February 10, 1832. The 1860 census lists him as 28 years old and a trader at Mayo Forge. Sergeant Thomas Green Penn was born on January 15, 1838. The census reports him as a 22-year-old merchant. Private William A. Penn was born on July 7, 1840. The census lists him as a 19-year-old clerk. Corporal John S. Penn was born December 4, 1842. The census reports him a 17-year-old student All the Penn brothers lived in the Mayo Forge section of Patrick County. Other Penns serving in Company H of the 42nd Virginia living in Horse Pasture of Henry County included Lieutenant Rufus G Penn, Private Samuel A. Penn, Captain Greenville B. Penn and Captain Edmund L. Penn.

On July 5, at Lynchburg, companies A, G (Henry Volunteers) and F (Leatherwood Fencibles) from Henry County, Company K (Franklin Invincibles) from Franklin County, Company B (Floyd Guards) from Floyd County, Company C (Buford Greys) from Bedford County, Company E, (Dixie Grays), from Roanoke County, and companies D (Lee Guards) and I (Campbell Guards) from Campbell County joined with Company H (Patrick Henry Volunteers) to form the 42nd Virginia Infantry. These companies remained unchanged during the entire war. The regiment made up of mostly farmers or farm laborers trained at Camp Lee on the Lynchburg City Fairgrounds under the command of Colonel Jesse S. Burks, an 1844 graduate of the Virginia Military Institute.

On July 18, 1861, the regiment, 867 strong, traveled to Staunton. It spent the summer and fall of 1861 in marches and skirmishes in the mountains of present day West Virginia. Like most of the other units, the men caught the measles, typhoid and diarrhea. Half of the men were ill at a time.

Staunton, Virginia, Sunday, July 21, 1861
Dear Ma,

    As you have learned through William or John Terrell the regiment had orders to march the next morning Thursday after I got to Lynchburg and I determined to accompany them to Manassas Junction. When we got to Charlottesville Colonel Banks, the colonel of the regiment, to which the boys belong received another dispatch ordering him to this place.

    The next day, Friday, they remained here and late in the evening of this day they were ordered to Monterey in Highland County this state 48 miles distant from this place together with Colonel Gillums Regiment, which had been here about a week. They left yesterday about 10 o'clock and camped 10 miles from this place. They have a fine turnpike all the way. A Georgia regiment left here the day before, and it is said that when the forces all arrive then that have left here in the last week, that they will be 10,000 strong. All left here in fine spirits and thus far have had pleasant weather for their march. I should have gone on with them, but to have hired a private conveyance would have cost me a good deal and I determined to wait until tomorrow morning and go by stage. I will then there about the time they will and I will spend a day two with them there. There is no enemy near there as this time, and it is impossible to tell whether they will remain there and fortify that point or whether they may be called to some other place.

    Four of John Penn's company were left here, with measles, young Adams, Via, Shelton and Murphey. They have appropriated the Deaf and Dumb Asylum to hospital purposes, and they are at that place pleasant situated, and getting on very well. Will be able to rejoin their company in a week, I think. Doctor Stuart of Floyd is their physician. He has an appointment in the Hospital Department here. I spent some time with him today and will call on them on my return. The militia of this county turned out yesterday in full strength, and the town and its vicinity. I saw Colonel Sam Kennerly yesterday and day before, but he was very much engaged in conversion with the military and was in his company only a few minutes. He said all were well.

    Before this reaches you, you will have heard of the great battle that is going on at this time at Manassas. It is reported here that the Confederates were advancing upon the enemy and there seems no doubt entertained but that the enemy will be badly whipped. Though I fear it will be at a heavy sacrfise of men on our side. Colonel Stedman passed here yesterday evening to join Governor Wise Legion in the direction of

Kanawha. Lieutenant Roome that was with Captain Rosser also went on our they thought… Company would be on in a few days. I think I will get home next Sunday. Will call and see Willie and if necessary will take him home. Though I expect to find him nearly well, as I know John Terrell will give every attention he possibly can.

  I will not write more, as the papers that you will get by the mail that carries this will give you more reliable news than I can now give as there are so many rumors afloat. They boys requested me to give you all their best love and say they will with every chance I will bring Edmond and Mary something.

         Your affectionate son
         G. W. Penn

Camp 17 miles NW of Huntersville, Friday, August 2, 1861
My Dear Ma,

  We were delighted to see Jimmy and all from our neighborhood. They reached our camp at Huntersville just as we had commenced packing up to leave. He can tell you all about our unexpected order to march etc and knows as much about the arrangements for the future as we do….

  In my letter from Huntersville I requested you to send me a pair of pants if there is any more passing. If you should have an opportunity it would be well to send each of us a pair of heavy coarse pants, and mine and Willies black hats….

  We can gather nothing concerning our future that would interest you, in fact I don't believe the Officers themselves are decided.

  You must not give yourself any trouble about us. Our forced marches are disagreeable, it is true, but when we stop we <u>enjoy</u> the <u>rest</u> and all keep in good spirits….Your affectionate son, Thomas Green Penn

Valley of Flat Top Mountain, Randolph County, Virginia,
August 7, 1861
My dear Ma (Mary C. Penn),

  I have just learned from the Colonel that a messinger will start in a short time to Huntersville and I must write you a line. The health of our company is improving. Many was recovering from the measles and I believe that about all have taken it who have not had it. Our Captain is down with it now at the camp we left this morning about four miles back. He was right sick for a while but is improving now and will soon be well if he is not imprudent.

  Johnnie and myself are well, but Bro is complaining of cold and disordered bowells but is going about and able to do duty. We are now encamped about a mile from the top of Flat Top Mountain 22 miles from Huttonsville. There are now between two and three thousand troops on top the mountain including cavalry and several pieces of artillery. The enemy are about nine miles from us. Their strength is said to be about ten thousand and they are fortifying their position.

Our forces will number between eight & ten thousand when all arrive. The Col'n thinks it likely that they the enemy will attack us soon though it is thought that our position is a strong one and I doubt whether or not they try it with their present force.

Though it is said that they intend to try to flank us by crossing the mountain at another point but there are forces at several points that could be brought to our assistance. General Lee is now at the camp on top the mountain. Our General Lowring also. With them at our head we feel that we could stand against most any force. We have heard nothing from Willie yet, nor the other boys at Lynchburg.

You must excuse this badly written letter. I have written in great haste.... I must close or my letter will be too late. Give my love to all.

Wm Martin was with us yesterday and said that Sam Hairston started but had to stop with Bob who was taken sick. We were greatly disappointed at his not coming on. It would have afforded us so much pleasure to have seen him. I was on guard while Mr. Martin was in camp and did not get to speak to him.

        Good bye.
        Thomas Green

Camp on Valley Mountain, Saturday, August 10, 1861
Dear Ma,

I wrote to you a few days ago but as I have an opportunity of sending another I will write again this evening. We received your letter dated the 31st this evening and were delighted to hear that you are all well. Nothing of importance has happened since I wrote last that I know of. We are kept very ignorant of the plans of the Officers and know very little of the movements of the enemy. It is said that they are fortifying about 10 miles from here and it is thought that we will have to make an attack soon.

It is reported that very heavy reinforcements are coming to us. We are encamped at the same place that we were when I wrote before though you will notice the heading of my letter is different. I made a mistake in the name of the mountain before. This is said to be part of Cheat Mountain but at this point is called Valley Mt.

General Lee was in our Camp yesterday, had an interview with the Colonel and returned to the camp above us. It is thought that if we make an attack on the enemy he will take command.

This is a wild and rough looking country, very thinly settled, and but little wealth. The nearest house is four miles from here.

There is still a good deal of sickness in our Regiment, mostly measles and its effects. It rains most all the time here and some of the citizens say that they have rain on an average of once a day through the year. But if we succeed in whipping back the Yankees, we will get to a better country North of this. Our boys are getting tired of the mountains and I believe all wish that the fight will come off soon, and none fear the result with anything near an equal fight, and General Lee at our head.

Brother is very much hurt at the story Sam wrote to his Pa and Sam positively denies that he ever wrote such a thing and says that he has not been treated amiss by Brother in a single instance and has never even thought hard of him for anything he has said to him. He pretends to be surprised that they took up such an idea from anything he wrote. But poor boy, the truth is not in him as his family and all who know him are aware.

Brother (Lt. Joseph G. Penn) has on different occasions when Sam Penn was misbehaving scolded him and advised him how he should do. but no one in the company will say that he has gone beyond his duty in the first instance. On the contrary he can get the certificate of the whole company that he has never mistreated him in any way if it is necessary. William Tatum has been in our mess all the time, eats and sleeps with us and he will testify to the same, and a more truthful young man is not to be found in our neighborhood. The fact is that Sam was at one time very anxious to go home and made this complaint thinking that it would induce his Pa to try to get him off....

Sunday morning (August 11, 1861)

I did not get my letter off yesterday and will add a line this morning. We are on the eve of starting out on picket Guard, to be out until tomorrow morning. All are well except a few who have not recovered entirely from measles. The Captain is improving. A young man belonging to Captain Lane's company named Manon died last night. his death was caused by taking cold when recovering from measles which caused a relapse. I keep uneasy about Willie. I fear he has had a severe spell by his not coming in, and dread the consequences of his leaving a comfortable house and coming into a damp tent and having to lie on a damp bed. We are getting hardened to it I hope and will be able to stand it. You must not give yourself so much uneasiness about us for we can stand ten times more fatigue and exposure here, than if we were staying at home....You mentioned that Dr. Hay has sent his Gum up for me. It will not be safe to send us any thing except by hand. Brother George promised to buy us something of the kind and I don't suppose we will need Dr. Hays. But if Bro George bought overcoats and did not get gum covers I would like if any of our friends visit us for them to buy us about two gum sheets to lie on or throw over us when it rains. They can be bought in Richmond now and I suppose they would come that way. Write to us often, Brother and Johnnie join me in much love to all. Don't you think Jimmie acted rather cowardly I know it was the sight at Charlottesville that…Tell him we all think so. Give our love to Cousin Bella. Goodbye dear Ma and all.

Your affectionate son
Thomas G. Penn

Camp on Valley Mountain, Pocahontas County, Virginia,
August 11, 1861
My Dear Ma,

    Thomas G. has written you a long letter but has not sealed it so I will write a few lines myself on the Sam subject. Sam has lied about my mistreating him. I have never scolded but very little but one time and that was in Lynchburg and then if I had of had my way with him I would have whipped him well. I was in my tent, and some of the boys came to me to look at Sam. He was walking with a negro girl about the encampment in the presence of the whole Regiment. I sent for him and when he came I talked to him as I thought he deserved he is the most low life boy I ever saw. If brother Jackson is dissatisfied I want you to let me know if he is. Sam shall not stay in my tent any longer.

    When I wrote to you last we had not had a death in our case, but since I commenced my letter we was notified of a burial. One of Captain Lanes men died last night with inflammation of the stomach he exposed him after having the measles his name was Manning, his burial was the most solemn one I ever saw about two hundred men present and hardly a dry eye in the crowd.

    All of our men are getting over the measles we left about 30 of our company behind we hear from them every few days some are on their way to camp. We haven't heard from Willie yet hope he is doing well. John said he should not want for attention. I have been unwell ever since I wrote until yesterday I am very well now my spell was caused by living too long on <u>beef</u> the day we left Big Spring I wrote on the off wheel horse riding in our wagon.

    It is reported in camp that Missouri and Maryland have seceded if the report is true peace will soon be made we are getting very impatient to make an advance on the enemy we heard last night they had fallen back 3 miles further our spies say the enemy have no idea of our number in this part of the State.

    We have Pickett on all the roads and paths leading to this place no one is permitted pass them without a permit. This is a hard country to live in we cant buy any thing at all to eat or ware, but we have meal and beef some <u>times</u> in abundance some coffee and sugar.

We get our supplies from Monterey. I have not seen but three newspapers since I left Lynchburg you may know by that how well we keep posted in public matters. We have Wm Murphy in our mess....

> Your affectionate son
> Joseph G. Penn

The 42nd Virginia learned quickly that United States troops were not the only enemies they faced. The regiment experienced bizarre weather fighting for Robert E. Lee in present day West Virginia. It rained for thirty seven days and on August 13 it snowed and the next the men endured ice falling on them. That same month three hundred men suffered from measles.

On September 8, 1861, the 42nd Virginia commanded by Lieutenant Colonel Langhorne became part of Colonel Burks Sixth Brigade in the Army of the North West along with the 48th Virginia Infantry and W. H. F. Lee's Cavalry. The next day along with the 1st Tennessee Infantry the 42nd saw its first combat at Mingo Flats.

Camp on Sewells Mountain, Fayette County, Virginia,
Tuesday, October 1, 1861
My Dear Sister,

I wrote you from Greenbriar Bridge. We were uncertain at that time what was our destination. On the next morning we started under forced march to join General Lee at this place. We came down the beautiful valley from the bridge by Lewisburg which burst upon our view just after climbing a long and rough mountain from the top of which we had a splendid view of the large nice farms and beautiful residences stretching as far as the eye could reach below. The scenery created a momentary change in the feeling of every soldier who ascended the mountain almost worn out with fatigue, and dispirited by nearly two months confinement among the mountains in Randolph County where we had not seen a respectable looking dwelling, nor a farm much larger than a roasting ear patch, and the air was made to ring for miles around with shouts from more than fifteen hundred voices.

It seemed to give new life to every one they forgot their fatigue, unfurled the banner and proudly marched through the neat villages and by beautiful residences keeping up a continuous shout and greeted everywhere by nice young ladies who waved their handkerchiefs from nearly every window. This is truly a beautiful country, one among few that I would exchange our home in old Patrick for.

For two days the dust was very disagreeable and many of the men had to fall out of ranks. On the evening of the second day of two Regiments not more than two hundred marched in camp together. I was one of eight in our company that continued in ranks. It went very hard with our men and we left many behind who gave out and had to stop on the way. I stood the march finely, did not have to leave ranks at all.

On the third day of our march it commenced raining and continued to rain till the next day. The water courses got very high, higher it is said than they have been for years, and we had many of them to wade. In one place we waded through back water for near a half mile, but I do not believe it hurt any of us. We camped on Meadow Bluff on last Saturday night where Floyd is encamped with part of his forces, and is strongly fortified. We met with Captain Lawson and many of his men, also some of Captains Ross and Conners men; among them Willie Price. He looks finely, and seems to stand the service very well. There is a good deal of sickness in Lawson's Company.

We are now where Wise was when Floyd fell back to his present position about 14 miles from here. Arrived here on Sunday night. We are about a mile and a half from the enemys camp only hidden from them by a body of woods. I went up on top of a mountain about three quarters of a mile from our camp from where I could see almost their entire encampment. It is situated on the side of a high hill in easy canon range of where I was.

I could see about four hundred units, could see the men plainly walking about and could see their flags waving in the air. We have canons on the hill that I was on and it is thought that the fight will commence by canonading from these two points. The enemy fired several times at our men on top of this hill several days ago but the balls went entirely over them. A Battle is expected hourly. Our tents and baggage are loaded every morning by light on wagons and carried some distance from camp.

It is thought that General Lee is waiting an attack from the enemy, but if they do not attack us soon, he will make it himself. I do not know the strength of our forces here but think they will number at least fifteen thousand. The enemys force is variously estimated at from ten to twenty thousand. We have I think between twenty and thirty pieces of canon. We have breastworks of rails and dirt thrown up I suppose near three miles long. It is thought that the enemy has strong fortifications also. The men are in fine spirits, seem to be anxious for the fight and all confident of success.

If we make the attack it is thought we will flank them on their right....Our Camp is on the turnpike leading from Lewisburg to Charleston, about thirty miles from the former....We have heard nothing from the Gum sheets yet........ We were not allowed to take any extra baggage in the Government wagons when we left the Bridge...A flag of truce was sent in to General Lee yesterday morning by the enemy proposing to go into winter quarters and suspend the war until spring. General Lee replied that he would accede to the proposition provided they would leave our land but that he would not go into winter quarters while they continued to invade our soil.

    Two Yankeys were taken prisoner by our pickets yesterday. On Saturday the Colonel of the 3rd Virginia Regiment in a drunken state rode into the enemy's camp and was killed. His horse turned and ran back to his men and they brought his corpse into camp. I have filled my sheet and it is all I have out of the trunk which is in the wagon....

                            Your affectionate brother
                                  Thomas Green Penn

Camp on Sewell Mountain, Fayette County, Virginia,
Tuesday, October 15, 1861
Dear Brother George,

    I wrote to Willie a few days since and as Mr. Craig will leave tomorrow for home I will write you a line tonight.... Since my last nothing of interest has transpired. We have had no news from the forces that have advanced towards Charleston, and I suppose we are awaiting the developments of that movement.

    If Floyd encounters the enemy and they prove too much for him I suppose we will be sent to his relief and if practicable an effort will be made to fight through to Charleston this winter. If not we will fall back either to Greenbriar Bridge or to some place for winter quarters.
I am surprised that you receive so few letters from us. I write by nearly every opportunity. I have of sending letters to the railroad or any point in a main mail route. I frequently write twice a week. There is very little certainty in sending letters from here though by mail carriers. They have to pass through the hands of Quarter Masters at different points and through their negligence many of them are lost...There is still a good deal of sickness in camp. some fever and a good many cases of Yellow Jaunders. We have had no deaths lately in our Regiment. Johnnie has been complaining for several days of pain in his head and stomach and has had some fever though I hope he will soon be relieved. If there is a probability of his having a spell I shall take him to some place where he can be made comfortable and receive the proper medical attention. Our Surgeon is sick and unable to attend to the sick which leaves Doctors Morris and Wingfield and a half witted man, I believe, named Muyer (Meire) to attend to them and the Regiment is almost entirely without medicines. I hope though that Johnnie will be well in a few days. I shall write again in a day or two and will let you know his condition.

    You mentioned in one of your letters that you thought it likely that Booker could get an appointment for me in the Regiment that he joined.... Unless I could get an office of some importance I would prefer continuing with Brother and Johnnie. In fact, I would dislike to leave them under any circumstances, and there are but few offices I would accept out side of this Regiment, that I am capable of filling. I have the office of fourth Sergeant in our company which makes my duty some lighter than a private. I have enjoyed good health since I have been in the service, and have undergone as much exposure of every kind as any man in the Regiment, and perhaps it will be better for me to remain where I am. At any rate I am content to do so while Brother and Johnnie are with me and do not believe that I would be satisfied to leave them under any avoidable circumstances.... As to the wagon if it has not started, I do not know what to advise. If we advance from here it is very uncertain how long we will remain as I think the result of that movement extremely doubtful on account of our great distance from the Rail Road, and the great difficulty of furnishing the army with provisions while the enemy have transportation facilities almost to their tents. It was lame management in the War Department to allow that valuable section of the state to fall into the enemy hands when with the troops that laid idle in Lynchburg Wise and Floyd could have easily kept them back.

    I fear it will take hard fighting to get it back. I forgot clearly to mention any thing about it in my other letter. In fact, this I considered it so uncertain that I thought but little about it unless...I made mention in my last letter of my willingness to dispose of my interest in the store if it is Mr. Zentmeyer's wish to conduct the business of his own hook. Tell Mr. Zentmeyer that I met with Nathan Purdy several days since the one that hauled metal for a while and he paid me six dollars which he thinks is the amount of his indebtedness at the store. He can enter it to his credit and charges to me. Send me a good strong pocket knife by the first opportunity.

                                  Your affectionate Brother
                                  Thomas G. Penn

Headquarters Green River Bridge, Pocahontas County, Virginia, November 9, 1861
Dear Daughter (Mary Jane Mason, Unseen Infant Daughter),

    I take my pen in hand to write you a few lines. This leaves me in the enjoyment of good health at present hoping they may find you and your Mother the like blessing. I have no news of importance to write. As it is the first time, I ever addressed a letter to you or anyone so near to me I scarcely know how to proceed feeling at the same time somewhat excited and begs to be excused for any mistakes you may find.

    Mary, you must be a good girl and obey your Mother remembering at the same time that you have a Father in the Army fighting for your Liberty and your country's rights and one is Daily yes hourly thinking of you and your kind Mother. One that dreams of you almost every night. I hope that you and your Mother will do well until I return. I hope that I may have the pleasure of being introduced to you between this and Christmas. I am going to try to come home when Captain Morris gets back. It may be I will not get off until after Christmas but I intend to come this winter without fail

You need not look for me till you see me coming. Mary, I have no idea you would know me if you was to see me but I hope the time is not far distant when we will meet each other face to face. I believe I will bring my letter to a close not forgetting to assign myself your affectionate Father until death…I will address a few line to you. If Mary James can't read her letter, you must read it for her. I have written many letters but my…beats higher than they ever have before.

James. M. Mason
First Lieutenant, Company G,
42nd Virginia Infantry.
Wounded at Second Manassas.
Died September 9, 1862.

Tragedy hit the Penn family on October 27, 1861, when John S. Penn died in present day Lewisburg, West Virginia. Thomas G. Penn, who acted as a nurse to his fellow Virginians, accompanied his dead brother home to Patrick County. The 5' 10" blonde haired, blue eyed, William A. Penn left the regiment in September at Big Spring in Pocahontas County, now West Virginia, due to disability. The following spring Thomas received promotion to fourth sergeant in April 1862, but Joseph failed in his reelection bid to Lieutenant and left the 42nd Virginia. Later in July 1862, Thomas hired a substitute, Alfred Cardinal, and left the ranks of the regiment. The regiment furloughed Samuel A. Penn at the end of October for sick leave, but he was back by January 1, 1862. He left the regiment in September 1862 before the Battle of Antietam after providing a substitute, James O'Hara, to take his place. Tobacconist and Lieutenant Rufus G. Penn left on sick leave in December 1861 and resigned due to disability in February 1862.

Other members of the Penn family soldiered on with the 42nd Virginia. Greenville B. Penn rose in rank to Sergeant by November 1861. He spent February through April 1862 recruiting in Patrick County until promoted to Lieutenant. Edmund L. Penn followed an identical path in rank and duties including recruiting and becoming Lieutenant in April 1862.

Patrick County, November 16, 1861
My dear Joseph,

Mr. Zentmeyer wrote…and informed you of Thomas Green having a very sore throat. We were fearful at first he was taking the fever, but he has but very little fever but one of his old sort of sore throats he is quite bad off but I hope it will break in a day or so. Dr. Ray lanced it on Wednesday & it was a most painful operation indeed. He said his throat looked a good deal like Diphtheria, but said it was not. He seems to have taken a good deal of cold he is most of the time in bed. I do hope he will soon be able to go into Camp....

The Captain has returned and is to be here to Day.... John A. Tatum is better I am informed.... My dear Jonny is in my mind nearly all the time dear child how strange to say he is dead & I am never to see his dear face no more on earth. Oh may we all so live as to meet him in a better place. My dear dear Jonny is gone but it does seem so strange to me for him to die away from home & be brought here & not to see him only the coffin they said held him Dear Jonny may your dear Spirit be in a happy world where no more fiting will be & no more exposure be felt or any kind of sorrow... Willy is about as he was when Mr. Zentmeyer wrote perhaps a little improved....

Mary C. Penn

Greenbriar Bridge, Pocahontas County, Virginia, November 21, 1861
Dear Ma,

I will nearly drop you a line to let you know that I am well. We have had snow one inch deep fell four days ago and it has rained ever since until yesterday this morning is looking like a spring morning and I hope will continue so as our company will commence cutting logs this morning to build our huts to winter in I think we will have them ready to go in two weeks. The snow on Elk Mountain five miles from here is eight inches deep. Our pickets are now picketting on that mountain. William Washburn, son of Thompson Washburn, died last night with fever. He has been sick ever since we reached here from Sewell. he was a good feller and a good soldier. He talked a great deal about his Mother said she was a Christian and he knew she prayed every day for him. He will be decently buried. All the rest of our company are on duty that are here except Charles Agee and Rufus Penn. Agee has got so he can walk about. Rufus has been rite sick for the last ten or twelve days. He has gotten leave of absence for 30 days to go home. Edd is now trying to get a furlow to go with him. He will go to Huntersville to day to see the General. I think he ought to go as Rufus is so feeble, though the Doctor thinks he has Pneumonia. they want to start home day after tomorrow.

Since I received Thomas G. letter Green has gotten one that said Thomas G was rite sick and had sore throat. I hope he is well by this time if he is not he ought to stay at home as long as he can, that is as long as a Physition will give him a certificate. I think he would be only doing his duty to stay as long as he could we are now building to go in winter quarters and he could not do much good here at this time and in fact if he would stay at home until spring by getting certificates it would be a good thing for him and nobody would blame him make him stay as long as you can. The Col told me a few days ago without my asking him that I should have a leave of absence between this and Christmas. I hope it will be so I can see you all soon. I have not more time to write now as I wrote brother George everything I could think of last week. My best love to all. The Colonel has recommended a furlough for Edd. They will start in a few days.

Your affectionate son
J. G. Penn

Greenbriar Bridge, Pocahontas County, Virginia,
December 6, 1861
Dear Ma,

I received your letter yesterday evening giving a list of eatables you had sent me by the wagon, and at the same time <u>we received</u> orders to leave we are ordered to Staunton but from what I can learn we will not remain there long if we stop there at all. From the talk in camp we will go to Winchester some think we will go to Kentucky. I hope not. I am very sorry you sent the things you did. I dont need any thing except what I wrote for but if we had staid here everything would have been very exceptable. I will insist now that you send nothing more but such things as I write for. The bedclothes the Captain got up I look upon as a <u>humbug</u> as he made it and excuse to get home. He had made a requisition for blankets some time before he left.... Enclosed you will find a very private paper that I fixed up some time since... About Thomas Green he ought not think of coming to us this winter if he could possible help it I know we are certain to have a hard time of it in all probability we will go to Romney or some other place as bad. dont let him come <u>unless</u> the Doctor think him <u>entirely well</u>. This is no place for an unsound man. that every body will admit and nobody will advise one to come unless they are perfectly sound. I will draw Thomas G and Willies money this morning. Willies will be about $50.00.

I wrote to Thomas G. to let me know what to do with pore Johny cloths. I shall keep them until I hear from him. I think they ought be sent home, his administrator will have to send a power of attorney to some one before his money can be collected. Thomas G. ought to make out his account so as to cover all expenses he was out. I know it would be Johny wish if he could let it be known. The wagons are coming in to be loaded so I will have to close. we will leave this morning

Your affectionate son
J. G. Penn

On December 5, the 42nd had 45 officers and 688 men present for duty. The regiment lost 38 men over the three months of 1861. The men spent Christmas at Strasburg with General Thomas J. Jackson's

Army of the Valley at Winchester. The weather was very cold that winter with considerable snow and sleet. The regiment continued to suffer from a lack of clothing. Colonel William Gilham took command of the brigade including the 21st Virginia Infantry, 1st Battalion Virginia Infantry, Marye's Battery of artillery and the 48th Virginia along with Colonel Burks reverting to command of the 42nd Virginia Infantry.

The 42nd spent the next three months in present-day northeastern West Virginia, northern Virginia, and Maryland. The Confederacy nearly lost Thomas J. "Stonewall" Jackson during the Romney Campaign. When the Confederate Secretary of War ordered the Army of the North West back to Winchester, Jackson threatened to resign. After a change in orders, Jackson stayed on beginning a spectacular military career.

Several small engagements with the enemy left a number killed and wounded. The worst losses occurred at Kernstown on March 23, 1862. In April, Colonel John A. Campbell assumed command of the Second Brigade of the Army of the Valley including the 21st, 48th, 42nd and 1st Battalion Virginia Infantry. On the twenty-first, the men of the 42nd unanimously reelected Colonel Burks to command them. Lieutenant Colonel William Martin replaced Langhorne as second in command.

In May, Captain John Penn assumed command of the Regiment for a time after the Battle of Winchester. During the summer of 1862, the regiment participated in "Stonewall" Jackson's famous Valley Campaign considered one of the most brilliantly executed campaigns in all history. In a period of seven weeks in May and June 1862, Jackson's 17,000 men beat armies with over 70,000 men, marched over 700 miles in almost continuous fighting, and chased the Federal forces north of the Potomac River. Jackson took his army to Richmond to aid in the city's defense against McClellan's Army.

Friday evening, May 16, 1862
Dear Ma,
      Today is set apart for fasting and prayer and we are permitted to rest. Stovall will not start until morning and I am sorry I did not know it sooner that I might have written my letter over. I wrote it on a borrowed sheet smoked and dirty and I am ashamed to send it.

      I have drawn up another petition for a transfer and had it recommended by Dr. Hunter and Smith, and approved by the Captain, Major Lane, and Col Campbell. It will now go to General Jackson and be forwarded by him to the Secretary of War. I learn today that it is very doubtful whether or not Col Burks will return to the regiment. But the staff officers are all filled and I do not think that there would be a likelyhood of Martin turning anyone out to give me an office. I prefer risking the cavalry service to the chance of getting an appointment and I do not think there is much doubt about getting a transfer now.

I shall write to C. Y. Thomas and request him to see the Secretary of War, and urge him to grant it. I know my service will be much harder as a private in cavalry than it is now and I will be equally as much exposed, but I believe I will enjoy better health, and will be relieved of the fatigue of long marches.

I would like for Brother to notice around and see if he can find a horse that will suit me if I get the transfer. I fear it will be a very hard matter to find the right kind.

I sold my sword and belt to Green Penn and he wants it sent by the first one that passes. I think the belt is in Brothers secretary....

Your affectionate son
Thomas Green Penn

Camp near Port Republic, Sunday June 8, 1862
Dear Brother,

Captain Withers will start home in a few minutes on sick furlough, and I will write you a few lines hoping that I may get it ready by the time he starts. Our movements have been so rapid and constant that I have not been able to write a full account of our movements, but suppose you have kept posted by the newspapers.

A gloom was cast over the whole army on yesterday morning by the intelligence of the fall of the brave General Ashby. I have heard since reports about the manner in which he was killed but suppose it is probbable that he was killed by the Maryland regiment which fired into his cavalry when they were returning from the pursuit of the enemys pickets, which were driven in day before yesterday evening by our troops. The same evening one of the Louisiana regiments fired into the 58th Virginia and killed twelve and wounded forty-one at one fire. I have not been able to learn whether any of the Patrick men were killed or not.

General Ashby was killed instantly, the ball entering under his right arm and passing out of his left breast. I consider we lose more by his fall than we had gained during the whole campaign. I understand that we lost about 200 killed and wounded the same evening, and I expect most of them by our own men firing into each other, but cannot learn any of the particulars. It occurred about two miles this side of Harrisonburg.

I think we will be bound to have another fight today or tomorrow, as the enemy drove in our pickets yesterday evening. It is said that Shields has gone from Swift Run and joined Banks and Rosencrans at Harrisonburg. We are now in a mile of Port Republic on the Shenandoah, and about 20 miles from Staunton. As the enemy has a superior force to ours, they could easily advance towards Staunton, and as the enemy is in possession of a portion of the Central R. R. they could send forces up to cooperate with them and get Jackson in a rather tight place. But he is watching them closely I expect and they will find it hard to catch him napping.

We are in about 8 or 9 miles of Uncle Sam Kennerlys and I tried to get permission to go to see him yesterday but the guards had instructions not to let anyone pass without a permit from General Jackson, and I could not go. If we go from here towards Staunton, we will pass in two or three miles of him and I will go by if I can.

I have met with Raine several times lately. He is First Lieutenant in the 23rd regiment. He seems to like the service very well and enjoys fine health. I also met with Whitten the day we passed Strasburg. Jimmie and myself were together and met him in the road. We only had a few minutes conversation with him. He was kept a prisoner by the Yankeys three months and was exchanged. He is Orderly Sergeant of his Company Martin is with us and will take command of the Regiment. today.

You have learned before this that Dr Smith has left us. Hunter will be our assistant Surgeon. I expect he is only commissioned assistant, and I do not know who will be our Surgeon. We could have Reid appointed if the proper effort was made but our officers are so careless about everything that I fear the effort will not be made till too late.

I have never heard anything from my petition yet for a transfer and fear it will not be noticed unless I can get some one of influence to give it their personal attention. Bocock has never replied to me. I fear he never received my letter. I sent it by Jos Koger and he may have lost it. I am very anxious for a transfer. I make no calculation on being promoted in this Regiment. Major Lane is the last man I expect any favor from. I have less confidence in him than I had in old Langhorne. I believe he is as deceitful as he can be, and he is becoming unpopular with the Regiment. In fact I do not aspire to any greater promotion than to be released from this Regiment and be allowed to join a cavalry company....

Greenville saw Jimmie yesterday. he is a little complaining but is attending to his business. Jimmie and myself visited the camp of Major Penn of the 7th Louisiana Regiment while we were at Winchester. We found him a very nice young man and he is very popular and considered a good officer. His father went from Bedford I think. He said he thought there was a son of A. G. Penns in the 9th Louisiana Regiment. who was severely wounded or killed in the battle at Winchester. He came to the Regiment as a recruit he thinks. Says he never made his acquaintance, and only learned he was there by seeing a box directed to him.

I received the shoes and sword sent by cousin Jeff. Green took the sword and belt at $17.50. He does not want the shoes. Tell Ma to please send me some scraps like my pants for patches by the first opportunity. Wm F. Mills is here and will leave Tuesday. I will try and write by him.

Thomas Green Penn

The 42nd participated in the action on the peninsula that succeeded in driving McClellan back beginning on June 17. During the Battle of Gaines Mill on June 27, the 42nd overran the camp of the 83rd Pennsylvania. Thomas G. Penn commented that the Union soldiers were "splendidly equipped." At the Battle on Malvern Hill on July 1, 1862, the regiment stayed in reserve near Willis Church. The 42nd Virginia camped near William Byrd's home Westover and then went into camp in Hanover County for several weeks. On June 29, Brigadier General John R. Jones commanded the brigade.

June 18, 1862
Dear Daughter (Mary Susan Dalton),

I was glad to get a few lines from you. I hope you will continue to write to one as often as you can I have nothing of importance to write you. I want you to try to learn all the children to read and write if you can try to improve your self all you can be kind to your man and all the children and to every other person try to keep your… from studying herself so much if you can and don't mistreat your aunt Elizabeth let her do as she may for she is your aunt she will be sorry of a… of things before she dies. I fear you must give my respect to Spencer Nowlin his wife and Arch and you Uncle Tom's family and your grandpa's family. I hope I will get home in a month of two some think peace will be made soon I hope so I do not believe I will ever want a gun in my hands anymore when peace is made. I can't tell when there has been a day that there has not been cannon and guns firing plenty. Until the last day or two we have now started some where I cant tell where Jackson has a great many regiments just come to hand. They are coming every day. There is now fifteen thousand rear force units in 12 miles of us and we got ten thousand 2 or 3 days ago. Frank and Rufus Penn has just got here. They say the road is lined with troops for Jackson. Some of our men say they are sent that we may rest a while. I hope that my be so though I don't believe it is Think Jackson is intend to give the Yanks a big blow some where soon for he now has a powerful force now you need not be surprised an anytime for Yanks and Jackson cant stay close together. For they must fight or run one I will write again soon as I find where I am going send your letter to Staunton will get there any how I have got all the letters from your man I have got six if not more I get all but do not get them regular yet they come I have sent about four every week and hope you get them. So farewell May remaining your devoted Father

Haman Critz Dalton

Company H, 42nd Virginia Infantry
Died of wounds received at
Antietam, September 1862.

Battle Ground, Friday, June 27, 1862
My dear Ma,

    I am seated under a tree right upon the battleground which is strewn with the dead and dying. Their groans are constantly heard from every side. Several dead men are in a few feet of me, and many wounded of the enemy. They will be cared for I suppose tomorrow after ours are taken care of. The smell of the blood is Sickening. I have just been ministering to one poor wounded fellow who belongs to the 83rd Pennsylvania. His Major was lying near him both mortally wounded I think.

    It has been a terrible battle. I never heard or read of such incessant firing. Our men making charge after charge and the enemy stubbornly contesting every inch of the ground. The ingagement became general I suppose about 1 o'clock. The canonading had been going on all day, with pretty heavy skirmishing all the morning.

    The 2nd Brigade did not get into the fight. We were held in reserve until late, then marched down near where the battle was raging, formed in line of battle, and advanced. but about that time our forces drove them from the field and when we arrived here they were pursuing them to the right and as many had fallen back to our front we were halted here to prevent their flanking our men on our right. It has been a terrible day. The loss on both sides I fear exceeds any that has occurred heretofore.

    I have no doubt but that the battle will recommence in the morning. if so we will be bound to be in the engagement. I think often when thus exposed of the prayers that you and others are daily making for our cause and for my safety to which I know the good Lord will not turn a deaf ear. But if it should be his will that I fall in this terrible struggle, you must my dear Ma give me up willingly, and consider me a sacrifice offered up for our dear cause, and consider that it is but the fate of many sons equally as dear to their mothers as yours. Though I feel that but few have such mothers as I have, and I am often grieved that I have not at times appreciated your worth and have lived such an undutiful life.

    The Yankeys left their knapsacks piled behind their breastworks and they have all been ransacked I suppose before this. I got one in which I found a very pretty pistol, a portfolio with some paper and envelopes, sundry articles of clothing all of which I threw away. I am writing with his pen and using the paper. Some found watches and other valuables. The knapsacks belonged to the 83rd Pennsylvania and they are splendidly equipped. If I can get Rufus to take them for me, I want to send the pistol home and a pipe for Brother George. I have a beautiful black plume that I should like to send, but I expect they will load themselves, and perhaps cannot take you any of the trophys gathered by me. I also have a good gum cloth I should like to send if I can.

The groans of the wounded are truly distressing. I wish the poor fellows could be attended to tonight. It is now I think about midnight. I am as well as usual. hop you are all enjoying good health. I must close. May God grant us all a happy meeting again at <u>our dear old home</u> here on earth and if not a happy one above is the prayer of

                              Your affectionate son
                              Thomas Green Penn

On August 9, 1862, the 42nd participated in the Battle of Cedar Mountain near Culpeper. Captain John E. Penn of Company H commanded the regiment at this point. Losses from this battle pitting Jackson against Union General Nathaniel Banks in the 42nd were 53 killed, 58 wounded and 8 captured. Lieutenant Greenville B. Penn received a wound in the shoulder in the shadow of Cedar Mountain. He returned to the regiment in November after several months of hospitalization.

On August 29, fighting in the Second Battle of Manassas with Jackson in an old railroad cut the 42nd attacked on the Union "Excelsior Brigade" of New Yorkers. Author John Chapla, who assisted with this chapter and the chapter on the 50th Virginia, described it this way "Rising from the prone position, the entire brigade charged with a yell and slammed into the enemy 'shattering, breaking and routing them'...The charge was irresistible."

The regiment lost eight killed at Second Manassas along with 54 wounded. In the past three months the men had marched over three hundred miles. The toil of constant campaigning saw a rise in desertion.

The regiment crossed the Potomac River on September 5 to fight in the Maryland Campaign. The lack of men showed in the command structure of the regiment. Captain John E. Penn commanded the brigade with Jones moving up to division level and Captain Robert W. Withers taking control of the 42nd. The men fought with Jackson at Harper's Ferry near Bolivar Heights resulting in surrender of the Union force.

At 1 a. m. on September 16, the 42nd moved towards Sharpsburg. They crossed the Potomac at Boteler's Ford by sunrise and reached the Dunkard Church by noon on Jackson's line on the left of Lee's line. On September 17, the regiment participated in the one day battle that took more American lives than any other in history did along the banks of Antietam Creek as Union General George McClellan began haphazard and uncoordinated attacks on Lee. Behind the 42nd on Nicodemus Heights, J. E. B. Stuart commanded the artillery supporting the Confederate defense. The attack began at sunrise with an "unprecedented iron storm" of artillery fire from the Yankees.

Captain John E. Penn received a leg wound that resulted in amputation after capture. After hospitalization at Frederick, Maryland, Union authorities sent Penn to Point Lookout Prison. Exchanged at City Point in December 1862, Penn received promotion to Colonel in 1863 to rank from August 1862 for his service. He left the army due to disability. The regiment lost 10 men, 36 wounded and 1 captured. Only 50 men remained in the 42nd at the end of the day ready to continue fighting. After recrossing the Potomac River on September 18, the men encamped near Martinsburg.

 John Edmond Penn

At this time, the 42nd almost fell apart after all of its officers resigned, transferred or were wounded. Among the wounded officers was Lieutenant Edmund L. Penn, who received a stomach wound at Antietam. Penn returned to the regiment in 1863 and received promotion to Captain. Lieutenant Henry D. Puckett of Company I assumed command. On November 30, Colonel B. W. Leigh replaced Puckett. On November 1, the 42nd with Leigh in command became part of Brigadier General John R. Jones' Second Brigade in Brigadier General William B. Taliaferro's First Division of Thomas J. Jackson's Second Corps in Robert E. Lee's Army of Northern Virginia.

On November 21, 1862, the regiment began the move to Fredericksburg, arriving on December 1, 1862. There were no tents, shoes and clothing were wearing out and the very cold weather caused the men to suffer terribly. They participated in the Battle of Fredericksburg and spent the remainder of the winter of 1862-1863 in camps along the Rappahannock River near Richard Corbin's home Moss Neck.

They received new clothing in February. On April 2, Lieutenant Withers took command of the 42nd in General Jones' brigade with the 48th, 21st, 44th and 50th Virginia Infantry in the division of Brigadier General Raleigh E. Colston. In May 1863, the 42nd fought in the Battle of Chancellorsville in General Jackson's flank march then served under J. E. B. Stuart after "Stonewall's" wounding. The 42nd lost 23 killed, 86 wounded and 6 captured during the campaign.

During 1863, Greenville B. Penn led Company H until wounded at Chancellorsville. He returned to duty at the end of July and received promotion to captain at the end of the year. Edmund L. Penn spent most of the year recruiting until he resigned at the end of the year due to health reasons. He spent the rest of the war enrolling and drilling recruits in Fluvanna and Franklin counties in Virginia.

After Chancellorsville, reorganization placed the 42nd under Captain Samuel Saunder in the brigade commanded by Brigadier General John M. Jones in Major General Edward Johnson's division in the corps of Richard S. Ewell. In June 1863, the 42nd marched with Lee's army into Pennsylvania and suffered heavy losses in the first two days of fighting at Gettysburg on Culp's Hill. After Gettysburg, they retreated into Virginia where they destroyed a section of railroad near Martinsburg.

By August 1, the regiment encamped at James Madison's Montpelier along the Rapidan River and saw little action for several weeks. In the previous two months, the unit marched 400 miles and fought in two major battles. Losses during the Gettysburg Campaign were 16 killed along with 78 wounded or captured. Of those captured nine died in Union prisons.

After about a month's rest, the 42nd moved north of the Rapidan to attack the Federals near Culpeper and saw action at Bristoe Station. One member of the regiment described the area as "the most perfect waste I have ever seen. It's almost like an uninhabited country." On November 3, the men crossed the Rapidan and went into winter quarters in Orange County. That same day, firing squads executed three deserters while soldiers of the regiment watched. On November 26, the men engaged an enemy unit in Orange County and lost 12 killed, 40 wounded and two captured.

The regiment went into winter quarters near Mt. Pisgah Church and constructed some log huts. During the bitterly cold winter, the clothing situation improved, but the food situation did not. Some men reported that they lived on a pound of flour a day with no meat. So many command changes occurred so frequently that the troops did not know who was in command. Discipline declined to a level that the men refused to obey orders.

Camp Orange Court House, September 18, 1863
Dear Brother,

    I set myself this morning for the purpose of answering your letter of the 6th. It afforded me much pleasure to hear from you. I had concluded you was not going to write to me at all. I received the letter you sent by Piles Hutcherson by mail. I did not see him. I do not know what company he belongs to. I don't expect I will get the tobacco you sent by him. I would be glad to get it. I am out and the tobacco is so high here. We are expecting a fight here every day. The Yankees have advanced to the Rapidan River, about 8 or 10 miles from this place. We have orders to be ready to move at a minute's warning. I think we will have a battle here before many days. I am in hopes not. I am getting tired of fighting. I don't believe fighting will do any good. This war will never be settled by fighting. I believe the more we fight makes it worse and worse. The army is in tolerable good spirits. I don't think there is any deserting going on in this Division. Andy, I would like to see your boy as you brag so on him. I recon it is good looking. We marched out to fight last Monday morning. The Yankees did not advance farther than the Rapidan River. We lay near the river 36 hours and came back to camp. I don't think we will stay here long. Longstreet's Corps has left his place. We have about 35 or 40 thousand men here. Enough to break the Yankees if they come on us. Andy, I hadn't heard from you or Pa for five or six weeks before I got this letter from you. I also received one from Pus yesterday. The army is in tolerable good health at this time. We had a very hard rain this morning.

To Cousin Mary,

    I believe you said the next time you heard from me I would be on my way home. No, if I live I expect to stay here until the Confederate Colors are stamped into the land. No, I think more of myself and folks than to desert. My life is very little satisfaction to me here. If I was to desert I know it would be worse. Desertion has stopped here since 10 men were shot out of the 3rd North Carolina. Give Uncle Nick and Aunt Mannie my best regards. I want you and Andy to write to me oftener than you do. I will be glad to hear from you anytime. I don't get a letter from home but about once a month. I must come to a close as I have nothing new to write at present. Direct all of your letters to Company H, 42nd Virginia Regiment, Second Brigade, Johnson's Division. Write soon as you get this. Fine times. Excuse all mistakes.

    Andy, tell Pa when you see him he can send that tobacco by Frank Penn. He is coming out here soon. Andy, write to me soon.

                              From your devoted Brother,
                              Hubbard V. Brown

The first four months of 1864 passed in relative ease with little fighting. By spring, the regiment had a full complement of officers and 32 new men bringing the total ready for battle to 328 men with Colonel Withers commanding the 42nd Virginia. On May 5, 1864, came the Battle of the Wilderness and General Grant's attempt to capture Richmond. Among those lost along the Orange Turnpike included Brigadier General Jones. Involved in the worst of the fighting, the 42nd lost many of its men to the Federal prisons for the remainder of the war. Union authorities sent several to Charleston, South Carolina, becoming members of the "Immortal 600," and placed under the fire of Confederate forces.

On May 8, the 42nd took part in the battles of Spotsylvania Court House in the Mule Shoe Salient with Company E of the regiment at the apex of the line pointing directly out to the Union forces. May 10-12 saw brutal fighting along this portion of Lee's line. On May 12, Corporal Charles L. Russell of the 93rd New York received the Medal of Honor capturing the battleflag of the 42nd Virginia Infantry. The regiment lost 5 killed, 11 wounded and 210 captured.

After the Battle of the Wilderness, the remaining members of the 42nd joined General Jubal A. Early and participated in his successful attempt to defend Lynchburg from General Hunter's Army. Early's troops drove Hunter into West Virginia. The regiment accompanied General Early and nearly captured Washington and with General Early as he tried to stop the advance of General Sheridan. Through the fall of 1864, the remainder of the unit marched a total of 1,260 miles up and down the Valley of Virginia and into Maryland. They fought in 24 skirmishes and 4 major battles.

Greenville B. Penn continued as a captain in the regiment until captured at Fisher's Hill on September 22, 1864. Sent to Fort Delaware Prison, the 5' 7" dark haired, dark eyed Penn spent the remainder of the war on Pea Patch Island in the middle of the Delaware River just south of Philadelphia. Released on June 17, 1865, the U. S. Provost provided him transportation home.

Camp near Petersburg, Virginia, November 14, 1864
Dear Friend,

    I take this opportunity to let you know that I am well and hoping that these few lines find you well and doing well. I have no news to write. We don't get half enough to eat at this time. I will tell you what we get to eat. We get beef and pork and corn meal and if we got a plenty we would do fine. I hope we will get more next time. I would be glad to see you and talk to you and get some food at your table and eat apples with you both and sit by the fire so I must bring my letter to a close by asking you to write.   Thomas Smith

At this time, James Anderson Purdy joined Company H of the 42nd Virginia. The son of John and Martha Custer Purdy and great-grandson of another James Purdy, who fought in the American Revolution, was born in 1840. He stood five foot two inches tall with dark eyes and light hair. Purdy originally part of Company G fought in "Stonewall" Jackson's 1862 Valley Campaign. He missed the Seven Days battles around Richmond due to the measles. He returned to fight in one hundred degree heat at Cedar Mountain on August 9, 1862. Purdy fought on at Second Manassas and Antietam.

He told of one time in 1862 when an exploding shell made members of the 42nd believe he was dead. Purdy replied, "Hell no, I'm not dead." At another battle, he played possum while passing Union soldiers thought him and others dead until he could make his way to back to the Confederate lines.

Purdy suffered from tuberculosis in the winter of 1862-63. The next year he took a job as mail carrier for the Confederate Postal Service, which made a profit under Postmaster General Reagan. Purdy walked fifteen miles between Danville, Virginia, and Yanceyville, North Carolina, every two days.

By July 24 at the Battle of Kernstown, Purdy was with the 42nd Virginia Infantry. Family tradition tells many stories James A. Purdy told his family after the war and related here. He had a hard time receiving pay for his military service due to a habit of losing his accoutrements of war such as lost ordnance of $54.43, a gun $36, a cartridge box $6 and other items totaling $54.73 between April and October 1864. He told he went seven days during this time without food and drank from mud puddles when it rained due to a lack of drinking water. The men of the company referred to James Purdy as "The Little Man" due to his slight size and ability to move around unnoticed. Purdy told how one winter night he decided to slip off and acquire a chicken. When challenged by a sentry he hit the man "up-side the head with a rock" and "went out to get me a chicken."

The fall of 1864 brought the 42nd to winter quarters at Fishersville in Augusta County with the remainder of General Early's Army, but in December the few remaining boarded a train at Waynesboro for Petersburg. The 42nd arrived in Petersburg on December 8, 1864, and the siege by U. S. Grant on Robert E. Lee's forces. The winter and the lack of food caused the use of extraordinary means. On February 12, five members lost their lives and 12 others deserted to the enemy. On April 2, 1865, General Grant launched a campaign that forced General Lee to evacuate Petersburg. The regiment lost its last man at Burkeville on April 7.

James Purdy was with those on the final march to Appomattox. On hearing of Lee's surrender, he proclaimed, "We ain't whupped yet!"

He described Ulysses S. Grant as, "as wide as he was tall. He rode his horse like a sack thrown crosswise on top of the horse. He slumped all over his horse."

Fourteen hundred and sixty-one men served in the regiment during the war. The United States paroled fifty-eight officers and men at Appomattox on April 11. At least six men of the at least 139 men from who served from Patrick County in the 42nd Virginia Infantry surrendered served.

James A. Purdy walked from Appomattox to Mayo Forge Post Office in Patrick County. To his dying day, Purdy said, "They didn't whup us, they starved us out, we won all the battles and lost the war." When his family complained of a lack of food he hushed them with stories of the sacrifice and starvation the men of the 42nd Virginia suffered during the war. One of the many characters from Patrick County to survive the war he passed down his thoughts on the war. He lived on until June 30, 1930, one of the last survivors of the war. Purdy rests today in the Koger Family Cemetery in Henry County.

The Penn family moved on from the war. Rufus G. Penn lived on until 1898 dying of heart disease. Edmund L. Penn died on October 26. 1903, of complications from the wound received along Antietam Creek in 1862. John E. Penn practiced law after the war and was instrumental in forming of Virginia Tech. He died on September 27, 1895.

1900 Reunion of Patrick County's Confederate Soldiers.

The Penn Brothers of the 42nd Virginia Infantry seated left to right are Joseph G. Penn and Thomas Green Penn. Standing are left to right John S. Penn and William A. Penn.

Chapter Six
"The Dear Old Hills of Patrick"
James Ewell Brown Stuart and Patrick County

One of Virginia's most famous son's roots reach deep into the red clay soil of the "Free State of Patrick." James Ewell Brown Stuart, the Confederacy's renowned cavalryman, grew up in Patrick County and always thought of it as home.

J. E. B. Stuart's maternal great-great grandfather was Irish-born Giles Letcher, who came to Virginia and settled near Petersburg. He married Hannah Hughes, who in 1750 gave birth to a son, William Letcher. The family moved up the James River through Richmond and Henrico County into Goochland and Fluvanna counties.

At 28, William Letcher wed Elizabeth Perkins, the daughter of Nicholas and Bethenia Hardin Perkins of Perkins's Ferry in Pittsylvania County. In March 1780, she gave William his only child, a girl called Bethenia.

History records little about Letcher's time in Patrick County (then Henry County) except for possessions and the major events of his life. William Letcher was a prominent and prosperous man. He grew corn and tobacco in the bottomland along the Ararat River. The farm included livestock with twenty head of cattle, ten hogs, and five horses. Nine slaves--David, Ben, Witt, Abraham, Dick, Look, Nunn, Randolph, and Craft--lived on the property. The inventory of William Letcher's estate lists many of the household and farm items that one would expect including saddlebags, rifles, three feather beds, and a looking glass.

Local people considered Letcher a leader. Tradition states that, as a member of the local Henry County Militia, Letcher was forthright about his support for the American Revolution. Pro-British Tories emboldened by the presence of a British army under Lord Cornwallis in the Carolinas, made Letcher a target.

In August 1780, a stranger came to the Letcher house and asked Elizabeth Letcher the whereabouts of her husband. She replied that he would be back shortly and invited the visitor to stay. When Letcher came home, the visitor identified himself as Nichols, a local Tory leader, and demanded Letcher's surrender as an enemy of the Crown. A struggle took place mortally wounding Letcher. The Tory fled, and the patriot died in the arms of his wife.

George Hairston, leader of the Henry County Militia, came to carry Elizabeth and Bethenia home. He later married the Widow Letcher and they had numerous children. They rest today in the cemetery at Beaver Creek Plantation in Henry County. Hairston paid taxes on the bottomlands along the Ararat River for his stepdaughter Bethenia where her father still rests in the oldest marked grave in Patrick County.

Bethenia Letcher inherited the Patrick County land of her father and married David Pannill. They lived at Chalk Level in Pittsylvania County. They had two children, William Letcher Pannill and Elizabeth Letcher Pannill. Today the Chatham Cemetery holds the remains of David and Bethenia Pannill, and displays a marker noting that they were General Stuart's grandparents.

Elizabeth and her brother divided the family estate, with Elizabeth receiving the Patrick County property called Laurel Hill. She married Archibald Stuart in 1817. The couple moved to Laurel Hill in the mid-1820s.

J. E. B. Stuart's paternal family also planted roots in Virginia. The first Archibald Stuart, a Scots-Irish Presbyterian from Londonderry, came to America in 1726 and lived for seven years in western Pennsylvania. When his wife and children were finally able to join him there, in 1738, the family moved to Augusta County, Virginia.

Archibald Stuart's second son, Alexander Stuart, fought in Colonel Samuel McDowell's regiment during the American Revolution and led the regiment in the battle of Guilford Courthouse. Major Stuart had two horses shot from under him and received a wound in the battle. The British captured him, but tradition states that they so esteemed his courage that they returned his sword when released. His later interest in education led him to become involved in the endowment for the college that subsequently became Washington and Lee University.

Judge Alexander Stuart, Major Stuart's youngest son, lived in Cumberland and Augusta counties in Virginia. As a member of the Executive Council of State, he spent time in Richmond. Judge Stuart served as a United States Judge in Illinois and a circuit court judge and Speaker of the House in Missouri. He returned to Augusta County on a visit and died in 1832.

Judge Stuart's oldest son, Archibald, was born in 1795 and as a youth served in the War of 1812 as an artilleryman. He studied law and represented Campbell County in the Virginia Legislature.

Archibald Stuart attended Virginia constitutional conventions in 1829 and 1850 representing Patrick County. In those conventions, he voted with the western counties of Virginia for a "white basis" for representation, excluding slaves from the counted population. The Patrick County tax records show his property taxes going up in 1831 due to the presence of new buildings at Laurel Hill. He served Patrick County in both houses of the Virginia Legislature and one term in the U.S. House of Representatives. He was Commonwealth Attorney of Patrick County from 1847 to 1851. Contemporaries described him as a man of talent and versatility, with a tremendous speaking and singing voice to go along with a good wit.

Elizabeth Letcher Pannill, a strict, religious woman with "no special patience for nonsense," worshipped with the Episcopal congregation in Mount Airy, North Carolina, and according to tradition was a good businesswoman who successfully ran the family farm.

On Wednesday, February 6, 1833, at 11:00 a.m., Elizabeth gave birth to James Ewell Brown Stuart. He was the eighth of her eleven children and the youngest of five sons to survive. Here on the family's fifteen-hundred-acre farm along the North Carolina-Virginia boundary line, he spent the first twelve years of his life.

Stuart's first biographer, H. B. McClellan, wrote, "She (Elizabeth Stuart) inherited from her grandfather, William Letcher, a beautiful and fertile farm in the southwestern part of Patrick County, which was named 'Laurel Hill'…The large and comfortable house was surrounded by native oaks and was beautified with a flower garden, which was one of the childish delights of her son James…The site commanded a fine view of the Blue Ridge Mountains, and near at hand was the monument erected to the memory of William Letcher by his daughter Bethenia…Amid these surroundings James Stuart passed a happy boyhood. He loved the old homestead with all the enthusiasm of his nature; and one of the fondest dreams of his manhood was that he might own the place of his birth, and there end his days in quiet retirement."

The Patrick County in which James Stuart grew up was half piedmont and half mountain. In many ways, it is a microcosm of the Commonwealth of Virginia, for it reflected the attitudes and values of both areas. Patrick County in the middle years of the nineteenth century consisted mainly of subsistence farmers who raised tobacco, corn and livestock. The county seat, Taylorsville, in 1849 contained only fifty buildings. Prominent families like Hairston, Staples, Wilson, and Reynolds owned much of the property of the county. The population of Patrick County in 1840 was 76% white and 24% black.

James Stuart grew up in a self-sufficient community of blacks and whites living and working together. Of the forty-one people living at Laurel Hill in 1850, nearly 30 were slaves. Of these slaves, eleven were less than ten years of age.

Young Stuart inherited his father's strong physical frame and zest for life. When he was not fishing in the Ararat or Dan Rivers, he was hunting in local forests. He spent many hours in the saddle, developing the skills that would someday make him the South's preeminent cavalryman.

As a boy, he never backed down from a fight and, indeed, often searched for a reason to start one. The most famous story of James Stuart's boyhood involved his attack on a nest of hornets, when he was nine years old. He and his older brother, William Alexander Stuart, were rambling through the pastures and woods surrounding their home when they came across a large nest of hornets. The two boys felt compelled to investigate the nest. When the hornets began to swarm, William Alexander fled the scene, but James stayed taking the stings until he knocked the nest down.

James learned his physical skills from his father, but it his mother gave him graces of the spirit. Elizabeth Stuart taught her son to have high standards, self-discipline, and a strong religious faith. When he was twelve she made him promise her that he would never take a drink of alcohol, and he kept that vow until receiving his mortal wound. She imparted sensitivity and a love of nature. Her flower garden fascinated him. Throughout his life, he loved animals, particularly dogs and horses.

In 1845, James Stuart crossed the Blue Ridge to begin his formal education. Stuart attended a boys' school run by attorney Peregrine Buckingham in Wytheville, Virginia, and later studied under Reverend George Whitfield Painter at Hillcrest, his home in the Draper's Valley section of Pulaski County. James also attended the music school operated by J.B. Wise and took voice lessons.

Young Stuart attracted the attention of several local ladies, including Miss Maria S. Crockett. He commented during this time that "I have gotten out with the girls. I believe they were just made for man's troubles." He took time from his studies to visit the family of his uncle James Ewell Brown at Cobbler's Springs on the Pepper's Ferry Road. Judge Brown married Archibald Stuart's sister, Nancy, and their son, Alexander Stuart Brown, corresponded for many years with J. E. B. Stuart.

While James was visiting Laurel Hill in the winter of 1847-1848, the house burned down. Stuart wrote to his cousin Alexander Stuart Brown of the "sad disaster." He noted that his father and brother, John, were living in the kitchen, an outbuilding separate from the main house. In 1996, an archaeological excavation located the sites of the house and the kitchen.

In the fall of 1848, James Stuart entered Emory and Henry College, the Methodist school located near Abingdon, Virginia. He entered as a special student still lacking in his studies, but in a show of dedication and discipline, he made up his deficiencies in his first year and entered his second year as a full sophomore.

The class load at Emory and Henry consisted of Latin, Greek, algebra, geometry, trigonometry, grammar, composition, and elocution. Sessions ran from August to January and February to July. Examinations were open to the public. The fees at Emory and Henry were fifteen dollars per session for tuition, fifty cents for library use, and one dollar and fifty cents for room and board. Despite the heavy load of coursework, academics were not his only interest there. Stuart joined the Methodist Church and the debating society.

He made many friends at Emory and Henry. John M. Davis said that he was "generous to a fault, genial in disposition, and vivacious in spirit." During the commencement ceremonies Stuart spoke of "The Triumph of True Principles." He gave his friends a turkey dinner the night before he left. He was so popular that, in what must have been an unusual gesture, the president of the college even visited to express his regrets at Stuart's departure.

In 1850, newly elected U. S. Congressman Thomas H. Averett appointed James Ewell Brown Stuart to the U.S. Military Academy at West Point. The young Stuart traveled through Salem and Lynchburg on his way to New York. He spent several days in Charlottesville meeting students at the University of Virginia, and found it necessary to comment that the women of the town were "the ugliest of the ugly." He visited Monticello, chipped off a piece of Jefferson's gravestone as a souvenir, and picked two roses from the garden there.

Stuart visited Congressman Averett to thank him for the appointment. In Washington, Stuart saw many of the famous politicians of his day including President Zachary Taylor and Vice-President Millard Fillmore. He described Daniel Webster as "the finest looking man in the senate" and Jefferson Davis as the most "pleasant speaker." He also saw Henry Clay and a distant kinsman, Sam Houston of Texas.

Stuart arrived at West Point on July 8, 1850. He was in distinguished company, for his class included a grandson of Henry Clay and a great-grandnephew of Napoleon Bonaparte. Military life came easily to him. He entered the summer encampment with delight, calling it "glorious," while other cadets less inclined to the military described it as "slavery." He did well in his studies at West Point, and in his second year received promotion to Corporal of the Corps of Cadets. By the end of that year, he ranked seventh out of a class of sixty.

Throughout his life, Laurel Hill seldom left Stuart's thoughts. During this time, far from home, he wrote, "Although every one deems his own home 'A spot supremely blest, A dearer, sweeter Spot than all the rest,' Yet experience has taught me that it is necessary to be deprived of it awhile in order to appreciate it properly. I might have rambled over the dear old hills of Patrick amid all pleasures of a mountain home for a life time."

J. E. B. Stuart circa 1850

In June of 1852, Stuart received a ten-week leave from the academy, and used it to visit friends and family. After a two-week stay at Laurel Hill he went to Beaver Creek, his Hairston cousins' Henry County plantation, where he spent most of his time walking in the garden or hunting blackberries with sixteen-year-old Bettie Hairston. Stuart returned to West Point to find a new man in charge of the academy Robert Edward Lee. During his four years at the academy, he met the other Lees as well: Custis, son of the Superintendent; Fitzhugh Lee, nephew of R. E. Lee; Stephen D. Lee, a cousin.

During his years in New York, he developed affection for various ladies, old and young. Among them was Mary Lee, daughter of the Superintendent, and Mary Pegram, sister of John Pegram, who said of Stuart, "he was the best hearted fellow I ever knew." Mrs. Winfield Scott, wife of the commanding General of the Army, became a favorite.

He often visited the Lee home during his last two years at the military academy and developed a lasting friendship with Mrs. Lee.

Others at West Point during Stuart's stay included William Dorsey Pender, Archibald Gracie, and Philip Sheridan. Oliver Otis Howard, a self-righteous, opinionated abolitionist from Maine, also encountered Stuart there. Howard later wrote, "I never can forget the manliness of J. E. B. Stuart... He spoke to me, he visited me, and we became warm friends." The two men met again as antagonists near a sleepy little crossroads in Virginia called Chancellorsville during the Civil War.

Stuart read more at West Point than at any other time in his life. The great romantics Sir Walter Scott and Lord Byron were among his favorites. Excellent work in the classroom and good behavior marked his first two years at West Point. However, the last two years tell another story. Fear that his good marks would put him in the engineer corps caused a deliberate slide in Cadet Stuart's grades and behavior. Family tradition holds that James wanted to be a cavalry officer and sabotaged his schoolwork in order to make this more likely.

In 1854 he graduated from West Point, thirteenth in a class of forty-six. His grades ranked him twenty-ninth in engineering, ninth in ethics, fourteenth in infantry tactics, thirteenth in artillery, and tenth in cavalry. The young graduate cut an impressive figure. He now stood five feet ten inches tall and weighed 175 pounds. He was short waisted with a barrel chest, which sometimes gave him the appearance of being overweight, but his long well-shaped legs made him look good on a horse. High foreheads made his chin seem weak and made his classmates award him the nickname "Beauty."

J. E. B. Stuart circa 1854 with Custis and Stephen D. Lee

After graduation, Stuart returned home by way of Williamsburg, Richmond, and Salem. He spent several weeks at Laurel Hill waiting for his orders and traveled extensively visiting Beaver Creek and Bettie Hairston. (Stuart wrote to her after he went west, but eventually their correspondence ended. She married her cousin J. T. W. Hairston who served on Stuart's staff during the Civil War.)

Stuart used this time to visit Cooleemee, the North Carolina house of his cousin Peter Hairston. Stuart assisted in the construction of the Greek pavilion-style home in 1852, and wrote Hairston saying, "I take pleasure in informing you that 'all's right' at Cooleemee hill." He told Cousin Peter that the brick had risen up to the second story of the house. Peter Hairston later joined his staff as a volunteer aide.

Stuart had another reason for visiting Cooleemee. Columbia Lafayette Stuart Hairston, the mistress of the plantation, was his favorite sister. During his visit, a fond Uncle James enjoyed playing with his niece and nephew, Elizabeth Perkins and Samuel.

Stuart visited Stokes and Forsyth Counties during his time on leave. Members of the Hairston family recognized him at Sauratown because of his resemblance to his sister. Stuart stayed at Panther Creek, the home of Colonel Joseph Williams in Forsyth County, and the home of Congressman Augustine Sheppard in Salem, North Carolina.

James E. B. Stuart received his commission as Brevet Second Lieutenant at Laurel Hill in the summer of 1854. Given some extra leave, he borrowed one hundred and fifty dollars from Peter Hairston and traveled to New York to equip himself for his trip west. In Richmond, he became ill and returned home for a last long stay with both parents.

To reach his new posting Stuart traveled through New Orleans to Texas, then went on a long overland trek across Texas to catch up with the Regiment of Mounted Rifles. Most of his first year in the army, Stuart patrolled the Texas panhandle and trans-Pecos country. He was supposed to be trying to control the Apaches and Comanche but never saw one, and the mission allowed him enough leisure to hunt quail and observe prairie dogs. His first commanding officer in Texas, Major Simonson, said of him, "Stuart was brave and gallant, always prompt in the execution of orders and reckless of danger or exposure. I considered him at that time one of the most promising young officers in the United States Army."

One of the more famous of these exploits took place when Stuart, in charge of transporting a cannon through rugged mountains, came to a fifteen-hundred-foot cliff with no roads down to the valley below. Ever resourceful, he devised a way for his men to lower the gun down the face of the cliff by hand using ropes. While in Texas, he grew his trademark cinnamon-red beard and chronicled his exploits for a

Staunton, Virginia newspaper. In Texas Stuart met James Longstreet and Richard Ewell, both future Confederate generals.

U.S. Secretary of War Jefferson Davis noted the exploits of young Stuart and others, picking them to join the First United States Cavalry. The Army sent Stuart to Jefferson Barracks near St. Louis, Missouri. There Colonel Edwin V. Sumner commanded the regiment with other officers including John Sedgwick. Sedgwick said that Stuart was the best cavalry officer "ever foaled in America." During this time, Stuart received his nom de guerre, the nickname of "Jeb," to distinguish him from Lieutenant George Stewart.

In 1855, the army assigned Lieutenant Stuart to Fort Leavenworth in the Kansas Territory. One of the first sights Stuart saw on arrival at Leavenworth was a lovely young lady named Flora Cooke skillfully controlling a wayward horse. She was a talented musician as well as an accomplished horsewoman, so her talents spoke both to Stuart's artistic and physical interests. Archibald Stuart's death in September 1855 saddened the couple, but they went forward with wedding plans and married on November 14, 1855.

A strong romantic bond tied Jeb and Flora. During the war, he tried to write to her every day, even if he could only manage to scribble a note with his leg across the pommel of his saddle. The marriage produced three children. The first child, Flora, preceded a son named for his maternal grandfather, Philip St. George Cooke. Their last child, Virginia Pelham Stuart, named for the Commonwealth and John Pelham, the famous artillerist under his command during the Civil War.

In 1857, the Stuart family moved to Fort Riley in the Kansas Territory. Colonel Sumner appointed Lieutenant Stuart to be Regimental Quartermaster. Being in charge of feeding and equipping the regiment taught him lessons used later during the Civil War. Stuart and the cavalry tried to quell the growing trouble between the anti-slavery "free soilers" and the pro-slavery factions in Kansas. Stuart encountered John Brown, who was leading raids on the pro-slavery towns and villages.

Colonel Sumner requested that Stuart assume the duties of Ordnance Officer for the First U. S. Cavalry. Since he was already serving as Adjutant and Quartermaster, Stuart balked at the additional responsibility, and Sumner returned him to his regular company.

The summer proved almost disastrous. In July, near a fork of the Solomon River in northwestern Kansas, Stuart and his men came under attack from Cheyenne. As Stuart saved the life of a fellow officer, a Cheyenne "dog soldier" shot Stuart in the chest. The bullet hit Stuart's sternum and bounced just under the skin. Stuart carried the bullet the rest of his life. The man he saved, Lunsford Lomax, served under him in the Civil War and later became President of what is today Virginia Tech.

Stuart and his new family visited his birthplace for the last time in 1859. In October 1859, his life changed forever. While he was in the War Department office to sell his patent for a saber-hitching device, Stuart observed the telegraph receiving messages about raiders attacking the U.S. Army arsenal at Harper's Ferry. Stuart immediately found Colonel Robert E. Lee and informed him of the situation. Together the two officers boarded a fast train and headed northwest to put down the disturbance.

They arrived in Harper's Ferry to find the raiders trapped in the firehouse near the arsenal. Lee sent Stuart up to the door under a flag of truce to ask for the surrender of the raiders. Stuart recognized the leader of the raiders known as Smith as his old antagonist John Brown. When Brown refused to surrender, Stuart stepped back and signaled the U. S. Marines to attack. He entered the building and took Brown's Bowie knife as a souvenir. After the John Brown raid, the War Department paid Stuart $5,000 for the patent.

The year 1859 was decisive in Stuart's spiritual life. In that year, he formally joined the church of his mother and wife and attended the Episcopal convention in Richmond. His commitment appears to have been deep and concrete, for he wrote to his mother, "I wish to devote one hundred dollars to the purchase of a comfortable log church near your place, because in all my observation I believe one is more needed in that neighborhood than any other that I know of…What will you take for the south half of your plantation? I want to buy it."

J. E. B. Stuart while in the United States Army.

In present-day Colorado, on the headwaters of the Arkansas River, First Lieutenant James Ewell Brown Stuart continued his career in the cavalry by directing logging operations to build Fort Wise. Flora stayed behind at Fort Riley, where she gave birth to their son Philip.

On April 17, 1861, Virginia seceded from the United States. Stuart, like other Southern army officers, faced a great moral choice. In early May he resigned from the United States Army. He had talked of practicing law, but when Virginia seceded, his mind became focused. He told his brother William Alexander that he would "rather be a private in Virginia's army than a general in an army to coerce her."

Lieutenant Colonel Stuart, then twenty-eight years old, returned east after seven years in the service of the United States Army's mounted arms. He arrived in the West single, and left with a wife and two children. Stuart arrived an inexperienced West Pointer and left as one of the best young officers in the army. In the cavalry, he learned the lessons of war, developed the skills necessary to move and supply large numbers of men, and acquired a keen eye for terrain and the tactics it suggested.

Virginia placed Stuart under the command of an eccentric professor of artillery from the Virginia Military Institute, one Thomas J. Jackson when he returned to Harper's Ferry. Jackson placed Stuart in joint command of the cavalry with Turner Ashby. General Joseph Johnston took command of the Confederate forces at Harper's Ferry and gave Stuart command of all mounted forces. On June 10, 1861, Stuart fought his first battle in the service of the Confederacy at Honeywood, in what is now West Virginia. With 313 men and 21 officers, Stuart's force captured or killed 100 of the enemy.

Stuart trained his men in cavalry operations. For a cavalryman, he told them, the best place to learn was in contact with the enemy. He taught through constant drill, seldom letting the men stay in camp and making amusing comments such as, "gallop towards the enemy and trot away." One of his favorite lines was, "a good man on a good horse can never be caught." His men began to see method in his madness and realized that his skill in getting them out of trouble made them effective soldiers.

His men said of him, "Jeb never says to us, 'go on'--with him 'it's c'mon, boys.' He leads us, he don't send us." Constantly in the face of the enemy, Stuart led his men from the front. His exploits continued. Stuart single-handedly captured forty-nine men of Company I, 15th Pennsylvania Infantry. Another time, he led a company of the First Virginia Cavalry into the Federal lines, once surrounded he led them out undetected.

His carefree manner kept the morale of his men at a high level. His men approvingly referred to him as a "laughing madman," happy as he courted danger. Once he traded horses with one of his men, got inside the Federal lines, and charged through the sentries, knocking them into ditches. Triumphant, joyous, oblivious to the storm of gunfire, Stuart laughingly asked his companion if he had ever timed the animal in the quarter mile. Exploits like that one filled his men with astonishment and admiration.

Stuart cultivated a dashing persona. He wore an old blue undress coat with long yellow cavalry gauntlets and a yellow sash around his waist, knee-high boots with gold spurs, brown trousers, and a gray waistcoat. His trademark hat waved an ostrich plume on one side while the other side a gold star pinned up the side. This unorthodox uniform, along with enormous physical strength and endurance, made him look the essence of a romantic cavalier, the stuff of legend. He once remarked that all he asked of fate is that "I may be killed leading a cavalry charge."

Near Winchester, Union General Patterson probed towards Johnston's line. Stuart and his men kept an eye on the Union flank. Stuart deceived Patterson into thinking that he was facing far more Confederate troops than were actually there: his men made noise, repeatedly rode back and forth to stir up dust, and lighted far more many campfires than his forces needed. These theatrics made Patterson cautious and delayed his movements.

Forty miles to the east, by a stream called Bull Run, Union General McDowell marched toward the troops of P. G. T. Beauregard. Johnston's Army of the Shenandoah moved to provide backup. Stuart's game with Patterson allowed Johnston the time he needed to move across the mountains and assist Beauregard. When his skilled maneuvering around Winchester was successful, Colonel Stuart and his command rode 36 hours to reach Johnston's army on the outskirts of Washington.

On Sunday, July 21, 1861, the first major battle erupted near Manassas. It started well for the Union forces, and as the day progressed the Confederates suffered under Northern pressure. Stuart, with no orders for cavalry, waited near Sudley's Ford and chafed to get into the fray. At last, he charged down the Sudley Road, hitting a unit of New York Zouaves and making the Yankees flee in terror.

Jackson and Jubal Early gave Stuart much credit for the rout of the Federal forces. While Stuart received little official recognition for his actions, Early said, "Stuart did as much as any subordinate who participated in it." Jackson said of Stuart, "he had the qualities to make him eminent in his branch of the service." A reporter asked who won and received the reply, "Jeb Stuart at the head of a body of yelling cavalry."

After the battle, Stuart served under the command of James Longstreet. He established Camp "Que Vive" near Fairfax Court House and from there went every day to Munson's Hill, where he could see Washington. Sometimes he slept there and he even took his wife Flora to see the capital. On September 24, 1861, the Confederacy commissioned J. E. B. Stuart a Brigadier General.

Late in 1861, General Stuart learned a hard lesson under the tutelage of Union General Ord. With 1,600 men in four regiments of infantry, 160 cavalry, and a wagon train, Stuart engaged 4000 Yankees near the northern Virginia town of Dranesville. Ord forced him to retreat. He regrouped and held his position for two hours, but lost twice the casualties that he inflicted. Stuart learned how crucial it was to thoroughly scout an area for potential combat and realized that there were serious deficiencies in the performance of his artillery.

A colorful and impressive set of characters gathered around him. One was the foraging preacher, Dabney Ball. Stuart liked his staff to include men of faith who could preach and fight, and Dabney could do both. John Esten Cooke, the most famous Virginia novelist of his day and a cousin of Flora Cooke Stuart, served as chief of couriers. John Singleton Mosby, the Confederate guerilla fighters, started his career on Stuart's staff. Heros von Borcke, a giant Prussian, was a source of great amusement for all around him and a favorite target for practical jokes.

Scouts on his staff were talented men like Will Farley and Frank Stringfellow. Stringfellow, who would one day become an Episcopal priest, was once trapped by Union soldiers while paying court to a young lady in Alexandria, and escaped the Yankees by hiding under the hoopskirt of a Southern woman. Another scout, Redmond Burke, had three sons riding with Stuart.

The bearded warrior from Patrick County was one of the most approachable of the Confederate generals. He rewarded women like Antonia Ford with honorary aide-de-camp commissions for their assistance in gathering information about Federal forces.

Morale among Stuart's men was high, not only because of military success but because of the high heart of their commander. A

Yankee captive commenting on the camp life around him said, "You rebels do have a good time." Stuart at this time had two setter dogs named Nip and Tuck and a raccoon chained to a cannon that would snarl at anyone who came close. A banjo player named Sam Sweeney rode with him, as did various guitarists and fiddle players. He loved to sing around the campfire with his little band. Some of his favorite tunes were "Lorena," "Dixie" and "Jine the Cavalry."

Stuart's fame grew with his "First Ride Around McClellan." This raid sanctioned by the new army commander, Robert E. Lee began at 2:00 a. m. on June 12, 1862, just north of Richmond. General Stuart gave his men an order: "Gentlemen, in ten minutes every man must be in the saddle." That morning Stuart's twelve hundred cavalrymen embarked on a ride that would make Stuart's reputation.

He led his men north out of Richmond and turned toward Hanover Courthouse. Near Old Church, the raid suffered its only casualty: Captain William Latane died leading a cavalry charge.

At this point Stuart had a choice. He could turn around and go back the way he came through the now-roused Federal cavalry, or he could ride around the Union forces. He took the bold course. He continued through Tunstall's Station into Talleysville, where his force fought with Union men on a railroad flat car. When it appeared the Union cavalry might be closing in, Stuart commented that his wish was "to die game."

The party continued to the Chickahominy River, where the exhaustion of the ride began to tell. Stuart helped his men build a bridge, singing as he put boards in place and exhibiting a peculiar habit of twisting his beard. The Confederates finished crossing the river just as Federal cavalry appeared on the opposite shore.

In the space of two days, Stuart's force had ridden a hundred miles around a Union army of 100,000 men and in the process had lost only one man. The ride gave Robert E. Lee, the new commander of the Army of Northern Virginia, critical information about the positions of the Federal forces under George B. McClellan. It gave Richmond, the beleaguered capital of the Confederacy, a much-needed morale boost. Moreover, it thoroughly embarrassed his father-in-law, Philip St. George Cooke, who commanded the Union cavalry. Stuart said of his father-in-law that his decision to stay with the Union forces was a decision he "would regret but once and that would be continually."

Governor John Letcher gave his cousin a sword in thanks for the maneuver. One newspaper reported the result of Stuart's raid as three million dollars' worth of damage, in addition to the capture of two hundred wagons, three hundred horses, and one hundred and seventy men. Stuart joked with General Longstreet that he had "left a general in his wake, general consternation." His venture secured him a promotion to Major General.

Throughout the summer of 1862, Stuart carried on his work for Lee, raiding the headquarters of Union General John Pope at Catlett's Station (Lincoln replaced McClellan with Pope and then restored McClellan). Stuart assisted Jackson at Second Manassas and supporting the Confederate left at Antietam using artillery on Nicodemus Heights. In October Stuart again rode around McClellan again prompting President Abraham Lincoln to say that, "Stuart's cavalry out marched ours having certainly done more marked service on the peninsula and everywhere since." Lincoln replaced McClellan with Ambrose Burnside.

Stuart's services continued to be invaluable to the Confederate cause. At the Battle of Fredericksburg in December of 1862, he supported the Confederate right. One of his subordinates, John Pelham, held off an entire union division for a time with only two guns. Stuart's cavalry closed the year with a raid on Dumfries.

No battle he fought during the war was harder to face than the death of his oldest child, Flora. He turned to his faith to bear the anguish of her loss and wrote to his sorrowing wife, "My duty is to remain here. Let us trust in the good God, who has blessed us so much that he will spare our child.... If it should please him to take our child let us bear it with Christian fortitude and resignation. At all events remember that Flora was not of this world, she belonged to another, and will be better off by far in her heavenly habitation."

The conflict Stuart suffered was enormous, as his devotion to his wife and children warred with the requirement to stay in the field and fight for his new country. Heros von Borcke said of him, "I have not found a soldier who loved his family more than Jeb Stuart, or one whose sense of duty burned with a clearer flame." As illustration, the Prussian wrote of the day Stuart stopped his staff while riding through a field of blue flowers, dismounted, removed his hat, and began to weep. When questioned, Stuart replied that he wept because the flowers were the same color as his late daughter's eyes.

After the Battle of Fredericksburg in December of 1862, Abraham Lincoln replaced General Burnside with Joseph Hooker. The resulting campaign led in May 1863 to the Battle of Chancellorsville, where Stuart's scouting was critical to Confederate success. Stuart reported to Lee and Jackson that the Union right flank, commanded by Oliver Otis Howard, rested on no natural barrier and was susceptible to pressure. Lee divided his army and sent Jackson on a twelve-mile march around the Union army. Jackson struck like a thunderbolt, pushing the enemy army back over two miles. However, the mistaken fire of his own men in the dark and confusion after the attack mortally wounded "Stonewall" Jackson. With Jackson wounded, Stuart took command of the Second Corps of infantry and led it throughout the rest of the battle considered to Lee's easiest victory. Lincoln soon replaced Hooker with George G. Meade.

During the turmoil Stuart found time to write to Flora, "The day has been beautiful, and I would like to be gathering violets with you on the hills of the Dan [River], but this war is <u>not</u> <u>over</u> and you must nerve your heart for its trials."

In June 1863, at Brandy Station, Stuart's men fought in the largest cavalry battle ever to take place in North America. One of the few times the cavalry was surprised brought unaccustomed criticism on Stuart. His role as cavalry chief included supplying Lee with timely information on the movements of the Union forces. Stuart did a superb job in reconnaissance and for this military science remembers him.

As June turned to July, the road of fate led the Army of Northern Virginia to the sleepy college town of Gettysburg, Pennsylvania, where Stuart's absence for the first day and a half of the battle continues to be controversial. Without the intelligence Stuart's cavalry might have provided, Lee was blind to the movements of the Union army. On the third day of the Gettysburg battle Stuart fought George Custer in the rear of the Union lines at the same moment that Pickett's men were marching steadfastly u

During the autumn, Stuart's thoughts continued to incline toward his boyhood home. Late in 1863, with the weight of the war and his own mortality resting heavy upon him, he wrote to William Alexander Stuart, "If I should survive the war I desire to settle down on a farm if I can get one to suit me—and devote my after life to agricultural pursuits; Flora now seems as anxious for this as myself. I am very partial to the old homestead at Patrick. I wonder if it could be bought?"

Ulysses S. Grant took command of all Union forces in 1864 and accompanied Meade's Army of the Potomac into Virginia. He came up against Lee for the first time in May at an unsettled tangle of woods called the Wilderness. As the two armies moved toward Spotsylvania Court House, Stuart put the infantry into line at a site named, like his home, Laurel Hill.

Shortly after, General Philip Sheridan raided toward Richmond. Stuart met him just north of Richmond at the Battle of Yellow Tavern. In the closing moments of the fight around 4:30 p.m. on May 11, 1864, one of Custer's men shot Stuart.

Stuart initially had the strength to stay on his horse, and then got off, remounted and made it to an ambulance, which carried him to Richmond. He arrived at the home of his sister-in-law, where he lived through the night and next day. He died at 7:30 p. m. on May 12, 1864. His last words were the simple ones of a Christian hero, "God's will be done."

The next day, Friday the thirteenth, as rain fell and Sheridan's guns thundered in the distance, Richmond buried James Ewell Brown Stuart in Hollywood Cemetery.

Patrick County noted his passing in Order Book Number Eight. "At a large meeting of the citizens of this county held on the 23rd of May 1864 at the Court House their respectful tribute to the memory of their distinguished county man General James E. B. Stuart the following resolutions were adopted, viz: The untimely death of our beloved and gallant countyman the chivalrous General J. E. B. Stuart who fell confronting the foe around our Capital, is an event deeply to be deplored by the county at large and more especially by the citizens of this, his native county. Feeling it due alike to his distinguished services and to our duty to place on permanent record a respectful tribute to his memory we resolve: First, that General Stuart was one who while living it delighted us to claim as our Own and now that he is dead we can pay this, the highest tribute to any man's memory – hold him up as a model to our young men and say, if you will imitate his virtues, his vices cannot harm you. Second, the loss at any time of a gifted and patriotic man who has forgotten himself in the sublime cause of his country, is an event that elicits all of our sympathies and brings fresh to memory the manly deeds of the departed; but for one thus to fall in the hour of danger and peril to the state, fills us with gloom and unfeigned sorrow. Upon the eastern frontier of this state many a threatened family have slept in sweet repose, knowing that Stuart and his bold troopers watched with sleepless vigilance the invading foe; and see it is a melancholy satisfaction for us to feel that from the Chickahominy to the Shenandoah bright eyes will grow dim and stout hearts will heave a sigh for him who has been called the Prince of Cavaliers and the Flower of Chivalry. Third, the brightest pages of our country's History will be enlivened by the slashing deeds that he achieved and children yet unborn will bear the name of the Christian Soldier, the unsurpassed Patriot and the cavalry chieftain. Fourth, that L. G. Rucker, Crawford Turner, and J. Thomas Clark be appointed a committee to express to the mother of the fallen hero and to Mrs. General Stuart the sincere condolences of the good people of this county with them in this their sad bereavement. Fifth, that these resolutions be published in the Richmond and Danville papers and that the county court be requested to have them spread upon their records which was ordered to be spread upon the records, and thereupon the court adjourned until the first day of the next time."

Stuart's brothers contributed to the Confederate war effort, and then moved on to successful lives after the war ended. William Alexander Stuart, the first child born at Laurel Hill in 1826, married twice--first to Mary Carter of Russell County, who died in 1862, and then to Ellen Spiller Brown, the widow of cousin Alexander Stuart Brown. As President of Stuart, Buchanan, and Company, he ran the salt works in Saltville during the Civil War. Afterwards, he moved to Russell County, founded the Stuart Land and Cattle Company and became the largest landowner in southwestern Virginia. His son, Henry Carter Stuart, became Governor of Virginia in 1914.

John Dabney Stuart, the next son born in 1828 at Laurel Hill, went to Wytheville then Emory and Henry for schooling. In Floyd, he studied medicine under his brother-in-law, Nicholas Headen, and practiced medicine there and in Wythe County. He married Anne Elizabeth Kent of Wythe County. John served in the Civil War as a surgeon. After the war, he farmed in Wythe County, where he died in 1877.

After her husband's death, Flora Stuart moved to Saltville, joining Stuart's mother and sisters, Mary and Bethenia, with William Alexander's family. Flora taught school there and later administered the Virginia Female Institute in Staunton. The Episcopal girl's school renamed itself Stuart Hall in her honor. She spent her final years in Norfolk raising the children of her youngest daughter, Virginia. In 1923, Flora Cooke Stuart went to rest beside her husband in Richmond's Hollywood Cemetery, on a hill overlooking the James River.

After the outbreak of hostilities in 1861, Philip St. George Cooke Stuart became J. E. B. Stuart, Jr. when his maternal grandfather did not join the South. The boy attended the Virginia Military Institute in Lexington and earned his living as a banker in Lexington and Richmond. Stuart, Jr. served as a captain in the Spanish-American War. At the turn of the century, Theodore Roosevelt made him a collector of customs and a United States Marshall. He worked for the war effort as a civilian during World War I and lived in New York City fathering three daughters and a son. He died in 1930 and rests today in Arlington National Cemetery.

The spirit of Jeb Stuart still rambles his "dear old hills of Patrick." In 1884, the county renamed Taylorsville in his honor. The Confederate Veteran's monument placed in 1936 in front of the courthouse marks General Stuart's contribution with a plaque on its base. Commemorations took place in 1964 during the Centennial of the Civil War with his grandson, J. E. B. Stuart III, speaking at the event. Twenty-seven years later, his great-grandson, J. E. B. Stuart IV, spoke at the bicentennial celebration of the county.

In 1859, Elizabeth Stuart sold Laurel Hill. She moved to Danville and later lived in Saltville with the family of her son, William Alexander. In 1952, members of the family moved the remains of Archibald Stuart from Laurel Hill to lie beside his wife and several of their children in Saltville. Laurel Hill passed through many different families including the Browns, Dellenbacks, Galloway, Hatchers, Hollingsworths and Mitchells. Robert E. Lee's biographer, Douglas S. Freeman, wrote the text for the historical marker erected by Virginia at Laurel Hill in 1932.

In 1990, the J. E. B. Stuart Birthplace Preservation Trust, Inc., the organization founded by this author to preserve the site of Stuart's birthplace, used living history events, symposia, art exhibits, lectures and direct solicitation to raise the funds needed to purchase part of the Stuart property. The Mitchell family sold the bottomland to the Dellenback family, who sold five acres of that land, which includes William Letcher's grave for preservation. Mr. and Mrs. George E. Brown who owned the land until 1991, when they gave an option for seventy acres through their nephew Joe Bill Brown and his wife, Edith, to preserve the property.

The College of William and Mary completed archaeological work there in 1996. The Virginia Historic Landmarks Commission and the National Register of Historic Places recognized the seventy-five acre site in 1998. In 2003, this author wrote and worked with the organization to install eight interpretive signs, a Virginia Civil War Trails interpretive sign and with the Commonwealth of Virginia to replace the roadside historic marker.

This region's most important historical figure often thought of his home when education and a military career took him far away from it. In 1863, J. E. B. Stuart told his brother, "I would give anything to make a pilgrimage to the old place and when this war is over quietly to spend the rest of my days." Today you may visit Laurel Hill to learn about its history and enjoy the peace that James Ewell Brown Stuart never knew.

Chapter Seven
"I owe the Southern Confederacy a debt"
George Stoneman's 1865 Raid

Virtually untouched by Union troops during the Civil War, Patrick County saw a change in the spring of 1865. During the second week of April 1865, family tradition tells of a lone horse carrying Dr. William F. B. Taylor of Elamsville on his daily rounds. Suddenly, in the distance, horse and rider glimpsed some of the 4,500 United States Cavalry under the command of George Stoneman. Dr. Taylor and friend prudently jumped a fence and raced into the forest. The animal spent the evening tied to a tree and the doctor spent the night at a friend's home.

Major General George Stoneman

Major General George Stoneman, born in western New York in 1822, graduated from the United States Military Academy in the fabled class of 1846. Other members of the class included future Union General George B. McClellan along with Confederate Generals A. P. Hill and George Pickett. Thomas J. "Stonewall" Jackson shared a room with the six foot four inch "powerfully built" Stoneman during their time at West Point. Stoneman served in the U. S. Army in the west for fifteen years. He traveled with the expedition from Fort Leavenworth to San Diego during the Mexican War (1848). When the Civil War broke out, Stoneman showed "the marks and experience of a man with long hard service."

Stoneman first led the cavalry for his classmate, McClellan, in what is now West Virginia, in the early part of the Civil War. After the Seven Days battles around Richmond, Brigadier General Stoneman led the First Division of the Third Corps and commanded the Corps at Fredericksburg. Promoted to Major General in March 1863, he took command of the 10,000 man Cavalry Corps of the Army of the Potomac under Joseph Hooker. Stoneman fought against J. E. B. Stuart, in early 1863. At the Battle of Chancellorsville, when his former roommate Jackson wreaked havoc on Hooker's right flank, he raided towards Richmond. Alfred Pleasanton replaced Stoneman, who was suffering from hemorrhoids, and fought Stuart at Brandy Station and during the Gettysburg Campaign.

Stoneman ran the cavalry bureau in Washington before transferring to the western theater. He joined William Sherman's army during the Atlanta Campaign. In March 1864, while commanding the Cavalry Corps of the Army of the Ohio, Stoneman set out to free the prisoners at Macon and Andersonville. Georgia Home Guards captured him on July 31, 1864, and sent him off to prison.

Exchanged in October 1864, Stoneman landed under the command of Major General George Thomas, the "Rock of Chickamauga," commanding the Department of the Cumberland headquartered at Nashville. Stoneman presented a plan to his immediate commander Major General John M. Schofield, who dispatched John Bell Hood and the remnants of the Confederate Army of Tennessee at Franklin in November 1864. Expressing that, "I owe the Southern Confederacy a debt I am very anxious to liquidate," Stoneman's plan called for a two-phase attack on the railroad in southwest Virginia and the Confederate munitions factory at Salisbury, North Carolina. Before a communication from the War Department relieved him from duty for his poor performance in Georgia, Stoneman set off to complete phase one to rousing success in December 1864. Schofield convinced Grant to revoke the dismissal order. His raid on Saltville, Virginia restored Stoneman's reputation and opened the way for phase two and the road to Patrick County.

An interesting sidelight to the raid on Saltville in December 1864 was the presence of the widowed Mrs. J. E. B. Stuart in the community with her two children. Young "Jeb" Stuart, Jr. heard gunshots and thinking that firecrackers were going off proceeded to investigate. Flora Stuart stopped the charge of young Stuart on Stoneman before any damage occurred on either side. Another story about this raid involves a Yankee trooper admiring a portrait of Archibald Stuart. When the

Yankee learned that it was indeed the father of Lee's cavalryman, he slashed the picture with his sword. The painting still displays a battle scar.

With U.S. Grant surrounding Petersburg and William Sherman moving through the Carolinas, Stoneman left Tennessee on a raid that would carry him through North Carolina and into Southwest Virginia. Stoneman, in command of the District of East Tennessee, was ready to begin phase two in February 1865, hoping to get to South Carolina and hook up with Sherman, but a shortage in horses delayed the movement. George Thomas had told Stoneman to "dismantle the country to obstruct Lee's retreat." General Grant told him to "leave nothing for the rebellion to stand upon." He wanted to free the prisoners at Salisbury and to "destroy, but not to fight battles." They intended to "throw the burden of the war on the disloyal citizens of the revolted province," but "all robbery, pillaging, sacking, rape, wounding, maiming, etc are prohibited." On February 17, 1865, Stoneman's objective changed. General Sherman reached Columbia on that day and with his future advance into North Carolina, there was no need for Stoneman to move south.

General Alvan C. Gillem

Stoneman with 4,500 men left "Strawberry Plains" at Mossy Creek, Tennessee, near Knoxville on March 21, 1865. General Alvan C. Gillem led his Cavalry Division of three brigades. Born in Gainesboro in 1830, he attended a military academy in Nashville with future Confederate Brigadier General Laurence S. Baker. Gillem graduated the United States Military Academy at West Point, New York, in 1851. At Mills Springs in 1862, Gillem acted as Quarter Master for George Thomas. The next year Andrew Johnson appointed him Adjutant General for the "the Volunteer State." A promotion to Brigadier General came in August 1863. In January 1865, forces of the "able but ruthless" Gillem's men killed the famous Confederate cavalry raider John Hunt Morgan.

Brevet Brigadier General William J. Palmer

Brevet Brigadier General William Jackson Palmer led the First Brigade of cavalry including the Tenth Michigan Cavalry Regiment under the command of Colonel Luther Trowbridge, the Twelfth Ohio under Colonel Robert H. Bentley and the Fifteenth Pennsylvania under Lieutenant Colonel Charles M. Betts. Palmer, born a Quaker in 1836 in Delaware, grew up in Philadelphia and served as a railroad engineer before the war. During the Maryland Campaign of 1862, Confederates captured Palmer and imprisoned him at Castle Thunder in Richmond. Exchanged, he served in the campaigns of Tullahoma and Chattanooga in middle Tennessee during 1863.

On January 14, 1865, at Red Hill, Alabama, Palmer "with less than 200 men attacked and defeated a superior force of the enemy, capturing their fieldpiece and about 100 prisoners without losing a man." Brevet Brigadier General William J. Palmer received the Congressional Medal of Honor on February 24, 1894 for this action.

Brevet Brigadier General Simeon Batcheldor Brown led the Second Brigade consisting of the Eleventh Kentucky under Major Frederick Slater, the Twelfth Kentucky under Major James B. Harrison and the Eleventh Michigan under Lieutenant Colonel Charles E. Smith. Brown, born and educated in New Hampshire, worked in the private sector before and after the war as a merchant, farmer and hotel owner.

Colonel John K. Miller and Bvt. Brig. General Simeon Brown

Colonel John K. Miller commanded the Third Brigade, including the Eighth Tennessee under Colonel Samuel K. N. Patton, the Ninth under Colonel Joseph H. Parsons and the Thirteenth Tennessee under Lieutenant Colonel Brazilliah P. Stacy. Miller, born and raised in Carter

County, Tennessee, served as Sheriff before the war and organized the 13th Tennessee Cavalry. Battery E of the First Tennessee Light Artillery under Lieutenant James M. Regan and a detachment of Signal Corps under Second Lieutenant Theodore Mallaby, Jr. completed the Union force. The Ninth Tennessee did not accompany Stoneman on the raid.

On March 23, 1865, Stoneman reached Morristown, Tennessee. He gave his men five days rations, one-day forage of corn, four horseshoes with nails and sixty-three rounds of ammunition. The local citizens in pro-Union East Tennessee received the raiders with open arms. There is an old Roman saying that "mountaineers are always free," and the mountain people of Eastern Tennessee loved the Union. In fact, Andrew Johnson, who succeeded Abraham Lincoln as President of the United States, lived in the area. Stoneman's raid allowed these people to voice their opinion.

Stoneman reached Boone, North Carolina, on March 28. Forced to attack the Home Guard, his command killed nine and captured 68 men. They burned the local jail. Stoneman accompanied Palmer and the artillery through Deep Gap to Wilkesboro. Another sad incident was the death of Jacob Council in Watauga County, killed by Union troopers after one of his slaves referred to him as an "infernal rebel." Gillem's "homegrown" troops received credit for these incidents and the burning of the Boone jail. The other brigades traveled through Flat Gap to the county seat of North Carolina's most unionist county. These units burned Patterson's Mills near Boone, which had supplied other Yankee troops. Gillem did not recognize neutrality among the Southerners and Stoneman rebuked him for this action.

They reached Wilkesboro the next day. During the occupation, they seized the horse of Confederate General James Gordon and paraded it around in front of the dead general's home. Gordon served in Stuart's cavalry and died a few days after him in May 1864. Stoneman's raiders behaved except for the "homegrown Tennesseans" of the Eighth, Ninth and Thirteenth Tennessee regiments. These units wanted to wreak vengeance on their Southern brethren. Stoneman called them a "fine body of Cossacks."

The flooding Yadkin River separated Palmer's men, who crossed to the north side, from the remainder of the force on March 29. Stoneman ordered a review of the remainder of the forces. The resulting review in the rain revealed the pillaging of Gillem's men as large numbers of men riding in stolen carriages and even a stagecoach with drivers fortified by Wilkes County moonshine. Stoneman reportedly "roared like a lion" and demoted officers on the spot.

On April 1, the commands still divided by the Yadkin River reached Elkin on the north side of the river and Jonesville on the south side respectively. They found sixty "flirty" girls working in a cotton mill in Elkin. The Union soldiers put the girls and two other mills to work grinding meal for the "Yankee boys." Stoneman sent Palmer's men full of honey, molasses, butter, chestnuts and smoking cigars down the river to trick the Confederate leaders on "All Fool's Day" that the raid was headed for Salisbury. Stoneman reunited his entire command on the north side of the river in Surry County at Rockford on April 2. P. G. T. Beauregard, then in command of Western North Carolina had a large force at Salisbury and could have repulsed Stoneman. Instead, the Yankee Cavalry made a diversion toward Virginia that led them to Patrick County.

A native of Surry County, James Gwyn, commented on the Yankee raiders as they came by his place on the north side of the Yadkin. "The Yankees passed along on both sides of the river. We were all agreeably disappointed. Those who passed acted very well. Indeed, only taking cattle, horses and mules and did not even enter our houses or do violence to our families and destroyed nothing, but a little corn and oats."

On April 2-3, Robert E. Lee and the Army of Northern Virginia evacuated Richmond and Petersburg. Brigadier General John Echols in command of Confederate forces in Southwestern Virginia had 3, 500 men spread out across Southwest Virginia, but was more concerned with joining Lee than fighting Stoneman. Stoneman's raiders moved through Dobson "not a very pretentious village" to Mount Airy.

The Yankees described the future birthplace of Andy Griffith as the "home of the famous Chinese (Siamese) twins, Eng and Chang, who after exhibiting themselves through Europe and this country and accumulating a large fortune married two ladies who were sisters, and built them an elegant home and settled down in this little Southern town." The Yankees raided the Mount Airy post office and read the letters for days after. While camping on the banks of the Ararat River, the men learned of a supply train that had just passed through on its way to Hillsville, Virginia. The pursuit ended with the capture and burning of seventeen wagons. A letter between two sisters in North Carolina at this time captures the local feeling of this event.

> "Dear Sister,
> I thought that I would write you a few lines. I know you would be uneasy. Sister, the Yankees have been here…I don't know how many there was but it was the most men I ever saw in all my life time. They were all Cavalry. Oh Sister you never saw the like in your life…They comensed coming about dark Sunday night and kept coming most all night. Most all the men in town left and run to the woods."

The raiders crossed the Blue Ridge Mountains at Fancy Gap, met slight resistance from the Home Guard and entered Hillsville on April 3. Stoneman divided his force sending Colonel Miller and five hundred men to Wytheville to destroy two railroad bridges over Reedy Creek. Miller ran into Confederates lost thirty-five men and rejoined the command at Taylorsville, now Stuart.

The remainder of the force moved to Jacksonville, now Floyd. They arrived on April 4 at noon. Two citizens came out with a white flag to surrender the town. A Pennsylvania trooper wrote, "These people have been so deluded by their papers that they are under the impression that to burn houses and rob them of all we can carry off is our mission here, and they are relieved when they find the mistake."

Stoneman sent Major Wagner and 250 men of the 15th Pennsylvania Cavalry to destroy the railroad bridges around Salem, Virginia. On April 7, Wagner reached the Peaks of Otter near the James River. Wagner got across Robert E. Lee's avenue of retreat on the outskirts of Lynchburg the next day. He returned to Stoneman after riding over 300 miles and avoiding the troops at Lynchburg and Martinsville.

Meanwhile, Palmer's Brigade destroyed railroad track of the Virginia and Tennessee Railroad east of Christiansburg. Brown's Brigade did the same west of the town. The troopers deceived telegraph operators in Lynchburg and had the Black women of Christiansburg cooking for them. Other regiments took possession of the railroad bridges and ferries over the New River and another detachment destroyed the bridge over the Roanoke River. With four separate detachments spread out over one hundred and fifty miles of track, the Virginia and Tennessee Railroad ceased operation.

On April 7, 1865, the entire command except for Wagner began to move towards North Carolina. The direct route ran through Patrick County. On the return, Palmer went through Martinsville where he ran into 250 Confederate cavalry. The result was one Union officer killed, Lieutenant T. C. Kenyon, "a noble young man," of the 10th Michigan Cavalry on April 8. General Gillem in his report said, "Colonel Palmer, commanding the First Brigade had been directed to send the Tenth Michigan directly on the railroad to Martinsville, by some misunderstanding he marched with his entire command." Palmer rejoined the command on April 9 in Danbury, North Carolina.

Colonel Miller's men made their way to Patrick via Hillsville on April 8. One of them reported, "During the night some of the men found two barrels of brandy and after the 'spirits' went down the men's spirits went up and many men and officers began to get merry," The merriment ended when an officer opened the barrels and left the contents on the ground.

The Second and Third brigades came through Patrick County and stopped on the evening of April 7. Theodore Mallaby, a Second Lieutenant in the newly formed Signal Corps wrote in a report in the *Official Records of the War of the Rebellion,* "April 6th command moved at 7 p.m. to Taylorsville via Jacksonville crossing the Blue Ridge at Mowbrey Gap. Went into camp at Taylorsville at 11 pm after marching a distance of 48 miles. April 9 marched at 7 am to Danbury." General Gillem in his report stated that, "at 10 pm we arrived at Taylorsville, Virginia and remained at Taylorsville during the eighth." General Stoneman stayed in Taylorsville, now Stuart, until the morning of the ninth with the majority of his command.

Stoneman's raiders received blame for many incidents in Patrick County at the end of the war. Problems with the jail are nothing new in the history of the "Free State." The condition of the jail plagued county officials throughout the Civil War. Early in the war, Floyd County held prisoners for Patrick and Henry did the same in 1863. The war produced larger numbers of prisoners and the facility in Patrick could not safely hold them. In 1862, the county charged the Confederate government $10.30 and Virginia $23.40 for jailing deserters. In October 1862, the "Gentleman Justices" voted to build a new jail and appointed a committee to look into a new jail for the county. Commissioners Crawford Turner and Silas Carter advertised to build a jail in July 1864, but received no bid within the limits. In October 1865, the Order Book stated the county could no longer use the jail.

In May 1896, Supervisor's Order Book #2 reports that the "repairing or building of a new jail be deferred until the board can ascertain something definite in regard to the claim of the county which is now pending in Congress against the U. S. for the jail that was burned at the close of the war." The county paid Mr. C. A. Powell for taking depositions relating to the burning of the jail. Claude Swanson, representing Fifth District including Patrick County in the United States House of Representatives of the Fifty-Fourth Congress, petitioned the War Claims Committee on April 30 to look into the possibility of funds to build a jail. The claim presented in the bill H. R. 8606 stated that the jail burned at the end of the war and the county deserved compensation of $10,000 for the damages. There is no official record of this claim's acceptance or funds allocated. The bill never reached the House floor for a vote and apparently died in committee. Stoneman's raid burned the jail in Boone, North Carolina, during the raid that included his visit to Patrick County, but that action took place in answer to an attack by local forces.

The timing of this action, taken in context, leads to an alternative reasoning. Grover Cleveland, the only Democrat elected President of the United States between Abraham Lincoln and Woodrow Wilson was in his last term. Cleveland, sympathetic to the South, had in a very controversial move had returned Confederate Battle Flags to several states. Acting in this climate county officials and Swanson may have acted to receive some patronage before the Republicans took back the White House. On August 15, 1896, the Supervisors authorized the building of a home for the jailer and a few months later authorization of fixing the roof of the courthouse and jail along with new cells of "Bessemer steel" for the jail without funding from the United States.

Patrick County Jail

On April 9, a Union trooper reported, "Started at 2 in the morning, passing through a fine section of the country, the home of the aristocratic Virginia tobacco planters. The houses are beautiful. Tobacco is so plentiful that all are smoking very fair cigars. We captured some fine horses, for although all the stock has been run off in the woods, the Negroes tell us where they are concealed, and if have time we go and get them." This same day Stoneman's entire command reunited in Danbury, North Carolina.

Jefferson Davis, President of the Confederacy, a day's ride away from Patrick County in Danville wrote Jubal Early's brother, Samuel, that day asking him to report to Robert E. Lee "information as to movements of the enemy through Patrick." Unknown to Davis and Stoneman on April 9, 1865, Robert E. Lee met Ulysses S. Grant to surrender the Army of Northern Virginia to the Army of the Potomac at Appomattox Court House, Virginia.

Confederate President Jefferson Davis and R. J. Reynolds

Another incident in Patrick County involved fifteen-year-old Richard Joshua Reynolds. The future tobacco magnate hid the family's horses in the woods during the raid. He returned to the family home, Rock Spring, to find it pillaged, but not burned. The raiders only took what they needed to feed themselves and their animals. A man named Staples gave a box of valuables to a poor man living in an obscure place. A malicious neighbor led some of the raiders to the poor man's house and took the treasure. Later, Staples traveled to Danbury to ask for his possessions back and received them.

Many slaves followed George Stoneman's United States cavalry when it passed through Patrick County in April 1865. The Reynolds' slaves followed the Yankee raiders. Hardin Reynolds told his other son Abram, "My son the Yankees have been here and torn up everything and my Negro men have all gone with them." Upon arriving in Danbury, Stoneman felt the number of former slaves following the raid endangered the future safety of all involved. Stoneman sent "several hundred" under guard to East Tennessee, where many of the men enlisted in the 119th United States Colored Troops. The regiment organized at Camp Nelson near Nicholasville, Kentucky from January 18 until May 16, 1865. Equipped with .577 caliber Enfield rifles, George Gray, Peter Gray, Edmond Hylton, Jacob Reynolds, Miles Reynolds and Samuel Tatum of Patrick County served under Colonel Charles G. Bartlett and Lieutenant Colonel Thomas R. Weaver. The regiment mustered out of the service of the United States on April 27, 1866.

Stoneman's raid continued down into Piedmont North Carolina going through Germanton and Bethania on the way to Salisbury. They described Germanton as, "without paint or whitewash, and laziness is apparent all over it." On April 10, the mayors of Winston and Salem came out to surrender their towns. The Moravians and Quakers of Piedmont North Carolina, who favored peace and the Union, were happy to see them. A solider wrote, "Here we met with a most cordial reception, very different from the usual greetings we receive. The ladies cheered us, and brought out bread, pies and cakes…The people showed much enthusiasm at the sight of the flag we carried, and many were the touching remarks made about it."

For several reasons the next target of General Stoneman was Salisbury, North Carolina. A munitions factory producing arms and ammunitions for the Confederacy employed 240 men and 60 women. The town contained a large hospital in fifteen buildings and the town's churches. Lastly, the town's prison camp contained over 10,000 Union soldiers. A young lady of the town reported on April 3, "People are looking for Stoneman to come here, his object seems to be to burn bridges. I have heard that the Yankees were only thirteen miles from Mr. Hairston's yesterday." Stoneman's men did not destroy Peter Hairston's house, Cooleemee, in Davie County.

Ulysses S. Grant, commanding all United States Armies, suspended prisoner exchanges in September 1864 resulting in the large number of prisoners in Salisbury. Confederate officials failed to get Grant to resume prisoner exchanges. He wished to apply the extra pressure of caring for Union soldiers on the Southern war effort. The prison is notable for several things. Prisoners played the first baseball game played in North Carolina. Many of the Yankee soldiers "galvanized," joining the Confederate service to escape being a prisoner. At one point in the war, there were 1,427 prisoners, 251 were sick, and one died. For the first quarter of 1862, there were 509 sick and only 3 died. These numbers made the prison a model of humanity compared with others on both sides. In February 1865, due to William T. Sherman's presence in North Carolina and Joseph E. Johnston replacing P. G. T. Beauregard in command of the Confederates, officials evacuated the prisoners from Salisbury except for the sick and lame.

Stoneman's men burned the prison, foundry, arsenal and other buildings on April 12. Palmer wrote, "We burned down the infamous Salisbury prison as we came along that way. It is only necessary to see one of these prison lots to know that the suffering inflicted has been intentional. Why leave thousands of men without a plank to shelter them from the sun or storm, compelling them to burrow in the ground and live like muskrats, when there is a primeval forest adjoining Salisbury, from which a small daily detail of these prisoners could fit us substantial shelter in a week? You can see murder on the face of it." A resident of the town stated that, "Salisbury's people will always hold Stoneman in grateful remembrance for the strict control exercized over his troops."

The next day Statesville hosted the Yankee raiders continuing the trend already exhibited by Tarheel males. A lady of town remarked, "Their return with the news that they brought, was a signal for a general movement of the male population toward the friendly forests." Mrs. Zebulon Vance, wife of North Carolina's Governor, witnessed Union troopers dividing the contents of her trunk. Stoneman returned the contents with his apologizes. On April 14, Stoneman at Taylorsville, North Carolina, heard of Lee's surrender. Stoneman returned to Tennessee on April 16 his raid complete, with prisoners bound for Camp Chase, Ohio.

Stoneman divided his forces with Gillem moving towards Asheville before he returned to Tennessee. Ina W. Van Noppen comments on this move, "Now that Stoneman had left the command the plundering and sacking of houses and mutilation of furnishings greatly increased." Palmer watched the Catawba River at Lincolnton, where they locals commented that his men "protected" them "from violence or molestation."

Palmer stayed in western North Carolina until receiving a message from George Thomas in late April to "pursue Jefferson Davis to the ends of the earth, if necessary, and never give up." Union officials offered $100,000 in gold for his capture. Governor Vance of North Carolina wrote of Davis after meeting him in Charlotte that he was "absolutely blind...to those things which his prejudice or hope did not desire to see." Palmer moved into South Carolina and then Georgia crossing the Savannah River north of Augusta. Palmer acted as a flanking agent on Davis' retreat. After the former Confederate President's capture in southern Georgia, a Michigan Cavalry Captain said, "Palmer drove the game into it."

The purpose of the raid had been to bring the war to the people of a region virtually untouched. It did a good job of destroying railroad bridges and tearing up track in Lee's line of retreat, but failed to free the Union prisoners at Salisbury. The officers behaved as gentlemen and restrained their soldiers, frequently protecting homes. Stoneman's time in Patrick County was a rest halt for his men before they moved back into North Carolina. The raiders' diversion into Southwest Virginia caused the people of North Carolina to ease up, and when the raiders returned they caught the populace off guard. Historians described this raid as "splendidly conceived, an ably executed attack upon the war potential and the civilian population of the south." A more civilized example of "Total War" than other more famous Union excursions into the South brought home to our area the power of Union forces. Almost every town in Piedmont North Carolina, including Danbury, Statesville and Dobson, has a marker describing Stoneman's raid in the spring of 1865. In 1996, this author worked with local historian Ruth Minick and North Carolina officials to have a marker placed on Rockford Street in Mount Airy, North Carolina, commemorating this important local event

Colonel William J. Palmer became a railroad man after the war and founded the city of Colorado Springs, Colorado, in 1871. In 1906, his horse threw him causing a broken neck and paralysis. The men he led changed their plans for a reunion in Philadelphia and traveled to Colorado in 1907. Palmer, in recognition, paid for all their expenses. He died in 1909 leaving over five million dollars to libraries, colleges, sanitariums and schools for the deaf and blind.

Alvan C. Gillem became colonel of the 28th Infantry in 1866 and commander of the Fourth Military District including Mississippi and Arkansas. He fell out of favor with Radical Republicans for his "conciliatory and moderate" views towards the former Confederates after Grant replaced Andrew Johnson as President. Gillem died at his home, Soldier's Rest, near Nashville in 1875.

After the war, Brevet Major General Stoneman commanded the First Military District, Virginia from June 1868 until April 1869 and the Department of Arizona until his retirement in 1871. He bought an estate near San Marino, California. President Rutherford B. Hayes appointed him to the Board of Indian Commissioners. He served as Commissioner of Transportation and became a Democratic Governor of California from 1883 until 1887. George Stoneman returned to New York in 1891 and died in Jamestown on September 5, 1894, having collected on his debt to the South.

Chapter Eight
"If I could get to old Patrick I would be a happy man."
Civil War Letters 1861-1865

This chapter presents these letters written by participants in the war and those at home to give the reader first hand examples of the lives led by both soldiers and their loved ones. Most writers have a direct connection to or are from Patrick County. The author corrected grammar and spelling mistakes in some cases o make it easier for the reader. Recognition to those who supplied the letters appears after each letter. Additional information added are relationships between writer, recipient and the fate of the soldier to give the reader a clearer view of those involved.

November 1, 1860
Dear Friend, (A. B. Clark in Texas)

I received your letter dated September 22 a few days ago and was sorry to hear you had so much sickness on the road and after you landed in Texas also; but was glad to hear that most of you were improving.

Sir, myself and family are as well as common. The children have bad colds some of them; and the fever has been worse here this season than common, that is. Those who have had the fever has been harder with them. Mr. Clifton and Frederick Dalton have been down some two months or more and their cases were hopeless for a long time. Dr. Peters was Clifton's doctor and Doctor Bishop Dalton's. Clifton had no nurse but his wife as anytime and then his wife was taken down and some of the children. I understand Clifton lay for 2 or 3 days at a time without help. The fever has got so much worse, the people have got more alarmed about it. Coleman Dalton's son William died with fever about one month ago…There have been several cases of fever in the county this season. Colonel Tatum lost two negroes, Riley and a woman with fever with Doctor Bishop in attendance.

Again you write me that most of you are very well satisfied and I am glad to hear that you all got to Texas and I hoped when you all get well you will be still better satisfied with Texas and the people in Texas. I learn from your letter that you had a good deal of sickness on the road which I was sorry to hear as it must be bad to be sick in a land of strangers; though sometimes strangers are the best of friends to travelers. I understand that Jacob S. Clark has sold the land he bought of you, sold for $850 to Will or James Harber, Mr. J. Smith has not moved yet and Davy W. Smith is in Danbury Prison for a debt against him. It is hard to tell when he will get out.

I will turn to the crops, wheat very sorry about three bushels to one sawing. Some few crops a little better. Rye, sorry. Oats, the finest crop I ever saw here. I made a good start to the bushel sawing this year for the first time I ever did. Corn crops some better than they were last year in this neighborhood and down the mountain to the courthouse they say they haven't had better crops of corn in ten years. The tobacco crop is over an average crop and there are a good many crops of old leaf tobacco in the county not sold. The leaf market is thought to be dull next spring. Some of our merchants wont' lay in any goods until the Presidential election is over and will be governed by that. Money matters are hard here with most of the people. There are several sheriff sales advertised for taxes in this neighborhood. There is some excitement about the election and the times. It is thought by some that there is a young preacher in this county who is a friend of abolitionists and you have seen the man. I suppose he is very friendly toward the blacks. From what I understand, he is judge very strong, etc.

I will say something about my mother. She is poorly, but keeps about. The first of July she was taken down to her bed and was confined about seven or eight weeks before she was able to walk without help. She had very little medicine given her during the time. It as mostly from the cancer she has on her face.

And sir, Mr. Boyd has just left my house and he said they were all were at Hamilton Joyce's last Sunday and Penn and wife and the Widow Norman were there. They were all well as common. Aunt Lizzie has another son. Tell Cousin Sally, Mary has another daughter born May 12 and its name is Harriet Columbia.

We are a long way a part and many rivers between us had lakes, but we must say something about the children and watch for them awhile as the rising generation might be led astray by false teachers on many point and I am afraid there are too many books and institutions before the children of these times.

To Mary, tell her to cheer up. She is not forgotten in the county for the day I got your letter there was a neighbor young man there. I will say who he was, Peter, and he was very anxious to hear the letter read and I came to where many was sick and he did not stay much longer. The day you left your place of residence I returned home and he passed my house in great haste going somewhere and afterwards called to see you in the afternoon, but you were all gone and he was badly disappointed. We are a long way apart, Cousin Mary, but we must pay some jokes freely no harm. I would like very well to see you all and talk with you.

Now I am afraid we will have something else to do if Lincoln is elected President of these United States. It is thought here that he will stand a good _____ for the White House the next four years. The people here are divided in this county with two parties of the South. We ought to unite and go for one man. I think these are some few Douglas men here, but mostly Breckenridge men, some Bell men.

Of the seasons of this year we had rain a plenty in the first of June and then day till corn seemed almost done, the rain came in part of this county and made very good crops here, but south of this is worse than it is here on Snow Creek and Dan River. Corn is $1 per bushel from the stack, so said.

The renters are moving about right smoothly in this county. We've had a great deal of rain this fall. The farmers have not sowed much wheat yet. The land is very soaked with rain here now.

The prices of merchandise are a little advanced in some things in this county. Coffee is thirty cents per pound. We have some ____ ____ but is was badly injured by the hail. We have had three of the heaviest hails here in my that I ever saw fall. The hail stones were from the size of small bird eggs to the size of goose eggs. Colonel Tatum weighed some of them and they weighed ¾ of a pound. After the rain was over some ½ of a pound. It ruined some wheat fields.

Mary to Cousin Sally and Mary. You have gone a long way and I am here yet; and from all news and circumstances I hear from the west I would not change my place of residence under present circumstances. I would like to see you very well, but the only way we can speak to each other is by pen and letter. We are far apart and I have nothing more at present. You must excuse my bad spelling and writing, etc.

But remember your ever and affectionate friends
G. L. and Mary E. Gunter

Until death and I want you to write to me as soon as you these few lines come in and let me know how you all are. It will be satisfaction to me to hear from you all as often as I can. Mary sends her love to you all and I wish my love to be given to you and family.

Yours with respect
Beverly S. Gunter

Meadows of Dan, Virginia, June 10, 1861

It affords us great pleasure to inform your readers that old Patrick is moving, and her sons at the sound of the bugle are enlisting to march in defense of their ever dear and renowned Old Dominion. The County Court of Patrick has made a levy of $1400 for the equipping of volunteers. There are four volunteer companies made up in this county. The first commanded by Captain A. M. Lybrook 98 strong, has marched to the seat of war. The second commanded by Captain Jefferson Lawson has swelled to 108, which will leave in a few days for its place of rendezvous, Lynchburg. In both of these companies, the "red-mouthed Yankees" will find some sharp shooters and brave boys to deal with.

We are all in good spirits. Men, women and children are rallying under the "Stars and Bars." We all feel that the God of Battles is on our side for our cause is the same that our fathers was in '76, righteous, duty and just.
P. (Author Unknown)

Richmond Daily Dispatch, June 17, 1861
Patrick County, June 12, 1861
Dear John and Polly (Potter),

I have long looked for a letter from you. We apply to the office every week expecting answer from you but find none. We answered yours right off and have been looking for an answer. I wrote to Tom and Tary at the same time I did to you and have got answers long since. What can be the matter? I fear some awful apprehension has taken place there as well as here. I sometimes think you are taken from your family and gone to the battleground to fight against your friends in this country. If you are not gone, I sincerely beg you to take up your little family and come to some southern state. Mother says please come home and fight. Your old father and mother and brothers and sister. What an awful thing to think of you. For you to stand on one side and Lim on the other and fire on each other. When I go town almost every one I meet with the first is Martha where is John and what does he say about war in the neighborhood. The same they say if they were in your place, they would pick up they're all and come home which hope you will. The country is in an awful fix. Old Virginia was slow to anger and suffered her self imposed on to have peace but could no keep it. After all, now her spunk is up. She is all up at once. There is some few abolitionist though they hang them fast as they show themselves and ever Negro that puts out threats or clash they swing him to a limb and leave him hanging there. Some Negroes volunteering to fight against north free Negroes or offering their services to wait on the soldier's wash cook and fight for them though men women and children will fight. Great many ladies are volunteering. They march the regiment with the voting and carry the flag. One lady run for first Lieutenant and was elected and is gone with her company. Old Virginia will loose the last drop of blood before she will come under Lincoln confederacy. One troop started two weeks ago from here. Another will go in a few days. I hope you will come here or go somewhere else to fight. I do hope I haven't got any brother in this world that has northern principles. The principles of the north is… so low life. I don't think any man with independence will support the north. I can't tell you half the trouble and distress Lincoln has brought in this country. I don't think he can be punished enough…no not half. In regard to our moving we will not undertake it now until times is settled more than they are now. Please write and give us the times in your country. I haven't seen brother Lum for some time. I understand he is gone to the Ohio line with a troop to guard the north. I pray God will direct us in the write way. Aliron Cheely is gone. Peter will go in few days. We have fine crops. Pa and mother and all of the rest of us is well. I look for Samuel to start to where in a few days.

   Write Soon Martha J. (Potter) Gilbert
   [Sister of John Potter]

Patrick County, Virginia, August 3, 1861
Dear Sons (William and Daniel Smith),

   I take the opportunity to drop you a few lines to let you know that I am well as common hoping this will find you both and all your folks well. My shoulder don't hurt me much now, but it is stiff yet. Boys, I want to see you the worst I ever did in my life. I am so uneasy for fear you will have to start from there or get to mustering or something and take a relapse. I have heard of some taken a relapse and did not get well. I want you to know of Jeff. What will be done about your coats. I want you to have them for you will need them if you live to get about. Saunders asked about them when he was in the courthouse and they said they wasn't enough of cloth to cut them. August the 6th, Bill Burwell has got your clover cut and stacked and your Father and Tom has cut your oats and they have commenced on the meeting house field today. I wanted some of them to go out and see you, but it looks like they have got so much to do they can't get off yet a while. Sanders and Tom was talking like going this week, but Tom's oats got ripe sooner than he expected and I don't expect they will get to go this week. I would be glad you both could come home and stay a while, but don't you to undertake to walk home if you thought you was able. I want to hear how you are the worst in the world, but it made me feel mighty bad to hear that you had nothing, but your arm for a pillow for your head while you was sick and while I am lying on my bed...Your bed is lying yet the same way you both left it. Dan, I want to know whether you have gotten so you can bake bread and turn it over? without it falling to pieces...A... bought us a cow and I am in hopes I can make us some butter. We got her of Richard Bowman and give $18 for her I want you to give my last respect to Albert Smith and tell him I shant forget him for his kindness to you. I am glad to hear you and your mess hung together. I want you to set an example for the rest. I must come to a close for Mr. Dunkley is in a hurry, but I remain your affectionate Mother until death
            Helen M. Smith

Camp Pryor, Prince William County, Virginia, August 10, 1861
Dear Brother,

After a long silence, I have again undertaken the pleasant task of conversing with you about the time we at Manassas… doing so much fighting, so much excitement then you know that I could not take time to scratch a line. The excitement of the battle has been over several days but I have had few opportunities to write since. I can't tell you nothing I guess of importance relating to the fight that you have not heard. This regiment was on the battlefield the 21st but did not fire a gun. I see though that some newspapers give it the glory of taking Sherman's Battery. General Early was so eager for a fight that he had the regiment running up and down the creek trying to come in contact with the Yankees that he missed them all. The battlefield was about seven miles long such a scene as the field presented at the close of the day and for several days afterward can by some be imagined but cannot be expected.

One does not shudder to see pieces of men or rather pieces of men knee high, but to hear the groans of the wounded and the calls for water is enough to make a demon tremble. I think the wounded were attended to as quickly as possible especially the wounded of the Southern Army. Those of the Northern Army who were suffering were treated very kindly. One soldier from Louisiana was walking over the field soon after the close of the battle and in passing a wounded man from the North he was called by the poor dupe and… for a drink of water "I for the sake of humanity give me one drop" The Southern Soldier happened to have a canteen nearly full promptly stepped forward and said "Here Sir, take canteen and all, while you were sound I was your deadly enemy and would have seen you in hell before I would have given you a drop, but now I am your friend, can I do anything else for you?" But this of course is an exception. I have seen a good many Yankee prisoners; some of them are very fine looking men. Their uniforms are very good from all appearances. The whole force that attacked us were much better equipped than we are. Some of the prisoners say they never had any desire to invade the South. They only volunteered to defend Washington City. If they ever get out of this…

Author Unknown

Camp Joe Johnston, Botetourt, Virginia, September 1, 1861
Mattie (Turner),

I take this opportunity of answering your letter when I have not received and I am thinking that is not half for I have not received but one letter since I left Patrick. I have written a dozen letters since I have been in camp to my friend's in Patrick and have not had my Answers I have no news of interest only we are all getting well of the measles Jimmie Ross is improving slowly but he will not be able to come home in sometime yet. Captain Ross has taken a relapse and he is very bad worse than he has ever been. We will march from here the 9th day of this so say the Captain but I don't hardly think we can get ready by that time. I like a soldier's life finely much better than I expected for I had heard so many horrible things that a soldier had to undergo. We all have a plenty to eat and not much to do at this time. I would like to see some of them good Patrick people but do not understand me that I want to be in Patrick for I would not be back in Patrick, as time is for money I will bring this disinteresting to a close for I think you are tired of such nonsense. Tell my friend if any to Direct their letters to Bonsack Depot in the care of Captain Conner 51st Regiment, Floyd's Brigade. Good by.

              Yours, H. C. (V. C.) Green

Camp Johnson, September 13, 1861
Dear Son (Charles F. Ross, Lieutenant, Company D, 51st Virginia Infantry),
  I read yours and Tinnies of the 11th of this month. I am glad to hear you and your mother arrived at home safely I am tolerably well but I have been housed up until I feel bad. Jimmie is no better than he was when I wrote last he sleeps a plenty and eats enough but he is frenzy nearly all of his time the doctor thinks there is some chance for him but rather a bad one the nerves of his head are affected he looks tolerably well there is a chance for him to get well. Your Uncle Lee is mending he eats pretty smartly he has quit taking medicine he looks poor but of a good color. They solders are here yet. Mr. Cruise and a few more wanted to leave last Tuesday but it was decided that they had better stay a few days longer. The wagons went on to Lewisburg and they will be back in nine or ten days from the time they started and then I expect very near all your company will be able to march and Captain Conners too. Your mess has fixed up their tent and put a fine chance of straw in it. It looks very comfortable they look well all but A. Nolen he improves. The rest of the soldiers looks tolerably well there is a few sick yet M. Agee is getting better. I. C. Adams is hauling for the soldiers. The commissary got out of coffee, sugar, and candies, but he has Reed and new supply Ran Canady got a sick furlough for a short time. I. P. Carter mends slowly he stays here of nights a Moomaus and goes to camp of days to eat. Sam Ross mends slowly but keeps strengthen. Peter Corn is well but weak. He has killed several squirrels for Lee and Jim. They like squirrel soup the best of any thing can get to eat. Mr. Stoner and the company are likely to fall out with each other. He charges $80.00 for keeping of them but I understand that he expects to get it from the War Department, but I have no idea he will get a cent that way. He charged Ewell Conner $8.00 for him and 3 ladies 2 nights and they eat off Captain Ross's Men's Provisions. I want to go and settle with him in a short time. There is a great deal of chat about his conduct towards the soldiers. They sent up there yesterday for a load of straw and he refused and they pressed it.

Some person has put up an advertisement about him and his wife rather shaming them for their conduct to the soldiers and the way he charged Ewell. We hear no news, but what you have I saw a letter Joel McAlexander and he states he was in a battle and our troops killed and wounded 160 and took 110 prisoners and we lost 4 killed and 14 wounded. Two wounded soldiers passed here a day or two ago and said they belonged to Floyd's Brigade and a few days before that time 150 of our men and 600 of the enemy engaged and our men whipped them and run them 15 miles. Killed 9 of the enemy as they know of and they wounded 4 of our men. These two were 2 of them. One was shot in the side and when the ball struck the rib it ranged round towards his back he had the ball. It was cut out of his skin. The other was wounded in the thigh. They were getting well fast. Mr. Moomau wanted them to come to the house and stay all night but they wanted to get home and stay until they got well and then they are going back. There is a great many soldiers going down every train. We can't get paper nor envelopes here. I will send to Fincastle and see if I can get some. It is now 4 o'clock since I wrote the above. The Doctor come to see Lee and Jimmie and he directed me to shave his hair off and blister it all over. I got Mr. Moomau to help me and we shaved his hair off and fixed a good blister and I am in hopes it will have a good effect. It is possible for him to recover yet. Lee is much better. He eats plenty, but he is very weak. We are going to see if he can sit up long enough for us to make up his bed this evening. You must all get along the beat you can. I will write to Tinnie or Buck so some of your in day or two tell you mother not to be uneasy about Jim for it wont do any good.

         Your Father, Charles L. Ross

Union Mills, Fairfax County, Virginia,
Wednesday, October 30, 1861
My Dear Brother
  After asking your pardon for not writing you several weeks since, I will endeavor to "write you a few lines." I have sealed myself. Kip, I guess, made it plain to you that we had no time to write after I received your letter owing to various marches that we were ordered to partake of. Kip arrived in camp night before last, but did not bring our boxes he could not get them on the cars at Christiansburg owing to the trains being loaded with provisions, clothing and for soldiers, says he could have brought them on by expressing by paying freight he concluded that would not pay and left them…We have not heard anything from them. Looking for them though on every train that comes. Colonel Terry says that Kip must go after them if they don't come soon.
  Last evening, at dress parade, orders were given for this regiment to cook two days rations and be ready to march this morning at eight

o'clock. At eight, this morning all were marched off except the sick and those that were detailed for guard. I have had a very bad cold for a few days back and concluded that I had best not go, though it's the first picket duty that I have failed to be on since I've been in service.

The regiment has gone to Lankses Station, which about four miles below this place. It is generally believed that the Yankees will advance on us in a very short time. General Early said this morning that there was no doubt about it. Think by my resting a day or so that I will be entirely ready for a big fight. I wish you could see the breast works that our men have thrown up, since we fell back just after Kip started home… these are the strongest that he had ever seen. Said he heard General Beauregard say that the Yankees should never get that place again while he lived. I suppose you have seen a full account of the splendid victory we gained at Leesburg (Leesburg is about 25 miles from here). The Eight Virginia Regiment covered themselves all over "with glory" (The 8th is composed of companies from this, Loudoun and Prince William Counties) one company in particularly Colonel Evans saw the Yankees and ordered one company to take a round about way to the River and conceal themselves and as soon as the Yankees advanced on him to go to their landing places, destroy all their boats they could then follow after the Yankees and fire on them in the rear. They did so and the plan acted finely so soon as the one company commenced firing, the Yankees fled in every direction. They thought, I suppose, they were surrounded, so much for these great boasting invaders… has the headache extremely bad when such news reaches us. He was left here this morning for camp guess he will have his head covered with handkerchiefs before night, poor fellow, we sometimes advise him to have his head taken off. The heart of our company is good. There are only fifty-nine privates and enlisted me of us. Thirteen of them are at home and at different hospitals, doing well as a general thing. Forty-six in camp, four of them reposted themselves sick this morning, nothing the matter, though I guess bad cold proverbially a foul stomach ache caused by eating too much. I was very sorry to hear of so much sickness in Lawson's Company. Thomas Hatcher wrote to Dan informing him of the deaths of John and Joe. Don't know when I was more surprised than I was on hearing of their deaths. One ought not to be surprised though on hearing of the death of any soldier…Author Unknown

Mount Jackson, Virginia, December 27, 1861
Beloved Cousin,

Yours of the 13th instance arrived here the first Christmas Day and it found me very sick, but I am glad to inform you that I have gotten a great deal better. I have been down with the jaundice and I am as ugly a white boy as you ever saw, for I am nearly as yellow as a pumpkin. I was very sorry to have to leave camp but I find it was a great deal better for me, as this is a very nice Hospital and a very good physician I have been here one week and I am in hopes I shall be able to return in a short time as it is very disagreeable to have to see men suffering so much cousin, I am very sorry to find that you are so low spirited as regards the war, but I assure you it is a horrible thing and such a war as this is very… But I am in hopes it will soon come to a close, you stated in your letter that we had to stay here two years longer, but you are mistaken about that, for we will be soon to come home when our time is out, and if I do not get a furlough before and if I can't get a furlough I will come then. If I am living I am very sorry that there will be so many married men that have to come but. There is a great many in the army at this time and there is a great many that are unmarried men at home yet, that will wait, thinking that there will be no salt for them at all. But they had just as well volunteer for they will have to come in a short time, all that are between 21 and 31 will have to come first.

    Cousin you wrote that you expected to take your Christmas in Henry and old Franklin and I would to God that was in my power to be with you, but sad fate was not, but I trust that it will be the last so long as I live as you can't imagine how lonesome and feel when I think, how it once was and then to think that I am away from all of my old acquaintances and the worst of all away from you and my Dear Old mother, cousin you can't imagine my feelings when I had to write to mother that I was gone to the hospital well knowing how unhappy she would be, but I am very thankful that it is so that I am able to inform her that my health is improving. I will have to close as my paper is short I want you to write me word how you spend your Christmas and if you have seen mother write me word how she is. There was several ladies here on yesterday and they looked very nice give my respects to all inquiring friend if any remember me to your Pa and family and believe me to be your true cousin, absent but not forgotten
                      William Herbert Cooper
                      24th Virginia Infantry Regiment.

Richmond, Virginia, April 9, 1862
Dear Wife,
    I take my pen in hand to let you know that I ain't well at this time hoping these lines may find you all well. I have got the mumps. Thomas has got the mumps too. A. J. Leceins, Saben Wright, Bill Hooker is here with us all got the mumps. There is about 15 of the recruits at other places sick with the measles and the mumps. I will give you our troubles since we got in camp. We had orders to leave our camp about twelve o'clock one day and then in about two hours we had orders to go back to our old camp and then in three days we had orders to start

again and then we went up to Orange Court House and we stayed there one night then we got on the cars and came down to…and then we went down to Yorktown yesterday. Then we came back last night we will stay here till we get well. I want you to write to me as soon as this comes to hand so I can hear how you all are getting along. You can't think how bad I want to hear from home. I want you to take good care of yourselves and little Bennet so I must close.

    A few lines to Pop and Mom. I didn't…I took them April 8th and Thomas took them April 6th and Tom's jaws is swollen tolerable bad but mine haint swelled much. I am well as all but the mumps. I think we stand camp life very well. Pap, I want you to tend to my things the best you can and write to me how everything is getting along and write to me soon and write me the news. Pap, you write to me whether the…is gone or not and have many lay out.

    A few lines to James. You must not volunteer because I can't think you could stand it. I want you to write to me when you hear from Richard, Jehu and Joel and I want you to write to me whether you are agoing to stay at home or not it is a dark day and I must come to a close by saying good bye to you all. I forgot to write that I haven't drawed any money, but I think the reason is that we have been on marching orders, but I will send some as soon as I get it.

                     Charles Barnard
                     Company I, 24th Virginia Infantry

To Mary Barnard and folks. Dear Father and Mother,

    I have the opportunity of writing to you once more to let you know that I am not well hoping when these lines come to hand. They will find you all well. I went to Orange Court House with the mumps and went to Yorktown and then I got so bad with the mumps and it was raining and they sent me back to Lynchburg to the hospital and I expect to stay here two weeks and if you will start a letter the first mail. I can't get it. I expect we will have a battle shortly on the eighth of April, they had a battle. So must come to a close. Direct you mail to Richmond, Virginia,…Royster Hospital.

                     Thomas A. Barnard
                     Company I, 24th Virginia Infantry.

Farrow Grounds Near Norfolk, Virginia, April 13, 1862
My dear wife and children,

    I take my pen in hand to write you a few lines to let you know that I am well and hope when you reach these lines they will find you all enjoying the same blessing. Sally, I received you letter last Thursday evening. I was glad to hear that you was all well. You wrote to me that

Larkin had been very sick. I was glad to hear that he was mending. We have a good deal of sickness down here. The fever and measles and mumps. One died from Franklin last Friday morning with the measles in one regiment. Two died with the measles over at the entrenchment camps the same morning. I heard from brother John a few days ago. He had the measles. They said he was getting better and was going about. Sally, you wanted to know how many… with me. We have twenty-six in our regiment. Daniel Shumate and all of his brothers. John Cahill, Marshall Jo Pace, George Gravely; It is too tedious to mention all. We all cook and eat together. We have a house to cook in. They all sleep in the house but six of us. They was so crowded that myself and Daniel Shumate and his brother and Tom Hardy and Armstead Eggleton all sleep in a tent. We all get together first rate, Sally. Ben Jones ain't in our company. We see him everyday. He is well. He talks about volunteering. There are a great many volunteering. Sally, I don't expect to volunteer. They ain't but very few that went from about here that has volunteered. They say they ain't going to. Major Taylor says them that don't volunteer will be drafted to fill up the old companies. If they do that, I can't tell where I shall get to Sally. I went down in town last Thursday. I went through the town to the boat landing. It was a great curiosity to see the old Merrimack. Started out last Friday morning, we men all marched down to Ambers Point battery to see the fight. They said it was eight miles to Sewell's Point. We could see the vessels very plain. The Merrimack taken three small vessels without firing a gun. I saw them bring them back. They said there was eleven white men and two negroes on them that was taken prisoner. The vessels were laden with hay. The old Merrimack centered about there all day but the Yankees wouldn't venture out. We could see the Yankee tents plain enough. They said it was ten miles to where they was. They are expecting a fight everyday at Newport News. It don't look like they even can get to Norfolk without being tore all to pieces. They have got breast works and cannons planted all along on both sides of the river. Sally, you said you wanted to know how I like to stay there. I don't like to stay one bit but I am a heap better satisfied than I expected. They say they are about to pass a law to send all over thirty-five years old home. If they do I may come home after while. Some say if that law passes, they will keep them all anyhow. If that be the case, I don't expect to be at home soon. Sally, as soon as the clover gets a good start you must have the hogs turned on it and try to save all the corn you can. John, you must try to get on with your work the best you can. Our…was very rough a long last week. This week we have had very good fare. Plenty of bacon, coffee and sugar and flour and some high-bread. Our wood we have to cook with is green pine. We haven't done nothing but cook and eat for five or six days. We have had a heap of rain this week. There are a cold east wind blowing every day. I

have wore my overcoat half the time since I have been here. Sally, some times I think maybe I come home after a little then again I get clean out of heart of coming home. Soon I want to come home and see you all very bad. Nothing more at present Sally, write to me every week and give me all the news you can. Goodbye to you all. You must write me soon. Nothing more. I remain you dear husband until death. Direct you letters to the Farrow Grounds near Norfolk, Virginia, care of Captain H. C. Wooton, Company E, 64th Regiment Virginia Military
      Meshach Turner
      Company E, 64th Virginia Militia.

April 15, 1862
Sally,
  I will write you a few lines this morning to let you know that I am well and hearty and hope when you get these lines they will find you all enjoying the same. Sally, all of my connections from Franklin is in the other regiment over at the entrenchment camp about a mile and a half away. They march over one hundred and sixty over to our camp and volunteered yesterday. Cousin Andrew Turner was with them. He said they was a heap of sickness in that regiment. He said they had seven or eight died at the hospital. Brother John has the measles but they say he is getting about again. Captain Jim Turner is down with the fever very low. Clayton Stone is very sick. Jo Pace has been sick. He is getting better. They are good many more sick in our regiment. Sally, write to me how you are all getting on with your work. Nothing more at present. Sally, I send howdy to you and all the children and sister Sally and her children. Nothing more at present. I remain your affectionate husband until death.
      Meshach Turner
      Company E, 64th Virginia Militia.

April 17, 1862
Dear Wife,
  I take my pen in hand to let you know that I am not very well at this time hoping these lines will find you all well. I have been sick for about two weeks. I have been sick ever since I wrote the last letter. I was taken with a headache and a puking and I have been puny ever since. I am getting better though tolerable fast. I had such a bad taste in my mouth I couldn't eat nothing at all. I did wish to be at home so bad for you to fix me something to eat that I could eat. Thomas keeps sorts puny. I am going to try to get a transfer to the company that Joe and Jehu is in. I wish that I had a helt on tell Joe and Jehu went back to their company and went with them. Mary, I hain't heard from you since I left home and I want to hear very bad. Mary write to me whether Bennett can walk or not and how he is getting along. Write to me whether you air again to start home or not. May I have wrote four or five letters to you and I

hain't received nary letter from you yet I wish I could hear from you. Mary, it seems like a long time since I left home. Be sure to write as soon as this comes to hand. Mary, I would send you some postage stamps, but I don't know whether you would get them or not. I have got plenty. I have got about 20 postage stamps, but not much money. I have spent about 5 dollars since I come here, but I couldn't eat what they had here and I was obliged to eat something and everything sells so high. I got plenty of sweet potatoes when I was sick, but I tell you they cost tolerable high. Mary, I want you to take good care of your sheep for you can do more with them than anything I left you. Mary, I want you to do the best you can till I get back if I should be so lucky.
      Charles Barnard
      Company I, 24th Virginia Infantry.

Headquarters 45th Virginia Regiment, April 19, 1862
Sir, (Major William Guerrant, Christiansburg, Virginia)
  I enclose to you, two notices, which you will deliver to the persons for whom they are intended, and, unless they furnish each a substitute who is "an able bodied man, well clothed" as the law directs, you will at once put their names upon the muster Roll of your county.
  The manner in which you left this encampment, (without furnishing the dates from which the reports as reports could be made out) was conduct highly unbecoming an officer, and will be reported to Headquarters.
      I am Sir Respectfully
      W. H. Werth, Major C. S. A.

Sitting on the banks of the Chickahominy, May 12, 1862

There needs an angels power
  In the tone and in the eyes,
To give the deeper meaning
  Of a tear, a vow, a sigh;

Or, to tell, in accents prosper
  The anguish of a heart
That loses hope forever,
  And smiles at its depart.

Oh! That this mystic language
  I could but learn to speak;
I'd tell why now unbidden,
  A tear in on my cheek;

I'd tell of hopes now blasted,
> Hopes fall of life and light
And that deeper anguish
> That clouds my soul in night.

Author Unknown.

Camp Winder, Henrico County, Virginia, May 8, 1862
Dear Father (Tirea Barnard),
>   I seat myself to let you know that I am getting pretty ni well greatly hoping these few lines may find you all well I received your letter this morning and you don't know how glad I was to hear that you was all well and to hear that Mary and Bennett was well you letter was the 27th of April and that is all the letters we have got I never heard from you all till yesterday and I happened to come across Uncle Charles and Pat and could tell me something about you all and it revived up mightily and then when we got the letter this morning you don't know how it revived me so that I stood a little too much and met legs pain me a little, but I expect to go to my regiment in a few days. I was so glad to hear that Mary was about well. It didn't pester me about Cardwell and Mister Epperson not doing the work, but I would rather they had stood up to their contract. I left the hospital May 7th and come up here and I left Thomas down at the hospital, but he got very bad off. He has a sore throat and he had something like the measles. The doctor said he had the measles. I was sick about two weeks and when I got a little better I broke out like I had the measles, but I reckon it won't. I heard from Thomas yesterday and he was about well. It is no use for me to write anything about the war for I hear so much that I had not got time to write it all to you. James, you must write to me. Direct your letters to Richmond, Virginia. So, I must close by saying I still remain your affectionate son until death.
>   Mary, I must write to you that I was very glad to hear that you was getting almost well. I have thought of you many times. I have been better satisfied since I heard from home than I have been since I have been in the army, but since I have been writing I have heard bad news. Our regiment is cut all to pieces. I hear that our general is wounded in the shoulder and our captain is mortally wounded and that Captain Jennings is killed and that about all the officers is killed or wounded. Also, I hear that our Colonel is shot in the mouth and that our Lieutenant Colonel is wounded too, but they say our men charged them and took their battery.
>   Charles Barnard
>   Company I, 24th Virginia Infantry.

May 9, 1862
Dear Mary,
    I went down today to see how Thomas cumin and he came up here with me. I think he is on the mend. I think that he will be able to go to the regiment again. I will close by saying I still your affectionate husband until death. Uncle Charley can tell more or war news than I can. Mary, you must write to me. I think you could get somebody to write for you. You don't know how lonesome I fell. I would be glad to get a letter every week. You must excuse my scribbling and bad spelling.
                      Charles Barnard
                      Company I, 24th Virginia Infantry.

Charles City County, Virginia, May 17, 1862
Dear Wife (Mary Barnard),
    I take the pleasure of writing you a few lines to let you no that I am well hoping these few lines will find you all well. We left camp Winder the 14th day and got to our regiment that same day and they had marching orders yet we was held in line to be in readiness to march. Doctor Elliot came to our company and told he was agoing to start home this evening and I thought I would write you a few lines and send you some money. I will send you all I have got. Don't know when I may loose it or get killed. I will send you 50 dollars. You must keep what you need and get Pap or Isham to pay it out for you must pay Bill Moir and R. J. Boyd and other little debts Thomas is well he sent his money by John Hatcher and I wouldn't send mine by him. I was afraid he would spend it and it would be gone. I will tell you about our hard times marched all day yesterday and about half rations of meat and we marched till about ten o'clock in the night. Will tell you the times we have been marching today. We have stopped awhile. They say we will give you Richmond, but I can't tell what I think myself. We are in about 5 miles of Richmond. They say the Yankees are in good spirits. They say they have got about a hundred acres of artillery, but I don't know hear so much. I hain't got time to write much I must say I still remember you. Your affectionate son until death. Write soon and direct your letters to in care of J. T. Clark. So good by to you all.
                      Charles Barnard
                      Company I, 24th Virginia Infantry.

May 1862
Dear Father and Mother,
    I take my pen to let you know that I feel better this evening than I have felt in two weeks, hoping these few lines may find you all well. I have no particular news to write to you of any importance. They has two of our company died right lately. Willaby Blackard and Joseph Plasters.

They is no use for me to aim to write to you the men that dies here. I believe the most that dies has got cold with the measles. Pap, I want you to write me all the news that is going I want you to write me how all my things is getting along you must excuse my bad spelling and writing. I must come to a close by saying I still remain your affectionate son. Direct your letters to Richmond, Virginia, in care of Captain A. M. Lybrook, the 24th Virginia Regiment. Write to me soon for I want to hear from you all real bad. Mary, you don't know how lonesome I feel since I left home. Mary, I must come to a close by saying I still remain your affectionate husband.

A few lines to Isham. I will write to something the word here the Yankees is leaving Yorktown. Don't know whether it is so or not and I hear some of our is leaving there too, but where they are going I can't tell. I don't have much news to write you, but I think I will be able to go back to regiment in a few days. Isham, I want you to write to me as soon as this comes to hand. I want you to write how long Joel stayed in and when you heard from Joel, Jehu and Richard last and how they was a getting. Isham, I must come to a close by saying I still remain your affectionate brother.

Charles Barnard
Company I, 24th Virginia Infantry.

July 11, 1862
My dear and lovin wife (Drucilla Wood),

I once more take my pen in hand to let you know that I am about but not well I hope this will find you all well. I have all your letters that you sent to me. I… but the last one and I wish I could I get it. I am pestered so bad I cant see no pleasure here and I don't expect see anymore if I don't get to come home where I can see you. For I want to see you the worst I ever did. Dru we have had powerful battle about here. We have run the Yankees back, but I don't know how long they will stay we have moved about 15 miles from what we was when we commenced fighting. We are between Richmond and Petersburg on Falling Creek. Dru I don't know which side killed the most but there was a heap killed on both sides. I expect they killed more of our men than we killed of them for we charged on their battery and they say our men just fell by… and we charged on their battery we had t fall back but they left that night. Dru I went on the battle field one day and seed where a heap of men was covered up and horses covered up. It was the awfulest site I ever saw in my life. The maggots was working out of the ground where some men where covered. I was in all of the battle but one evening. I give out and left them about 12 or 1 o'clock and they commenced fighting about a half an hour after I left. Dru, the bombshells fell around us. It was mighty dangerous the next morning. I seed nine men laid out side and side.

Some of them was hit in one place and some in another. It looked mighty bad. Dru I bought me a ginger cake today and give 25 cents for it about a 10 cent cake and I have bought some butter and give $1.00 and 25 cents a pound for it. Dru, I have got nine dollars yet and we haven't got no pay yet and I don't know when we will but if I could get to come home I would not care for it home sweet home. Oh how I long to see it Dru. Tell father to write me and tell him direct his letters to Richmond Virginia to 6th Virginia Regiment in the care of Colonel Rogers company and tell him I would write to him but am scarce of paper and stamps and when I have the change to write I feel like I must write to your. Father wrote to John that he did not know how to write to me. I thought he could tell by your letters since he did not know Captains name. His name is John Ludlow and our First Lieutenant N.M. Stokes and 2nd Lieutenant is George Croley and 3rd is Waite. These is our officers name. Dru, tell Lilly Martin that Joshua is dead. Sam has wrote about it but I don't know whether he got it or not. I will close my letter by saying I remain you affectionate husband so far well for this time.

      James M. Wood
      Company D, 51st Virginia

Camp Near Richmond, July 18, 1862
To Captain Clark,
  I wrote you a few lines a few days ago concerning the company papers I want you to send me the muster roll… was made at… if you have it if you haven't got it send me a list of everything that happened in March… and a list of all the clothes the company… and all you know of marched and get well I come back. I want to see you very but the health of the company is about the same it were when you left us… reports every morning. I don't think my of… is very dangers. I want you to be… send them papers to me I will stop writing not knowing whether you are at home or at Danville.

      Your Friend, Joseph E. Hatcher, Company D,
      51st Virginia Infantry

August 28, 1862
Dear Sir (Captain Thomas Clark),
We have returned from Yankee land to Richmond and we are in Bird Island Hospital and our regiment is gone to General Jackson and we learn that you are in Danville and we are in want of some money. We would be very glad if you would make a deserters list and send it to us. We are here unwell and thin of clothing and wish to have some money to by us some extra snacks and clothes. We had a tolerable rough time of it with the Yankees we was only two months and if it is necessary for you to any information about our height or size I will give it. I am about… six foot high…John Michal and mustered into service and have received

no pay only my bounty. Hardin Spencer and Robert Radford is about six felt one inch high and is in his 46 year and weighs about 160 or 70 and wish you to attend to this as soon as you can and send them to us at Bird Island Hospital Richmond Virginia in care of Doctor Garnet. So I hope these lines may find you well and doing well and you will please excuse my awkwardness in writing. So, I remain yours

      Thomas Clark
      Hardin Spencer
      Robert Radford
      Company I,
      24th Virginia Infantry

Berkeley County, Virginia (Now West Virginia) near Martinsburg, September 22, 1862
Dear and affectionate wife (America E. Fitzgerald Gilbert),

 I take my pen in hand to let you know I am well at this time. Hoping when this reaches you it may find you and all the rest enjoying the same good blessing. It has been a long time since I have written you. I reckon you think I have forgotten you, but the reason I have no written is I have not had the chance. I have been on the march now ever since the 16th day of August. I have been in 5 fights since. Two large ones, the rest small ones. I have been hit twice, but did not hurt me. I came very near being torn all to pieces with bombshells but some unseen Power protected and brought me out safe. We have marched through Maryland and had some tall fighting over there. We lost a heap of men and got rather more there than we bargained for, but we have got to old Virginia once more now. If I could get to old Patrick, I would be a happy man. America, I received the letter Emily wrote a few days ago. I was glad to hear from you and hear you was all well. We are out here in an old field. I don't know how long we will stay here. Not long I reckon. We are not out of hearing of the Yankees yet. I can hear a cannon every now and then while I write.

 America, I have seen the hardest times that I ever saw. I am in hopes they are over, at least for a while. America, I hope the time will soon come when we can sit and stay with each other. I want to see you and the children so bad I am nearly crazy. I cannot write very much, if I could see you I could tell a great deal. Our Company has been killed and wounded and deserted till we have but 12 men rank and file. A. J. Winginton, William Clifton, Henry Haley, William Coleman have all deserted. Tom Wigginton has gone to the hospital. He was very sick when he left. We have lost five men in battle. Anderson Tuggle was killed at the Battle of Manassas on the… and on the 14 of September we lost four men missing. It was George Lawless, Arthur Lovyns, Floyd Bowlen and A. M. Kesster.

America, I have got some thing for you. I will send you a ring. You must write to me about how you like it and I have some I cannot send in a letter. You must write to me as soon as you get this and let me hear from you and Flood and sis and kiss them for me and tell them about Pa and tell me what Flourney says. I have wrote all I can think of so direct your letter to Winchester, Virginia, Company I 24th Regiment Virginia Volunteers. I will close now by remaining your… and affectionate husband until death.

George, I will write to you and Pa and Mother and Emily and John Fed and Brother all at once for this is all the paper I have got. You can see all the news in America's letter. You must all write to me and give me all the news. I think there is some by this time that think about all the other. George, tell Luvenia Critz I saw Haman this morning. He eat breakfast… he wants to get home any of the bad. George, you don't know any thing about hard times. I have been through more hardship in the last 40 days than I ever went through in all my life. Tell John Fed I will not answer his letter now but will answer it time enough to let him know whether I can do any thing for him or not. I forgot to tell America one thing. She wanted to know what I meant by telling her not to spree about. It was only a joke of mine because she wrote to me she had been to the Courthouse and guessed she took a spree. Bucket says he reckons Jeff and Bose has gone home. They were sent back. Rick, tell America I will not send the ring this time. I will have to send my letter without stamps. I have not got any and cannot get any. Write soon and let me hear from you.

     Samuel S. Gilbert
     Company I, 24th Virginia Infantry
     Killed at Gettysburg on July 3, 1863.

In my room, December 25, 1862

This has been a delightful day not a cloud to dim the sun. Roads in excellent order, atmosphere mild and pleasant as a May Day. I took a ride. Went as far as Mr. Kings. Called for a Christmas gift and got some fine apples.

But Oh! What a sad Christmas. How sadly out of harmony with the annunciation of the Creators will made 1862 years ago, by the angelic host, "Peace on Earth, Good Will To Man." We have war, and we have its bereavements to mourn, its hardships to bear. The wickedness of man has come between us and the happiness which heaven would bestow. But, while we endure these wits, it is our privilege to be able to appeal to the ruler among nations and the searcher of hearts to vindicate the purity of our motives and the justice of our cause. We have desired to wrong no man.

     Author Unknown.

Camp Near Quency (Guinea) Station, January 20, 1863
Dear Brother (Sam Gilbert),

    I embrace the opportunity of answering your letter. I received it yesterday and was happy to hear from you all and to hear that you was well. Sam, I field as well as ever did in my life though I am weak yet. I feel a little bad today by being on guard last night. Me and John was on guard last night. Hoping these few lines we find you enjoying the blessing of health. Sam, me and John and Pen and Whit Boswell messes together. Sam, Cumpsy did mess with us but he has took Willis Dalton's place of cook for the company. We have plenty of bacon on the shelf but not much bread. Sam, we are here yet I can't tell how long we will stay here. We may stay hear all the winter and we may go away from here before night. We don't know. Sam, you wanted to know if I was willing for you to make a road through my field. I have no objections. You can make a road down the fence side if you want to. Sam, I expect for you to have my meter according to contract and as t the rent we wont fall out about it. Sam, I told Bob before I left home that you was to have the meder. Sam, you can make a line fence between us if you will make a good fence. Sam, I had rather you would so my meder…if it will suit you. Sam, John says tell Jane to answer his last letter. He told her not to answer it but the order is countermanded. Tell her to direct his letter to Richmond, Virginia and it will come to him. So nothing more at present only remain your affectionate brother until death. Sam, we can't get postage stamps here to put on our letter.
                        John F. Gilbert
                        Company I, 24th Virginia Infantry

Camp Quencies (Guinea) Station, January 22, 1863
Dear Brother (Samuel L. Gilbert),

    I now take the present opportunity of writing you a few lines to let you know that I am not very well at this time. My hip and back hurts me very bad this morning. Dow is as well as common. He sees he is very hungry. Hoping these few lines may find you all enjoying good health. Sam, I think there is a fight close at hand for was ordered last night to be ready to march at a minutes warming. Though we are hear yet we hear the cannon fire this morning over on the river. We expect to be engaged in a fight over here. Sam, I will put my trust in God to spare my life. Sam, it is a very wet time and very muddy. Sam, I dread to have to march but I will have it to do in a short time. Sam, I received your letter on the 19th and I was happy to hear from you all and to hear that my family was well. Sam, I am very sorry that you was put to so much trouble to get salt for my wife and at last could not get it. Sam, I sent one hundred and ten dollars home by Murray Turner and I wrote to Jane to pay you ten dollars for me. Sam, I am due you ten thousand thanks for your kindness to my dear wife and children. Sam, I want Jane to pay you for your services. Sam, I want you to aid Jane is getting some salt. Sam, I am afraid that Jane's meet wont keep if you cant get any salt. I want some more put on the meet for I am afraid the meet won't keep with quantity of salt was put on it. Sam, we can't get no stamps here. You must not think hard of our sending letters without paying the postage on them.

      Write soon,
      John F. Gilbert
      Company I,
      24th Virginia Infantry

Lenoir County, North Carolina, March 27, 1863
Cousin Sam and Martha (Samuel L. and Martha Jane Potter Gilbert),

  I seat myself to answer your kind letter, which came last night, and I was glad to hear from you all and hear you was all well. This leaves me well and doing very well down here in North Carolina in the Pines and I sunned until I am as black as any Tarheel North Carolinian you ever saw. Martha, you said you would write to me to let me know I was not forgotten. I am glad to hear you say so for it looks very much like the most of my old friends have forgotten me, as I don't get any letters from any of them. I have not had but one letter from home in a month. Show this to Ross folks and America and tell them I have written three of four letters to them and have had but one answer to them. America can see from this I am well and that as much as I can hear from her and I hear it by some one else's letter for I don't get any from her. If she writes I don't get them. Sam, I am boiling some peas for dinner. I wish we could eat some soup together but I don't want us to eat together here. <u>Sam you are out of this war and my advice to is stay out if you can.</u> Some men in our Company is mean enough to be mad with a man if he keeps out of it carefully, but a grunt is all that can be expected from a hog. Martha, you said when America moved to Pa's you would go to see her. Thank you. I am glad you think enough of her to visit her. You must visit her often and comfort here all you can. <u>Martha, I am so glad Sam got a discharge.</u> I know he will do any thing for any of the women that is left destitute of some one to do anything for them. Sam, you must not let America suffer for anything you can do for her. She has got money enough to pay you for it. I was not uneasy about her as long as poor George was at home and now he is gone and I can't be ever where to so I can write to him. I have never heard from him since he left. It is a very nice country here but the water is not very good. We can dig a well and wall it in three hours. We are drawing bacon peas and corn meal. We have to eat the meal without sifting and the bacon is as large as ten cents. We get plenty to eat but it is very rough fare. Sam, you must write again as soon as you get this and give me all the news you have and remember me in your prayers. I will bring back my lines to a close. Write soon. Farewell till I hear from you. Direct your letters to Petersburg for we are as apt to go back there as to stay here. They will come to the Regiment. Let us go where we will.

                            Samuel S. Gilbert
                            (Son of Samuel L. and Lucy
                            Sharp Gilbert)
                            Company I, 24th Virginia
                            Killed at Gettysburg, July 1863.

Camp Narrows, April 5, 1863
Dear Sister,
      Your letter by Mr. Tuggle came to hand this evening and as Lieutenant Terry expects to start for Patrick in the morning. I will answer it but I haven't any news to write that would interest you I wrote to you by Colonel Bennett but suppose you had not received it when you wrote I have also written to Buck by T. M. Hubbard the weather has moderated a little it has been very severe I suppose the farmers are very backward with their work. Well Tinnie, we came very near having a wedding a few days ago Quince Stovall has been trying to marry a girl at Peters Town but failed to get their license was all that prevented it. G. W. Cheely has been writing to a girl in Henry by the name of Griggs and she has written to him and promises if any girl writes to him they may expect for the company to read the letter there is some sickness in camp at this time. Elijah Vaughn has been very sick for some time but is improving slowly and I think he will get well with care. There is no talk of leaving this place. I think it is quite likely that we will stay here all the summer. The boys generally in very good spirits and we have a very lively time generally. We get plenty to eat. Plenty of bacon and bread and rice and sugar. I understand that Jimmie Woolwine and I. S. Adams are likely to marry soon in fact it has been reported that they were all ready married. It is reported that G. Anglin is out here on a courting expedition but I can't find but will be back Wednesday and I will write again you must all write to me. You wrote that you had chicken to eat. We had an egg pudding last night. No more at present.
      P. S. I am well and hearty think I can stand camp fine. Don't show the badly written letter to anyone I sent one hundred and fifty dollars by Colonel Bennett and want Pa to lend it out if he can I want you to send me my Jeans pants if you can conveniently. I can draw pants at anytime but had rather have them.
                            Remain your brother
                            Charles F. Ross
                            Company D, 51st Virginia Infantry

Camp Glade Spring, April 25, 1863
Dear Sister,

    As Mr. Harbour starts for Patrick in the morning, I will write you a few lines have nothing of interest to write. I am in fine health I think am heavier than when I left home. We left the slat works yesterday morning and are now in camp at Glade Springs immediately on the railroad…have but little to do. Tis thought we will go back to the Narrows or somewhere in that country. Jenkins command left here this morning. I think they were going back to where they came from to Salem it was a false alarm that brought us to this place a fellow by the name of Menifee, a Colonel in the State Line Troop, killed a man by the name of Newburg and put out the report that the Yankees were advancing on the salt works in order to pass himself off for a courier so as to make his escape but was arrested somewhere in Tennessee so I guess it will be apt to swing the gentleman report says that the Yankees are advancing by the way of Lewisburg we will not be apt to stay here very long. They are making good deal of salt at the works in fact more than they can get transportation for I think I will go to Wytheville of Abington in a few days to get my teeth plugged there is nothing more to write of interest you must write soon give me all the news. Tell Buck and Pattie they must write to me no…

                Charles F. Ross
                Company D, 51st Virginia Infantry

Caroline County, Virginia, May 16, 1863
Dear Wife ("Kit" Bowling Rorrer),

    I take the opportunity of writing you a few lines in answer to your kind and very welcome letter which to hand yesterday and found me tolerable well as to health but broke down marching and fighting. I was fighting all day the 3rd of this month, the day that you wrote your letter to me. I can inform you that we lost six men killed and nine wounded of our company. General Jackson was killed. D. B. Barnett and Rubin Via was killed. A. H. Roberts' son was wounded. That is all of the Patrick men that was hurt in this battle. Captain Daverson killed. He was Peter Rorrer's Captain. Peter came out safe. I saw him after the fight was over. He came… when we was coming…. It is reported that General Hooker was wounded. I don't know whether the report is true, but I hope… is the one that… Chancellorsville. But we give them a decent whipping and ran them back across the river. They are camped on one side of the Rappahannock River and us on the other side in sight of each other but I don't think we will have anymore fighting to do here soon at least I hope we will not for I am getting very tired of fighting. Tell Isaac Akers' wife that he is well. I truly hope that this letter may find you all in good health and doing well. I have no good news to write to you at this

time. I want to come home and see you all very bad but I see no chance for me to come home soon unless we could have peace and I see no prospect of peace at this time. As I have no news to write that will interest you I will come to a close by asking you to write soon and often. Direct your letters to Guinea Depot, Carolina County care of Captain C. W. Fry, Orange Artillery, Major Carters Battalion. So no more at present. I will write you a few lines more. I sent you and Susan a ring piece in a letter. I want you to let me know whether you received them or not. Tell Susan, Seph, State and the baby howdy for me. Let us all never forget each other. Nothing more at present. Only remember yours until death.
        William Anderson Rorrer
        Orange Artillery

Hanover Junction, May 28, 1863
Dear Sam (Samuel L. and Martha J. Potter Gilbert),
  I have been trying to get the chance to write to you for a long time. I don't care so much about hearing from you as I do from Martha. I have been writing to several of my old friends and they have been very prompt in answering my letters but they have never been able to give my any satisfaction that I want to hear. They seem to know nothing about Martha. I am writing to you and not to Sam and if you have any idle moments I would be glad that you would devote them to giving me the general news in the neighborhood. They say the young widows are going it red eyed. I received a letter from a young lady a few days since. She says that the women whose husbands have died in the Army don't give the girls any change at all. The widows must be very unpopular with the girls. I should like to see them flying around. I hear these young widows frequently spoken of, but I never hear a thing said about the girls. I would like to know what has become of the girls in our neighborhood. What has become of Miss Agnes Stoop and Lisa, Miss Mattie McIntosh, Roby Howell, Miss Ruby and Cal use to write to each other but some thing has broken it up. I have nothing of importance to write. I am waiting in order to get the points. If you don't know what is going on no lady does. Times are hard but I am in hopes no lady will suffer. I suppose Father is doing all he can for some of the widows. Give my respects to every lady. John (Frederick) and Sam are well. Dow's (Lorenzo Dowell) health is rather bad, but he is improving. Give my support to Sam (Samuel S. Gilbert) Pet (William Preston) and Ab (John Albert). Have a pot of crust by the time I get home. I will close by saying I remain your friend.
      Henry C. Aistrop Company I, 24th Virginia Infantry

Camp near Culpeper County, June 11, 1863
Dear Cousins (Samuel L. and Martha J. Potter Gilbert),

Dow is gone to the country to hunt him some corn bread. His health is common at this time. You did not say much about me in your letter but I would write to you as John has gone to take his mess and Dow is to full of melons to write and I like to write to you anyhow. I would like to see you too but I want to see you at home. I would like to see this day. To eat something that is clean and good. We don't have anything here but white oat bread and maggoty bacon and not enough of that. Some of it you can smell then feet off. Sam, I think the prospect for a fight here is null but our Cavalry and the Yankee Cavalry had a fight about ten miles from here on Monday and they whipped our men and made a run in the county and took off all the horses and cows they could find and everything they could that suits to carry on war. They never interrupted any Negroes as I heard of. They are not as bad as a heap of people make out they are. They do not tear up and destroy a county where they go as bad as our own men do. Sam, I have no news of importance to write. I want to see home very bad. If I knowed how I would go deranged but home. But, I have not got sense enough.

  The boys are all well now. All they lack is something to eat. Every thing is burnt up in this Country for rain. The dust is shoe top deep in the road. We cannot see a man twenty steps and we have had some of the hard marching to do for the last eight days. Pet, you and Ab must not grow too fast. If you do you might have to serve a tower in this sweet war. Tell Jane she must not quit writing if John gets home. Sam, you must write to me and Dow as soon as you get this and tell me all about everything. I will close by remaining your cousin until death.
      Samuel S. Gilbert
      Company I, 24th Virginia Infantry

Headquarters Cavalry Division, Army of Northern Virginia, Near Middleburg,
June 20, 1863
My Dear Flora (Care of Major Langhorne, Lynchburg, Virginia),
  Your letter of the 14th enclosing newspaper slips was received yesterday. The newspapers are false <u>in every statement</u> except as to the victory. General Lee wrote me a very handsome letter after reading my report which of the large number of the kind I have received from him is the only one I ever allowed to be published. All the papers are to publish it. Dr. Brewer will attend to it as I sent him the letter. The papers ought to apologize. <u>I pleasure myself on my vigilance</u> and the Yankee accounts show I was not surprised. The story about my Head Quarters amounts to this. The high hill on which I slept the night before called Fleetwood was a fine military position and about noon we had a fight for it and there we captured the Yankee artillery. My Head Quarters were transferred to the saddle at daylight and when the enemy was advancing on the hill, I was

leading my squadron against them to victory, the greatest triumph I ever had.

Not a vestige of my Head Quarters was left. All the baggage having been sent to the rear in the morning. We have had several fights up here, always successful and have captured over 500 Yankee cavalry in battle, horses, etc. Yesterday in a fight with the enemy near Middleburg, my gallant Major von Borcke was very severely wounded by a Minie Ball through the neck. He is doing well, but the wound is a very serious one. I pray he may recover. He was near me at the time the ball passed me to hit him. He is at Dr. Eliason's at Upperville and is well nursed. May God bless you and ours.

Ever yours,
J. E. B. Stuart

Orange County, Virginia, September 1, 1863
Dear Cousin (Matilda Rorrer),

I seat myself to drop you a few lines to let you know that I am well at this time hoping these few lines may come to hand and find you well and do well. I have nothing strangely to write to you. I got one letter from you and was glad to hear from you and hear that you was well and doing well. You have my best desires and well wishes. I would like to be there and pass off time with you though I cannot at this time but I hope the time will soon come when we can all be at home in peace and happiness again then I can see you and my other good friends when I wish truly tell… and all the balance of my friends they have my best respect and you may obtain a good portion for yourself. I want you to write to me and not be afraid to write. There is no danger of you retiring…. I would like to say something about though I will not at present you may guess at the balance you must answer these lines if you can read them and direct your letters to Richmond to be forwarded to Scales Brigade 14 North Carolina Troops Company B. Answer these line and give… all the news of the country and as much more as you please. May the Lord bless us all is the prayer of your friend. I will add no more at present I subscribe myself your cousin and friend until death.

Javis B. Callahan, 16th North Carolina Infantry

Richmond, Virginia, November 6, 1863
Dear Cousin,

While autumns cooling appearance intrudes itself upon us with it's rough and disagreeable frost. The bitter of the cool morning and sometimes quite intolerable nights with bitter north wind making us glad to hold ourselves closely in our cabin overcoats. I take this convenient opportunity to send you a few lines that the chain of our correspondence may not be entirely broken consequently that those intelligent letters which I occasionally may not be withheld to intercept from me those who of knowledge and friendship combined give my heart a pleasant thrill of joy surmounting the many daily occurring trouble that intrude themselves on us and acts as a salve.

    I am growing very anxious to visit Old Henry and Patrick again. I think I shall come home Christmas if I have to run the devil. I often think of the pleasant hours we have spent together. Will this war ever end and let us return to our peaceful homes…cousin. I have but very little duty to do here but I cannot be contended here. I don't expect to stay here very long. The health of the army is very good at present. We have every few… here now. I have but little to do. We have a very fine meeting going on here. I go to church very often and when this meeting is over I am taking off these lonely hours the best way I can. This meeting commenced about two weeks passed and is going on yet so you may guess I have quite a nice time. Well I will close for the present. I heard from home some few days passed all of our relations were well. Please don't let any person see this badly written letter. I hope that you will answer my last letter. Give me all the news when you write.

    Through pestilence and famine that we are atoning for our wickedness. We might learn by these plaques to love one another and keep his commandments inviolate from sin cousin Ruth. I suppose you have heard of the death of poor brother. He died in Hagerstown. If I only could have seen him before he died. I think I could have given him up much better though I don't think I ought to grieve after him for I feel like he is at rest. He has gone where there is no more war. He was one of the best brothers I had on earth. He was kind to all persons, all of his company loved him, cousin. It is very hard to give up a dear brother though I feel like he is much better off than I am. Well, I must soon close as it is getting very late. My respects to all. Remember my love to cousin Sallie. I hope you will excuse bad writing and all mistakes and the shortness of this for it was written in haste. I remain your same devoted and affectionate cousin. Write, write soon, very soon.
                       Benjamin S. King
                       Company I, 24th Virginia Infantry.
                       Killed at Drewry's Bluff, 1864.

Camp near Charlottesville, Virginia,
Monday, January 18, 1864
My Dearest Friend,

    When I sent my little missive forth upon the delicate errand of asking for your correspondence and friendship. I little dreaming that it would so soon make me the recipient of such a nice complimentary letter. It relieved my heart of a heavy burden and filled it with emotions of inexpressible joy for I had anxiously awaited it's coming fearing that perhaps it would be returned with an indictment of presumption and conduct prejudicial to the modern code of etiquette. But happily, thrice happily am I to find these doubts mere hallucinations of an over anxious brain and in accepting of your proffered friendship and as an evidence that a continuance of this correspondence is desirable I hasten this morning to reply. From the kind and gentle tenor of your letter, I believe that friendship will flourish with but little culture in such a sail as your heart. Tis said the delicate flower can only flourish in the bosom of the truly brave and intelligent of man, and the sincerely good and affectionate of woman. I already feel for you an attachment of warm and enduring friendship and by frequent intercourse through the medium of the pen the frail texture of the tie which now binds our stranger souls to such other may be so strongly formed that neither time nor space will be able to burst it asunder. The frigid winds of adversity will only serve to knit our hearts more closely together in the bonds of a pure and holy amity. I cannot accord with the poet who said, "I have too well studied mankind to be amused with friendship. Tis a name inventive merely to betray credulity. Tis intercourse of interest, not of souls in my estimation, tis a beautiful enabling emotion. Its purifies and elevates the heart above the sordid passions of every day life" Yes, rest assured Miss Mattie, you will ever find in humble correspondent a true friend not a "summer friend", who will stand firmly by you while the sun of prosperity shines brightly above your head and flee far hence when the murky storms of adversity lower over your pathway. But a friend who will prove true amid all the varying phases of fortune and I beg you Miss Mattie never to believe that I will so far forget the lofty principles that constitute a gentleman as to indulge in petty speculations when writing to you. Know when writing to you my letters shall always be indicted with the highest regard for the noble principles of truth. I will be sincere and candid at all times. Do me not the injustice, dear Miss Mattie, to think that I would use my letter as a cloak of simulation. Nay, I would myself if I believed that my heart could prove so base as to speculate upon the credulity of such a gentle creature.

  Ah! Tis indeed a sweet pleasure to have a congenial spirit to condole with us when the pitiless storms of adversity from forth their fury upon our defenseless honor. When grief and trouble and all things better waters over our bosoms, washing out every vestige of past happiness. How to have the consolation sympathies of some kindred spirit. I to have the sympathies of some kindred spirit. If there was less treachery among friends there would be more happiness in this gainsaying world. But alas! So few regard as sacred their noble principles.

  I recon you have long ere this come to the conclusion that I have drawn the black curtain of oblivion between me and thy image and rallied your name into the dark specter of forgetfulness. But when I recount to you the reasons why I have not answered your kind letter sooner I am sure you gentle heart will not hesitate to forgive. The next day after writing to you we moved to this place with the expectation of going into winter quarters, But alas! How soon were there flattering expectations to be blasted. The very next morning after getting here we were ordered to the valley of Virginia and have just closed in that quarter one of the several campaigns it has ever been our misfortune to endure. In fact, it stands without a precedent in history. Our father doubtless suffered much to gain our independence, but this sufferings and privations in comparison with ours dwindle into utter insignificance. We marched day and night hourly the whole time. I recon though you have had a graphic account of the campaign through the newspapers so I will not weary you further with another from my dull pen. If I could only feel that the good people at home were ready to make such sacrifices, there would my heart leap with emotions of joy at the prosperity of a speedy and honorable peace. Is not the prize well worth the sacrifice? If we leave this most abject slavery that ever cured the human family will be our lot. If we win it will be our high privilege once more to inhale the pure untainted atmosphere of liberty and freedom. Tis true dark and lowering clouds overhang our national horizon at present but we must grow weary and faint at heart. We cannot stop the war. If were overcoming to humanity as religion to surrender the principles involved in this conflict. It would be treason against truth, God and every feeling of national pride. The only and great issue now is liberty or death. Let us go forth investing in the righteousness of cause, the goodness of Providence and feel when liberty is gone there remainth freedom in the grave. Hope throws his dazzling rays among the passing shadows of today and cheers our dishonoring hands with the... of hope for better and brighter times tomorrow.

   This is the third year of the war. These years ordinarily pass away like summer clouds, but when laden with the storms of war the days have a weary length and while it has been needlessly long it is still short. Not half the period of our forefathers struggle for independence. Many hearts now buoyant with hope and continuances bright with joyous anticipations will have ceased to beat and have passed away forever from the scene of mortal action in the newborn year shall him run its course! Many hearts will have been made devotion by crushed hopes and disappointed expectation. Many fair forms now becoming with jubilation and radiant with joy will be stumbling amongst the pale nations of the dead. Sincerely do I pray neither of the sad lots recounted may be your fate. But let us not anticipate evil. I must beg you Miss Mattie not to call me Mr. Jordan. It is a title I am wholly unused to and besides it sounds so cold and formal when from you especially would I have words of endearments. Call me anything else except Mr. I am pleased to inform you that Jimmie Jones has gotten his discharge and gone home. He is a good, nice young man. Made a most excellent soldier. We are…disbanded to go home. Anticipate a nice time. But the fortunes of war are truly uncertain and we may be disappointed. Please excuse the length of this. I must close by claiming New Years Gift and wishing you a very happy new year. Goodbye. May God Bless you.

                         Affectionately yours, William
                         Lieutenant J. W. Jordan,
                         3rd Virginia Cavalry Regiment

Wigwam (Orange County, Virginia), February 8, 1864
My Dearest Flora (Flora Cooke Stuart),

    It will be impossible for me to spend a day in Richmond, unless the present excitement from the direction of the Peninsula should draw me in that direction. I hope Brother Alex did something in the matter before leaving, concerning the house. Yesterday a bold demonstration of the enemy prevented Divine Service again. We punished them, however, at Morton's Ford, capturing about 80 and killing quite a number.

    I have not been able yet to get the things you wished purchased. I am, however, looking out for them and feel very confident of getting all we have in St. Louis. But say as little about it as possible. I am glad old Schofield has left St. Louis. I was very near being arrested by his wife when I was passing through. Governor Gamble's death is announced in the Yankee papers, also Thackeray's. Major Mosby has arrived and brought me a superb pair of heavy gauntlets.

    I see you are still considering me as the culprit and say nothing whatever of your own failure to write for about two weeks. As to being laughed at about your husband's fondness for society and the ladies, all I can say is that you are better off in that than you would be if I were fonder of some other things that excite no remark in others. <u>The society of ladies will never injure your husband,</u> and ought to receive your encouragement. My correspondence with the ladies is that kind of correspondence which pertains to the position I hold, and which never could obtain with me were I a subordinate officer, such no doubt as you hear insinuations from. Such men have not sense enough to understand it but I am thankful to say I have – and I hoped that my wife could not for one moment be made a prey to any twinge or unpleasant feeling at anything of the kind. I have Jimmy's wheelbarrow and will have it repaired. What do you think? The ladies at Mr. Scott's made up their minds when I sent for it that the Army was about <u>to move.</u> No wonder when the size is considered. Jimmie may truly be said to have commenced life with a wheelbarrow. Richmond is a queer place with a <u>few</u> queer people in it. If anyone speaks to you of subjugation, tell them is shows a total ignorance of what constitutes <u>our armies.</u> Long after the inhabitants crouch to the conqueror, our armies will tread with the triumph of victorious freemen over the dead bodies of the vainglorious foes. North Carolina has done <u>nobly in this army.</u> Never allow her troops to be abused in your presence. Tell me of the acquaintances you make. It is strange how you seem to be ill-inclined to those who have treated me with such openhearted kindness. Try and overcome it.

P. S. If Brother Alec has returned without making the purchase you had better see about the house yourself, but before closing the purchase, get Dr. Brewer to make close inquiries about the neighbors as some are very objectionable. Some of the most modest looking houses in the city were pointed out to me as gambler's dens. There will be but one result to your partnership, but go ahead – success to the firm. If you take in Nannie, too the firm ought to fare well. "Steward Brewer & Cooke" Kiss my little Virginia and tell Jeb Pa's horse Maryland is getting well. Love to Dr. Brewer and Maria. Tell Mary to write to James to come on – I need him now. Bob is again at Orange. Rosser made a splendid haul on the enemy the other day in Hardy. I have not been mistaken in any of the officers I have recommended for promotion. I have the slippers. They are a great comfort. Remind Major Von Borcke of my sabre-attachment he promised to have made. Dr. Corey went off expecting to return in a day but no news of him yet. Give dear little Posey a kiss from Uncle Jeb and tell her he hopes old "Mrs. Bates" is better of the chicken pox.
        Yours,
        J. E. B. Stuart

Camp Near Orange, Virginia, March 7, 1864
Dear Cousin (Matilda Rorrer),
   I seat myself to let you know that I am well at this time… hoping that these few lines may come to hand and find your lady ship in good health. I have no news to communicate to you at this time. I would like to be there to enjoy myself with you and tell you of my trials. You said that you would like to see me but not better than I would like to see you. I would to god that this war would stop so we could all… in peace and enjoy the sweets of liberty one time… and the good pleasures of my friends and connections. I would like to be there. I write but I cannot at this time… I expect to stop writing to her through you and you can let… the people will I mistrust you and yet I don't want that to happen. You may tell her that I have nothing against her and I take her to be a lady worthy of any gentleman's attention alterations and I wish to be remembered by you and I will not forget her… give my…friends my best respects…. May the lord bless you is the prayer of your cousin till death.
        Javis B. Calahan
        16th North Carolina Infantry

Patrick Court House, alias Taylorsville, Virginia
May 11, 1864
My Dearest Laura,

    Again I resume the pleasing task of continuing our weekly correspondence, which seems a dearer and sweeter privilege as the intervening time and distance lengthens our separation. Today four weeks ago, we parted and today two weeks hence. Providence permitting, I fondly hope to enjoy once more your charming presence.

    On Saturday last, we Henry Court House en route for this place, where we arrived safely on Sunday evening after traveling over forty miles of the most mountainous and rugged roads in the state. Saturday night we were all, by special invitation, kindly entertained at a Mr. Penn's house about half way from this place to Henry Court House. It is almost impossible adequately to describe to you the cordial welcome and princely hospitality that greeted our arrival and cheered us during our brief sojourn under this hospitable room. His fair daughters and several other fairer guests invited were there for our entertainment, vied with other in generous emulation to contribute to our enjoyment on the occasion, music, flowers, wine and ice cream, cake and all the other delicacies of the table were prodigally lavished upon us on all sides "comme d'habitude." I hastened to find out and make my special "decoirs" to the gayest and most charming of these fascinating mountain nymphs, a Miss Fannie E. Scoles, an invited guest on the occasion and one of the reigning belles of this county whose dazzling accomplishments in music and sprightly conversations were altogether irresistible and quite won my heart, beguiling it at times of its tedium of homeward yearnings, which become more and more overwhelming as the lengthening distance and receding time prolong the weary void of our separation.

    Of course on this occasion as all others, I was compelled to act out the unmarried man in order to play off as the engaging gallant and according to my comrades, I succeeded in the assumed character "a hurrielle." But a short time previous to our parting, by some secret intuition, they suspected my real situation and threatened to inform you by letter my carryings on. But jesting apart, they were kind, genteel and most hospitable people and are justly entitled to our warmest and lasting gratitude for the generous good cheer showered upon us.

    This family is connected with the Reverend Mr. McDonald's family in Essex, i.e. Mr. Penn's wife is a sister of Mr. McDonald who lives near Mrs. Ray's Bloomfield. The family is also connected with Mr. Staples' family who married Miss Caroline Harris DeJearnett of Caroline County, the sister of Honorable DeJarnett who acquaintance I formed years ago when a child at Dewsville and renewed again at Bettie Dew's marriage in 1863 at Uncle Frank Dew's. She also claims acquaintance with you and Aubrey and has made many enquiries about my darling Laura, which of course endears her much to me.

Mr. Penn lives in considerable style and affluence and entertains us with the most generous and engaging hospitality. We will remain here until Friday morning, when we will commence our journey to our last, but own station, i.e. Carroll Court House, forty miles distant, thence to Liberty, Bedford County, where we are due on the 20th and whence I shall start home on the 22nd, "ultimo."

Patrick County is composed almost entirely of mountains and gorges, contains 8,000 inhabitants (and 1700 to 2000 slaves). The county seat, i.e. Taylorsville, whence I write, is a small crossroads village of some dozen or more houses. The courthouse and jail are situated on a small gradually sloping knoll on all sides and completely encompassed by overbearing mountain peaks, which stand out in bold relief like high Cyclopian Towers over shadowing, as it were, the very heart of the village, seeming so near that one is almost inclined instinctively to reach out his hand to touch them. The soil is adapted chiefly to the growth of tobacco, though now all the lands are cultivated in corn and wheat to raise supplies for the Government and Army. There is one strange anomaly to be found in the District altogether astounding to me and quite disappointing, that is that notwithstanding its complete isolation, exemption from all occupation by the Army or our troops, still it seems quite as much or more in need of necessary supplies as our dear and down trodden First Virginia District.

I come now, my dearest Darling, to speak of home and its sacred associations. Can you believe me, that I have not heard from you since your letter of 26th of April? I was sorely disappointed in not hearing from you by early mail here on Monday morning, but fondly hope and pray for glad tidings from you on Thursday next. You can not imagine, dearest Laura, how apprehensive I am about you and our treasurers. I am undergoing, when not otherwise directed, almost daily torment of trembling suspense in regard to your situation, dependent as it is for the fate of the coming or perhaps the actually engaging battle between Lee and Grant. I am so much afraid of our being cut off or separated by Lee's failing back to Richmond. God grant it may never be! I can not advise you at this distance, save to say you must be on the alert. Watch out and try and save all you can from the Yankee clutches and do not, for Heaven's sake, allow them permanently to separate us, for believe me dearest Laura life is vain and but an empty void without thee and our darling little cherubs. May Heaven bless, protect and bring us all together once more in happy reunion, is my wish by day, prayer by night and dream in sleep.

Do not allow them to get my two riding horses and should there be any danger of their being permanently cut off from me, you had better send them over to Richmond and get J. Taliaferro at the Ballard House to telegraph to me at Liberty, Virginia, where I shall be by the 20th inst., informing me of their arrival in Richmond, so that I may hasten to make arrangements for bringing them up to Danville at once, where they will be fed and cared for at public expense, as will appear from the certificate forwarded to you in my last letter from Henry Court House written by Dr. Ficklen. I would advise you to have a sort of weekly inspection of all the horses at least once a week by having them brought into the yard for your personal observation. So that you may see whether or not they are attended to, etc. Of course the colt and my riding horse are turned on the marsh by this time. If not, they should be; so as to save all the corn and fodder possible. How comes on the supply of corn in our barn? I hope we will have enough to last. How many hogs have you and how many sheep or lambs, and calves?

  Have you been annoyed by the enrolling of free negroes in the First District? I hope not. If you have, I herewith enclose the accompanying certificate, to save you of all further trouble, and which certificate will save Jesse and Philip from all interruption in my business. What has become of Water and Aubrey?

  When will the strawberries be ripe? How is the ice keeping in both houses? How are the farm and garden operations progressing? How comes on our fish supply? What of the Loyalty of our servants and also of Miss F.

  Be sure to look out for me about 21 or 22nd May. If the Yanks are in my way in the regular route, I shall certainly come through in some way, by New Town or otherwise. Now if there are no Yanks in King William or New Kent, be sure to send over for me on the 24th ulto. either in buggy or horseback as may be most convenient to Tunstalls Depot. An in case I can not come that route safely, suppose you meet me in Miller's on 23rd ulto. en route to Forest Hill to the wedding. But his only in case it is not safe to come or send me to the York River Railroad, of which you can better judge at the time.

  Now then, be sure to write exactly what you intend doing, by return mail without fail and direct your letter to me at Richmond, care of Mr. J. C. Taliaferro, Ballard House, so that I may shape my conduct according to the import of your letter. Don't forget to bring my wedding vest to Forest Hill for the wedding occasion, my white silk vest. Now then, don't fail to come over to Forest Hill on the 23rd evening, i.e. on Monday evening so that Jesse may come for me at Tunstalls Station on Tuesday morning by 10 or 11 o'clock, i.e. if there are no Yanks in the way. Just go according to directions in my last letter to you from Henry Court House.

  Do you know "mother" that I am intensely curious to know whether you are making any progress towards introducing me to young

Mr. "John Paul Jones G." In your letter to me, in answer to this, which you must write at once, and direct to Richmond, care of Mr. John Taliaferro, Ballard House, let me know what you want me to bring you from Richmond and also say what way you are going to send for me; whether in buggy or on horse.

    Now farewell my dearest darling and little cherubs,
    Very fondly and devotedly your loving husband
        H. Gresham

Camp near Waynesboro, Virginia, June 10, 1864
Father and Mother,

    I am well as to health, but am very sorry to tell you that I am alone. My Dear Beloved Brother Daniel was killed dead in the fight last Sunday near Staunton, Virginia. He was shot through the head with a Minnie ball. It is a hard thing to write of my brother… but I think he died in a righteous cause and I am only to hope to meet him a shining in realm of victory and glory.

    Mother, do not grieve for him for I hope he is gone to a world of peace and happiness…I would rather go like Daniel went than James. We are expecting a fight every day. We have lost good men from our regiment this spring. Nothing more.

        Your sons,
        Joseph Cox, A. Cox
        36th Virginia Infantry Regiment.

July 10, 1864
Dear Friend,

    I take my pen in hand to let you know that I am well hoping when this reaches you it will find you well. I want to have my age proved that I han't been laying out none. Write to me whether you…your corn or not and how you are getting along. Write how brother is getting along with his corn and whether he is hired anybody or not. I am in the guardhouse instructing…in the care of Major Dorman.

        Tirea Bowman

Chester Station, July 20, 1864
Dear Dow (Lorenzo Dowell Gilbert),

    I received a copy of the extension of your furlough, which expired about the 15th of June. I approved it and it went back I supposed to the board and you have been absent without leave ever since you furlough expired. It is now the 20th of July. I have not reported you absent without leave yet but I shall have it to do if you do not have your furlough legally extended. I do not want to report you absent without leave nor none of the balance of the boys. Neither do I intend to if I can get over it but in obedience to an order issued a short time since I will be bound to report you and all of the balance of the company absent without leave unless you have your furlough legally extended. I will put it off as long as I can. Captain Barrow is commanding the Regiment and he is a perfect a tyrant as Colonel Moury. There is no such thing as pleasing him. He is a very nice man and a particular friend of mine but he tries to do things up to Gunter. He wants every man reported absent without leave if he has been absent more than 24 hours. Tell Henry Haley and the balance of the boys who are not able for duty to try and have their furlough extended. If you were reported absent without leave for a short time I could keep you from being punished but you would loose you wages for the time. Dow give them galls all of my kindest regards. I have been sick for some time. I am at the Division Hospital now but I am going to the Regiment in a few days. I suppose you have heard that Bryant was killed. He was killed on the 18th of June in a skirmish. Dow tell John Fed's wife I received her letter a few days ago. I will answer it in a few days. I received a letter from Pen's wife a few days age. She wanted to know where he was. Let her know if you have a chance he is dead. Dow give my father's family my love and all my friends if I have any. Dow do the best you can. Give Cal and Jack Wiggington my respects. Tell Cal to write to me. Give Sam Fed's family my respects and all of the balance of the dear Gilberts.

July 24, 1864
  Dow I have been working to see if I could get over reporting you absent without leave and I find that I will be obliged to do it unless you have your furlough legally extended. I suppose Cal has gotten worse. Tell Haley he will have to do the same and all the balance whose furlough have expired. Dow write to me and give me all the news. Tell Mrs. Dalton's family that Willis is well. Conrad Plaster is here sick. Bill King has been but he has gone back to the Regiment. Dow give Pat and Taylor my love and tell them to try and keep out of this war if they can. Give Pete Cassell and Nancy my best respects. Tell Pete I wrote to him a short time after I got back to the Regiment and I have received no answer as yet. Tell him dam him to write to me. I will close as it is getting so dark I cant see what I am doing. Dow write as soon as you get this and give me all of the counts.
  P.S. Dow I would have sent you a description before now but the Company papers are all the Brigade and I have not seen them in time.
      Your Friend Flint (Henry C. Aistrop)
      Company I, 24th Virginia Infantry

Camp Near Winchester, Virginia, July 23, 1864
Brother David,

Through the kind mercies of God, I am once more permitted to write a few lines. I received a letter from you and father today dated the third instance. I was glad to hear from you once more. I saw from the way you wrote that you had not heard that Brother Daniel was dead. Poor Brother was killed dead in battle at New Hope. I wrote to you about the thirteenth of June is the last chance I have had till now. We have been on march and fighting ever since I left home. We have been all through Maryland. We was in sight of Washington City. We fought nearly every day on our march and whipped the Yankees badly all the time. We brought out a great many horses and cattle and all other kind of government property. We made the greatest raid that ever had been made and now have to take up a line of march again to follow the Yankees.

I suppose we fought a heavy battle yesterday, killed and taken a great many Yankees…Poor Richard Nolen was very badly wounded. I fear he will never get well though I hope he will. He is shot through the thigh close t his body. Since I commenced this letter we have started on after the Yankees again. We are close to the Maryland line again. Send Father this letter or write to him. I know they want to hear I have not a chance to write anymore at present. Write soon. Direct to A. Cox Company C, 36th Virginia Volunteers, Smith's Brigade, Breckinridge Corps. Tell Richard Nolen's fold about him. He was wounded on the twenty-fourth of July. He is in the Valley at New Town.

        A. Cox
        D. R. Cox
        36th Virginia Infantry

Camp Near Charleston, Virginia, August 23, 1864
Dear Tinnie,

As I have an opportunity this evening, I will write to you. Have but little news to write. The 17th of this month our Division was engaged at Winchester and between sunset and dark. Our line moved forward drove in their line of skirmishers and came to their regular line of battle, which broke in great confusion. The next thing was the fort of the heights close to Winchester. We pushed forward to get the Battery that had been playing on us all the time and was all that did any harm but when we got to the Fort they had left carrying their Artillery with them. We had one man killed and five wounded. Charlie Smith was killed. John Pendleton, Buddy Rorer, Jonathon Brammer, David F. Hall and private William T. Akers was wounded and left at Winchester besides good many others stunned and bruised. Budy Rorer is the only one dangerously wounded. He had arm broke and wounded in the thigh severely but not broken. Pendleton flesh wound in shoulder. Brammer shoulder and leg. Akers in heel. There was not very many men killed out of the Division, but good many wounded. We captured good many prisoners. After we got possession of the fort it got so dark we had had to halt for the night lay in line of battle until morning. The Yankees all left during the night. Since we have drove them to Harper's Ferry. Have had some skirmishing nearly every day. We have been moving backwards and forwards up and down the valley ever since we came from Maryland and are getting very tired of traveling one road so much. We stayed several days at Fisher's Hill and expected a fight every day while there was an order for furloughing one for every fifty men and any person that furnished a recruit before the first of May. I sent in one for thirty days. We only get one from this Company. They were sent in the 10th of this month and we have heard nothing from them yet so I suppose we will not get them.

You wanted to know if I knew anything of Creed Conner. I saw him while we were at Winchester. Belongs to Dobbins Co. He says he came very near being captured at Mayfield at the time that McCauslin was surprised. His horse got shot and he lost him. George Conner is with us and is well. The company is generally in good health. We are faring tolerable well. Have had good deal of rain for the last few days…of Longstreets Corps is now with this command. I do not think we will stay in this country very long. I have not heard from home since Lieutenant Akers came up. We drew four months wages few days ago. I heard a few days ago that Uncle Lee was at home by this time. Buck looks very well and stands the service very well. Wharton is commanding our Division and Breckinridge the Corps. Forsberg commanding the Brigade. We all like Breckenridge very much. Much better than we do Early. This is a very plentiful country, but the army will soon strip the country if they stay here long. The Yankee Army in this country is reported to be 4000 strong and are well equipped but is seems they will not stand a charge. The Yankee papers say that the Kernstown fight was the most shameful thing on the part of the Yankees that has ever been known. We captured some of the finest guns at Winchester that I have ever seen. Some of them shoot thirty six times. I understand Cain Harbour has had his leg shot off. Lem Joice was at our camp few days ago. Our regiment is holding up very well. It is the largest regiment in this Army. I think corn will be very good in this country and there would be good corps if the armies did not destroy it but it is just now…good roasting ear and I tell you that eat and destroy a sight. Charlie Smith was killed with a shell and the same shell killed and wounded some fourteen or fifteen men. I got a good pistol in the Kernstown fight, but could not get the chance to send it home and I sold it. I have not heard from Thomasville since I left Southwest nor have heard nothing from Uncle Abe Fosters. Only what you wrote. I do not know whether I will have a chance to send this letter or not. Our mail is very uncertain. I have not received a letter by mail for several months. I have written home nearly every week since we came from Maryland. I will close my sheet is full. Tell Pattie she must write to me.

I remain truly your brother
Charles F. Ross
Company D,
51st Virginia Infantry

Mercer County, Virginia, September 23, 1864
Dear Brother (Abner Cox, 36th Virginia Infantry Regiment),

    I have wrote this makes five letters to you and had no answer. I have nothing interesting to write. My health is better than common. I am trying to sit a little. I want you to write. I have heard for the last month you was dead. The deserters are very numerous yet Whitlock and our Dave has gone to Yanks. I want you to write to Father's folks for me. I have not heard from them since you left. I want you to try to come and see me this winter. Brother Louis is well and laying in the brook.

    I want you to write to me what Brandy must sell at. If Brother David is alive write to him to come and see me. I think I will make grain plenty to do me. Crops is great in Mercer. The hogs is all dead though and there is a great… You must excuse my scattering lines for the boys is in a hurry to start. I hope God may shield you from the flying bullets and roaring cannon for ever God Bless you, dear Brother.
    W. Cox

Waynesboro, Virginia, September 29, 1864
Dear Tinnie,

    I got to the Company last Sunday. Found them at Brown's Gap about 20 miles below Staunton…they had been falling back and fighting…. the 19th they fought…. and the yanks were two…. forth and they fell back to Fisher's Hill then the Yanks flanked…. stampeded them. In the fight… Winchester Company D lost 30 men. I will send you a list of them. When they left Fisher's Hill…was on the right…had to take the mountains…. good many of them has not come up get. Bucky is missing…him and Lum Rakes was together last time they were seen. Sam Akers left them in the mountains. The stragglers are still coming in and they say that good many has gone on across to Charlottesville and I think Buck and Lum will be up in a few days. Clabe Akers says he heard from them and they were on the other side of the mountain if so they are safe. The Yankees are reported at Staunton. We got to this place yesterday. Will Woolwine is Captain…. Akers…we have about thirty men in the Company, only half of them fit for duty there is none of my mess left. G. W. Conner and John Washburn was both captured at Winchester. I am camping with David Washington and Samuel Critz. I. M. Akers and Sam came out safe. They think Nat was mortally wounded in the hands of the enemy was shot through. I will close and write to you as soon as I hear from Bucky. Write soon to your brother.

Charles F. Ross
Company D, 51st Virginia Infantry

Camp near Druses, Virginia, October 4, 1864
Dear Mother (Martha J. Potter Gilbert),
    I this eve with great pleasure seat myself this evening to write you a few lines to let you know that I am tolerable well and I truly hope these few lines may find you all well. Mother, I have got some good news to write this time. All of our Battalion is moved from here, but our Company and Captain Perkin's Company from Henry. We will have to go to town and go into winter guard and it is supposed that we will be held as Provost Guard. We will go to our barracks at town. They say that we will get furloughs then. If you all are not to busy I would like for you to continue to send and or bring me some things like fruit and a broom and some potholders and coffee. Tell Pa if Mr. Stovall come that he must let Ab come with him or anybody else that come for I can show him some very great curiosities and tell Uncle Dow that he must come down too. You all must write. I don't get half letters enough. You must all turn out to writing. I must close.

                    I remain yours,
                    William P. Gilbert
                    Company I,
                    5th Battalion Virginia Reserves

Mount Sidney, Augusta County, Virginia, October 6, 1864
Brother David,
    I have just received your letter dated the thirteenth of September. Was glad to hear that you got home. I wrote several letters to you since you left here. It seems to take a letter a long time to go on home. Brother David, we are expecting a big fight every day. Our noble cause in which we are engaged is my shield that I wave in all battles and fortunately is standing ready and willing for the next battle. Any day it may come. David, attend to all our affairs the moment you can. I think the end of this war is coming near. I hope I will live to see it come so that I may meet you all again…I am very uneasy, but poor little Charlie you must write often as possible. Here is a letter from Brother Wellington. Read it and send it to father's folks. He requested me to write to them for him. I think we will come to the west this winter. Nothing more. Write soon and after.

                    Your brothers
                    A. Cox, D. R. Cox
                    36th Virginia Infantry Regiment

Patrick Courthouse, October 14, 1864
My dear Sir,
  In reply to your letter of the 4th inst., which I received nearly a week after its date, I regret to have to inform you that after diligent inquiry throughout this county, I can hear of no detailed man who has one bushel of wheat to dispose of. All the surplus grain in the region of the county has been absorbed by the Confederate Government, the wives and widows of soldiers and by the order of the county court. The quantity of wheat refereed to in your letter can easily be purchased (I presume) but for not less than $50 per bushel.
  In answer to your inquiry if there is a small house and lot in this village to rent. I will inform you that there are two tolerably comfortable houses with a lot to each which can be rented for the next year. I am not informed as to the price but if you desire it I can easily obtain the necessary information and write you.
  I have a comfortable dwelling house with a kitchen, smoke house and garden attached which I have partially engaged to occurrence will probably render the gentleman's occupancy of that house impractable. If this be true you can have the use of it upon very moderate terms. The house contains three comfortable rooms with two passages and is quite a neat one. The enclosure around the house is by no means a very good one. Sufficient however with very trifling repairs to keep out stock. The garden is in good condition.
  If not rented soon as indicated above, you have the house and lot for the rent year or longer if you desire it at $200. This sum will hardly pay the terms, however, in Confederate money.
  This leaves us well. Since your visit to this place Mrs. Staples has been blessed with a daughter, now one month old. She being the only daughter in the family, is regarded as being perfect in every respect.
  We would be pleased to receive a visit from you and Mrs. Grehsam whenever it will suit your pleasure to pay us one. Mrs. Staples joins me in kind regards to yourself and family.
            Very truly your friend,
            Samuel G. Staples

Near Petersburg, Virginia, October 21, 1864
Dear Friend,
  I take my pen in hand to let you know that I am well hoping that these few lines may find you well. I received you kind letter dated 12th and was glad to hear that you was well. I was very sorry to hear that the frost had bit the corn, but I hope it taint hurt as bad as you think. I was glad to hear from Jehu and James and to hear that they was well. I was glad to hear from Thomas Barnard. You wrote that he was at Ohio at Camp Chase. I han't much news to write to you at this time. Times is

still hard at this time…will remain…this war ends if…any end to it. I…to see you and talk with you. I hope it won't be too long till I can come home to see you again. I think this war will soon end. We get plenty to eat at the present time. Tell the girls that I am alive yet and hope to come home to hug them once more. Tell them that I han't forgot them yet and I hope they han't forgot me yet tell them that…die in my heart. I think of you study. I hain't forgot you yet and I hope you will not forget me…will satisfied her…So well as if I was at home with the girls. I will close by asking you to write me as soon as you get this letter and give me all the news that you have. So farewell until I hear from you remain your dear friend until death. I would like to know what has become of Isham and Richard. So no more at present.

       Tirea Bowman

Montgomery County, Virginia, October 31, 1864
Brother David (David R. Cox),

  I am now in Blacksburg with a captured Negro. The deserters aimed to release him from me, but they failed. I have nothing interesting to write. I want you to come out and see me as soon as you can. I want you to write to me when you heard from Brother Abner. I started you a letter three weeks ago. Brother James is well. He thinks hard of you all for not writing to him. I have to go to Princeton to get license for Jack Bolen (Bowling) and Celina Pence. Ceily Meadows is married and gone to the Yankees. God give my respects to Rusty and George Thomas. God Bless you. I did not tell you where the deserters were. They were at Newport in Giles County.

       W. Cox.
       36th Virginia Infantry

Camp 10th Virginia Cavalry, November 9, 1864
My Dear Sister,

  When we parted I expected to get back home in two weeks, but after getting to Camp Lee I found than an order had been published that no man would be permitted to join the cavalry unless recommended by the medical board. I stayed there until I got tired of the place. Thomas was transferred from field service and recommended for cavalry will come to this regiment. Brother George was transferred for light duty, his detail papers renewed. You have heard of poor Willie's case. He was sent to Infantry 24 Regiment. I received a letter from him yesterday. He wrote that the had been tolerable well ever since he has been in the army, but I fear that he will not be able to stand it this winter and I fear that Thomas Green will have another spell of sore throat if he has such a spell as he has every winter. I fear he will not be able to stand it, but the officers are more indulgent in the cavalry than they are in Infantry and in cases like his they are sent to the country. I hope to be able to get Willie in this regiment by hiring some man to take his place in Infantry, but I believe that Ma can go to Richmond and with the aid of Goode and Staples can get him off and I shall advise her to try it. I have not received a word from home since I left as no one near where I went to. Well I must tell you about my escape from Camp I found that I was bound for the service so I went to the Passport to get a pass and how do you reckon I got passed myself off for a porter got my pass made my way to this regiment with a friend. This Burgess Mr. Hairston knows him. He sends his respects to Mr. _____. He would run the risk of a court martial for too such looking men so we are. Caskie is our Colonel. I met with him in Richmond once he knew me as soon as he saw me. He is very strict, but I think a nice man come among us and talk to us as if we were all on an expreslity. Halley is our Captain. I am in the same company with George Dillard Wooton Schofield another. I have no horse but expect to get a start in a few days to go home as I have no fighting to do until I get one. They will give me 20 or 25 days to go after my horse and the Colonel has promised to disband the Company for three months this winter as it was in all last winter and the balance of the regiment was disbanded consequently.

     I don't expect to be in the service all the winter. I am better satisfied than you would think. I could be in the army and intend doing my duty if I am treated right. We are getting good rations of flour, beef or bacon, peas, rice, pure coffee and sometimes sugar…long potatoes, sweet turnips and… Mr. Mays has joined this regiment is in the company with Jimmy, Sam Martin are in Rassus old company has been sick several days but is better. I was over a part of the ground that the last fight was fought on that Grant pretended was a small affair after there is a one doubt but he intended to get to the Southside Railroad for all the prisoners said that the order was to take it at all hazards.

                                                 Joseph G. Penn

Camp near Petersburg, Virginia, November 15, 1864
Dear Friend,
     I seat myself to let you know that I am well and hearty and truly hope that when these few lines come to hand they may find you well and hearty. I hain't no news worth writing to you about at this time. I would like to see you and talk with you. We have very good times here at this time. We have nothing to do only go and guard every third day. Times is hard down here and likely remain, so I hope this war will soon come to a close so all the soldiers can return home once more. I am getting tired of this war and I don't think I am the only one neither. I thin they are all tired of it now. We don't get more than half enough to eat. I han't got no money and I would be glad if you would send me some in a letter if you

please. I will close write soon. Excuse my short letter. I will try to write more next time.

  A few lines to brother to let him know that I am well truly hoping when these few lines come to hand they might find you well and hearty. I would like to see you and talk with you. I han't no news worth writing to you at this time. I hope you will have Sam Mayes to write to me. I want to get a furlough this winter to come home to see you if I can. Write soon.

Tirea Bowman

Camp Rockingham County, Virginia, Army of the Valley,
November 18, 1864
Brother David,

  I read your letter this morning…I was very glad to hear from you. I have no news of interest to write. I am well and living well as could be expected. I have plenty to eat of the best pork and beef, cornbread and wheat bread. Me and Jim Crawford killed a hog the other day that would weigh 200 pounds. It is plenty of meat to do our mess a good while. We have not drew any money yet money is very scarce with us so is tobacco…and brandy is scarce with us. We hope it will not be so long.

  Brother, I am very sorry to hear of Father's being drunk. Every time I hear from him though I cannot help what he does. He never writes to me at all. I suppose he can't take time from drinking.

  Brother, we are about six miles above New Market in camps. I don't know how long we will be here. We have drawn some clothing lately, but not much. Brother, you must do the best you can with all our things till I come home. I think I will get to come home before long. I cannot tell you anything to do. Tell or see about some…. Do the best you can is all I can tell you.

  Abraham is reelected President and has called a million more men to crush the rebellion

Your Brothers
A. Cox, D. R. Cox
36th Virginia Infantry

Camp Near New Market, Rockingham County, Virginia,
November 26, 1864
Dear Milly (Milly A. Turner),

  I enclose this happy…which will inform you that I am well truly hoping those few lines may reach you and find you well. I have no muse to write this time when you write next time you must write how much corn you got and how much meat you will have and whether Fanny gives milk… I am afraid you wont have enough to eat next year times is hard when rations is short our wagons have been gone seven days after food for the horses and hasn't got back yet. We haven't had but one feed for horses in four days and the grass is all killed with cold. I don't think we will stay when long before we will move up to Staunton that is fifty miles west from where it is thought we will take winter quarters near Staunton. I don't know whether we can winter there or not. I think this Confederacy is gone up dead. The quicker the better for us. I think this is the third year of the war. The years ordinarily… away like summer clouds. But when burden with storms of war the days have a weary length and while it has been needlessly long it is still short not half the period of our fore fathers struggle for independence. Many hearts now buoyant with hope and containing bright with joyous anticipation will have cause to beat and have fanned away forever from the scene of mounted action. If the new born year shall him run it's cover. Many hearts will have been made devotion by hopes and disappointed expectations. Many fair forms now will be stumbling among the pier… of the dead… Milly, the weather is very cold where the snow is on the ground that fell last Tuesday night and the rain is falling where now and is very cold and disagreeable. I fell for you and Susan today. I don't now how you are to make out this winter you must write how you make out for wood and whether you can get any hold or not. I will close for this time. I remain your friend, Martin A. Ratliff

Camp near Chester Station, December 12, 1864
My Dear Sister,
    I have been prevented from answering your much esteemed letter for several days on account of the irregularity of our mails caused by the impressments of the cars to convey troops from the Valley to Richmond, Petersburg and other places along our lines to be ready for the big fight which has been expected to come off for a week or two.
    You cannot well imagine the pleasure that it affords me in reading letters written by the hands of those I love so dearly as I do each member of our dear family and if I do not write as often as you think I ought to you must not conclude it is for the lack of the will, but time and opportunity. Our duties are so hard now that I cannot write near so often as I desire. We have to go on picket every third evening and remain a day and night besides drilling and doing other duties about camp when we are not on picket. I was on picket last Friday night and it was snowing, raining, and sleeting all night and a greater part of the next day and I heard a good many of the old soldiers say that they never had experienced a more disagreeable time in their lives. I suffered a very little though with cold as we had a large log fire at our post all of the time. My health still continues tolerable good and have suffered but very little indeed with my eyes since I have been in the army.

Thomas Green got to his command I think the last day of last month and was in a right severe cavalry engagement the next day. After he arrived in which two members of his company were wounded. Young Mays was one of them. He was wounded about two inches above his old wound fracturing the same bone that was broken before. He was sent to Richmond and expected to go from there to Ma's to stay until he gets able to go to his fathers in Alabama.

I have understood that there has been some very hard fighting for the last but three or four days down below Petersburg in which the 10th Cavalry lost I have understood some eight or ten men killed. I saw two men yesterday just from the 10th Cavalry. They told me that Brother had gone home after his horse and that Thomas Green had a very bad boil in his wrist and was not in the fight, which occurred last Wednesday night.

I received a letter from him two or three days ago written the 6th of the month in which he said that he was not well with the exception of a boil on his wrist. I also received one from Ma written on the third. All were tolerable well when she wrote.

We have had some right brisk picket firing in our front for the last two or three weeks. I have been on picket two or three times when firing was going on and fired myself three or four times, but don't know whether I done any execution or not. Several balls passed very near me, but did not strike any person. One man has been wounded very badly in our regiment in the last few weeks and several killed and wounded in the brigade. Our men killed some of the Yankees (Negroes) but it is not known how many. The Negroes have been removed from our front through now and then is no firing kept up between our pickets and the Yankee picket on our line.

Captain Barrow requested me to give you all his best respects, and to tell Mr. Hairston he wishes this war would end soon so he could go to see him that he knows he would have a fine time of it. As it is time for the mail to be in for our letters, I must close or I may be late to mail my letter. You must tell Mr. H. that I have not received his letter yet. Give my best love to him and each member of your dear little family and expect the same for yourself. You must all write often.

     Your ever devoted Brother,
     William A. Penn

Patrick County, Virginia, December 26, 1864
My Dear Son, (T. S. Penn, Yadkin River)

I will only write a few lines. I wrote last Monday. We are all well. All our friends got a letter from Elizabeth. All well there. George is here, Joseph gone to a ____ at Harrison Floyds. Jimmy and Lucinda and a good many others I suppose all will be here Wednesday. I mean Joseph and Jimmy's families. It is a displeasing Christmas to me as you and

Thomas Green are in the army and all the time exposed in ___ very ___. I heard news reach your regiment were ordered to Georgia. Oh, it seems a long ways from home so very easy to get anything to you. I fear you will never get your box and so great loss you overcoat and shirts and many other valuable things, but we can't help it. I will try and have more made as soon as I can. Let me know what you need and I will try to and get them to you. George is here, came day before yesterday, is quite straight and pleasant. No news storming. Joseph's horses has the scratches badly and he is gone to try and get Ridgeway to give him protection in a few days longer. He went to Carter on Wednesday after Monday and Ridgeway not give him protection he will have to go on. I hope he will. Oh, how I shall miss him as I do you and poor Thomas Green. I here fear you have both suffered awfully this dreadful cold weather enough it seems to hold both of you and will rest the nearly Thomas Green you are both safe. I have not got any letter either yesterday and the papers did not come either. Can't see what is the matter. Zentmeyer got a letter from Richmond and the papers did not come. I heard the enemies expected to make a raid on the Danville and Richmond Railroad. No one here this Christmas. Oh, I am always uneasy about you and dear Thomas Green. I shall send my petition down to Richmond to get your officers to endorse it as soon as Waller Staples goes to Richmond and this is about the 10th of next month. I think Congress meets about the 10th. It seems a long time to be kept in surprise. I hope and pray your officers may let you off by endorsing favorably. Though it is all wrapped in uncertainty but I must hope and pray it may be granted your release. Try and be patient and resigned under all circumstances. I will do all I can to get you off. You had better both to your officer and regiment and get them prepared for the petition. I have it reaches you. Edwin and Pet at home. Edwin has a bad rising on his face and both had sore throat before they left. I am… for the mail… so God bless you my dear child. May you be kept in safety in the constant and sincere prayer of your

        Write soon, Mother
        Mary C. Penn

Camp near Belfield, Virginia, January 1, 1865
My Dear Sister,
  The weather during the latter days of the "old year" was disagreeable and this New Years morning. The sun rose bright and beautiful. The reflection of it's rays from the sun which fell on yesterday producing a painful effect upon the eyes for a moment after stepping from our law dark little shantys. May this happy change in the weather and this bright greeting of the New Year's morning be obvious of a brighter day in the early future of our country's cause. I consider that

there has been no darker period since the commencement of the war than at present. I am not yet discouraged about our ultimately gaining our independence but my vices have made a change of late as to the effect the war is to have on the institution of slavery. I adhere to the opinion that I have for a long time entertained that the war is to continue for years to come, but do not believe that we can ever become so exhausted as to be held by the enemy as a conquered province. But I do believe that before it ends almost every foot or our territory will be over run by the enemy and that slavery will cease to be our institution with us and that all who desire freedom and many who do not will be liberated of have it in their power to be. I think it an unsafe business for those whose property now consisted mainly in slaves to depend upon holding them, but believe it would be a better policy to turn at least a portion into safer capital. It is useless to say that any portion of our country is safe from the savages of the enemy. Had we been told in the commencement of the war that the enemy could yet possess of the whole Mississippi Valley and march with a ground army through Tennessee and Georgia to Savannah without forcing us into submission, we would have thought it impossible but I believe that before we have peace the enemy must learn that though Richmond, Charleston, Wilmington and all other important towns fall into their hands and almost every foot of territory be trampled over by their armies we will not even then be conquered. My firm conviction is that all this be effected before we have peace.

Before another new year's day there will be many another blood stained battlefield and many who are now enjoying perfect health, buoyant and cheerful in spirit must gasp his last breath upon the cold ground many demand even a burial this thought was forcibly presented to my mind as he came on to this place. Saw a dead Yankee lying near the road stripped of every rag of clothes and a portion of his body enter up. After passing many places where large comfortable dwellings had been burned to the ground during the recent raid upon Belfield and seeing the destruction to property of every description on their route. I was wicked enough to whisper to myself what many spoke audibly. There is one side which who has met his just doom, but after short reflection my feelings change. I thought that in all probability that man had a mother, a wife, sisters, brothers and now revolting the thought of ones own dear relatives having to share such a fate and we know not how soon it may be the case thought with us it would be a consoling thought that they die in a just cause.

I reached the command on the 30th November. Next day the enemy burned Stoney Creek Station on the Weldon Railroad and the 10th Regiment was ordered out to meet them. I borrowed the necessary accoutrements and went with my company. We met the enemy about 10 o'clock.

The squadron to which I belonged was ordered forward. The squadron consists of two companies and the order soon give to charge the enemy who appeared about a regiment strong in our front. The captain discovered that the road or lane was so blockaded with sails that a charge would be impracticable ordered us to deploy on the right in a field as skirmishing which orders was promptly executed and we immediately engaged the enemy who returned the fire briskly and kept their ground till a small party of us dashed around upon their right to interrupt their retreat when they broke in full retreat but after passing us made a feeble stand in a thicket of pines. It was here that young Mays was wounded which you have doubtfully heard of this. He is a brave boy and was very popular nearly every man in the regiment knew him.

As I have digressed thus far from my descriptions of the battle I will add that Mays was wounded about three inches above his old wound the ball passing through and fracturing the same bone which was before broken. He started next morning for Richmond and was sent to the Chimborazo Hospital where he remained till the 24th instance when he wrote to Abe that he had a sixty days furlough and expected to start next day to Patrick. He will make his home at Ma's. He said he was just able to hobble about a little on crutches. I have no thought he will ever be able again for field service.

To return to my description of the fight we charged the enemy and drove them through the pines for over half a mile to the railroad when there was a very extensive steam mill on fire. The burning mill right upon the road and a deep cut in the railroad prevented our charging them at this point. So, after fighting them for some time across the road we formed a skirmish line again and advanced upon the driving them from their position. We then crossed the road and dashed forward through a field to a piece of wood where they had blockaded the road and made another stand. We made no halt, but charged upon their works when they broke and ran at full speed to a swamp where they again made a halt for a few moments but as soon as we formed and command advancing upon them they fell back again. This maneuver of fighting continued till we had driven them about six miles when night prevented a further pursuit. We only lost eight men wounded whilst the enemy left six dead upon the field and the citizens report that their ambulances were filled with wounded. They destroyed the depot and several other buildings besides a considerable quantity of forage at Stoney Creek. During their raid upon Belfield our regiment was not engaged. They burnt many houses destroyed about 28 or 30 miles of railroad and a vast amount of food stock and property of every description.

The enemy a few days since attempted a raid upon the Central Railroad at Gordonsville or Charlottesville and we were ordered off on the right of the 22nd to meet them, but when we got within seven miles of Petersburg we went into camp for the night and next morning received order to rest that day (the 24th) and start back the next to this place. The enemy having been foiled.

We were within thirteen miles of Willie's camp and I got permission to visit him. I found him enjoying his usual health but somewhat reddened in flesh. I took a Christmas breakfast with him. I must tell you what he had. We had an excellent eggnog before breakfast and turkey hash, fried cabbage, coffee and sugar, nice wheat bread and butter all well served up and we enjoyed it much. He told me that they had not been drawing enough to eat for several days but he had recovered a box from sister Sarah and two of his misfortunes had received boxes so they were faring well. I only had permission to stay on night and had to leave him next morning. It was a great trial for me to part with him. He seems like one alone there and is so anxious to be with Brother and I. If Ma fails to have him detailed to attend to her business we will try very hard to have him transferred.

Brother has not returned from home, but his furlough is about out and I will look for him in a few days. I took the liberty of opening your letter which came after he was gone. I do not suppose you felt at all slighted at the enemy's not paying your section a visit while passing through your state. I was much gratified when I learned that they had passed you by. We are tolerably comfortably quartered here most of the men have built log huts, but our provisions are rather rough. We get the poorest beef you ever saw, coarse corn, meal without sifting and coffee and sugar once in 8 or 10 days and flour occasionally. This section has been stripped of everything nearly by the Yankees and our men who are nearly as bad. So we can buy but little. The latest news I have from home is dated 19th. All men well. I have written most of my letter by firelight and while a crowd was around me talking. So you must excuse bad writing and mistakes.

I know you all will not give my letter a second reading if you get through it. Give much love to Mr. H and all the children and tell all to write often to me. I have so much writing to do that you must not expect me to be a punctual correspondent, but I will promise to write occasionally. Direct your letter to Company G, 10th Virginia Cavalry, Chambliss Brigade, W. H. F. Lee's Division, Army of Northern Virginia. All your acquaintances are well. Sam Martin is with his company and is well. Can't you send me a box of ground peas. They are worth $4 per quart here and sweet potatoes $25 per bushel.

          Ever your devoted brother,
          Thomas Green Penn

Camp Near Belfield, Virginia, January 4, 1865
My Dear Miss Addie,

We have last completed our quarters and began to feel quite at home. I have been busy building a stable for my horse since we finished our shanty and have now a dry and comfortable place for him. I am on guard today and while I am waiting for my turn I will devote a portion of the time to writing to you our monotonous life here affords but little in the way of now that would interest you. It would surprise you to see what a large town we have built. It covers many acres of ground and is laid off by streets with some pretensions of _____. The houses vary in size and structure as much as the building of very low. You have ever visited but unlike other towns you can form but little idea of the different classes of the inhabitants by the style in which they live; many of those who live in the most comfortable style at home occupy the smokiest and most ordinary looking huts here. While those who are laborers at home, and live in ordinary style have the neatest and most comfortable quarters here. Company G as the credit of occupying the neatest looking portion of the city and I believe we have for the most comfortable quarters of any other company of the regiment.

Our duties in camp are light besides having to get wood, cook, attend to our horses, etc. We have to go on picket in 12 or 13 days and will remain eight days. I dread the picket duty as we will be without shelter and there is no telling what kind of weather we may have.

I am very impatient to hear how you spent Christmas. I believe I will send you that little piece of poetry now as it has been a long time since I received a letter from you. I attribute the failure of letters to come to the negligence of officials in the mail routes as I believe you have been faithful to your promise and I have heard complaints from many of their failure to get letters since we have been so far from Petersburg.

Letters would probably come sooner directed to Belfield but we never know when we may move and it is best to direct to Petersburg or to the Army of Northern Virginia without designating any place. They will then be sure to reach us no matter where we go. I hope you had a merry time since Christmas. How many parties did you attend.

I received a letter from Ma dated the 26th she said there would be several parties in her neighborhood. Brother was fortunate in being put to so much trouble to get to cavalry. He accomplished all he desired in being assigned and after being kept for several weeks off duty, he got his furlough just in time to allow him to be at home Christmas and Ma wrote me that he expected to attend the parties that I alluded to. Fewer of our family were together at dear old Poplar Grove than ever before on Christmas. It has been the custom of our family to assemble together every Christmas on earth. It is a sad thought though this time that families when once so scattered as ours now is, rarely ever all meet together again. I am enjoying greatly good health and think I will stand the service right well. I am still of the opinion that the war is to last many years and the changes of the most robust and healthy who are now in the service to service it are few. There is at present no prospect of our being disbanded this winter and it will in all probability be next winter or possibly longer before I can go home. If any furloughs are granted they will be given to those who have been longest in service. I suppose it will be justice and I am willing to submit to it. How's your brother Edward standing the service.

  If he is still at Joel on I have no doubt he is faring as well as he would any other in the Confederacy. Our course rations are rather slim now but we do not suffer. If Ma lived nearer the railroad she could send us boxes of provisions, which would be very acceptable now. Brother is in time just our and so much more satisfactory to sending one from home than to receive letters. If you desire to be…I have read in a little testament. I have been getting on very slow. I can now average much more than a chapter a day and our duties are the same on Sabbath as other days. I am now reading Mark. You will get on Miss ____. It is a close…do…very disagreeable to be out on guard but I only have to it on very two hours at a time. I will have to go one in a few minutes and will close. Goodbye May God ever bless and direct you…

          Yours as ever,
          Thomas Green Penn

Near Chester Station, Camp of the 24th Virginia Infantry,
January 4, 1865
My Dear Ma,

  I received your letter written the 19th on yesterday. Was glad to learn that you were all well. I suppose the reason that your letter was so long on the road was that the clerks in the Post Office Department must have taking Christmas. I have been informed that they had been making just preparations for that event.

  Will I suppose you would like to hear something about our New Years dinner that you have seen an account of in the newspaper. My mess got some cold beef turkey ham… apple butter and I think there was a… of drink and probably a piece of… and of our Company got a piece of an apple… Well, I got about as much about eating at… but a great many of the soldiers were inclined to make fun of it. The division never came in until the second day of the month and as our… it. We never got ours until yesterday after we came off for better. It commenced snowing yesterday we and the ground is covered with snow morning about an inch and a half deep and a great many of the soldiers are having their own fun catching and shooting rabbits. There are a great many rabbits and birds about here. I never saw so many ____ in my life as there are about here. I have just looked out my door and counted fifteen soldiers after on rabbit. I think as a general thing they are large in this part of the country than they are in ours.

      The pencil points you sent me came safe. I wouldn't be surprised if the box you sent is in Danville yet. One of the new… Company had a box sent him some time ago and it staid in Danville about a month and Captain B's Negro boy found it there about tow or three weeks ago as he was on his way home and started it on and it came through safe it was on the road 46 days. It seems that there is but little risk in sending boxes if they can be gotten by that place. I am getting on very well with what clothing I have. I have been patching and dressing my sock and find that I can fix them up first rate better than I expected. Thomas Green was with me and was snowing stayed all night with me the night before. We had an eggnog together next morning and I had a very nice breakfast for him also that in to be fixed up in the army. Tell Sister I will try and write to him in two or three days… I have filled my half sheet and it is time for the mail to start out so I must close. Give my very best love to each member of our family. You must all write often.

      I got a plenty of paper here. You must use that of where that you will find in one of the drawers of the bureau in the big room upstairs.

                                   Your ever devoted son, William Penn

January 9, 1865
My Dear Brother,

      I have been disappointed in my calculations every week since you started in writing to you, by various hindrances and now am writing too hurried to give satisfaction. Mr. Zentmeyer is busy fixing off to Henry Court and it is freezing cold. We had not mail on yesterday and consequently I will have to send my letter of Mr. Zentmeyer to Henry Courthouse to be mailed. Ma received a letter from you, and one from dear Will on last Thursday, and they both afforded us all great pleasure and much relief from a painful anxiety. We always suffering about you dear brothers in the Army. You both gave such a touching account of your meeting Christmas eve. Your social engagement reflections about home and your parting. I shed many tears over those dear precious letters, and breathing a sincere prayer for the safety and preservation of my dear brothers. And oh, may Heaven grant us a speedy peace, and a happy relief from this terrible war. There seems to be a general impression that it can't last many months longer.

Sunday night, January 15

      I commenced writing this letter on last Monday to send to Henry Court House and the snow and rain commenced falling and turned so excessively cold. Mr. Zentmeyer declined going as we have had no mail since Spoll Read is acting very trifling. Ma was here this evening quite well and all our friends in the neighborhood are as well as usual. Your servants and Joe are doing pretty well also.

I hope dear Joe has reached you in safety before this Poor dear fellow had a rough time for his hovel and I fear he will suffer from it severely in some way. So let us hear from you all as often as possible, for it is a great source of relief and comfort.

I suppose Joe has told you of this if his little surprise party he played off on Ma Christmas his inventing a parcel of the girls and young gentlemen and Ma's nice little supper. Linda and I assisted her about. Oh my dear brother if you and dear Willie could only have been here but the vacuum you both left could not be filled by other guests, it made me fell so sad to miss those dear precious ones. May our Heavenly Father grant that we may all meet at that dear old home next Christmas render happy auspices.

Edwin and Peter came home a week before Christmas and are still at home. They will start back in a few days. Edwin has been suffering very much from a large boil and painful we were alarmed about it fearing it might make his knee stiff, but it is now entirely well. Edwin is much improved, and has grown considerably taller than his Pa. They are much pleased with the school but have Army fare.

Mr. Mays is at Ma's just returned from Brother Jackson spent nearly a week there and speaks of going to Mr. Pannills tomorrow in the buggy to spend several days; his leg is much improved can walk on it some. He says he will ever love you dearly for your kindness to him when he was wounded said a mother could not have been more watchful than you were, none more constant and faithful than you.

Dear Thomas Green,

Mother's eyes have given out and she has requested me to close this letter for her and say that all are well at Sarah Lucinda and Jackson Penn. Have heard nothing from Eliza for some time. My own health has been quite good of late but I have had enough to break me down. Now Mr. Andrews has left me and I feel that I have more on me than I can possibly attend to. Were it not for the very heavy expense of living I would close the store, but if I do that it will soon take all I am wroth to pay expenses.

I made another effort to have the district divided but Green refuses positively to do it. Colonel Gress had agreed to take the office in Henry. I suppose Martha has written you all the news of the neighborhood. We here are quite discouraged about the condition of affairs. I do hope some happy times may take place in affairs to end our troubles. Old Johnny Koger is quite ill of the flux. Your Ma joins us in best respects to Captain Kelley. Tell him we heard from his family

yesterday. They were well. We send this by Marion Koger which going to Henry Courthouse tomorrow.
Yours truly, J. N. Zentmeyer

Give our best love to Jo Edwin Peter. Join us in this Edwin would be much pleased to receive a letter from you. Tell Jo Martha will write to him soon. Lizzy a fine boy in doing well. Your little geranium is alive, green and flourishing and I enclosed a leaf from it to show you how well I have nursed it you and dispose of the leaf as you chose I can guess.   Author Unknown

Camp 10th Virginia Cavalry, Belfield, Virginia,
January 30, 1865
My Dear Sister,

It has been just fifteen days today since I returned to the regiment and I know you think I might have written before this but when you learn the reason I have been so long writing you will excuse me. The day after I returned we went on picket thirty five from this place, was out ten days on the out sick lines, part of the time we had rain, sleet and snow, but my health is pretty good and we are living well enough for soldiers. This morning we had for breakfast, cornbread, biscuits, fried ham, beef steak, pure coffee with sugar (not as good as Mrs. Bococks) and syrup. We drew it with Confederate money and besides Sarah sent Thomas Green and me a nice box a piece with just such articles as we were needing. The army rations are tolerable scant. I have Granville Stuart with me and think by letting him forage I can live pretty well. I am messing with George Hylton, John Burgess and John Coan. We are in winter quarters, have a log hut eight feet by ten with a chimney and covered with boards and over beds are fixed about a foot from the ground with boards in the place of feathers. Our camp is one mile north of Belfield on the Weldon Railroad. Thomas Green received your letter yesterday 17 and you have no idea how we were delighted to hear from you all and that you were all well and still undisturbed by the Yankees.

The army is very despondent in this State and the men are deserting daily while we were on picket line of this regiment. Went to the Yankees and if all going the spring that says they it will leave few of us to fight. While we were on picket we had orders to shoot any infantry men that tried to cross the creek that we were picketing on. Some say that they are willing to fight as long as a man is left but a large majority say that they can't see how they can stand another campaign. I do hope the authorities will do something by spring. It seems if they don't our army will be too small to meet the enemy. If none deserted but cowards it would be different but some are deserting that has been good soldiers ever since the war commenced. They get $50 in greenbacks a new suit of clothes and transportation to any place they wish to go to and if they take a horse with them they get $200 for it.

 I suppose some of them at home wrote to you about our Christmas. I never enjoyed myself more in my life. Everybody seem to forget the war and were determined to enjoy themselves in spite of Old Abe's War. The tables look like old times and after being in camp three months you may know it did me good to eat. Our division is under marching orders but I hope we will have to leave this place as we are so snugly fixed. Thomas Green is well and looks better than he did when he came here. Samuel Martins is well and requested me to give his regards to you and Mr. Hairston. I heard from Willie a few days since he was well. Ma has been rite sick since I left but when the last letter was written from home she was almost well. She had something like cholic. I hope by this she has entirely recovered.

          Thomas Green Penn

On picket at Monk Neck Bridge, Dinwiddie County, Virginia, February 16, 1865
My Dear Sister,
 I was sorry to learn through your letter of the 16th January that you had never received my letter written a few weeks after I reached the army but hope that it had reached you and satisfied you that I am not altogether deserving the good soldiering you gave me for not writing to you. I should have answered your letter before now but Brother wrote a few days after I received it and then the demonstration made upon the sight of our lines last Tuesday a week ago called us from our winter quarters at Belfield and we have been so constantly on the move since that I have had but little chance to write. I am writing now with a doubt in my mind whether my letter will ever reach you or not fearing that the enemy has before now cut off unit communication with Georgia, but I trust it is not the case. What our authorities can be thinking of to allow Sherman to march, unmolested where he pleases through Georgia and South Carolina I cannot image. It seems that we are feeling our deficiency in numbers of fighting men now more sensibly than ever to fore. This is truly a dark period with us and the great despondency of the people at home is very disheartening to the soldiers who are constantly receiving letters from their friends written in the most discouraging tone telling them that we are whipped and that it is useless for us to fight longer. I do not believe we will ever be subjugated, but this feeling will prolong the war a great while, I fear and if we are whipped it will be in account of the spirit of our armies being broken by this feeling among the masses out of the army. What course will you pursue in the event of the enemies cutting off railroad communication with Georgia? Will you not return to Virginia by private conveyance? I know you would not

fancy the idea of living at the Hunter Place, but I think your objection is not a good one at such a time as this. It is time that is an out of the way place, but you would be in short visiting distance of your relations where you could hear from them and be heard from often. I will advise no one now to run from the Yankees for it seems that they are to over run every section of our country, but then it is so much more satisfactory to be near our friends and relatives than to be cut off from them entirely, so that neither can know the fate the other often times.

    Our regiment was held in line of battle on Tuesday while the fighting was going on near Burgess Mills, but the enemy only made his appearance twice on our front or few rounds suffering each time to drive him back. Willies regiment was not in the engagement. I received a letter from him dated the 7th. He was in his usual state of health. We are making an effort to get him in this regiment, which I hope will succeed. We agreed to pay a young man $1200 to exchange with him and the petition had bee approved by all the officers whose approval was necessary except General Lee when it was last heard from. The latest news from home was about the first of the month. All were well then. We are entertaining her morning and evening by the music in the enemy's camp, which is very near us. There is frequent firing by the pickets during the line on our left, but we have had none on our post yet. I saw Brother day before yesterday. He is very well. He is now on duty at another post on our left. My general health is better I believe in camp than at home. I suffered a good deal when I first got to camp with my stomach some times, but it rarely ever gives me any pain at all. Our rations have been part of the time rather rough consisting of corn meal ground about as coarse as hominy without sifting and lean beef but as a general thing we got enough and frequently draw nice flour and good pork. We have made out very well with what we have bought in the country and we have received a nice box sent us by sister Sarah filled with good things. Also, one from Ma and Aunt Martha, but their co-partnership boxes don't pay. My expenses are enormous I expect the service will about sum up the little that I have and but for having that with us I should never have advised him to come to cavalry though apart from the expense it is preferable to infantry service.

    I was very sorry to hear of old Mr. Cole's death. I fear Mr. H. will not be able to get another man who will take the same interest in his business that Mr. Cole did. You must write as often to as you can my dear sister and tell Mr. H. and the children to write often too. My address is Company G, 10th Virginia Cavalry, Chambliss Brigade, W. H. F. Lee's Division, Army of Northern Virginia. Give much love to Mr. H. and the children accepting a large share for yourself.

                                         Your affectionate brother
                                         Thomas G. Penn

Trenches of the 24th Virginia Infantry, February 19, 1865
My Dear Ma,

After my return from preaching a few moments ago I learned that I would have an opportunity of sending a letter to Richmond by a member of my company to be mailed and thinking that you may receive it sooner than to send it by mail from here I have intended to write you a few lines to let you know that I am still to be able to write.

I received your letter sent by Uncle Jo… to be mailed on day before yesterday was very glad to hear that you were all well. I wrote you in my very last letter that there was a chance for me to get with my brothers into cavalry. I have received a letter from Thomas Green since I sent my petition back to his regiment. He wrote me that his General approved it but that he was rather fearful that General W. H. F. Lee would not. But I do hope that it has been approved and that I will soon be with them. If it has been approved I shall begin to look for Brother as Thomas Green.

The box that I started home I had directed to Mr. Zentmeyer in the care of Danville. I will send the receipt in my letter so that if it has not come to hand Mr. Zentmeyer can make the railroad company pay for it. I put some stuff for the box that we get here to make a kind of vegetable soup of. One of the prices is for Franklin Mitchell's wife. And the other two prices she put in for you to try. The way it is made is to put it in water and let it simmer about a half hour and it will drop all to pieces and then you put in a little meat and whatever else you please and boil it for something like an hour and it will be for use.

There is a man to be shot in our brigade tomorrow for desertion. We will have to witness the execution. It is such a horrid sight to look at. I will try and get off from going if I can. If you will hear I have no doubt before this reaches you of the fall of Columbia, South Carolina that will put an end to our receiving letters from dear Sister Eliza. It seems that Thomas Green ____ his letter and had to go on picket. I will write to him this week. Give my best love to all of the family. You must all write often. I have nothing on interest to write. Hoping that I will get an opportunity of seeing you before long I will close.

Your ever affectionate son
William Penn

Penn's Store Virginia, February 19, 1865
Dear Sir (William A. Penn),

I recon you have almost concluded that I was not by any means a man of my word but I have been so very busy ever since I got home and would forget mail after mail to write. You must excuse me and I will do better next time.

I did not forget to look after your box at Richmond and Danville and also at the stations along where the cars stopped long enough. I could hear of nothing of it hope you have before now gotten it all right as I know such things are very expectable with the men in the old 24th.

William, I mailed your letter to Martinsville as I came up. Guess it has been received by your folks long since. I have not seen any of your mother's family since I returned home except Mr. Zentmeyer yesterday at the Patrick Henry Lodge. I hear no complaint.

William, there is nothing in the way of news to write in the county. Time as very dull and getting worse the lonesome nest county you ever saw. The people are very much discouraged at the gloomy prospects of peace as our commissioners did nothing while gone in the way bringing those troublesome difficulties to an end. I see no chance of peace soon unless the different states a hold a convention and faces up the thing in that way.

William, as I have nothing that will interest I will come to a close by asking you to write to me again and give Ma all the war news. Let me know how you all are making out. News about something to eat. Whether or not your rationing was increased or decreased since I left.

Give Mr. Mitchell and Mr. Clark my respects. Tell them to let me hear from them. Tell Mr. Mitchell I left his coffee at Horsepasture Store and Mr. Abington promises to take it to his mother. Tell Mrs. Mitchell Deshazo Carter and Dillon to write me and give me all the news and tell Nat Deshazo for he don't write I shall just let Star… tell Ed Mitchell to let not along about Star for he has improved he throws that right hind foot exactly right. Give all the boys of my acquaintance my best respects be sure to write me on receipt of this.

                        Respectfully,
                        P. L. Young

Bivouac on White Oak Road, Ten miles from Petersburg,
February 19, 1865
My Dear Ma,

I have received several letters from you which are unanswered, but you will not expect me to answer each one promptly for since I received letters from several members of the family it will always be my aim to write to some one of you every few days and my letters to the others are of course intended as much for you as for those to whom they are directed.

I have received several letters from Sister and one from Lucinda. I have written to Sister, but have not yet answered Lucinda shall answer it soon. We are out of our winter quarters for good I reckon, but I think it will probably be no disadvantage to us as we have to be out so much it will be best for us to become seasoned to it. So that we will not be so liable to contract cold from the change. My powers of endurance have been well tested I think. The old members of the regiment say they have now experienced a harder time they have had this winter, and my health is better now I believe than it was at home. Brother is present and is very well. He says he wants his boy Pete disposed of as soon as possible. He is anxious to get rid of him. I suppose he is constantly fearing that he will get into some other meanness and the neighbors will I have no doubt censure him for keeping such a terrible fellow. I regretted much to hear of the great difficulty that Marshall and Pine got into. I hope Pine may recover, and the he may… by this lesson. I think Marshall is not much to blame for if he had any natural affection for his wife. I do not think he could have helped acting as he did from the impulse of the argument. I was sorry to hear of the death of poor John. His loss will be felt by the whole community. I think of Bill has commenced his thieving on such a large scale you ought to send him off the place. I do not think he will ever do enough work without an overseer to pay for his salt and time every way. I am very much pleased at the trade with Langhorne for Ballard's services. If I had a colored I would let them all go on such terms. I think Amanda was very well hired too. I think now, as Barbara's work will not be worth anything on the plantation and you have not hired her out. You had better take her in the house and put Catharine in the field, so as to make a regular hand of her. It will be necessary for you to make every edge cut to make expenses.

Please do not let anyone ride my horse and as I think there is now a good prospect of getting Willie to this regiment you had better not sell the old grey if he has not been already sold but have him swapped for one that will suit you for a riding horse. We have not yet seen Mr. Fratwell but have found out that he is in Company F of this regiment. We just came off picket day before yesterday, Friday, and I went yesterday to Petersburg and came by the camp of the 2nd Mississippi Regiment to see Haynes. I spent last night with him, found him quite well, living as well as a soldier ought to desire and in fine spirits. I enjoyed my stay with him very much. He promised to visit us in a few days if we do not move. We are looking though for orders to move now. General Lee has issued orders for the men to be kept in camp and be held in readiness to march at an hours notice. The enemy is preparing to advance massing their forces on our right. And as soon as the ground becomes firm enough for our army to move we expect a general engagement. Brother says tell Ma that cold disagreeable weather is the kind we love to see. That it lets us live longer. The success of Sherman in the South is causing the soldiers to grow more despondent. They think that if it was necessary to feed them upon short rations while we have had Georgia, Carolina to draw supplies from and could buy a large amount of provisions through blockade... now that both of these sources will probably be lost to you it will be impossible to keep the army provisioned though it rather the gloomiest time we have experienced but I have not yet and hope a few months wills change affairs greatly to our advantage. I think we will have to fight for many years to come to gain our independence and it is best for us to prepare our minds for it. Give yourself as little uneasiness on our account. My dear Ma's as you can. It is wrong to be always imagining what misfortune may happen to us but you should always hope that all is going well with us. It may be that... you are spending your most miserable moments uneasiness about us. That we are enjoying ourselves. All of your acquaintances believe are well except... He has a very bad cold and has been complaining a good deal for several days though. He is some better than he ...If Mr. Z or Dr. Hay have any nice calico that would be able for making shams to wear over my shirts I would like to have two made to wear on some occasions in the spring summer as my shirts will be faded and it now seems...family in a few days. I will be sorry to see him leave. He is very kind to me and there are few better captains I think. He sends his respects to the family.

    The enemy is preparing for a soldier to have a genteel appearance when he can go among nice people of foraging expeditions. I think it best to make them with a plain hem down in front, and sufficient him on each side. The calico should not have too much white in it. Most any neat small fit calico would suit. Captain H has kindly offered to bring me anything I need from home if he succeeds in getting a furlough. Give much love to all and we all write.

Ever your affectionate son,
Thomas Green Penn

April 6, 1865
My Dear Ma,
    I am so glad to hear from you and to get poor dear Joe's letter, but if has been written so long. I wish Jimmie could go to see them and after court, which is next week, if things are quiet I think it more than probable that he will go if it is considered safe for him to venture. There has been great excitement down this way and on the turnpike, but I believe everything has quieted down. Jimmie and Uncle John Cobb started out early yesterday morning in the direction of Mt. Airy to find out what route the Yankees had taken. They went up the turnpike about fourteen miles and they said there was a ...among the people all along the road they was expecting the Yankees every hour, as they went on. They would some times...men that would say they were at Patrick Court House and then some are else would come on and say they were coming down by George Hylton's just a few miles up the road and the people all along the road were having such rumor all day and frightened half to

death a great many had their meat and corn carried off and hid. Peyton Tatum sent several wagon loaded with meat and corn, and his and Larson Murphy darkies to an old barn over at the back of our field, and they stayed there until this morning, it is right laughable now all danger is over I can't help feeling amused. I felt as calm all the time as I do now but I was cooking out for them all day. Jimmie and Uncle John stayed at Martin's Store until the pickets come back that had been up not far from John Smiths which is in the neighborhood of Mt. Airy and they updated the enemy falling back in the direction of Hillsville. Jimmie did not get back until eight o'clock last night. It is reported that the enemy is at Madison, North Carolina and that their intention is to go to Danville, if they get there and destroy the railroad the Confederacy will go up. I would not be surprised to hear that raiding party had returned to Mt. Airy. They might not have gone a mile from there, and they met with so many good Union friends they will be apt to go again. I heard this morning that Richmond and been evacuated Johnson has left Sherman and gone to Lee so he can now go on his way without interruption.

    I reckon we are subjugated if we knew it I fear so anyhow. Jimmie has gone out again to summon men. So attend Superior Court, will be back tomorrow or next day. You must write to him immediately after he gets back from court. I know it would afford him great pleasure so go down to see them and carry them something good to eat.

    I feel better today than I have since you were here. The children were mightily pleased with the pies they come in good times while they were eating dinner. Hearing of the arrival of Mrs. Smith bring so fresh to my mind everything connected with the death of my dear dear brother how I hear longed to press the hand of that dear friend that kind honor that bathed this poor dear head and to look upon here from which was among the last on which his dear eyes rested. I would like so much to see here and to hear her talk about him. Give here my warmest love. I hope you can go so are back soon. When I saw Rufus coming I thought he had come to tell me of dear Wills arrival. I do hope he will soon be home I am glad to hear of sister's improvement. The little ones send kisses to dear Grandma and thanks for the little pies. Goodbye dear Ma.

                                      Your fond child
                                      Lucinda Staples Penn

Born in Ararat, Patrick County, Virginia, James Ewell Brown "Jeb" Stuart is the most famous person from Patrick County involved in the War Between the States. Below, a reenactor portraying Stuart shakes hands with J. E. B. Stuart IV in 1990 at the first Civil War Encampment at Laurel Hill, the birthplace and boyhood home of J. E. B. Stuart.

Chapter Nine
Regimental Histories of Patrick County Units

"Henry Reserves," Company I, 5th Battalion Virginia Reserves

This regiment organized in September 1864 only saw action at the end of the war. At least seven men from Patrick County who served in this unit lost their lives. Major Abram David Reynolds commanded the Patrick unit in this regiment. Being late in the war, its soldiers were either old men or young boys, with the exception of a few who had dropped out of other units because of medical or other reasons. While records are not complete, at least 99 men from Patrick County served in the 5th Reserves out of 117 in all Reserve units. Patrick Henry Giles, John P. Stovall and Edward Davis from Patrick County served as lieutenants. January 1865 saw the unit stationed in Danville, Virginia. On February 26, 1865, the unit had 24 officers and 363 men present.

Cardwell Reynolds

6th Virginia Infantry Regiment

While those who entered the Confederate States Army in 1861 were volunteers, most men who entered after that time came into service via conscription under an act of the Virginia General Assembly passed in early 1862. These draftees went to units where the need was greatest at the time. Some joined units formed from volunteers in 1861 as replacements or into some new companies formed from these draftees.

In May 1862, about 24 draftees from Patrick County joined the 6th Virginia Regiment of Infantry formed in Norfolk the year before. This regiment was under the command of Colonel William Mahone, who later became the "Hero of the Crater." After the war, Mahone, active in the railroad business, elected United States Senator, became the most powerful person in Virginia government for several years.

The 6th Regiment participated in the Peninsula Campaign of 1862 driving General McClellan's troops from the Peninsula. The unit fought in the Battle of Second Manassas. The regiment fought with Lee in the Maryland Campaign at Crampton's Gap on September 14, 1862 and at Antietam. The 6th fought at Chancellorsville, Gettysburg, Wilderness and Cold Harbor.

Involved in the defense of Petersburg, as part of General Mahone's Brigade in Longstreet's Corps, the 6th experienced the Battle of the Crater on July 30, 1864. The Federals exploded 8,000 pounds of black powder under the Confederate lines making a hole 170 feet long, 60 feet wide and 30 feet deep killing nearly 300 Southerners. The Confederates kept the Federals from exploiting the explosion to any great extent. Twenty-three members of the 6th died along with 43 wounded and 14 missing. The last action of the regiment was at Saylor's Creek on the way to Appomattox. One hundred and sixteen men surrendered at Appomattox, a few of which were Patrick Countians. At least 47 men from Patrick County served in the 6th Virginia Infantry.

Company D, 12th Virginia Infantry Regiment

The 12th Virginia Infantry originally organized from the "State Guard" units from Petersburg and Richmond, included many wealthy, prominent, and educated men from that area. The regiment started with about one thousand officers and men. A large number resigned an option available at the beginning of the war. In March 1862, in order to bring the regiment up to strength, a number of men from all over the state joined the regiment. Among these were about seventy soldiers from Patrick County. The 12th claimed it was the "best educated" regiment in the army before the Patrick boys came, who being mostly illiterate farm boys had a hard time among the educated city boys. Although they saw limited action before the Patrick men joined that changed in May 1862. Federal warships gained control of the James River and threatened the defenses at Drewry's Bluff between Petersburg and Richmond. The 12th spread out along the James River fired upon any Federal vessels attempting to go up the river. When General McClellan decided to approach Richmond from the land instead of the river and moved to the defense of Richmond.

They went into camp just east of Richmond and came under the command of General Mahone. The 12th engaged heavily in the Battle of Seven Pines in early June. General Joseph E. Johnston commanded all forces defending Richmond was lost to a wound early in the struggle. General Robert. E. Lee took command and stationed the regiment along the Charles City Road after the battle. The men engaged in several battles including Malvern Hill where the unit lost 112 men killed, wounded, and captured. After Federal General McClellan left the Peninsula, the unit moved across the river near Drewry's Bluff where several Patrick men died of disease.

On August 17, 1862, the 12th moved by train to Orange Courthouse to aid in preventing General Pope from moving on Richmond from the north under the command of General Thomas J. Jackson. They fought in the Second Battle of Manassas. On August 31, where they occupied the Henry House Hill, where the roughest fighting in the First Battle of Manassas took place. They lost 69 men killed, wounded, and captured in this battle. After three months of difficult fighting, the first day of September saw only 150 men in the regiment, down from the June 12 listing of about 800 men. General Lee had his headquarters at one time near the 12th and the Patrick men had a chance to see all of the Confederate Generals.

Those left in the regiment accompanied Lee's forces on the Maryland Campaign. On the way, they marched through Frederick, Maryland and camped just west of the town. Here General Lee's lost battle plans made their way into Federals hands and proved costly to the Confederate cause. The 12th fought at Crampton's Gap on September 14, 1862, and lost about 60 of the 100 men remaining. The men broke in confusion, but Stuart's cavalry arrived in time to restore order and get the survivors away to safety.

Following the Battle of Antietam, the army re-crossed the Potomac safely moved into Virginia near Winchester. Some of the lost and wounded returned to ranks and new recruits joined the regiment. The 12th took part in the Battle of Fredericksburg along with several other units containing Patrick Countians.

During the winter, men from the two armies often talked with each other across the river and sometimes even visited each other. This was particularly true of the officers, some of whom had been classmates at West Point. As was true of most Confederate soldiers and in all of the winters, shelter was poor, food was scarce, and clothing was inadequate.

In the spring, "Fighting Joe" Hooker took command of the Federal armies in northern Virginia. On April 27, 1863, he moved his troops across the river near where the 12th was camped bringing on the Battle of Chancellorsville. The 12th boasted a strength of nearly 400 men before this battle, but 36 died or suffered wounds and 51 fell into enemy hands. On roll call on May 6, only 100 men answered. In a few days, a number of men returned to the unit with miscellaneous stories concerning where they had been. The great victory at Chancellorsville did much to restore the morale of the regiment.

The 12th did not get to Gettysburg in time for the first day's action but took its place on the northern section of Seminary Hill opposite the Gettysburg Cemetery. The regiment saw little action and did not participate in Pickett's Charge on the last day of fighting. They did play an important part in covering Lee's retreat from Gettysburg. Several members deserted on the way back to Virginia.

General George G. Meade, in command of the Federal Army, pursued the Confederate Army into Virginia. The two armies again faced each other across the Rapidan and Rappahannock Rivers. Lee attempted several times to chase away Meade's Army, but was unsuccessful. He finally moved back across the Rapidan River. The 12th took part in these actions all winter of 1863-64.

William Henry Smith

In the spring of 1864, General U. S. Grant took command of the Federal forces in northern Virginia and began his relentless drive to capture Richmond with the battles of The Wilderness and Spotsylvania Courthouse. On one occasion, some of the men suffered friendly fire from members of their own regiment. General Lee, in spite of inferior numbers, stayed between the Union army and Richmond. Grant, not able to get to Richmond from the north, decided to go around and attack from the south beginning an almost yearlong siege of Petersburg. Transferred to the defense of Petersburg, the 12th stayed in the trenches north of town. The last action involving the regiment took place at Farmville after the evacuation of the Confederate Capital. About 180 of the regiment reached Appomattox, but very few Patrick Countians were in that group. Samuel C. Turner and Charles Ferguson may have been at Appomattox, but only Jackson A. Collier surrendered.

The only Patrick Countians commissioned officers in this regiment were Rufus Turner and James P. Critz. Turner served as Second Lieutenant but died of diphtheria June 19, 1862. Critz, elected Captain May 1, 1862, but resigned after becoming sick and returned home to take care of his widowed mother. Eighteen Patrick Countians died of disease before the end of their first year of service. At least 86 men from Patrick County served in the 12th Virginia Infantry.

Company G, 21st Virginia Cavalry Regiment

The 21st Virginia Cavalry Regiment organized in August 1863 with men from Floyd, Franklin, Henry and Patrick counties. The men came from companies reduced in numbers including the Virginia State Line troops and new some recruits. The Patrick Countians served in Company G, formerly Company I, under Captain Armstead O. Dobyns of Floyd County. Approximately 35 Patrick Countians served in Company G of the 21st Regiment of Virginia Cavalry.

The 21st saw action at Cloyd's Mountain and at Crockett's Gap under John Hunt Morgan near Wytheville in May 1864. In June the regiment help drive David Hunter from Lynchburg in the brigade of Bradley T. Johnson with Colonel William E. Peters commanding. The next month the unit joined in the burning of Chambersburg, Pennsylvania under John McCausland and in August at the cavalry disaster at Moorefield. Among these soldiers was Lee Baliles, great-grandfather of Governor and Patrick native, Gerald L. Baliles. In September, the unit saw action at Third Battle of Winchester and Fisher's Hill.

At least 123 men from Patrick County served in various cavalry regiments during the war. At least 31 men served in the 32nd Battalion of Virginia Cavalry, which became the 24th Virginia Cavalry Regiment. A few served in the 10th Battalion of Cavalry and the 5th Battalion of Cavalry.

Company I, 24th Virginia Infantry Regiment

Captain Andrew M. Lybrook organized Company I on May 31, 1861, at Patrick Courthouse. Lieutenants Daniel G. Hatcher, Aaron

Blackard and John D. Mitchell later commanded the company. This unit joined the 24th Regiment of Virginia Infantry at Lynchburg under the command of Colonel Jubal Anderson Early, a West Point graduate and a native of Franklin County. William R. Terry commanded the Regiment after Early received promotion. The 24th transferred to Manassas Junction and participated in the Battle of First Manassas. The regiment spent the fall and winter of 1861-1862 in northern Virginia.

In April 1862, the regiment moved to Richmond to defend the city from the advance of General McClellan's forces. The unit engaged in the battle of Williamsburg, where Captain Lybrook received a wound. The regiment took an active part in the battles of Seven Pines, Mechanicsville and Gaines' Mill, serving in Brigadier General Samuel Garland's Brigade.

Willis Dalton

After the Peninsula Campaign, the 24th moved to Gordonsville and then to the Second Battle of Manassas serving in James L. Kemper's Brigade of Longstreet's Corps. Casualties, killed, wounded or captured reached forty percent of the regiment.

When General Lee invaded Maryland in 1862, the regiment fought in the Battle of Antietam. After the Maryland Campaign, the 24th participated in the Confederate victory in the Battle of Fredericksburg at the end of the year.

In February 1863, the 24th moved near Petersburg. On March 21, the regiment took the train to Goldsboro, North Carolina and then to Kinston, but an expected action did not take place. After a few days, the men returned to Suffolk where they spent three weeks before moving to Hanover County, Virginia.

In June 1863, the regiment marched to Gettysburg. In Pickett's Charge, the 24th's losses included 18 men killed, 71 wounded, 40 taken prisoners and 50 missing. At least two from the 24th died. Eight or more Patrick Countians from the 12th and 50th infantry regiments lost their lives in the Battle of Gettysburg.

After Gettysburg, the 24th returned to the Richmond area and spent the remainder of the summer and fall. In January 1864, the regiment went to eastern North Carolina to retake several forts under Union control. Although it succeeded in taking a few towns, the Confederates could not drive the Union forces away and returned to Virginia.

The 24th spent the remainder of the summer and fall of 1864 in the area between Richmond and Petersburg. It suffered heavy losses in the Battle of Drewry's Bluff on May 16, 1864. Six Patrick County soldiers died in this battle. During the fall and winter of 1864-1865, the regiment stayed busy on picket duty and in occasional skirmishes. When Petersburg finally fell in early April 1865, the 24th saw action at Five Forks west of the town where nearly all the men became prisoners. Only 23 members of the 24th Regiment reached Appomattox Courthouse. Approximately 156 men from Patrick County served in the 24th Virginia Infantry.

Arthur J. Lovins

Company E, 29th Virginia Infantry Regiment

Most of the volunteers serving in the Confederate armies from the western section of Patrick County belonged to Company E of the 29th Virginia Infantry. Organized at Fancy Gap in Carroll County, it included men from both counties. Captain Alexander Haynes, a native of Patrick County, commanded the unit. Organized in early September of 1861, five companies from Carroll, Wythe, Smyth, and Russell Counties composed the regiment. Colonel Alfred Cleon Moore, born in western Patrick County, commanded the regiment. The men trained at Camp Fulkerson near Abingdon drilling without any guns until late November. When guns did arrive, they were old, reworked, obsolete weapons. These were the only guns the regiment had for about two years.

On December 4, the regiment transferred to Prestonburg, Kentucky. After marching across the Clinch River, the men refused to go farther until they were paid. After four days, they resumed the march to the Kentucky where they again stopped because some of the men had gone home to cut firewood for the winter. The unit waited for these men to return.

The regiment arrived at Paintsville, Kentucky on December 28 and joined the regular army under the command of Brigadier General Humphrey Marshall, a political appointee. The Army of Eastern Kentucky tried to keep the area under Confederate control. James A. Garfield, who later became President of the United States, commanded the Federal Army in that area. A small battle fought on January 10, 1862, at the Middle Creek of the Big Sandy River costing the regiment 5 dead and 7 wounded.

The biggest enemy of the Confederate forces at this point was the lack of food. By mid-January, the men hunted corn left in the fields, shucking and shelling it and taking it to the local mills. Near the end of January, the 29th moved back into Virginia and spent the remainder of the winter there. On May 16, the regiment along with the 51st drove the Federals from Princeton. General Marshall kept the unit inactive during the summer of 1862.

Members of the 29th came down with measles, mumps, chicken pox, and typhoid. As noted earlier, lack of sanitation led to polluted water with flies and mosquitoes plentiful. Living mostly on a diet of bacon and cornmeal, poor nutrition was common as well.

On September 6, 1862, they left camp at Castlewood in Russell County and headed for General Marshall's home state of Kentucky. By the 21st, the regiment was at Mt. Sterling where it stayed a week. By October 5, the 29th was in Lexington. Although near the Battle of Perryville, the ineptness of General Marshall prevented the regiment from seeing action. After lingering around Danville and Harrodsburg for a few days, the unit headed back to southwest Virginia when General Bragg decided to evacuate Kentucky. The 29th went through quite an experience in Kentucky without firing a gun.

In December 1862, orders came to transfer the unit to eastern Virginia. Encamped in Bland County, it marched to Wytheville where the troops took a train that arrived in Richmond a few days later. The regiment traveled to Petersburg where it remained until March 1863. This was the best winter the unit had during the war. One soldier remarked that the young ladies of Petersburg were very sociable to the soldiers.

Colonel Moore, disappointed over a lack of promotion to brigadier general, resigned and left the army. As with all other units, AWOLs and desertions were problems. More diligent than those in some other counties, Carroll officials shot at least two deserters. Disease also took its toll. Twenty men died during the stay in Petersburg.

On March 23, 1863, the 29th joined James Longstreet's Corps in the division under the command of General George E. Pickett in Southampton County. This unit skirmished with Federal troops on boats in the Nansemond River. Although under the command of General Pickett, the regiment guarded the Richmond area and did not fight at Chancellorsville or Gettysburg. After Gettysburg, it marched to the Shenandoah Valley to aid the retreating army in case General Meade attacked Lee's Army. The regiment engaged in a few skirmishes but returned to Petersburg where, on September 14, it boarded a train for east Tennessee. After engaging a small Federal force there, the 29th returned to southwest Virginia where remained until January 25, 1864. Then, it again entrained for Petersburg and onto Kinston, North Carolina in an attempt to recapture New Bern from the Federals. After several attempts to take the town, they returned to Petersburg.

General Lee's Army fought in a desperate attempt to prevent Grant's Army from capturing Richmond from the north. At the same time, General Benjamin F. Butler attempted to advance on Richmond from the south. Along with several other units containing Patrick County soldiers, the 29th fought on May 16, 1864, in the Battle of Drewry's Bluff on the James River between Richmond and Petersburg. Although considered a Confederate victory, this battle was costly for Patrick Countians, as at least six of them lost their lives. Major Alexander Haynes, the first captain of Company E, suffered a wound in his leg resulting in amputation. He died a few days later and was posthumously appointed Lieutenant Colonel.

After Drewry's Bluff, the 29th moved north of Richmond. When General Grant made his attempt to capture Richmond to the south side of the city, the regiment moved in that direction. The 29th stationed along the Howlett Line on the Bermuda Hundred was one of the Confederate units that opposed him almost the entire time. During the siege, Union forces captured some and sent north to Federal prisons.

The 29th fought at Dinwiddie Courthouse and Five Forks in April 1865 suffering high casualties in killed, captured and wounded. The unit's last action occurred at Saylor's Creek on the way to Appomattox resulting in capture for most of the men. Only about 30 men received paroles at Appomattox. Of approximately 80 Patrick Countians who served in the 29th, existing records show only two reached Appomattox.

54th Virginia Infantry

Company H with 64 men under the command of Sparrell H. Griffith enlisted on October 1, 1861. Joseph H. Scales, James R. Scales, Lewis A. Buckingham and Peter S. Banks led the company later in the war. This regiment made up of men mainly from Floyd County included at least 24 men from Patrick County.

The regiment fought future President James A. Garfield at Middle Creek on January 10, 1862. Griffith left with the reorganization in May 1862. At the Battle of Kelly's Store in Southampton County in January 1863, the 54th fought along side the 50th Virginia Infantry.

The 54th joined the Army of Tennessee fighting at Chickamauga in September 1863 and Missionary Ridge near Chattanooga in November. The Atlanta Campaign in 1864 occupied the regiment fighting at Resaca in May, Atlanta in July and Jonesboro in August under the command of Joseph Johnston and John Bell Hood.

John Bell Hood "played hell in Tennessee" the remainder of the year into 1865 with the 54th Virginia participating except for the disaster of Franklin in November. The 54th joined Nathan Bedford Forrest at Murfreesboro in December 1864. Johnston replaced Hood in January 1865. The 54th with 235 men moved towards North Carolina in February traveling through Augusta, Georgia to Charlotte. On March 19, 1865, the 54th fought its last battle at Bentonville, North Carolina losing four killed, 5 wounded and losing 30 prisoners.

"Patrick Grays" Company H 58th Virginia Infantry Regiment

Captain George E. Booker organized and commanded the Patrick County Grays, Company H, 58th Virginia Infantry. Booker, a graduate of Randolph-Macon College and an Episcopal minister, swore his men into service for one year at Patrick Courthouse on July 6, 1861, and joined the regiment on September 5.

The regiment encamped at Staunton in September 1861. Second in command of this regiment was Lieutenant Colonel Samuel Houston

Letcher, a brother of Virginia Governor John Letcher and a cousin to J. E. B. Stuart. Captains William S. Penn and Henry W. Wingfield eventually commanded the regiment. Lieutenants included James W. Frashure, James W. Hatcher, and George W. Hylton.

In October, the regiment went into winter quarters at Monterey in Highland County. Early in the spring, it joined Stonewall Jackson's famous Valley Campaign fighting at McDowell on May 8, Harrisonburg on June 6, Cross Keys on June 8 and Port Republic on June 9, 1862. The 58th went with Jackson to the defense of Richmond and engaged on the peninsula between the York and James Rivers in the Seven Days Battles including Gaines Mill on June 27.

Alexander R. Fulcher

The regiment traveled to northern Virginia, fighting in the Battles of Cedar Mountain and Second Manassas. Taking part in the Maryland Campaign as a part of Jackson's Corps, it captured Harper's Ferry. At Sharpsburg, the 58th fought off Federal forces while the army re-crossed the Potomac into Virginia territory. In December 1862, the regiment fought in the Battle of Fredericksburg. The men spent the remainder of the winter of 1862-1863 drilling and on picket duty while enduring cold and poor living conditions.

The regiment fought at Chancellorsville, but did not go to Gettysburg. It guarded the northern Virginia area. The winter of 1863-1864 involved preventing Federal armies from penetrating deeper into northern Virginia.

This regiment fought at the Battle of the Wilderness and at Spotsylvania Courthouse in May 1864. Heavily engaged in the Battle of Cold Harbor and at Rutherford's Farm, it returned to the Valley of

Virginia and fought with General Early against General Sheridan in the Shenandoah Valley. They fought at Winchester, Fisher's Hill and Cedar Creek losing men at each of these engagements.

In 1865, the regiment served at Petersburg and fought at Saylor's Creek on the way to Appomattox. The 58th, one of the last to fight at Appomattox, surrendered seventy men including nine men of Company H. Patrick County gave at least 109 men to the 58th.

The Orange Artillery

First organized in May 1861 and reorganized in March 1862 under the command of Captain Charles William Fry as part of the Army of Northern Virginia, at least 45 men from Patrick County served in a light artillery company from Orange County, Virginia. Fifty-nine men from Patrick County served in various artillery regiments during the war.

Roster of Confederate Soldiers From Patrick County

Key To Abbreviations

1910C. Listed in 1910 U. S. Census of Patrick County as Confederate Veteran.
BPC   Buried in Patrick County. See: Pilson, O. E. *Tombstone Inscriptions of Patrick County, Virginia*.
CDAR Confederate Disability Application Receipts
http://eagle.vsla.edu/al/virtua-basic.html
CPA   Confederate Pension
http://eagle.vsla.edu/conpen/virtua-basic.html
Index to Confederate Pension Applications.
http://lvaimage.lib.va.us/collections/CW.html
Collection: Confederate Pension Rolls, Veterans and Widows.
KIA   Killed in Action.
LCA   Robert E. Lee Camp Confederate Soldiers' Home Applications for Admission
http://ajax.lva.lib.va.us/F/?func=file&file_name=find-b-las16&local_base=clas16
MIA   Missing in Action.
PCDR Patrick County Death Register.
POW   Prisoner of War.
UDC   United Daughters of the Confederacy Cross of Honor Application. On file at the Patrick Historical Society in Stuart, Virginia.
WIA   Wounded In Action.

ABELL (ABLES) Joseph. Company I, 26th Battalion Virginia Infantry. CPA.
ADAMS, Abram (or Abraham) (August 10, 1830-March 29, 1871). Company H, 58th Virginia Infantry. Medical discharge July 2, 1863. BPC. CPA.
ADAMS, Isaac C. (November 18, 1824-November 21, 1905). Company G, 61st Virginia Infantry. BPC.
ADAMS, Giles. Company C, 10th Battalion Virginia Heavy Artillery. Died May 14, 1862 of measles.
ADAMS, James W. Company D, 51st Virginia Infantry.
ADAMS, John Henry (July 7, 1843-February 10, 1916). Company C, 10th Battalion Virginia Heavy Artillery. WIA, Malvern Hill. CPA. BPC.
ADAMS, John Sparrell (1830-1881). Company K, 6th Virginia Infantry. WIA Malvern Hill, July 1, 1862. Medical Discharge. CDAR.
ADAMS, Joshua J. Company H, 42nd Virginia Infantry. Disabled 1862. BPC. CPA.

ADAMS, Joshua J. Born in Patrick County 1843. Moved to Surry County, North Carolina and served in Company E, 53rd North Carolina Infantry. POW near Washington, D.C. on July 11, 1864 and died of diarrhea in Point Lookout Prison, Maryland, November 24, 1864. CPA.

ADAMS, Joshua Thompson (November 13, 1832-August 19, 1902). Company G, 21st Virginia Cavalry. WIA. POW, Point Lookout Prison, Maryland. Son of Reverend Joshua Adams. BPC. CPA.CDAR.

ADAMS, Nathaniel P. Company D, 51st Virginia Infantry. KIA, Battle of Winchester, 1864.

ADAMS, Thomas S. Company D, 6th Virginia Infantry. Paroled at Appomattox. CDAR.

ADAMS, William A. (November 20, 1829-March 25, 1905). Company B, 24th Virginia Cavalry. Company A, 42nd Virginia Infantry. BPC. CDAR. CPA.

AGEE, Austin (1820-1890). Company I, 5th Battalion Virginia Reserves. BPC. CDAR. CPA.

AGEE, Charles L. Company H, 42nd Virginia Infantry. PCDR, chronic diarrhea at Elmira, New York Prison, February 19, 1865.

AGEE, Edmund H. Corporal, Company H, 42nd Virginia Infantry. Medical Discharge, March 15,1862. Re-enlisted October 1862. WIA, Payne's Farm, November 27,1863. CDAR.

AGEE, Garrett William. Company H, 42nd Virginia Infantry. Court-martialed for desertion but reinstated. WIA. CDAR.

AGEE, George M. Company D, 51st Virginia Infantry. POW, Waynesboro and Released from Fort Delaware Prison June 15, 1865.

AGEE, James H. Company H, 42nd Virginia Infantry. POW, paroled May 14, 1865.

AGEE, John Tazewell. Company D, 51st Virginia Infantry. Died of disease September 10, 1863.

AGEE, John Tazewell. Company I, 5th Battalion Virginia Reserves. BPC. CPA.

AISTRIP (AISTROP), Patrick. Company I, 5th Battalion Virginia Reserves.

AISTRIP, Henry C. Lieutenant, Company I, 24th Virginia Infantry. POW, Sailor's Creek, April 6, 1865 and Released from Johnson's Island Prison June 1, 1865. CPA.

AKERS, Elisha A. Company D, 51st Virginia Infantry. Probably lived in Franklin County and served from Patrick.

AKERS, George. Mountain and Orange Artillery.

AKERS, Henry P. Orange Artillery, Company K. 10th Virginia Cavalry.

AKERS, Isaac N. Company D, 51st Virginia Infantry. Mountain and Orange Artillery. Treasurer of Patrick County 1879-1882. BPC. CPA.

AKERS, John A. Lieutenant Company D, 51st Virginia Infantry. KIA, August 25, 1864.

AKERS, Nathaniel Claiborne. Company D, 51st Virginia Infantry. BPC. CPA.

AKERS, Samuel R. (November 25, 181843-October 17, 1923). Sergeant, Company D, 51st Virginia Infantry. WIA, Fayetteville, West Virginia. BPC. CPA.

AKERS, William Tyler. Company D, 51st Virginia Infantry. Replaced David L. Ross as Captain. Promoted to Major in 1864. Served in Virginia House of Delegates. Died at Stoneville, North Carolina. CPA.

AKERS, W. T. Company D, 51st Virginia Infantry. Enlisted in Patrick County and lived in Franklin County. Died of wounds.

ALEXANDER (McALEXANDER), William. Company I, 5th Battalion Virginia Reserves.

ALLEN, Anderson. Company E, 29th Virginia Infantry.

ALLEN, Bailey F. (P.) (April 2, 1846-December 25, 1897). Company I, 25th Virginia Cavalry. BPC.

ALLEN, Creed G. Company D, 51st Virginia Infantry.

ALLEN, George L. (July 4, 1844-December 29, 1917). Corporal, 24th Virginia Cavalry. BPC. 1910C.

ALLEN, James Henry. Company H, 42nd Virginia Infantry. Born Mississippi and enlisted at Spoon Creek in Patrick County. WIA, Cross Keys June 8, 1862.

ALLEY, John Wesley. Company H. 58th Virginia Infantry. Died Staunton Hospital, October 24, 1861.

ANGLIN, James Phillip. Corporal, Company K, 42nd Virginia Infantry. WIA, Chancellorsville. POW, Spotsylvania Court House. Exchanged. Died in Patrick County in 1925. CDAR. CPA.

ANTHONY, John Virgil (1840-1900). Company D, 51st Virginia Infantry. POW, Waynesboro March 12, 1865. Released from Fort Delaware Prison June 19, 1865. BPC.

ARNOLD, John. Company I, 24th Virginia Infantry. Died of typhoid September 7, 1861 in Fairfax County, Virginia.

ARRINGTON, Sparrel G. Sergeant, Company H, 51st Virginia Infantry. Living 1907. CPA.

ARRINGTON, William H. (February 7, 1837-February 3, 1925). Company K, 50th Virginia Infantry. BPC. CPA.

ATKINS, Booker C. M. (May 30, 1832-January 17, 1878). Company H, 51st Virginia Infantry. BPC.

ATKINS, Obadiah. Company H, 51st Virginia Infantry.

ATKINSON, J. E. Company H, 24th Virginia Infantry. CPA.

AYERS, Anderson (January 4, 1846-April 29, 1929). Company E, 29th Virginia Infantry. 4th Virginia Reserves. WIA, Dinwiddie Court House, Virginia, March 29, 1865. BPC.

AYERS, Elkannah H. Company C, 24th Virginia Infantry. WIA. POW, Hatcher's Run, April 2, 1865, Point Lookout, Maryland. CDAR.

AYERS, James Jackson (1815-April 12, 1898). Company E, 29th Virginia Infantry. Discharged in 1862 being over age. Died in Carroll County.

AYERS, James J. Company H, 58th Virginia Infantry. Died in Staunton Hospital, July 6, 1861.

AYERS, Joel. Company H, 21st North Carolina Infantry. Born in Patrick and moved to Surry County, North Carolina. WIA, Hatcher's Run near Winchester. Died in Surry County after 1900.

AYERS, Joshua. Company E, 29th Virginia Infantry. WIA, Cold Harbor. POW, April 6, 1865. Released from Point Lookout Prison, Maryland, June 23, 1865.

AYERS, Madison. Company E, 29th Virginia Infantry. Died of pneumonia at Petersburg April 19, 1863.

AYERS, William H. (October 2, 1842-March 21, 1914). Company K, 50th Virginia Infantry. BPC. UDC. CPA. 1910C.

AYERS, William. Company H, 51st Virginia Infantry. WIA, Lee Town. CDAR. CPA.

AYERS, William (June 24, 1841-April 7, 1916). Company E, 29th Virginia Infantry.

AYERS, William R. Company E, 29th Virginia Infantry. Born 1814. Discharged 1864 being over age.

BAKER, C. J. Company D, 51st Virginia Infantry.

BAKER, James H. Sergeant, Company G, 42nd Virginia Infantry. POW. WIA. CPA.

BALILES, George W. Born circa 1814 in Patrick County. Company D, 51st Virginia Infantry. Paroled at Appomattox. Died in Henry County, 1889.

BALILES, Lee. Company G, 21st Virginia Cavalry. Served July through September 1864. Great-grandfather of Governor Gerald L. Baliles. Died in Little Rock, Arkansas 1907.

BARBOUR, Andrew J. Company D, 12th Virginia Infantry and wagon master for 6th Virginia Cavalry. CPA.

BARNARD, Charles (April 20, 1818-June 10, 1872). Company I, 5th Battalion Virginia Reserves. BPC.

BARNARD, Charles. Company I, 24th Virginia Infantry. PCDR, hospital at Danville of typhoid June 30, 1862.

BARNARD, James William (1844-1923). Company K, 50th Virginia Infantry. POW, Spotsylvania Court House May 12, 1864, Point Lookout, Maryland and Elmira, New York. CPA.

BARNARD, Jehu (1840-1933). Company K, 50th Virginia Infantry. BPC. CPA.

BARNARD, Richard (April 4, 1835-March 6, 1871). Company K, 50th Virginia Infantry. BPC.

BARNARD, Richard Joseph. Company K, 50th Virginia Infantry. POW, Wilderness, May 5, 1864, Elmira, New York. Died September 22, 1864 of typhoid.
BARNARD, Thomas A. Company K, 50th Virginia Infantry.
BARNARD, Thomas A. Company I, 24th Virginia Infantry. POW, Camp Chase Prison, Ohio. Released May 8, 1865.
BARNARD, William Patterson. Company K, 50th Virginia Infantry.
BARRETT, William. Company H, 51st Virginia Infantry.
BARRETT, James. Company I, 24th Virginia Infantry. Died of disease at Liberty (Bedford County) Hospital, February 6, 1863.
BEASLEY, Richard. Company K, 50th Virginia Infantry.
BEASLEY, Robert M. Company I, 24th Virginia Infantry. POW, Burkeville April 6, 1865 on way to Appomattox. Released from Point Lookout Prison, Maryland, June 23, 1865. BPC. CDAR. UDC. CPA.
BELCHER, Costly (Causely). Company D, 51st Virginia Infantry. POW, Winchester, September 19, 1864, Pt. Lookout Prison, Maryland. Exchanged, March 15, 1865. Living in 1909. CDAR. CPA. BPC.
BELCHER, Daniel. Company D, 51st Virginia Infantry. PCDR, October 1861, Raleigh County, West Virginia, of fever.
BELCHER, John. Company H, 51st Virginia Infantry. CPA.
BELCHER, Noah. Company D, 51st Virginia Infantry. Died after 1909.
BELCHER, Peter B. Company D, 51st Virginia Infantry. POW, Winchester, September 19, 1864, Point Lookout Prison, Maryland. Exchanged, March 15, 1865. BPC. CDAR. UDC. CPA.
BELCHER, Reed (May 23, 1844-June 2, 1931). Company D, 51st Virginia Infantry. BPC.
BELTON, Hamilton. Company H, 58th Virginia Infantry. BPC. CPA.
BENNETT, Bluford. Orange Artillery.
BENNETT, Alexander C. (1829-1863). Company H, 58th Virginia Infantry. Died of typhoid, Albemarle County.
BENNETT, Henry C. (1841-1863). Company I, 24th Virginia Infantry. KIA, Gettysburg.
BENNETT, Howard (June 26, 1821-November 20, 1903). Company G, 21st Virginia Cavalry. POW, Front Royal, Virginia, November 12, 1864. Exchanged. BPC.
BENNETT, J. H. Company D, 12th Virginia Infantry. WIA near end of war.
BENNETT, Jacob. Orange Artillery.
BENNETT, John. Company D, 51st Virginia Infantry. Died 1927.
BENNETT, Richard. Company I, 5th Battalion Virginia Reserves.
BENNETT, Venith Thomas. Company K, 10th Virginia Cavalry. KIA.
BENNETT, William H. Company D, 12th Virginia Infantry. Died of pneumonia and smallpox at Chimborazo Hospital, Richmond March 4, 1863.

BERNARD, (BARNARD), William. Company D, 12th Virginia Infantry.

BIGGS, Robert T. Company H, 23rd Virginia Infantry. LCA. CPA.

BISHOP, Andrew J. Company C, 10th Battalion Virginia Heavy Artillery. CPA.

BISHOP, John Terrill. Company C, 10th Virginia Battalion Heavy Artillery. UDC.

BISHOP, Dr. Joseph (1830-1862). Company I, 24th Virginia Infantry. Died at Christiansburg en route home. BPC.

BLACKARD, Aaron. Lieutenant, Company I, 24th Virginia Infantry. Resigned in 1862. 1910C. BPC. CDAR, CPA.

BLACKARD, William. Company I, 24th Virginia Infantry. Died of disease at Richmond Hospital, April 27, 1862. CPA.

BLACKARD, Willoughby. 24th Virginia Infantry. Died of disease, April 20, 1862. CPA.

BLACKBURN, Thomas J. Company F, 21st Virginia Infantry. CDAR.

BLANCET, James M. (1834-1918). Company G, 54th Virginia Infantry.

BLANCETT, Samuel. Company H, 51st Virginia Infantry.

BOAZ, James Russell (April 20, 1828-January 5, 1906). Company B, 24th Virginia Cavalry. BPC. CPA.

BOAZ, Robert W. (1835-February 15, 1862). Company H, 58th Virginia Infantry. Died of disease.

BOAZ, Thomas Jefferson . Private. Company B, 24th Virginia Cavalry.

BOLT, Leroy. Corporal, Company K, 50th Virginia Infantry. Lived in Carroll County.

BOOKER, George Edward (April 11, 1826-May 3, 1894). Major, Company H, 58th Virginia Infantry. Promoted to Major. Died in Maryland, 1894. BPC.

BOOKER, Marshall. Sergeant, Company H, 58th Virginia Infantry. Surrendered at Appomattox.

BOSWELL, John W. Company K, 50th Virginia Infantry. BPC. CPA.

BOSWELL, Whitmel T. Sergeant Company I, 24th Virginia Infantry. Died at home during war.

BOWERS, Jacob. Company D, 51st Virginia Infantry.

BOWLES, Henry Chapman (November 20, 1831-August 6, 1918). Company F, 2nd Virginia Cavalry. 1910C. BPC. CPA.

BOWLING, Henry T. Company D, 51st Virginia Infantry.

BOWLING, James Tyler. Company K, 50th Virginia Infantry. Transferred to 42nd Virginia Infantry. CDAR.

BOWLING, John W. Company D, 51st Virginia Infantry. POW, Waynesboro. Released from Fort Delaware Prison, June 19, 1865.

BOWLING, William Waller. Company K, 50th Virginia Infantry. BPC. CDAR. CPA.

BOWLING, Wiley F. Company I, 24th Virginia Infantry. POW, South Mountain. Exchanged.
BOWMAN, Aaron (1835-1909). Company I, 45th Virginia Infantry.
BOWMAN, Aaron. Company H, 51st Virginia Infantry. BPC.
BOWMAN, Anderson. Company I, 45th Virginia Infantry. CPA.
BOWMAN, Austin. Captain, 50th Virginia Infantry. POW, Point Lookout, Maryland and Elmira, New York.
BOWMAN, Charles H. Company H, 51st Virginia Infantry. POW, Strasburg, October 1864. Exchanged. UDC. CPA.
BOWMAN, Coleman C. Possibly in 10th Virginia Cavalry. PCDR, acute dysentery at Richmond, Virginia, June 23, 1862.
BOWMAN, Crockett. Company K, 50th Virginia Infantry. KIA, Gettysburg.
BOWMAN, Crockett (or Crickett). Company I, 5th Battalion Virginia Reserves, 1864. Living in 1907. CPA.
BOWMAN, Ewell. Company D, 12th Virginia Infantry. Died in Richmond General Hospital #7 of intestinal infection, July 13, 1862. CPA.
BOWMAN, Galen. Company K, 50th Virginia Infantry. 1910C. BPC. CPA.
BOWMAN, Henry. PCDR, May 1862 in Norfolk of measles.
BOWMAN, Isaac Henry. Company K, 50th Virginia Infantry. POW, Gettysburg, Point Lookout, Maryland.
BOWMAN, Hugh. Company K, 50th Virginia Infantry.
BOWMAN, Isham. Company K, 50th Virginia Infantry. Died of fever in Bland County. CPA.
BOWMAN, Jefferson. Company K, 50th Virginia Infantry. BPC. CPA.
BOWMAN, John H. Company H, 51st Virginia Infantry.
BOWMAN, John. Company K, 50th Virginia Infantry.
BOWMAN, John. Company E, 6th Virginia Regiment Infantry.
BOWMAN, John J. Company D, 12th Virginia Infantry.
(Note. A John Bowman is listed in the County Death Register as having Died of fever on August 13, 1862, but which of the above is the correct soldier is not known.)
BOWMAN, Preston. Company K, 50th Virginia Infantry. KIA, Fort Donelson, Tennessee.
BOWMAN, Raleigh. Company K, 50th Virginia Infantry. General Order 31, April 16, 1864.
BOWMAN, Reuben (Rhuel). Company K 50th Virginia Infantry. CDAR.
BOWMAN, Robert. PCDR, May 20, 1862, Norfolk of consumption.
BOWMAN, Ruel. Company K, 50th Virginia Infantry. Living 1907. CDAR. CPA.

BOWMAN, Samuel Godfrey. Company F, 58th Virginia Infantry. Company A, 3 rd Virginia Reserves. Company I, 5th Virginia Battalion. Living 1909. BPC. CPA.
BOWMAN, Thomas Franklin. Company I, 65th Virginia Infantry. CPA.
BOWMAN, T. H. Company A, Wood's Confederate Cavalry Regiment.
BOWMAN, William D. (February 14, 1836-Aug 30, 1914). Company D, 12th Virginia Infantry.
BOYD, T. Caleb (May 2, 1827-June 12, 1919). Company H, 51st Virginia Infantry. BPC. CPA.
BOYD, Charles J. PCDR, September 22, 1861 of fever.
BOYD, Charles M. Sergeant Company H, 51st Virginia Infantry. WIA, Gaines Mill. Died in Richmond Hospital of the wound, June 7, 1864.
BOYD, Francis M. Company D, 12th Virginia Infantry. Died of typhoid in Winder Hospital, Richmond, June 14, 1862. Buried in Hollywood Cemetery, Richmond (Death Register states July 16, 1862 as death date).
BOYD, German. Company I, 5th Battalion Virginia Reserves.
BOYD, George W. Company D, 51st Virginia Infantry. BPC.
BOYD, Howard Hiram. Company H, 51st Virginia Infantry. Living 1907. BPC. CPA.
BOYD, Isaac, Company D, 51st Virginia Infantry. PCDR, Giles County, December 8, 1861, of fever. CPA.
BOYD, Israel. Company H, 51st Virginia Infantry. PCDR, April 7, 1862, of fever.
BOYD, Jacob C. Teamster, Company I, 54th Virginia Infantry. CPA.
BOYD, James H. 4th Battalion Virginia Reserves. CDAR.
BOYD, John. Company D, 12th Virginia Infantry. Died July 1862.
BOYD, John A. Company E, 29th Virginia Infantry. WIA, Drewry's Bluff.
BOYD, Martin V. (June 8, 1843-August 7, 1862). Died shortly after entering service, cause unknown.
BOYD, R. J. Company K, 50th Virginia Infantry.
BOYD, Samuel S. (September 13, 1837-June 22, 1920). Company D, 51st Virginia Infantry. BPC.
BOYD, William. Company I, 26th Virginia Cavalry. BPC.
BOYD, William. Company D, 51st Virginia Infantry. POW. Living 1907.
BOYLES, Lee. Company G, 21st Virginia Cavalry.
BRADLEY, M. W. Company D, 51st Virginia Infantry.
BRAMMER, Elkanah. 6th Virginia Infantry. UDC.
BRAMMER, Henry T. (July 6, 1832-May 31, 1900). Company H, 51st Virginia Infantry. BPC. CPA.
BRAMMER, John H. (1821-1864). Possibly in Company F, 151st Virginia Militia. POW, Exchanged, Died of pneumonia at Wytheville en route home.

BRAMMER, John W. Mountain and Orange Artillery. Died of disease, February 4, 1863.
BRAMMER, Jonathan L. (1833-1908). Company D, 51st Virginia Infantry.
BRAMMER, Madison L. (1845-1903). Company D, 51st Virginia Infantry.
BRAMMER, Tazewell Perry. Company D, 51st Virginia Infantry.
BRAMMER, William Davis. Company D, 51st Virginia Infantry. WIA, Gordonsville, September 1862.
BRANCH, John, Company H, 51st Virginia Infantry.
BRANCH, Joshua. Company D, 51st Virginia Infantry. Went North. Served in 140th Indiana U. S. Infantry. Living 1907. BPC.
BRANCH, William (1847-February 4, 1864). Company H, 58 Virginia Infantry. Died in war of unknown cause. Substitute for Harman Critz.
BRANSON, Augustus S. Company E, 29th Virginia Infantry.
BRANSON, Greenberry M. Company E, 29th Virginia Infantry. POW. Released, July 1, 1865.
BRANSON, John W. (1839-1863). Company E, 29th Virginia Infantry. Died of typhoid fever at Richmond, September 15, 1863.
BRANSON, Stewart L. Company E, 29th Virginia Infantry. WIA, Dinwiddie, March 31, 1865. Living in Carroll County in 1880.
BRAY, Robert F. Company B, 2nd Battalion North Carolina Infantry. 1910C. CPA.
BRIDGEMAN, George H. Company E, 18th Battalion Heavy Artillery (Alexandria Artillery).
BRIDGEMAN, Robert F. Company D, 12th Virginia Infantry. Died at Naval Hospital in Norfolk May 9, 1862.
BRIM, Phillip W. Company H, 58th Virginia Infantry.
BRIM, Nicholas. Company H, 58th Virginia Infantry.
BRIM, Rice Osborne (1832-1899). Company H, 58th Virginia Infantry. Lost eye at Cedar Creek. CDAR. CPA.
BROCK, Talton F. Company E/F, 57th Virginia Infantry. KIA Gettysburg, July 3, 1863.
BROOME, James E. Company H, 51st Virginia Infantry.
BROWN, Abram (or Abe). 24th Virginia Cavalry. Born in Patrick County but enlisted in Henry County.
BROWN, H. Private, Company B, 24th Virginia Cavalry.
BROWN, Hubbard P. Sergeant, Company H, 42nd Virginia Infantry. POW, Antietam, Maryland. Exchanged, December 1862.
BROWN, James A. Company K, 51st Virginia Infantry. Died in Giles County, August 18, 1862 of typhoid, age 19.
BROWN, John Marshall (b. April 8, 1841). Company H, 42nd Virginia Infantry. Died January 9, 1862 of typhoid fever after coming home. BPC. CPA.

BROWN, Joseph Henry, Sr. (September 6, 1843-January 13, 1940). Company G, 24th Virginia Infantry. POW, Five Forks and released from Point Lookout Prison, Maryland, June 23, 1865. 1910C. CPA. Last surviving Civil War soldier in Patrick County. BPC in the Critz Baptist Church Cemetery.

BROWN, Robert (1841-1900). Company H, 42nd Virginia Infantry. Medical discharge.

BRYANT, Abner J. Company D, 51st Virginia Infantry. Living in 1907.

BRYANT, Alexander N. Company D, 51st Virginia Infantry. Died, September 18, 1875.

BRYANT, Ambrose. Company B. 42nd Virginia Infantry. WIA, Cedar Mountain and Kernstown. PCDR, wounds, August 25, 1862, age 41.

BRYANT, James. Company D, 51st Virginia Infantry. Served in 24th Virginia Cavalry.

BRYANT, John Wesley. Company D, 12th Virginia Infantry. Living in 1909. BPC. CPA.

BRYANT, Jackson. Company G, 21st Virginia Cavalry.

BRYANT, William. Second Company F, 29th Virginia Infantry. PCDR, August 12, 1862 while "in Army."

BRYANT, William C. Company I, 24th Virginia Infantry. KIA, Hewlett House, June 18, 1864.

BRYANT, William F. Company D, 51st Virginia Infantry. POW, Winchester, September 19, 1864. Exchanged March 15, 1865.

BURGE, David C. 24th Virginia Cavalry. Died April 20, 1906. BPC. CPA.

BURGE, Robert W. Company H, 42nd Virginia Infantry. Discharged 1862, over age.

BURKHART, Ephraim W. Private. Company F, 47th North Carolina Infantry. Born in North Carolina. POW, Gettysburg. Prisoner at Old Capital Prison, Washington D. C. and Point Lookout, Maryland. Exchanged. Furloughed for illness and suffered paralysis of the leg for the remainder of his life. Moved to Patrick County, married and had 19 children. BPC. CPA.

BURNETT, Abram Dandridge (1839-1907). 24th Virginia Infantry. WIA, Battle of Seven Pines. Right arm amputated. Died in Floyd County.

BURNETT, David Bluford. KIA, Battle of Chancellorsville. Mountain and C. W. Frye's, Orange Artillery.

BURNETT, Frank. Company I, 24th Virginia Infantry. Died in hospital.

BURNETT, George W. Company H, 29th Virginia Infantry 45th Virginia Infantry.

BURNETT, Jacob John. Mountain and Orange Artillery. Died in Richmond November 12, 1862.

BURNETT, Jeremiah (April 24, 1842-September 22, 1927). Company H, 51st Virginia Infantry.

BURNETT, John Adam (June 19, 1836-May 25, 1892). Lieutenant, Company D, 51st Virginia Infantry. POW, Winchester, June 19, 1864. Released from Fort Delaware Prison, August 17, 1865.

BURNETT, John A. Company H, 29th Virginia Infantry. Born in Patrick County. Died in Tazewell County.

BURNETT, W. H. Company I, 24th Virginia Infantry. KIA, Gettysburg.

BURROUGHS, George T. Corporal, Company H, 51st Virginia Infantry. KIA.

BURROUGHS, Robert D, Company H, 51st Virginia Infantry. MIA, Fort Donelson, Tennessee.

BURROUGHS, Thomas J. Company H, 51st Virginia Infantry. POW, Waynesboro, March 2, 1865. Released from Fort Delaware Prison, June 19, 1865.

CALLAHAN, Javis B. Company B, 16th North Carolina Infantry.

CAMPBELL, James M. Company K, 50th Virginia Infantry. 21st Virginia Cavalry. Living 1907.

CAMPBELL, John P. Evans. (1835-1909). Company K, 50th Virginia Infantry. POW, Gettysburg, Fort McHenry and Point Lookout, Maryland and Fort Delaware. UDC. CPA. BPC.

CAMPBELL, James William. Sergeant, Company K, 50th Virginia Infantry.

CANNADAY, Constant. Company I, 5th Battalion Virginia Reserves. Discharged, over age.

CANNADAY, Marshall. Company D, 51st Virginia Infantry. Discharged, 1863.

CANNADAY, Pleasant. Company D, 51st Virginia Infantry.

CANNADAY, Randolph. Company D, 51st Virginia Infantry. Born in 1827 in Patrick County. Died in Dickenson County, West Virginia at over 100 years of age.

CANNADAY, Stephen H. (1825-1879). Company D, 51st Virginia Infantry. WIA, May 30, 1864. POW, Waynesboro, March 3, 1865. Released from Fort Delaware Prison, June 19, 1865.

CARTER, E. N. Company D, 51st Virginia Infantry.

CARTER, James Franklin. Company H, 23rd Battalion Virginia Cavalry. CPA.

CARTER, George Robert. Company H, 58th Virginia Infantry. POW, Spotsylvania Court House, Fort Delaware.

CARTER, James L. Company H, 58th Virginia Infantry. Died of pneumonia, July 15, 1863, at Lynchburg Hospital.

CARTER, James W. (1834-1865). Company H, 58th Virginia Infantry. POW Spotsylvania Court House, May 12, 1864. Died in Fort Delaware, May 24, 1865.

CARTER, John. Company I, 5th Battalion Virginia Reserves.
CARTER, John Jefferson. Company E, 6th Virginia Infantry. Died in Pittsylvania County while on furlough September 15, 1862 of consumption.
CARTER, John P. Corporal, Company D, 51st Virginia Infantry.
CARTER, Robert. Company H, 58th Virginia Infantry. 42nd Virginia Infantry. WIA, Cedar Mountain August 9, 1862. CDAR. CPA.
CARTER, William. Company H, 58th Virginia Infantry.
CARTER, Walker. Company I, 5th Battalion Virginia Reserves.
CASSADAY, Anderson. Company H, 58th Virginia Infantry. POW, Spotsylvania Court House. Died Fort Delaware, August 4, 1864.
CASSELL, Brice W. Company K, 50th Virginia Infantry. BPC.
CASSELL, Carter. Company K, 50th Virginia Infantry. KIA, Chancellorsville.
CASSELL, Joseph H. Company K, 50th Virginia Infantry. Died December 17, 1868, age 23.
CATES, Solomon R. Company H, 24th Virginia Infantry.
CHANDLER, John. Private, Company A, 28th North Carolina Infantry. Born in 1831. Enlisted in Surry County, North Carolina, 1862 while living there. Discharged April 15, 1863 for chronic rheumatism.
CHANEY, Steven B. Company I, 5th Battalion Virginia Reserves. CPA. BPC.
CHAPMAN, Andrew J. Company H, 58th Virginia Infantry. Medical discharge, August 31, 1863.
CHAPMAN, William H. Company H, 58th Virginia Infantry. WIA, Winchester, July 20, 1864. CDAR. CPA.
CHAPPELL, Alexander. Corporal, Company I, 26th Virginia Cavalry.
CHAPPELL, Henry Alexander (1847-1921). Company E, 29th Virginia Infantry. POW, April 2, 1865. Released from Point Lookout Prison, Maryland, June 8, 1865.
CHAPPELL, Isaac. Company C, 29th Virginia Infantry. Died in Carroll County.
CHAPPELL, James. Company D, 29th Virginia Infantry. Discharged 1862 over age. Also, with 5th Reserves. WIA, Saltville.
CHAPPELL, James F. (June 2, 1845-March 3, 1924). Company E, 29th Virginia Infantry. WIA, Drewry's Bluff. POW April 2, 1865. Released from Point Lookout Prison, Maryland June 24, 1865.
CHAPPELL, William. Company E, 29th Virginia Infantry. Father of James F. and Henry A.
CHEELEY, Graves W. Lieutenant, Company D, 51st Virginia Infantry. WIA, Winchester September 18, 1864.
CHEELEY (CHESLEY), John A. Company I, 5th Battalion Virginia Reserves.

CHEELEY, Peter P. Company H, 51st Virginia Infantry. Died May 13, 1863. Buried at Emory and Henry College, Washington County, Virginia.

CHEELEY, Richard G. Company D, 51st Virginia Infantry. WIA. POW, Winchester, September 18, 1864. Released from Point Lookout Prison, Maryland, March 3, 1865.

CHILDRESS, James H. Company F, 4th Battalion Virginia Reserves.

CHILDRESS, Maston. 1910C.

CHILDRESS, Robert. Company I, 24th Virginia Infantry.

CLARK, Alexander D. Company H, 42nd Virginia Infantry. Medical discharge, July 1, 1862.

CLARK, Christopher C. Company I, 24th Virginia Infantry. POW, Williamsburg. Exchanged. Enlisted in Cavalry. CDAR.

CLARK, George W. M.D. (February 7, 1826-March 19, 1913). 1910C. CPA.

CLARK, Hughes Dillard (February 14, 1846-April 9, 1865). Co E, 24th Virginia Infantry. Enlisted April 26, 1864 at Taylorsville. WIA. Left leg amputated at Farmville hospital where he died April 9, 1865. BPC

CLARK, Jackson. Company D, 51st Virginia Infantry. POW, Waynesboro. Released from Fort Delaware Prison, June 9, 1865.

CLARK, James W. (1827-1884). Sergeant, Company H, 58th Virginia Infantry. POW, Fredericksburg May 3, 1863. Exchanged from Fort Delaware May 23, 1863.

CLARK, Jefferson Thomas (February 13, 1838-May 2, 1884). Captain, Company I, 24th Virginia Infantry. WIA, Seven Pines. Served as County Treasurer and Clerk of the County Court after the war. BPC. UDC. CPA.

CLARK, John Henry. Company D, 12th Virginia Infantry. POW, Burgess Mill, October 2, 1864. Point Lookout Prison, Maryland. Served in Company A, 34th Virginia Militia. CPA.

CLARK, John R. Company D, 51st Virginia Infantry. POW, Waynesboro, March 2, 1865. Released June 19, 1865.

CLARK, Joseph H. Company H, 58th Virginia Infantry.

CLARK, Robert Moorman (June 10, 1822-July 5, 1911). Captain, possibly in Assistant Adjutant Inspector General Office. 1910C. BPC.

CLARK, William A. Company H, 42nd Virginia Infantry. Paroled at Lynchburg April 15, 1865. Blacksmith. Died Patrick County 1908. BPC. CPA.

CLARK, William Harrison. (November 12, 1840-March 13, 1862). Company H, 58th Virginia Infantry. Died of disease, March 13, 1862 in Huntersville, Alabama.

CLEMENT, James T. W, Sr. 6th Virginia Cavalry. POW, Yellow Tavern, May 11, 1864. BPC. CDAR. CPA.

CLIFTON, Andrew Martin. Company D, 12th Virginia Infantry.

CLIFTON, Daniel. Company K, 50th Virginia Infantry.

CLIFTON, James C. (July 20, 1843-December 2, 1912). Company K, 50th Virginia Infantry. BPC.
CLIFTON, James M. Company K, 50th Virginia Infantry. CPA.
CLIFTON, Samuel (January 14, 1844-1922). Company K, 50th Virginia Infantry. CPA.
CLIFTON (Clifford), William J. (July 30, 1834-November 12, 1918). Company I, 24th Virginia Infantry. Transferred to Confederate States Navy, 1864. BPC.
CLOUD, Benjamin F. Lieutenant, Company K, 50th Virginia Infantry.
CLOUD, George M. D. Company E, 29th Virginia Infantry. 26th Virginia Cavalry.
CLOUD, James L. Company E, 29th Virginia Infantry. WIA, Howlett House. Died in Carroll County, 1885.
CLOUD, William H. Company E, 29th Virginia Infantry. Died in Sullivan Company, Tennessee after 1900.
COBB (Cobbs), John S. Died September 10, 1861 at Augusta, Georgia of fever. PCDR, April 10, 1861.
COBB, John T. Corporal, Company H, 42nd Virginia Infantry. Medical discharge, August 13, 1864.
COBB, J.T. Private, Company B, 24th Virginia Cavalry.
COBB, Thomas H. Company B, 24th Virginia Cavalry.
COCK, Joel Hubbard (January 26, 1848-December 12, 1928). Company K, 50th Virginia Infantry. Patrick County Home Guard. BPC. CPA.
COCKRAM, Alexander (1833-1909). Company H, 51st Virginia Infantry. Medical discharge, May 9, 1862. CPA.
COCKRAM, Andrew G. Company K, 50th Virginia Infantry. KIA, Wilderness. CPA.
COCKRAM, Charles. Company D, 51st Virginia Infantry. POW, Lee Town, August 25, 1864, Camp Chase, Ohio. Exchanged March 18, 1865.
COCKRAM, David. Company D, 51st Virginia Infantry. BPC.
COCKRAM, German (June 9, 1838-June 30, 1916). Company H, 51st Virginia Infantry. BPC. CPA.
COCKRAM, Isham (June 4, 1831-January 23, 1929). Musician, Company D, 51st Virginia Infantry. BPC. CPA.
COCKRAM, John. Company D, 51st Virginia Infantry.
COCKRAM, Nathan. Company K, 50th Virginia Infantry. CPA.
COCKRAM, Peter. (June 4, 1841-April 28, 1915). Company H, 51st Virginia Infantry. BPC.
COCKRAM, Richard. Company H, 51st Virginia Infantry. BPC.
COCKRAM, Spencer. Company F, 29th Virginia Infantry. Paroled at Lynchburg, April 15, 1865.
COCKRAM, William. Company K, 50th Virginia Infantry. WIA.

COCKRAM, William Harvey. (Jan 1, 1843-December 15, 1936). Company D, 51st Virginia Infantry. WIA. POW, Winchester, September 19, 1864. Exchanged February 20, 1865. BPC. CDAR.
COLEMAN, James. Possibly in Company H, 23rd Virginia Cavalry. 1910C.
COLEMAN, Samuel. Company H, 51st Virginia Infantry. 1910C. UDC. CPA.
COLEMAN, William. Company I, 24th Virginia Infantry. POW, South Mountain, September 15, 1862. Exchanged November 1862.
COLLIER, Jackson A. Company D, 12th Virginia Infantry. POW. Exchanged. Paroled at Appomattox.
COLLINS, Andrew J. Company H, 51st Virginia Infantry. Medical discharge. CDAR.
COLLINS, George. Company H, 42nd Virginia Infantry.
COLLINS, Jackson. Company I, 5th Battalion Virginia Reserves.
COLLINS, James Madison. Company G, 53rd North Carolina Infantry. BPC. CPA.
COLLINS, Jesse. Company H, 23rd Battalion Virginia Infantry. Company H, 51st Virginia Infantry. CPA.
COLLINS, Joseph H. (September 7, 1842-July 26, 1931). Company H, 23rd Virginia Cavalry.
COLLINS, Levi Patterson (September 2, 1837-May 7, 1917). Company H, 23rd Virginia Cavalry. BPC. UDC. CPA.
COLLINS, M. V. Company K, 22nd Virginia Infantry.
COLLINS, R.S. Company A, 2nd Battalion North Carolina Infantry. Company E, 29th Virginia Infantry. CPA.
COMBS, Zadoc (1843-1863). Company E, 29th Virginia Infantry. Died of smallpox at Petersburg Hospital.
COMPTON, James R. Company G, 17th Virginia Infantry.
COMPTON, William A. Company H, 51st Virginia Infantry.
CONNER, Abram. 1900 Reunion.
CONNER, Allan. PCDR, September 20, 1862. KIA.
CONNER, Alexander. Company D, 51st Virginia Infantry. KIA, September 20, 1862.
CONNER, Daniel Creed (1846-1864). Company G, 21st Virginia Cavalry. Died of smallpox, November 10, 1864.
CONNER, David Euell (July 29, 1843-November 29, 1884). Sergeant Company H, 51st Virginia Infantry. BPC. CPA.
CONNER, George W. (1847-1881). Company D, 51st Virginia Infantry. POW, Winchester, September 1864. Released from Point Lookout Prison, Maryland, June 21, 1865. BPC. CPA.
CONNER, Greenville (Granville) H. Captain and organized, Company H, 51st Virginia Infantry. Resigned in 1862. BPC.
CONNER, James. Company H, 51st Virginia Infantry.

CONNER, John. Company K, 50th Virginia Infantry. Moved to Wythe County after war.

CONNER, John, Jr. Corporal, Company H, 51st Virginia Infantry. POW, Waynesboro. Released, Fort Delaware, June 1865. BPC. CDAR. CPA.

CONNER, Reed W. (December 22, 1847-February 28, 1920). Company I, 5th Battalion Virginia Reserves. BPC. CPA.

CONNER, S. D. Company H, 51st Virginia Infantry.

CONNER, William. Corporal, Company H, 51st Virginia Infantry.

CONNER, William B. Lieutenant, Company H, 51st Virginia Infantry.

CONWAY, Benjamin D. (December 7, 1842-March 8, 1902). Company I, 24th Virginia Infantry. WIA, May 16, 1864. BPC. CDAR.

COOPER, Dr. James D. (November 18, 1834-August 12, 1900). Enlisted, May 3, 1862. Company K, 10th Virginia Cavalry. POW, December 13, 1864. Released, Point Lookout Prison, Maryland, June 6, 1865. BPC. CPA.

COOPER, William Herbert. (September 9, 1835-May 10, 1970). Company K, 10th Virginia Cavalry. 24th Virginia Infantry. CDAR. BPC.

CORBIN, Benjamin (September 5, 1825-January 8, 1920). Company B, 13th Battalion Light (Ringgold) Artillery. CPA.

CORN, Peter (February 26, 1834-February 7, 1920). Company D, 51st Virginia Infantry.

CORN, Richard (March 16, 1829-March 27, 1891). Company D, 51st Virginia Infantry. BPC.

COX, Alvin (Abner). Company C, 36th Virginia Infantry. Teamster.

COX, Daniel R. Company C, 36th Virginia Infantry. Medical discharge, January 10, 1864.

COX, David R. (July 29, 1841-February 25, 1900). Company E and C, 36th Virginia Infantry. CPA.

COX, Elijah (1845-1863). Company D, 51st Virginia Infantry. Died of typhoid, June 10, 1863. Buried at Emory and Henry College, Washington County.

CRADDOCK, Jackson. Company I, 5th Battalion Virginia Reserves. Died in Federal prison.

CRADDOCK, James M. Company H, 42nd Virginia Infantry. Died in Standardsville Hospital.

CRADDOCK, James. Company D, 51st Virginia Infantry.

CRADDOCK, John H. Company H, 58th Virginia Infantry. Died of disease, Staunton Hospital, Virginia, October 27, 1861. Buried in Staunton.

CRADDOCK, Joshua T. Company H, 58th Virginia Infantry. WIA, Sharpsburg, September 1, 1862. POW, High Bridge April 6, 1865. Released from Point Lookout Prison, Maryland, June 10, 1865. CDAR. CPA.

CRADDOCK, Peter J. (1837-1918). Company K, 58th Virginia Infantry. BPC. UDC. CPA.
CRADDOCK, William Isaac. Company H, 58th Virginia Infantry. Living 1909. UDC. CPA. BPC.
CRAIG, Peter D. (July 19, 1838-May 28, 1929). Company G, 42nd Virginia Infantry. POW, May 12, 1864, Spotsylvania Court House. Point Lookout Prison, Maryland and Elmira Prison, New York. Exchanged, March 20, 1865. BPC. CPA.
CRAIG, Greenville. Company A, 42nd Virginia Infantry. Died of measles at Staunton, July 1862.
CRAIG, William. Company G, 42nd Virginia Infantry. WIA, Sharpsburg, Maryland and Gettysburg, Pennsylvania. Died July 13, 1863.
CRANFORD (Crawford), William Elvira. Company K, 50th Virginia Infantry. Living in 1907.
CREASEY, James D. Company I, 26th Virginia Cavalry.
CREASEY, J. H. Company F, 25th Virginia Infantry. BPC. CPA.
CRITZ, Haman. Company D, 12th Virginia Infantry. POW, Point Lookout, Maryland, Exchanged Aiken's Landing, March 28, 1865.
CRITZ, Haman (Herman). Company H, 58th Virginia Infantry. Hired substitute in 1863. CPA.
CRITZ, James P. Captain, Company D, 12th Virginia Infantry. Resigned May 1, 1862.
CRITZ, John William. Captain, Company A, 42nd Virginia Infantry. WIA, Kernstown and First Manassas. Medical discharge.
CROAF, Henry F. Company F, 57th Virginia Infantry.
CRUISE, David. Company A, 3rd Confederate Engineer Troops.
CRUISE, James. Company F, 51st Virginia Infantry. PCDR, fever, Mercer County, West Virginia, November 18, 1861. CPA.
CRUISE, John Martin. (1837-1900). Lieutenant, Company H, 51st Virginia Infantry. POW, Waynesboro, March 2, 1865. Released Fort Delaware, June 17, 1865. BPC. CPA.
CRUISE, Samuel A. PCDR, gunshot wound, May 17, 1864 (or May 27, 1865).
CRUISE, William B. 1910C. CPA.
CUMMINGS, Dr. Woodson Riley (January 8, 1838-May 20, 1907). Company C, 30th Battalion Virginia Sharpshooters. Served from Craig County, but moved to Patrick after war. Practiced medicine near Critz and was a Baptist preacher. CPA.
CUNNINGHAM, John J. Company G and B, 23rd Battalion Virginia Infantry. Company G, 53rd North Carolina Infantry. 1910C.
CURTIS, John P. On list of Civil War veterans in Patrick County Order Book #18.
DALTON, Andrew J. Company C, 24th Virginia Infantry.

DALTON, Coleman J. Company D, 12th Virginia Infantry. POW, Burgess Mill, October 27, 1864, POW, Point Lookout Prison, Maryland, Exchanged Aiken's Landing, March 28, 1865.
DALTON, Frederick. Company K, 50th Virginia Infantry. Died March 11, 1920. BPC. CDAR. CPA.
DALTON, Haman Critz (born 1822). Company H, 42nd Virginia Infantry. PCDR, wounds at Antietam, October 20, 1862. BPC. CPA.
DALTON, Isham (1827-1913). Company H, 58th Virginia Infantry. BPC. UDC. CPA.
DALTON, James R. Sergeant, Company H, 58th Virginia Infantry. Died of disease, Winchester Hospital, September 5, 1861.
DALTON, James W. Company H, 58th Virginia Infantry.
DALTON, Nicholas. Company H, 42nd Virginia Infantry. WIA, June 9, 1862. POW, Spotsylvania Court House May 12, 1864. Died of chronic diarrhea at Elmira Prison, New York, January 13, 1865 and was buried there.
DALTON, Peter Washington. Lieutenant, Company H, 42nd Virginia Infantry. POW, Spotsylvania Court House May 1864. One of the 600 Confederate officers who were imprisoned in Charleston, South Carolina Harbor where they would be fired upon by Confederate cannon ("The Immortal 600"). Released June 16, 1865.
DALTON, Samuel P. Corporal, Company H, 13th North Carolina Infantry.
DALTON, Willis. Company I, 24th Virginia Infantry. POW, Farmville, April 6, 1865. Released from Point Lookout Prison, Maryland, June 1, 1865. BPC. CPA.
DAVIS, Edward. Lieutenant Company I, 5th Battalion Virginia Reserves. Living 1907.
DAVIS, Samuel Wesley (1825-1879). Lieutenant, Company H, 51st Virginia Infantry. POW, Waynesboro, March 2, 1865. Released from Fort Delaware, June 20, 1865. BPC. CPA.
DEAN, Alfred Washington. Company E, 29th Virginia Infantry. Died Carroll County, 1921.
DEAN, Calvin Nathan (1840-1902). Company E, 29th Virginia Infantry. WIA, New Bern, North Carolina. Paroled at Appomattox.
DEAN, Josiah. Company E, 29th Virginia Infantry. Died of smallpox at Petersburg Hospital, January 9, 1863.
DEATHERAGE, Emery. Company H (or K), 50th Virginia Infantry.
DEATHERAGE, Leabon, Company H (or K), 50th Virginia Infantry.
DEATHERAGE, Sampson H. Company K, 50th Virginia Infantry. PCDR, KIA, Charleston, West Virginia, September 13, 1862.
DEATHERAGE, William A. Company A, 33rd North Carolina Infantry. 1910C. CPA.

DeHART, Aaron Pleasant. Company D, 51st Virginia Infantry. PCDR, typhoid, Mercer County, West Virginia, December 1861. CPA.

DeHART, Daniel C. Company I, 24th Virginia Infantry. Medical discharge.

DeHART, Eleazor (October 10, 1842-April 4, 1909). Company D, 51st Virginia Infantry. POW, Strasburg, October 19, 1864. Released from Point Lookout Prison, Maryland, May 13, 1865. BPC. CPA.

DeHART, Eli H (February 2, 1843-March 20, 1923). Company D, 51st Virginia Infantry. BPC. CDAR. CPA.

DeHART, Green. 51st Virginia Infantry. PCDR, November 1, 1861 in Raleigh, North Carolina (or Raleigh County, West Virginia).

DeHART, Green W. (May 6, 1847-February 20, 1934). Company I, 5th Battalion Virginia Reserves. BPC. UDC. CPA.

DeHART, Henry C. (December 4, 1839-November 28, 1924). Company A, 24th Virginia Infantry. Transferred to 51st Virginia Infantry. POW, Frederick, Maryland, July 10, 1864. Exchanged at Elmira Prison, New York March 2, 1865. BPC.

DeHART, James A. Company I, 24th Virginia Infantry. WIA, Drewry's Bluff. Returned to duty.

DeHART, Jesse H. Company A, 24th Virginia Infantry. WIA. POW, Gettysburg. KIA.

DeHART, John. Corporal, Company I, 5th Battalion Virginia Reserves. BPC.

DeHART, John S. Company D, 51st Virginia Infantry.

DeHART, John W. Company D, 51st Virginia Infantry. BPC.

DeHART, Jonathan, Company I, 24th Virginia Infantry. KIA, Drewry's Bluff, May 16, 1864.

DeHART, Joseph C. Company D, 51st Virginia Infantry. POW, Halltown, August 24, 1864. Released from Point Lookout Prison, Maryland, June 16, 1865.

DeHART, Paul. Company D, 12th Virginia Infantry.

DeHART, Pleasant A. Company D, 51st Virginia Infantry. POW, Waynesboro, Released from Fort Delaware, June 20, 1865. Living in Patrick County, 1909.

DeHART, Robert R. Company D, 51st Virginia Infantry. Medical discharge, 1862 (or 1863). BPC. CDAR.

DeHART, Stephen Hubbard. (November 30, 1834-November 8, 1921). Company I, 53rd North Carolina Infantry. CDAR. CPA. BPC.

DeHART, Thomas. Company A and I, 24th Virginia Infantry. BPC.

DeHART, Thomas. Company H, 58th Virginia Infantry. WIA, Payne's Farm, November 26, 1863. Medical discharge, July 2, 1864.

DeHART, Thomas J. Company H, 51st Virginia Infantry. POW, Waynesboro, March 2, 1865. Released from Fort Delaware, June 20, 1865. CPA.

DeHART, Thomas T. Company D, 51st Virginia Infantry. POW, Waynesboro, Virginia, March 2, 1865. Released from Fort Delaware, June 19, 1865. CPA.

DeHART, William. Company H, 51st Virginia Infantry. POW, Lee Town, August 6, 1864. Camp Chase Prison, Ohio, and Point Lookout Prison, Maryland. Exchanged March 28, 1865. Living in Patrick County, 1909. CPA.

DeHART, William Green. (February 9, 1843-November 1, 1861). Company H, 51st Virginia Infantry. Died at Raleigh Court House, West Virginia, 1861. BPC.

DeHART, William T. Company A, 24th Virginia Infantry. Died in Richmond June 25, 1862, of wounds received at Battle of Seven Pines. BPC.

DeHART, W. T, Sr. (August 30, 1837-December 31, 1916). Company H, 51st Virginia Infantry. BPC. CDAR. CPA.

DENT, McHenry H. Company D, 28th Virginia Infantry.

DICKERSON, Floyd S. Sergeant, Company K, 50th Virginia Infantry.

DICKERSON, Leonard. Company I, 58th Virginia Infantry. PCDR, KIA, 1862. CPA.

DILLON, Abram M. born 1842 or 1843. Company G, 42nd Virginia Infantry. BPC. UDC. CPA.

DILLON, Edward Lee. Company G, 42nd Virginia Infantry. POW, Spotsylvania Court House, May 12, 1864. Exchanged from Point Lookout Prison, Maryland, January 21, 1865.

DILLON, H. H. Company A, 42nd Virginia Infantry and Company H, 24th Virginia Cavalry. WIA, Chancellorsville, May 3, 1863.

DILLON, James Marion. Company A, 24th Virginia Infantry. PCDR, pneumonia, July 15, 1862, in Chimborazo Hospital, Richmond.

DILLON, John G. Company I, 5th Battalion Virginia Reserves.

DILLON, John Purris. Company A, 24th Virginia Infantry. Furloughed because of illness. Died at home, November 3, 1862.

DILLON, John Reid. Company I, 5th Battalion Virginia Reserves.

DILLON, William Davis. Possibly in Company K, 38th Virginia Infantry. Born in Patrick County, resided in Henry County. Died at Camp Chase, Ohio, November 25, 1864 at age 39. CDAR.

DILLON, William J. Company D, 51st Virginia Infantry.

DISON, John. Company B, 2nd North Carolina Cavalry.

DODSON, John. Mountain and Orange Artillery. Conscripted April 1, 1862.

DODSON, F. William. Company D, 51st Virginia Infantry.

DONATHAN, George. Company H, 51st Virginia Infantry.

DOSS, Joel A. Company I, 5th Battalion Virginia Reserves. CPA.

DOSS, William W. Company B, 24th Virginia Cavalry. Born in Patrick County circa 1833

DRAUGHN, William. (June 3, 1838-November 28, 1915). Company A, 28th North Carolina Infantry. BPC. CPA.

DUGGINS, (DURGINS), Edward C. Company D, 51st Virginia Infantry.

DUNCAN, Andrew J. Company H, 51st Virginia Infantry. Living in Patrick County 1909.

DUNCAN, James Martin. Company H, 51st Virginia Infantry. 45th Virginia Infantry. POW, 1864, Exchanged from Point Lookout Prison, Maryland, March 28, 1865.

DUNCAN, John H. Company K, 50th Virginia Infantry. CPA.

DUNCAN, Joel H. Company E, 6th Virginia Infantry. Leg amputated at Spotsylvania Court House, May 12, 1864.

DUNCAN, John. Company I, 24th Virginia Infantry. Died of typhoid and pneumonia at Manassas, August 4, 1861.

DUNCAN, John. Company I, 6th Virginia Reserves. Enlisted 1864.

DUNCAN, William. Company I, 29th Virginia Infantry. Died in Tazewell Company, Virginia, 1890.

DUNKLEY, Samuel Harden (August 9, 1841-March 1, 1932). Sergeant, Company H (or K), 50th Virginia Infantry. BPC. UDC. CPA.

DUNKLEY, William Harvey (June 16, 1834-April 18, 1918). Company E, 6th Virginia Infantry. Company H, 51st Virginia Infantry. BPC. CPA.

DURHAM, Caleb C. 16th Virginia Infantry.

DURHAM, John. Company B, 21st Virginia Cavalry. Died May 26, 1918. CPA. 1910C.

EAST, Golden. Company E, 29th Virginia Infantry.

EAST, William A. (H.) (1846-1930). Company I, 6th Virginia Reserves. BPC.

EASTER, George Abraham. Company D, 29th Virginia Infantry. 45th Virginia Infantry.

EASTER, Robert Seth. Company D, 29th Virginia Infantry. Died 1916, Surry County

EDENS, Claiborne (March 10, 1834-December 12, 1910). Company K, 50th Virginia Infantry. BPC.

EDWARDS, Abram. PCDR, of measles in Chattanooga, Tennessee on April 1, 1862. CPA.

EDWARDS, Albert. Company I, 6th Virginia Reserves. Enlisted 1864.

EDWARDS, Joseph W. Company I, 24th Virginia Infantry. POW, Gettysburg. Exchanged. Paroled at Appomattox. CPA.

EDWARDS, Larkin V. (or J). Lieutenant, Company G, 21st Virginia Cavalry. WIA.

EDWARDS, Thomas Jefferson. Company E, 29th Virginia Infantry. 22nd Virginia Cavalry.

EDWARDS, William Albert. Company E, 29th Virginia Infantry.

EDWARDS, William H. Company H, 42nd Virginia Infantry. WIA, Cedar Run. Discharged because of age, November 4, 1862. BPC. CDAR. CPA.

ELGIN, Alfred or "Abb" (July 23, 1823-December 29, 1909). Company H, 51st Virginia Infantry. WIA.

EMBERSON, Jabez. Orange Artillery. Discharged 1862.

EMBERSON, Wade A. (June 6, 1836-May 5, 1922). Company K, 10th Virginia Cavalry. BPC.

EMMERSON, S. T. Mountain and Orange Artillery.

EMMERSON, Wade A. Mountain and Orange Artillery. CPA. BPC.

EPPERSON, Benny (Berry). Company K, 50th Virginia Infantry.

EPPERSON, Hillery Tippett, Company E, 6th Virginia Infantry. Furnished a substitute, Discharged due to health. CPA.

EPPERSON, John. Company K, 50th Virginia Infantry. BPC.

EPPERSON, Nicholas. Company E, 6th Virginia Infantry. PCDR, Richmond Hospital, October 28, 1862 of fever. CPA.

EPPERSON, William M. (May 6, 1847-May 22, 1930). Company I, 5th Battalion Virginia Reserves. CPA. BPC.

FAIN, Abraham M. Company K, 50th Virginia Infantry. Died in Elmira Prison, New York, September 7, 1864. Grave #218.

FAIN, Henry. Company I, 5th Battalion Virginia Reserves. CPA.

FAIN, Jacob W. Company D, 12th Virginia Infantry and Company I, 6th Virginia Reserves. Living 1909. BPC. UDC. CPA.

FAIN, William. Company H, 51st Virginia Infantry.

FARLEY, Christian Pearis. Company D, 51st Virginia Infantry.

FARLEY, Thomas A. Sergeant, Company H, 58th Virginia Infantry. POW twice. Released from Point Lookout Prison, Maryland on June 16, 1865.

FEAGANS, George W. Company I, 24th Virginia Infantry.

FERGUSON, Charles. Company D, 12th Virginia Infantry. Teamster.

FERGUSON, Harden. Company H, 51st Virginia Infantry. KIA, Fort. Donelson, Tennessee.

FERRELL, James M. Company A, 38th Virginia Infantry. Teamster and ambulance driver.

FISHER, Henry. Company K, 6th Virginia Infantry.

FISHER, Joel. Company D, 51st Virginia Infantry.

FISHER, Nathaniel. Company D, 51st Virginia Infantry.

FLEMING, William W. Died of measles, Norfolk, Virginia, May 9, 1862.

FLIPPIN, Samuel. Company E, 45th Virginia Infantry. POW, Winchester, September 9, 1864. Died in prison at Point Lookout, Maryland on March 8, 1865.

FLOYD, John. Company I, 5th Battalion Virginia Reserves.

FODDRELL, S. Columbus. Company B, 24th Virginia Cavalry. Born in North Carolina.1910C.
FOLEY, Andrew J. Company I, 20th Virginia Cavalry.
FOLEY, Bluford. Company D, 51st Virginia Infantry. Died after 1900. BPC.
FOLEY, Fleming (1830-1864). Company D, 51st Virginia Infantry. Died June 1864 in Petersburg Hospital.
FOLEY, James W. Company D, 51st Virginia Infantry.
FOLEY, Peyton (1840-1928). Company D, 51st Virginia Infantry. POW, Waynesboro, March 2, 1865. Released from Fort Delaware, June 30, 1865. BPC. CDAR. CPA.
FOLEY, Reed Marshall (June 20, 1838-August 7, 1928). Company D, 51st Virginia Infantry. Company G, 36th Virginia Infantry. BPC. CDAR. CPA.
FOLEY, Stephan. Mountain and Orange Artillery. Died of fever in January 1863 in Caroline County. CPA.
FOLEY, William G. (1846-1914). Possibly 51st Virginia Infantry. BPC.
FOLEY, William Lee. Company D, 51st Virginia Infantry. CDAR.
FOREST, Joseph W. Company H, 58th Virginia Infantry. Paroled at Farmville, April 21, 1865.
FOSTER, Abram Penn (January 31, 1842-March 20, 1919). Company I, 5th Battalion Virginia Reserves. CPA. 1910C. BPC.
FOSTER, George J. Company D, 12th Virginia Infantry.
FOSTER, Hardin. Company E, 17th Virginia Cavalry. In list of Confederate Veterans from. Patrick County Order Book #18.
FOSTER, Peyton M. Company D, 51st Virginia Infantry. POW, Charlottesville, March 5, 1865. Released from Point Lookout, May 13, 1865. Living 1909. CDAR. CPA.
FRANCIS, John. Possibly in 25th Battalion Virginia Infantry. BPC.
FRANKLIN, W. A. Company H, 51st Virginia Infantry.
FRAZIER, Albert. Company I, 24th Virginia Infantry. POW, Lexington, June 11, 1864. Enlisted in U. S. Navy.
FRAZIER, Benjamin T. Company I, 24th Virginia Infantry. WIA, Second Manassas, but Died of disease at Lynchburg, April 6, 1863.
FRAZIER, Brice M. Lieutenant, Company I, 24th Virginia Infantry.
FRAZIER, James W. Company C, 4th Virginia Infantry. Killed on January 12, 1864, by a deserter while home after being WIA in 1863.
FRAZIER, Peter F. Company A, 42nd Virginia Infantry. WIA, Kernstown, March 23, 1862. Discharged for disability, but re-enlisted in 1864.
FRAZIER, Samuel C. Company I, 24th Virginia Infantry. Died of pneumonia, May 1, 1862, at Charlottesville, Virginia
FRAZIER, William James. Lieutenant, Company H, 58th Virginia Infantry.

FRAZIER, Zackery Taylor. Lieutenant, Company I, 5th Battalion Virginia Reserves.
FREEMAN, Andrew J. Company H, 22nd North Carolina Infantry. BPC.
FREEMAN, Jesse M. Corporal, Company H, 58th Virginia Infantry. WIA. POW, Winchester, September 19, 1864. Exchanged at Point Lookout Prison, Maryland, October 26, 1864.
FREEMAN, William W. (1837-1862). Company H, 58th Virginia Infantry. PCDR, disease, February 21, 1862, Monterey Hospital.
FRENCH, Gordon C. (1816-1864). Company D, 51st Virginia Infantry. Died in Winchester Hospital, July 27, 1864, of gunshot wound.
FRY, John. Company I, 5th Battalion Virginia Reserves.
FRY, John H. Company H, 51st Virginia Infantry. Living 1909. CPA.
FRY, Louis A. Company H, 51st Virginia Infantry. POW, Winchester, September 19, 1864. Exchanged, March 15, 1865.
FRY, Richard. 24th Virginia Cavalry.
FRY, William H. Corporal, Company B, 24th Virginia Cavalry. Company K, 50th Virginia Infantry.
FULCHER, Albert (Alexander) R. (1841-1899). Sergeant, Company H, 58th Virginia Infantry. POW, Spotsylvania Court House May 12, 1864. Released from Fort Delaware, June 20, 1865.
FULCHER, Edward. Company D, 12th Virginia Infantry. UDC. CPA.
FULCHER, Gabriel F. Company D, 6th Virginia Infantry. WIA, Crampton's Gap. PCDR, Chimborazo Hospital in Richmond, September 11, 1864 of typhoid. Buried Oakwood Cemetery, Richmond. CPA.
FULCHER, Peter H. Company D, 12th Virginia Infantry. PCDR, KIA, Spotsylvania Court House, May 12, 1864.
FULCHER, Spencer S. Corporal, Company H, 58th Virginia Infantry. WIA, Fredericksburg, May 3, 1863. POW, Bethesda Church. Died in Elmira Prison, New York, on April 1, 1865. Buried Woodlawn National Cemetery.
FULCHER, William Lee (May 13, 1837-July 22, 1888). Company D, 12th Virginia Infantry. BPC. CPA.
GATES, Virgil Thomas. Company K, 50th Virginia Infantry. PCDR, Russellville, Kentucky, February 2, 1862, congestion of bowels.
GATES, William Benjamin (January 1, 1824-March 28, 1895). Company I, 5th Battalion Virginia Reserves
GEORGE, Andrew J. Company K, 50th Virginia Infantry. PCDR, Kanawha Valley, typhoid, August 23, 1861.
GEORGE, John W. Company A, 2nd Battalion North Carolina Infantry and Company H, 23rd Battalion Virginia Infantry.
GILBERT, George W. (February 1, 1829-June 22, 1902). Company H, 42nd Virginia Infantry. WIA. POW, Gettysburg. Exchanged from Point Lookout Prison, Maryland, on April 30, 1864. BPC.

GILBERT, John Frederick. Company I, 24th Virginia Infantry. POW, Williamsburg. Died of pneumonia in Richmond Hospital, May 20, 1864.
GILBERT, John R. Company G, 21st Virginia Cavalry.
GILBERT, Pendleton. Company I, 24th Virginia Infantry. Died, June 8, 1864 at Chimborazo Hospital (Richmond) from wounds at Drewry's Bluff. CPA.
GILBERT, Lorenzo Dow. Company I, 24th Virginia Infantry. WIA. POW, Gettysburg. Living 1909. UDC. CDAR. CPA.
GILBERT, Robert. Company I, 5th Battalion Virginia Reserves. CPA.
GILBERT, Samuel Lafayette (1821-1903). Possibly in Company E, 37th Virginia Militia. BPC at Wayside Church Cemetery lists him as Confederate veteran.
GILBERT, Samuel S. Company I, 24th Virginia Infantry. KIA, Gettysburg on July 3, 1863. CPA.
GILBERT, Thomas J. Company D, 12th Virginia Infantry. POW, Burgess Mill. Paroled at Point Lookout, February 18, 1865. CPA.
GILBERT, William Preston (December 20, 1846-July 9, 1939). Company I, 5th Battalion Virginia Reserves. Second from last Civil War soldier to die in Patrick. BPC. CPA.
GILES, Patrick H. Captain, Company I, 5th Battalion Virginia Reserves. CPA.
GILES, Smith Samuel. Company H, 42nd Virginia Infantry. Discharged after hiring substitute. Returned late in war.
GILLIE (GILLEY), Fountain. Company H, 42nd Virginia Infantry.
GILLEY, Greenberry B. Company H, 42nd Virginia Infantry. Died of typhoid fever, March 12, 1863, in Richmond Hospital.
GILLEY, Hagwood (Haygood). Company H, 38th Virginia Infantry. WIA, Drewry's Bluff, May 16, 1864.
GILLEY, Leftridge. Company H, 42nd Virginia Infantry. Died of disease, July 7, 1862, Charlottesville, Virginia
GILLEY, Peter D. Company H, 42nd Virginia Infantry. WIA, Kernstown, 1910C.
GILLEY, William. Company I, 24th Virginia Infantry. Died of typhoid fever in Chimborazo Hospital, Richmond, December 6, 1861.
GILLEY, William R. (1842-1910). Company F, 16th Virginia Infantry. POW, Burkeville. Released from Point Lookout Prison, Maryland, June 27, 1865. CPA. BPC.
GILPIN, Little B. Company H, 51st Virginia Infantry. Buried Edge Hill Cemetery, Charles Town, West Virginia.
GILPIN, Thomas. Company I, 24th Virginia Infantry. WIA, Fredericksburg.
GLIDEWELL, James A. McCarthy's Company, Richmond Artillery. WIA, Antietam.

GOAD, Henry J. Company H, 42nd Virginia Infantry. PCDR, KIA at Cedar Run, August 9, 1862.
GOARD, William M. Orange Artillery.
GOIN, James. PCDR, October 1, 1861.
GOIN, Perrin. Company K, 50th Virginia Infantry. KIA, Gettysburg.
GOINGS, Leroy. Company H, 51st Virginia Infantry. Company H, 23rd Battalion Virginia Infantry. POW.
GOINS (GOINGS), Ewell. Company K, 50th Virginia Infantry. CPA. BPC.
GOINS, Lee. Company D, 6th Virginia Infantry.
GOINS, Morgan. Company E, 53rd Regiment North Carolina Infantry. Born in Patrick County in 1842. Living in Surry County, North Carolina when he enlisted in the Army. Went North and took oath of allegiance to United States in April 1864.
GOINS, William Harden (1831-1864). Company E, 53rd Regiment North Carolina Infantry. Born in Patrick County but enlisted in Surry County, North Carolina in 1862. Died in January 28, 1864.
GOODE, Jonas. (June 23, 1830-May 8, 1907). Company B, 5th Virginia Infantry. POW. Exchanged. Paroled at Appomattox. CDAR. CPA. BPC.
GRADY, Patterson. Company I, 24th Virginia Infantry. PCDR, Richmond, Virginia, August 1862, breast complaint.
GRADY, Peter D. Company H, 58th Virginia Infantry. PCDR, measles, Staunton, February 6, 1862. Buried Thornrose Cemetery, Staunton, Virginia.
GRADY, William. Company H, 58th Virginia Infantry. CPA.
GRAHAM, Jackson. Company D, 51st Virginia Infantry.
GRAHAM, James. Company D, 51st Virginia Infantry.
GRAHAM, Noah B. Company H, 51st Virginia Infantry. KIA, Lee Town.
GRAHAM, Parris M. Company H, 51st Virginia Infantry. Lived in Floyd.
GRAY, John Floyd. Company D, 12th Virginia Infantry. WIA, August 1864 at Battle of Weldon Railroad, North Carolina. Living 1909. BPC. CPA. 1910C.
GREENWOOD, Thomas. Company D, 12th Virginia Infantry. PCDR, measles in Norfolk, May 5, 1862.
GREGORY, Christopher (February 17, 1837-March 24, 1908). Company B, 38th Virginia Infantry. BPC. CDAR. CPA.
GRIFFIN, Samuel J. Company H, 24th Virginia Infantry.
GRIFFIN, William F. Company H, 42nd Virginia Infantry. PCDR, measles, Charlottesville, Virginia, May 5, 1862.
GRIFFITH, James H. Company H, 58th Virginia Infantry. WIA. POW, Fredericksburg May 3, 1863. Exchanged. WIA, Wilderness May 6, 1864. CDAR.

GRIFFITH, Jehu. Mountain and Orange Artillery. Went North in 1865. Born in Franklin County.

GRIFFITH, Michael H. Corporal, Company D, 51st Virginia Infantry.

GRIFFITH, Perry. Company D, 51st Virginia Infantry.

GRIFFITH, Sparrell (1846-1920). Captain, Company H, 54th Virginia Infantry. Company H, 4th Virginia Reserves. BPC.

GRIGGS, Louis S. 42nd Virginia Infantry.

GRIGGS, William James (February 21, 1842-July 22, 1906). Company A, 42nd Virginia Infantry. WIA, Cedar Mountain, August 9, 1862. Leg amputated. BPC. CPA.

GROGAN, James Alexander. Company D, 10th Alabama Infantry. Born in North Carolina. CPA.

GROGAN, William D. Possibly in 64th Virginia Militia. 1910C.

GUNNELL, A. F. 1910C.

GUNTER, Beverley L. Company H, 58th Virginia Infantry. WIA, Wilderness, May 6, 1864 and at Hatcher's Run, February 6, 1865. CDAR. CPA. Also, Company K, 50th Virginia Infantry.

GUNTER, George B. Company I, 24th Virginia Infantry. BPC.

GUNTER, Joseph H. Company I, 24th Virginia Infantry.

GUNTER, William Wade. Company H, 53rd North Carolina Infantry. UDC. CDAR. CPA. BPC.

GUSLER, John. Company D, 12th Virginia Infantry. Died of chronic diarrhea at home in Patrick County June 22, 1863. CPA.

GUYNN, Aaron. Company E, 29th Virginia Infantry. WIA, Howlett House, May 18, 1864. POW April 2, 1865. Released from Point Lookout Prison, Maryland, June 11, 1865.

GUYNN, James. Company E, 29th Virginia Infantry. Discharged because of over age. Later served in 28th Virginia Cavalry.

GUYNN, Lemuel. Company E, 29th Virginia Infantry. Tradition states he was killed by the Carroll County Home Guard.

GUYNN, Levi. Company E, 29th Virginia Infantry. Died in Patrick County, November 12, 1864. Buried in Old Willow Hill Cemetery. CPA.

HADEN (Hayden), Seaton or Ceaton (1840-1921). Company H, 51st Virginia Infantry. BPC. UDC. CDAR.

HADEN, William H. Company I, 24th Virginia Infantry. WIA, Second Manassas. POW, Burkeville, April 6, 1865. Released from Point Lookout Prison, Maryland, June 13, 1865. UDC. CPA.

HAGOOD (HAGWOOD), William R. Company K, 6th Virginia Infantry. Company G, 21st Virginia Cavalry. POW, Point Lookout, Maryland. CDAR.

HAIRSTON, James Thomas Watt. Born in 1835 at old Fort Mayo, Major in Confederate Army. Assistant Aide-de-camp and Assistant Adjutant General for J. E. B. Stuart January 16, 1862 until March 1, 1863.

HAIRSTON, Samuel Harden. Major, Company H, 24th Virginia Infantry. On staff of General J.E.B. Stuart May 5, 1862 until March 31, 1863. Born at old Fort Mayo, 1822. Killed in state capital disaster, 1870.
HALE, Jerry L. Company H, 51st Virginia Infantry. Living 1909.
HALEY, Grissom M. F. Company H, 51st Virginia Infantry.
HALEY, James R. Company D, 51st Virginia Infantry.
HALEY, Samuel R. H. Company I, 24th Virginia Infantry. Company G, 21st Virginia Cavalry. WIA. POW, Gettysburg. Exchanged. Furloughed. CDAR. CPA. BPC.
HALL, Adam. Died April 7, 1865 of typhoid.
HALL, Andrew J. Private. Company E, 53rd Regiment North Carolina Infantry. Born in Patrick in 1834. Inducted at Raleigh, North Carolina April 30, 1862. PCDR, Camp Mangum, Raleigh of pneumonia on June 14, 1862.
HALL, Burwell R. Sergeant, Company D, 51st Virginia Infantry.
HALL, David T. Company D, 51st Virginia Infantry. PCDR, KIA, Fort Donelson, Tennessee, February 14, 1862. CPA.
HALL, David Thomas (April 15, 1838-November 27, 1931). Company D, 51st Virginia Infantry.
HALL, Elijah Harden. Company H, 51st Virginia Infantry. Living 1909. BPC. CPA.
HALL, Henry. Company H, 58th Virginia Infantry. WIA, Fredericksburg, May 3, 1863.
HALL, Henry. Mountain and Orange Artillery. CDAR. CPA.
HALL, Henry. Company H, 51st Virginia Infantry. 1910C. Born in North Carolina.
HALL, Jackson. Possibly in 54th Virginia Infantry. KIA, Battle of Chickamauga, September 13, 1863.
HALL, James Franklin (1841-1909). Company D, 51st Virginia Infantry. Medical discharge. Re-enlisted. POW, Waynesboro, March 2, 1865. Released from Fort Delaware Prison, June 20, 1865. BPC. CPA.
HALL, James P. Company B, 24th Virginia Infantry. POW, Chaffin's Farm, October 2, 1864. Exchanged March 28, 1865. BPC. CPA.
HALL, Jasper R. (1826-1916). Company D, 51st Virginia Infantry. WIA, Winchester, July 24, 1864. POW, September 19, 1864. Exchanged, March 18, 1865. CPA.
HALL, John C. Company D, 51st Virginia Infantry.
HALL, John H. Company H, 51st Virginia Infantry. Living 1907. CPA.
HALL, Lemuel. Killed in Wytheville, Virginia, December 20, 1862 by train.
HALL, Nathan R. Lieutenant, Company H, 51st Virginia Infantry. POW, Lee Town, August 25, 1864. Released from Fort Delaware Prison, June 16, 1865. BPC. UDC. CPA.
HALL, Russell. Company I, 5th Battalion Virginia Reserves.

HALL, Samuel S. Company K, 50th Virginia Infantry.
HALL, Waller. Company I, 5th Battalion Virginia Reserves. Living 1907. BPC. CPA.
HALL, William Crawford (April 15, 1848-Dec 6, 1929). Company E, 6th Virginia Infantry. BPC.
HALL, William Henry. Company G, 53rd North Carolina Infantry.
HALL, William Lee (September 18, 1844-October 4, 1926). Company D, 51st Virginia Infantry. POW, Waynesboro, March 2, 1865. Released from Fort Delaware, June 20, 1865. BPC. CPA.
HANBY, David S. (1821-1890). Company K, 50th Virginia Infantry. BPC.
HANBY, Henderson Harrison. Company H, 51st Virginia Infantry. Killed September 1861.BPC. CPA.
HANCOCK, James A. Sergeant, Company E, 50th Virginia Infantry. POW, Fort Donelson, February 16, 1862. POW, Wilderness, May 6, 1864. POW, Point Lookout, Maryland and Elmira, New York.
HANCOCK, John. (1834-March 3,1897). Company B, 2nd North Carolina Infantry Regiment. Moved to Surry County, North Carolina in 1857 and volunteered there in 1861. POW, paroled. POW, Gettysburg, Point Lookout Prison, Maryland. Later sent to Savannah, Georgia. Exchanged.
HANCOCK, John Henry (June 6, 1841-July 8, 1927). Company H, 42nd Virginia Infantry. Medical discharge, September 1861. BPC. CPA.
HANCOCK, John T. Company D, 51st Virginia Infantry. POW, Waynesboro, March 2, 1865. Released from Fort Delaware, June 20, 1865.
HANCOCK, Lewis D. Sergeant, Company E, 50th Virginia Infantry. POW, Wilderness, May 6, 1864. POW, Point Lookout, Maryland and Elmira New York.
HANCOCK, Lewis P. Company I, 5th Battalion Virginia Reserves.
HANDY, Harrison H. Company H. 51st Virginia Infantry. KIA, September 17, 1861.
HANDY, James Preston. Company E, 6th Virginia Infantry. WIA, Charles City Road, June 21, 1862. Buried Oakwood Cemetery, Richmond. PCDR.
HANDY, John R. Company K, 50th Virginia Infantry. CPA. BPC.
HANDY, Nathaniel J. J. (1842-1924). Company H, 51st Virginia Infantry. Living 1907. BPC.
HANDY, Peter. Company H, 51st Virginia Infantry. POW, Waynesboro, March 2, 1865. Released from Fort McHenry, Maryland, May 1, 1865. CDAR. CPA.
HANDY, Samuel Isaac. Company K, 50th Virginia Infantry.
HANDY, Sanders W. 1910C.
HANDY, W. R. Company K, 50th Virginia Infantry. Living 1907.

HANKS, Pugh H. Company D, 51st Virginia Infantry.

HARBOUR, Abner J. "Zack" (1840-1925). Lieutenant Company D, 51st Virginia Infantry. Company G, 21st Virginia Cavalry. POW. BPC. CPA.

HARBOUR, Ahira J. "Hick" (January 20, 1843-May 26, 1915). Company D, 51st Virginia Infantry. WIA, Fayetteville, September 10, 1862. BPC. CDAR. CPA.

HARBOUR, Chapman J. (December 8, 1829-March 10, 1910). Company D, 51st Virginia Infantry. Medical discharge for tuberculosis. First Board of Supervisors of Patrick County. BPC.

HARBOUR, Charles J. Company D, 12th Virginia Infantry. KIA, Battle of the Crater, Petersburg, Virginia, July 30, 1864.

HARBOUR, Elkana J. (1830-1864). Company G, 21st Virginia Cavalry. WIA, New Creek, West Virginia. Leg amputated. Died August 20, 1864 at age 33. Buried at New Creek.

HARBOUR, Joshua T. Company D, 51st Virginia Infantry. PCDR, wounds at Fayette Court House, West Virginia September 10 or 20, 1862.

HARBOUR, Marion J. (March 16, 1836-October 16, 1903). Company K, 6th Virginia Infantry. Medical discharge. BPC. CPA.

HARBOUR, Moses Green (1833-1910). Captain, 73rd North Carolina Militia. Born Patrick County. Moved to Surry County, North Carolina. CPA.

HARBOUR, Richard Harrison "Tip" (May 19, 1841-June 9, 1915). Mountain and Orange Artillery. BPC. CDAR. CPA.

HARDY, Joseph H. Company G, 42nd Virginia Infantry.

HARMON, Essais (born circa 1842-Died after 1911). Second Company G, 21st Virginia Cavalry. BPC. UDC.

HARRELL, David Kent. (January 25, 1842-November 23, 1921). Corporal, Company K, 50th Virginia Infantry. WIA, Wilderness, May 5, 1864. BPC. UDC. CDAR. CPA.

HARRELL, Enos Sylvester. Company E, 29th Virginia Infantry. 1910C.

HARRELL, Thomas G. (October 14, 1830-February 4, 1908). Company K, 50th Virginia Infantry. BPC.

HARRELL, William B. Company K, 50th Virginia Infantry. Died in Point Lookout Prison, Maryland. CPA.

HARRIS, George L. Company D, 51st Virginia Infantry. WIA, Fayette Court House, West Virginia, September 10, 1862. Living 1909.

HARRIS, George L. Corporal, Company D, 51st Virginia Infantry. Died of measles, Charlottesville, April 17, 1862. CPA.

HARRIS, George S. Company I, 24th Virginia Infantry.

HARRIS, Greenville R. Company H, 51st Virginia Infantry. Medical discharge, February 16, 1862 for rheumatism. Died December 14, 1890.

HARRIS, Hiram. Company D, 12th Virginia Infantry. POW, Crampton's Gap, September 1, 1862. Exchanged, October 1862. WIA, Cold Harbor, June 1864. Died at Stuart Hospital, Richmond, June 25, 1864.

HARRIS, Israel Thomas (1837-1914). Company H, 42nd Virginia Infantry. WIA, Kernstown, March 23, 1862. BPC. CPA. 1910C.

HARRIS, James H. H. Possibly in 37th Virginia Infantry. PCDR, Richmond, January 17, 1864 of smallpox.

HARRIS, Newman. Company H, 51st Virginia Infantry.

HARRIS, Phillip. Company H, 51st Virginia Infantry. Native of Floyd County.

HARRIS, Samuel Green. Company K, 50th Virginia Infantry. Living 1909. BPC. CPA.

HARRIS, William H. Company H, 42nd Virginia Infantry. Medical discharge, January 24, 1862.

HARRIS, William. Company I, 24th Virginia Infantry.

HARRIS, William. Company H, 51st Virginia Infantry. Died August 30, 1863 of cause unknown.

HARRIS, William T. Company D, 51st Virginia Infantry. POW, Waynesboro, March 2, 1865. Released, Fort Delaware Prison, June 20, 1865.

HARROLD, Henry. Company D, 12th Virginia Infantry. WIA, Maryland Campaign, 1862. POW, Burgess Mill, October 27, 1862. Released June 1, 1865 from Point Lookout. BPC. CPA.

HARROLD, T. M. Company E, 29th Virginia Infantry.

HATCHER, Charles. Company I, 18th North Carolina Infantry. Born in Patrick County 1817. Moved to Surry County and enlisted at Wake County, North Carolina. Died in Surry County 1864.

HATCHER, Daniel G. Lieutenant, Company I, 24th Virginia Infantry. WIA. POW, Gettysburg. Released from Johnson's Island, South Carolina, March 14, 1865. CPA.

HATCHER, Eden T. Company D, 51st Virginia Infantry. POW, Waynesboro, March 2, 1865. Released from Fort Delaware Prison, June 20, 1865.

HATCHER, Elkanah (Ephram). (August 19, 1842-September 11, 1901). Company D, 51st Virginia Infantry. POW, Waynesboro March 2, 1865. Released from Fort Delaware June 20, 1865.

HATCHER, James C. Died May 17, 1865 of typhoid fever.

HATCHER, James Wellington (1838-1895). Lieutenant, Company H, 58th Virginia Infantry. WIA, at Gaines Mill, 1862, and Spotsylvania Court House, 1864. Surrender at Appomattox. CDAR. CPA.

HATCHER, John B. Company D, 51st Virginia Infantry. Medical discharge, 1863.

HATCHER, John H. Company K, 50th Virginia Infantry. Died at Blue Sulphur Springs of fever, October 7, 1861.
HATCHER, Joseph. Company K, 50th Virginia Infantry. Died October 14, 1861 of fever at White Sulfur Springs.
HATCHER, Robert. Company H, 42nd Virginia Infantry. 1910C.
HATCHER, Rush E. (January 24, 1845-November 18, 1912). Company I, 5th Battalion Virginia Reserves. BPC.
HATCHER, Thomas J. Company K, 50th Virginia Infantry. PCDR, Elmira Prison, New York, September 20, 1864 of scurvy.
HATCHER, William. Company H, 58th Virginia Infantry. Died, Bedford, October 2, 1861, typhoid. CPA.
HATCHER, William H. Company H, 42nd Virginia Infantry. WIA, left thigh at Kernstown, March 23, 1862. Court-martialed for desertion, but received lenient sentence for previous good record. Reinstated. POW, Spotsylvania Court House. Released from Point Lookout Prison, Maryland, May 12, 1865. CPA.
HAWKS, Pugh H. Company D, 51st Virginia Infantry. Died, Jackson Hospital, Richmond, July 24, 1865. Buried at Hollywood Cemetery, Richmond.
HAYMORE, D. H. Company D, 29th Virginia Infantry. UDC. CDAR. CPA.
HAYNES, Alexander. Lieutenant Colonel, Company E, 29th Virginia Infantry. Born in Ararat, Virginia. WIA, Drewry's Bluff May 5, 1864. Died at Richmond Hospital on May 30, 1864. HAYNES, Columbus (October 16,1839-May 21,1881). Company I, 54th Virginia Infantry.
HAYNES, Ferdinand (February 19, 1839-June 20, 1916). Company G, 42nd Virginia Infantry. WIA, Gettysburg. POW. Exchanged from Fort Delaware Prison in February 1865. BPC. CDAR. CPA.
HAYNES, George S. PCDR, measles, Charlottesville, April 17, 1862.
HAYNES, John. Company E, 29th Virginia Infantry. Tradition states he was killed by Carroll County Home Guard.
HAYNES, Lafayette (1841-1881). Company B, 54th Virginia Infantry. POW, November 25, 1863, at Missionary Ridge, Tennessee. Enlisted in U. S Army on October 14, 1864, at Rock Island, Illinois for service on the frontier.
HAYNES, Littleberry. Company E, 29th Virginia Infantry.
HAYNES, Stephen M. Company E, 29th Virginia Infantry. Discharged because of over age. Later in 4th Virginia Reserves.
HAYNES, Virgil S. (1845-1864). Company G, 21st Virginia Cavalry. POW, September 12, 1864, at Front Royal. Died in prison at Point Lookout, Maryland.
HAYNES, William H. Company E, 29th Virginia Infantry. Discharged. Re-enlisted. Died 1903 in Carroll County, Virginia

HAZELWOOD, Edward. PCDR, Strasburg, Virginia, May 20, 1862 of fever at age of 23.
HAZELWOOD, Hiram G. Company D, 51st Virginia Infantry. CPA.
HAZELWOOD, Hiram. Company H, 58th Virginia Infantry. PCDR, typhoid, February 12, 1862 at Camp Zollicoffer, Huntersville, Alabama. CPA.
HAZELWOOD, Robert F. Company G, 12th Virginia Infantry. POW.
HEADEN, William D. Company I, 24th Virginia Infantry.
HEARD (HURD), Ira. Company G, 21st Virginia Cavalry.
HEFFLEFINGER, Henry A. Company K, 50th Virginia Infantry. POW, Snickers Gap July 18, 1864. POW, Washington D. C. and Elmira, New York. Died, February 9, 1922. Buried Hollywood Cemetery, Richmond. LCA.
HELMS, Adam (1836-1915). Mountain and Orange Artillery. BPC. CDAR.
HELMS, George M. Company A, 42nd Virginia Infantry.
HELMS, Joseph. Company D, 54th Virginia Infantry.
HELMS, Thomas J. PCDR, Raleigh County, West Virginia, November 1861, typhoid, age 22.
HELMS, Samuel. Died June 8, 1862 of fever.
HENDRICKS, Nathaniel J. Company D, 29th Virginia Infantry. Living 1870 in Carroll County
HENDRICKS, R. D. Tombstone inscription states he was a Confederate veteran. BPC. CPA.
HENDRICKS, William. Third Company C, 19th Battalion Virginia Heavy Artillery.
HENSLEY, Alexander. Company H, 42nd Virginia Infantry. POW, Cedar Creek, October 19, 1864. Exchanged from Point Lookout Prison, Maryland, March 30, 1865.
HENSLEY, Robert A. Company H, 42nd Virginia Infantry. POW, Spotsylvania Court House, May 12, 1864. Exchanged, November 15, 1864.
HIATT, Anderson. Company E, 29th Virginia Infantry.
HIATT, Jesse E. Company E, 29th Virginia Infantry.
HIATT, John. Company D, 12th Virginia Infantry. PCDR. Died Saint Charles Hospital, Richmond, July 12, 1862 at age 33. Epileptic. CPA.
HIATT, Uriah Franklin. Company E, 29th Virginia Infantry. Received medical discharge.
HIATT, William (March 12, 1835-December 9, 1909). Company E, 29th Virginia Infantry. BPC. CPA.
HIGH, William H. (b. 1807). Company H, 58th Virginia Infantry. Discharged.
HILL, Hyram. Company H, 58th Virginia Infantry. WIA, Fredericksburg.

HILL, Nathaniel Davis (1825-1903). Company H, 23rd Battalion Virginia Infantry. POW November 6, 1863. Exchanged from Fort Delaware Prison. Sent to Chimborazo Hospital in Richmond. Medical discharge. BPC.

HILL, Phillip. Company D, 12th Virginia Infantry. Died at home in Patrick County, May 29, 1862 of pneumonia, age 32.

HILL, W. D. Company F, 5th Battalion Virginia Reserves.

HINES, James H. Company H, 51st Virginia Infantry. Living 1907. CPA.

HODGES, Robert. Company D, 51st Virginia Infantry.

HOGAN, Abram. Company D or H, 51st Virginia Infantry.

HOLLAND, James Ballard, Company K, 50th Virginia Infantry. Died, October 16, 1863 at Point Lookout Prison, Maryland. Buried at Finn's Point National Cemetery, Salem, New Jersey.

HOLLANDSWORTH, Thomas L. Company D, 51st Virginia Infantry. KIA.

HOLLEY, David. Company D, 51st Virginia Infantry. Tombstone inscription states that he was member of Company A, Tuttle's Virginia Troops. BPC.

HOLLEY, James R. Company D, 51st Virginia Infantry.

HOLLEY, Thomas R. Company D, 51st Virginia Infantry.

HOLLEY, William. 21st Virginia Cavalry. POW, Moorefield, West Virginia, August 7, 1864. Released from Camp Chase Prison, Ohio February 23, 1865.

HOLLINGSWORTH, John Jackson. Company D, 6th Virginia Infantry. WIA, Crampton's Gap, Maryland, October 8, 1862. Hospitalized remainder of war.

HOLT, William. Company K, 50th Virginia Infantry. POW Waynesboro, March 2, 1865. POW Fort Delaware.

HOOKER, Ephraim. Company I, 5th Battalion Virginia Reserves. CPA.

HOOKER, James. Company D, 12th Virginia Infantry. Medical discharge, July 11, 1862.

HOOKER, James E. Company I, 5th Virginia Infantry. Living 1907.

HOOKER, John W (M). (1833-1915). Orange Artillery. Enlisted April 1, 1862. Discharged June 10, 1862. Grandfather of Judge John D. Hooker.

HOOKER, Leroy. Company D, 12th Virginia Infantry.

HOOKER, Samuel H. Company H, 51st Virginia Infantry. Medical discharge, July 25, 1862.

HOOKER, Samuel (1830-1900). Company K, 50th Virginia Infantry. CDAR. CPA.

HOOKER, William. Company I, 24th Virginia Infantry. Died in hospital.

HOPKINS, Harvey D. (July 5, 1835-March 14, 1922). Company D, 51st Virginia Infantry. POW, Waynesboro, March 2, 1865. Released from Fort Delaware Prison, June 20, 1865. BPC.

HOPKINS, James M. Company H, 51st Virginia Infantry. POW, Waynesboro, March 2, 1865. Released from Fort Delaware Prison, June 20, 1865.

HOPKINS, John. PCDR, May 15, 1862 of fever.

HOPKINS, John H. Company H, 22nd North Carolina Infantry. POW. MIA.

HORSLEY, Reuben C. Company D, 51st Virginia Infantry.

HOUCHINS, Abram W. (December 16, 1827-March 19, 1916). Company D, 51st Virginia Infantry. BPC. CPA.

HOUCHINS, John Burwell. Company K, 50th Virginia Infantry. Living 1907.

HOUCHINS, John T. Company K, 50th Virginia Infantry. Left in Tennessee, February 1862.

HOUCHINS, Moses Lee (1834-1862). Orange Artillery. Became ill in camp near Richmond. Died in Burkeville on way home.

HOWELL, Caleb. Company D or H, 51st Virginia Infantry.

HOWELL, Isaac L. Company D, 51st Virginia Infantry. POW.

HOWELL, Samuel. Company K, 50th Virginia Infantry. KIA, 1864.

HOWELL, Thomas D. (September 4, 1840-July 18, 1917). Company G, 21st Virginia Cavalry. BPC.

HOWELL, J. C. Company H, 51st Virginia Infantry. POW, Waynesboro, March 2, 1865. Released from Fort Delaware Prison, May 1, 1865.

HOWELL, John W. Company D, 51st Virginia Infantry.

HOWELL, William A. Company H, 51st Virginia Infantry.

HUBBARD, Benjamin B. Company H, 51st Virginia Infantry. POW, Winchester, September 19, 1864. Exchanged from Point Lookout Prison, Maryland, March 17, 1865.

HUBBARD, James W. Company D, 12th Virginia Infantry. POW, May 12, 1864 at Spotsylvania Court House. Exchanged March 1865. Furloughed sick.

HUBBARD, Jefferson. Company I, 5th Battalion Virginia Reserves.

HUBBARD, John C. Company H, 51st Virginia Infantry. CDAR. CPA.

HUBBARD, Jonathan W. Company D, 51st Virginia Infantry. POW, Waynesboro, March 2, 1865. Released from Fort Delaware Prison, June 20, 1865. BPC.

HUBBARD, Steven W. Company D, 51st. Virginia Infantry. Died in service.

HUBBARD, Thomas M. Company D, 51st Virginia Infantry. POW, Waynesboro, March 2, 1865. Released from Fort Delaware Prison, June 20, 1865. LCA.

HUBBARD, W. J. Company I, 5th Battalion Virginia Reserves.

HUBBARD, William. Company H, 51st Virginia Infantry. Died May 20, 1863 at Emory and Henry College Hospital, Washington County, Virginia of cause unknown.

HUDNALL, Claudius B. Company A, 42nd Virginia Infantry. Teamster. Surrendered at Appomattox.
HUDSON, John. Company D, 51st Virginia Infantry.
HUFF, John H. Company H, 51st Virginia Infantry.
HUGHES, James Matthew. Company H, 58th Virginia Infantry. Died of disease, Lynchburg Hospital, October 4, 1861.
HUGHES, John J. Company H, 51st Virginia Infantry. Living 1907. BPC.
HUGHES, R.P. Sergeant, Co B, 24th Virginia Cavalry.
HUGHES, Rutledge Powell. Lieutenant, Company I, 24th Virginia Infantry. Medical discharge, May 10, 1862.
HUGHES, William J. 51st Virginia Infantry. Died of fever, Mercer County, West Virginia, November 9 (or 15), 1861. CPA.
HUNLEY, Edward C. HUNDLEY (HUNLEY), Edward C. Company H, 42nd Virginia Infantry. PCDR, measles, Charlottesville, May 1862.
HUNDLEY, George H. Corporal, Company H, 58th Virginia Infantry. Killed, Fredericksburg, May 4, 1863. CPA.
HUNDLEY, James S. Company I, 24th Virginia Infantry. Died of pneumonia, May 31, 1861 (or December 5, 1862) at Camp Windsor, Lynchburg.
HUNDLEY, John Lee. Company A, 42nd Virginia Infantry.
HUNDLEY, William F. 42nd Virginia Infantry. UDC.
HUNGATE, Thomas. Company D, 51st Virginia Infantry. Enlisted 1864.
HURD, William B. Company H, 58th Virginia Infantry.
HUTCHINS, John W. Company H, 53rd North Carolina Infantry.
HUTTS, James B. Company H, 42nd Virginia Infantry. Died November 17, 1862 of typhoid at Staunton Hospital. Buried in Thornrose Cemetery, Staunton.
HUTTS, Owen. Company H, 42nd Virginia Infantry. PCDR, Winchester, January 8, 1862. Death Register states January 13 of pneumonia.
HYLTON, Ballard. Company A, 24th Virginia Infantry.
HYLTON, Gabriel. Sergeant, Company D, 12th Virginia Infantry. Furnished substitute and was discharged.
HYLTON, George Wade (September 7, 1823-August 12, 1898). Lieutenant, Company H, 58th Virginia Infantry. Resigned May 1, 1862. Returned to service by October 29, 1864 and was at Camp Lee in 10th Virginia Cavalry. POW, Petersburg. Released from Point Lookout Prison, Maryland June 14, 1865. BPC.
HYLTON, Harden. Company H, 51st Virginia Infantry. CPA.
HYLTON, Ira A. Sergeant, Company D, 51st Virginia Infantry. Died of typhoid fever, September 9, 1862, at hospital at Emory and Henry College, Washington County, Virginia.
HYLTON, Jacob. Company D, 12th Virginia Infantry. Died August 4, 1862 of acute hepatitis at General Hospital, Petersburg. CPA.

HYLTON, James A. (April 15, 1844-August 6, 1923). Company K, 50th Virginia Infantry. Company I, 5th Battalion Virginia Reserves. BPC. CDAR. CPA.
HYLTON, Levi. Company E, 18th Battalion Virginia Heavy Artillery.
HYLTON, William B. Company D, 51st Virginia Infantry. CPA.
INGRAM, George W. Company A, 5th Battalion Virginia Reserves.
INGRAM, Richard L. Company H, 51st Virginia Infantry. Took oath and went North.
INGRAM, William Green (November 26, 1847-September 6, 1933). Company I, 62nd North Carolina Infantry.
IVIE, George Gilbert. Company H, 58th Virginia Infantry. Died Monterey Hospital, March 20, 1862.
IVIE, John H. Company H, 58th Virginia Infantry. Died of erysipelas, September 1862, Gordonsville.
JACKSON, Charles. Company H, 51st Virginia Infantry.
JAMES, Rufer. Family tradition states that he served in Civil War. BPC.
JAMES, Willis (1840-1916). Served in Company F, 21st NC Infantry. Born in Patrick. Moved to Surry County, North Carolina. POW. Released from Point Lookout Prison, Maryland, July 28, 1865.
JANNEY, John. Company D, 51st Virginia Infantry.
JARRELL, Albert H. Company A, 2nd North Carolina Infantry.
JEFFERSON, John Pinkwood (July 6, 1842-1883). Company D, 51st Virginia Infantry. POW, Winchester, September 19, 1864. Exchanged from Point Lookout Prison, Maryland, March 15, 1865. Died Hancock County, Tennessee.
JEFFERSON, Moses Peter (1842-1928). Company H, 51st Virginia Infantry. Orange Artillery. WIA, Totopotomy Creek, May 30, 1864. BPC. CPA.
JEFFERSON, Peyton Graves. Company E, 6th Virginia Infantry, Company H, 51st Virginia Infantry. WIA, Totopotomy Creek, May 30, 1864. Brother to Moses P. Jefferson. BPC. CDAR.
JEFFERSON, Thomas T. Company H, 51st Virginia Infantry. BPC.
JEFFERSON, William J. (1846-1923). Company D, 51st Virginia Infantry. POW, Waynesboro, March 2, 1865. Released from Fort Delaware Prison, June 7, 1865. CPA.
JENKINS, George W. Company H, 42nd Virginia Infantry. Died of typhoid fever in Staunton Hospital, Virginia, May 1862.
JENKINS, Peter. Company I, 5th Battalion Virginia Reserves.
JENNINGS, Luther. Company C, 45th Virginia Infantry.
JESSUP, Elijah S. (April 23, 1831-July 12, 1904). Company D, 12th Virginia Infantry. POW, Crampton's Gap, Maryland, September 14, 1862. Exchanged, Fort Delaware Prison, October 1862. BPC.
JESSUP, Sanders. Possibly Company K, 50th Virginia Infantry. BPC.
JOHNSON, David. Company I, 24th Virginia Infantry. UDC. CPA.

JONES, Henry. Company A, 29th Virginia Infantry.
JONES, Preston. Company G, 29th Virginia Infantry.
JOYCE, Abram. Company I, 5th Battalion Virginia Reserves. CPA.
JOYCE, Calvin R. (April 18, 1846-November 10, 1895). Company C, 10th Virginia Cavalry. Company I, 5th Battalion Virginia Reserves. BPC. CPA.
JOYCE, James M. Company H, 42nd Virginia Infantry. Died in Charlottesville Hospital, August 8, 1864, of wound received at the Battle of the Wilderness.
JOYCE, James W. Company H, 58th Virginia Infantry. WIA, Manassas, 1862 and 1864.
JOYCE, John W. (December 24, 1834-August 28, 1906). Corporal, Company B, 22nd Battalion North Carolina Infantry. Born in Patrick Springs. Moved to Surry County, North Carolina circa 1857. Volunteered for Confederate on August 10, 1861. POW, Roanoke Island. Paroled. Regimental Teamster. Died in Surry County, North Carolina.
JOYCE, John William. Company I, 24th Virginia Infantry. PCDR, rubella, April 22, 1862 at Charlottesville Hospital. Native of Stokes County, North Carolina.
JOYCE, L. G. Company G, 21st Virginia Cavalry. WIA.
JOYCE, Thomas. Company H, 51st Virginia Infantry.
JOYCE, R. M. Company C, 6th Virginia Infantry.
JOYCE, William. 24th Virginia Cavalry. CPA.
JOYCE, William H. Sergeant, Company H, 58th Virginia Infantry. Died of pneumonia, Charlottesville, June 28, 1862.
JOYCE, William L. Company G, 42nd Virginia Infantry.
JOYCE, Willis (1840-1916). Company F, 21st North Carolina Infantry. POW. Released from Point Lookout Prison, Maryland July 28, 1865.
JUSTICE, John Caleb. Company I, 5th Battalion Virginia Reserves. Died at Lee Camp Soldier's Home, November 4, 1935. Buried in Hollywood Cemetery. LCA.
JUSTICE, John. Company D, 51st Virginia Infantry. PCDR, July 22, 1861, on way to army after induction.
KASEY, John F. Company H, 58th Virginia Infantry. Died of disease, December 22, 1861, Staunton.
KASEY, William P. Company H, 58th Virginia Infantry. CPA.
KEATON, Hansford J. Company H, 42nd Virginia Infantry. Medical discharge. Died of old age at Critz, Virginia in 1900. CDAR. CPA.
KEATON, Harris. Company I, 5th Battalion Virginia Reserves.
KEATON, Hiram. Company D, 51st Virginia Infantry. Medical discharged, February 1, 1863.
KEATON, Hiram Lee (June 16, 1843-November 5, 1921). Company H, 42nd Virginia Infantry. POW, Payne's Farm, November 27, 1863. Exchanged, March 16, 1865. BPC.

KEATON, James M. Company D, 51st Virginia Infantry. Living in 1909. CPA.

KEATON, McAlexander. Company I, 24th Virginia Infantry. PCDR, Charlottesville, April 6, 1864 of measles, age 18.

KEATON, Madison (Matt). Company I, 24th Virginia Infantry. Died of chronic diarrhea at Elmira Prison Hospital, New York, December 20, 1864. CPA.

KEATON, White. Company I, 24th Virginia Infantry.

KEATON, William S. Company H, 58th Virginia Infantry. POW Harrisonburg, Virginia, June 6, 1862. Paroled. WIA, Fredericksburg. Died February 24, 1892.

KEESLING, Ephram. Company H, 51st Virginia Infantry. Died Saint Louis, Missouri. Buried, Jefferson Barracks National Cemetery.

KEISTER, Andrew M. Company I, 24th Virginia Infantry. POW. Exchanged February 13, 1865.

KENDRICK, John H. Company H, 5th Battalion Virginia Reserves.

KENDRICK, William. Company A, 42nd Virginia Infantry.

KENNELLY, Edward C. Died of measles, Charlottesville, Virginia, May 1862 at age 35.

KIMBALL (or Kimble), William. Company K, 50th Virginia Infantry.

KING, Benjamin S. Company I, 24th Virginia Infantry. KIA, Drewry's Bluff 1864.

KING, C. Henry. Company K, 50th Virginia Infantry.

KING, George Robert. Company K, 50th Virginia Infantry. Died circa 1930 in Patrick County. CDAR.

KING, John B. Possibly in Company I, 54th Virginia Infantry. CDAR.

KING, Henry J. (1823-1886). Tombstone states he was veteran of Civil War. BPC. CPA.

KING, Robert F. Company K, 50th Virginia Infantry. Living 1907. BPC.

KING, S. B. Company D, 50th Virginia Infantry. UDC.

KING, William. Company K, 50th Virginia Infantry. Company I, 24th Virginia Infantry. Died of fever March 18, 1865 in New York.

KNOWLES, Naamon William. Company H, 51st Virginia Infantry. POW, Waynesboro, March 2, 1865. Released from Fort Delaware Prison, June 17, 1865.

KOGER, Daniel King. Company H, 42nd Virginia Infantry. KIA.

KOGER, James M. Company H, 42nd Virginia Infantry. WIA, Chancellorsville. POW, South Mountain, Pa, July 4, 1863. Died in prison at Point Lookout Prison, Maryland, December 14, 1863 of chronic diarrhea.

KOGER, Joseph H. (January 12, 1834-August 2, 1923). Company H, 42nd Virginia Infantry. POW, Spotsylvania Court House. Released from Elmira Prison, New York, June 19, 1865. BPC. 1910C.

KOGER, Middleton. Sergeant, Company G, 42nd Virginia Infantry. POW September 1864. Prisoner at Point Lookout, Maryland.

KOGER, William Lee. Company H, 24th Virginia Cavalry. CPA.

LACKEY, George (April 3, 1841-July 3, 1863). Company B, 57th Regiment Virginia Infantry. KIA, Gettysburg.

LACKEY, James. (December 8, 1843-September 12, 1862). Company B, 57th Virginia Infantry. Died September 12, 1862 of diphtheria in regional hospital, Lynchburg.

LACKEY, James Marshall. Company D, 51st Virginia Infantry.

LACKEY, John (May 15, 1838-October 4, 1863). Company B, 24th Virginia Infantry. Died of pneumonia at Hanover Junction, October 4, 1863.

LACKEY, John Elcaney, Sergeant Company D, 51st Virginia Infantry. Company G, 21st Virginia Cavalry. POW, Winchester, September 13, 1864. Died of smallpox at Camp Chase Prison, Ohio on December 20, 1864, (grave #638).

LACKEY, Josiah (December 19, 1830-November 24, 1864). Company B, 57th Virginia Infantry. Died Chimborazo Hospital, November 20, 1864, of disease.

LACKEY, W. C. Company H, 51st Virginia Infantry.

LAMB, John. Company B, 24th Virginia Cavalry.

LAMBERT, Columbus C. Company K, 50th Virginia Infantry. Died of fever October 13, 1861 at White Sulphur Springs.

LANCASTER, Nathaniel. Company D, 51st Virginia Infantry.

LANCASTER, Thomas J. Company D, 12th Virginia Infantry. POW, Burgess Mill, October 27, 1864. Released from Point Lookout Prison, Maryland, June 26, 1865.

LANKFORD, James. Company D, 5th Battalion Virginia Reserves. 1910C. Born in England.

LAW, William J. (May 18, 1824-May 4, 1907). Possibly in Company E, 20th Virginia Cavalry. Lived in Henry County. BPC.

LAWLESS, Andrew Jackson. Company I, 24th Virginia Infantry. KIA, Drewry's Bluff.

LAWLESS, Francis Marion. Company I, 24th Virginia Infantry. PCDR, measles, August 9, 1862 in Richmond. Buried in Hollywood Cemetery.

LAWLESS, George Washington. Company I, 24th Virginia Infantry. WIA, Gettysburg. Living in 1909. CDAR. CPA.

LAWLESS, McNealy C. Company I, 24th Virginia Infantry.

LAWLESS, Thomas Jefferson. Company I, 24th Virginia Infantry. POW, Williamsburg. Escaped from prison and returned to duty. Another source says, "left behind in Pa."

LAWRENCE, William R. Company H, 24th Virginia Infantry. CDAR. CPA.

LAWSON, Abram T. Company K, 50th Virginia Infantry. POW. Died of measles at Point Lookout Prison, Maryland (or Elmira Prison, New York).

LAWSON, Andrew J. Company D, 12th Virginia Infantry. POW, Burgess Mill, October 2, 1864. Released from Point Lookout Prison, Maryland, May 13, 1865.

LAWSON, Beverage Monroe (May 9, 1844-October 6, 1863). Company D, 51st Virginia Infantry. Died of typhoid fever at White Sulphur Springs, October 6, 1863. BPC.

LAWSON, Claiborne T. Sergeant, Company K, 50th Virginia Infantry. Living in 1907. CDAR. CPA. BPC.

LAWSON, Clifton M. Captain, Company K, 50th Virginia Infantry. POW, Spotsylvania Court House, May 12, 1864. POW, Fort McHenry. Died, Baltimore Hospital, October 18, 1864. Buried Loudon Park Cemetery.

LAWSON, Hampton. Company I, 24th Virginia Infantry. Medical discharge, November 16, 1861.

LAWSON, James M. Company D, 51st Virginia Infantry. Medical discharge, January 16, 1863. Re-enlisted. POW, Waynesboro, March 2, 1865. Released from Fort Delaware Prison, June 20, 1865. CPA.

LAWSON, Jefferson Thompson. Captain, Company K, 50th Virginia Infantry. Organizer of the company. State Senator after war. BPC.

LAWSON, Lafayette. Company D, 12th Virginia Infantry. Medical discharge, July 27, 1862 for tuberculosis. Later member of Company D, 51st Virginia Infantry.

LAWSON, Madison T. (Matt). Major, Company G, 21st Virginia Cavalry. Discharged to become County Surveyor of Patrick County. Died November 4, 1893. CPA. BPC.

LAWSON, Silas. Company K, 50th Virginia Infantry. Moved to Missouri after the war.

LAWSON, W. J. Company D, 51st Virginia Infantry.

LAWSON, William Zackery Taylor. Company K, 50th Virginia Infantry. KIA, Battle of Seven Pines, May 1862.

LAWSON William S. (July 27, 1845-January 25, 1921). Company G, 21st Virginia Cavalry. BPC. UDC. CPA.

LAWSON, Wilson T. (1841-1913). Sergeant, Company A, 24th Virginia Infantry. CDAR. CPA.

(Note. Abram T, Claiborne T, Jefferson T, Madison T, William Z.T. Lawson, and Wilson T. Lawson were all sons of Reverend William and Anna (Thompson) Lawson. All have tombstones in the family cemetery near Meadows of Dan.)

LAYMAN, William C. Company F, 51st Virginia Infantry. Medical discharge for tuberculosis, March 14, 1862. BPC.

LEAK, Thomas J. Company I, 24th Virginia Infantry.

LEARY, William. Company D, 51st Virginia Infantry.

LEE, Harden H. (November 1, 1843-March 25, 1918). Company H, 42nd Virginia Infantry. WIA, Cedar Creek. BPC. CDAR. CPA.

LEE, John. Company D, 51st Virginia Infantry. CPA.

LEE, Marion F. PCDR, exposure, Mercer County, West Virginia, November 25, 1861, age 18.

LEWIS, Andrew J. (1842-1924). Company K, 50th Virginia Infantry. Living 1907. CDAR.

LEWIS, Anthony F. Company E, 29th Virginia Infantry.

LEWIS, William M. Company C, 3rd Virginia Infantry.

LIGHT, Henry Clay (February 2, 1844-July 5, 1917). Corporal, Company I, 24th Virginia Infantry. WIA, Drewry's Bluff and at Five Forks. BPC. UDC. CDAR. CPA.

LIGHT, James M. Company E, 6th Virginia Infantry. Died of disease, March 20, 1863, at Alsop's Station, Virginia

LINDSEY, Henry. Company D, 29th Virginia Infantry. Killed in Augusta County, December 28, 1864, while cutting timber in winter.

LINDSEY, Henry. Company I, 50th Virginia Infantry.

LOVELL, David A. Company D, 51st Virginia Infantry.

LOVELL, James K. Company D, 54th Virginia Infantry. BPC.

LOVELL, Thomas. Company D, 51st Virginia Infantry.

LOVING (LOVINS) Arthur J. (1833-1863). Company I, 24th Virginia Infantry. Died from wound received at Battle of Gettysburg. CPA.

LOYD, John. Company H, 58th Virginia Infantry.

LOYD, Patrick. Company F, 52nd Virginia Infantry.

LUSK, Eli. Company H, 51st Virginia Infantry.

LYBROOK, Andrew Murray (January 18, 1832-January 1, 1899). Captain, Company I, 24th Virginia Infantry. WIA, Williamsburg. Attorney and State Senator after war. BPC.

LYON, Elijah. Company H, 51st Virginia Infantry. PCDR, measles August 17, 1862.

LYON, James D. Company D, 12th Virginia Infantry. POW, Seven Pines. Died July 28, 1862 at Fort Delaware Prison. Buried at Finn's Point, New Jersey.

LYON, Silas T. Company H, 51st Virginia Infantry. Living in 1907. CDAR.

LYON, William, Jr. Possibly in 51st Virginia Infantry. Died early in war.

LYON, William, Sr. Company H, 51st Virginia Infantry. Discharged because of age, November 20, 1863.

MABE, Jesse. Company H, 58th Virginia Infantry. POW. Released from Elmira Prison, New York, June 30, 1865. BPC.

MABE, Matthew. Company H, 58th Virginia Infantry. WIA, Sharpsburg (Antietam). PCDR, pneumonia at Staunton, Virginia, December 12, 1862.

MABE, Samuel N. Company K, 50th Virginia Infantry. POW, Spotsylvania Court House, May 12, 1864, Point Lookout, Maryland and Elmira, New York. Died, May 1, 1865.

MABE, William C. Company H, 58th Virginia Infantry. Company I, 24th Virginia Infantry. Medical discharge, August 15, 1861. BPC. CDAR. CPA.

MANON, William. Company D, 51st Virginia Infantry.

MANKINS, Claude (Cloyd). Company K, 50th Virginia Infantry.

MANKINS, Faulks. Possibly in 50th Virginia Infantry. Died November 15, 1862 of pneumonia.

MANKINS, Jesse Ewell. Company E, 29th Virginia Infantry. PCDR, June 1862 of measles. Buried at Emory and Henry College, Washington County.

MANKINS, Joel. Company K, 50th Virginia Infantry. POW. Died at Point Lookout Prison, Maryland, November 20, 1863.

MARSH, John Henry. Corporal, Company C, 51st Virginia Infantry. POW, Waynesboro, Fort Delaware. Alive 1912.

MARSH, Thomas D. Company C, 51st Virginia Infantry. Alive 1912. Buried St. Paul Cemetery, Wythe County.

MARSHALL, Elijah (May 10, 1846-February 17, 1922). Company I, 5th Battalion Virginia Reserves. BPC. CPA.

MARSHALL, Leroy. Company E, 29th Virginia Infantry. Company D, 12th Virginia Infantry.

MARSHALL, William Lee (1847-1923). Company K, 4th Regiment Virginia Reserves. BPC.

MARTIAL, Leroy. Company D, 12th Virginia Infantry.

MARTIN, A. W. Company K, 50th Virginia Infantry.

MARTIN, Abram Walter. Company I, 24th Virginia Infantry. Listed as Civil War soldier in The Enterprise. BPC

MARTIN, Alexander G. (1835-August 31, 1864). Sergeant, Company G, 54th Virginia Infantry. Born and married in Patrick County. Lived in Carroll County.

MARTIN, Alexander W. Company I, 24th Virginia Infantry. WIA, Williamsburg. Never returned to duty. Living in 1909. CPA.

MARTIN, Andrew J. Company E, 54th Virginia Infantry. Tombstone inscription states that he served in 6th Virginia Reserves. 1910C. BPC. CPA.

MARTIN, Charles Jackson. Company D, 12th Virginia Infantry. Orange Artillery. Living in 1907.

MARTIN, Charles Thomas (August 16, 1831-July 26, 1911). Company H, 58th Virginia Infantry. BPC. CPA.

MARTIN, Crawford. Company D, 51st Virginia Infantry. WIA, Totopotomy Creek and at Cold Harbor. Living in 1907.

MARTIN, Daniel. Company I, 5th Battalion Virginia Reserves and 24th Virginia Infantry. Died in Elmira Prison, New York, September 23, 1864.

MARTIN, David Harbour (July 11, 1846-January 25, 1920). Company D, 51st Virginia Infantry. POW, Waynesboro, March 2, 1865. Released from Fort Delaware Prison, June 20, 1865. BPC. UDC. CDAR. CPA. 1910C.

MARTIN, Edward Noah (June 1, 1837-November 3, 1924). Company D, 51st Virginia Infantry. POW, Waynesboro, March 2, 1865. Released from Fort Delaware, June 20, 1865.

MARTIN, Gideon A. Company K, 5th North Carolina Cavalry.

MARTIN, Harvey. Company D, 12th Virginia Infantry.

MARTIN, Isaac. Company I, 5th Battalion Virginia Reserves, also, Company H, 58th Virginia Infantry. CPA.

MARTIN, J. B. Orange Artillery. Arrested three times for desertion. Alleged to have been a member of a lawless gang in Southwest Virginia. Shot by firing squad March 9, 1864.

MARTIN, James. Company I, 5th Battalion Virginia Reserves. Living in 1907.

MARTIN, James. Company I, 24th Virginia Infantry. Died of fever at Chimborazo Hospital, Richmond, July 22, 1864. CPA.

MARTIN, James J. Company H, 58th Virginia Infantry. BPC. UDC. CPA.

MARTIN, Jesse. Private, Co H, 58th Virginia Infantry. WIA, Winchester, September 19, 1864. Living in Patrick County 1888.

MARTIN, J. J. Company H, 51st Virginia Infantry.

MARTIN, John James (October 9, 1841-November 11, 1882). Orange Artillery. BPC.

MARTIN, John K. Company H, 22nd North Carolina Infantry. UDC. CPA.

MARTIN, John W. Company I, 24th Virginia Infantry. Absent sick, 1861 and did not return to duty.

MARTIN, Joshua T. Company H, 51st Virginia Infantry. Died October 10, 1863, in Giles County, Virginia of disease. BPC.

MARTIN, Joshua W. Company D, 6th Virginia Infantry. WIA, Charles City Road, June 29, 1862. PCDR, July 1, 1862. Buried Oakwood Cemetery, Richmond.

MARTIN, Larkin T. Company D, 51st Virginia Infantry. Died in service, details not known.

MARTIN, Lewis. Died February 20, 1862 of pneumonia.

MARTIN, Marshall. Company A, 24th Virginia Infantry.

MARTIN, Noah (1837-1924). Company D, 5th Virginia Infantry. CPA.

MARTIN, Reid (1836-1862). Company D, 12th Virginia Infantry. Died of disease, July 1862.

MARTIN, Richard, Company I, 5th Battalion Virginia Reserves. Living in 1907.

MARTIN, Samuel Isaac (1843-1925). Company D, 6th Virginia Infantry. BPC. CDAR. CPA.

MARTIN, William. Company I, 5th Battalion Virginia Reserves.

MARTIN, William. Company K, 50th Virginia Infantry. UDC.

MARTIN, William Abe (1836-1916). Company H, 58th Virginia Infantry. POW, Charleston, West Virginia, October 16, 1862. Exchanged. POW, Winchester September 19, 1864. Exchanged at Camp Chase Prison, Ohio, March 2, 1865. CPA. 1910C.

MARTIN, William Franklin. Company K, 24th Virginia Infantry. Listed as Civil War soldier in Patrick County Order Book #18. BPC. 1910C.

MARTIN, William G. Company D, 51st Virginia Infantry. POW, Loudon Company, July 16, 1864. Released from Elmira Prison, New York, May 29, 1865. UDC. CPA.

MARTIN, William H. Company I, 24th Virginia Infantry. Died of fever December 22, 1861 at Culpeper, Virginia.

MASON, James M. Lieutenant, Company G, 42nd Virginia Infantry. WIA, Second Manassas. Died September 9, 1862.

MASSEY, Cadwallader. Company C, 29th Virginia Infantry.

MASSEY, John A. Company I, 60th Virginia Infantry.

MASSEY, William Taylor (1846-1926). Company K, 50th Virginia Infantry. BPC.

MASSEY, Wilmouth O. Company K, 50th Virginia Infantry.

MAY, Joseph T. Company E, 6th Virginia Infantry. WIA, Crampton's Gap, September 14, 1864. POW, Germana Ford, April 29, 1864. WIA, Battle of the Crater, July 30, 1864.

MAY, William C. Company K, 50th Virginia Infantry. PCDR, Wytheville, Virginia, May 22, 1862, of pneumonia.

MAYS, Abram Fountain (April 6, 1844-July 12, 1915). Corporal, Company K, 50th Virginia Infantry. WIA lost an arm. BPC. UDC. CDAR. CPA.

MAYS, George W. Company K, 50th Virginia Infantry. POW. Died in prison, Elmira Prison, New York.

MAYS, James. Private, Company B, 32nd Battalion Virginia Cavalry.

McALEXANDER, Alexander. Company D, 51st Virginia Infantry.

McALEXANDER, Charles F. (or P.) (January 11, 1841-July 20, 1926). Company D, 51st Virginia Infantry.

McALEXANDER, Daniel. Company D, 51st Virginia Infantry. Company G, 21st Virginia Cavalry. WIA. POW near Front Royal, November 12, 1864. Released from Point Lookout Prison, Maryland, June 29, 1865.

McALEXANDER, Darius. Company D, 51st Virginia Infantry. Died of rheumatism, December 14, 1861, Mercer County, West Virginia.

McALEXANDER, David (July 5, 1837-December 24, 1927). Company D, 51st Virginia Infantry. BPC. CDAR. CPA.
McALEXANDER, James C. Company D, 51st Virginia Infantry. PCDR, fever, December 14, 1861 in Mercer County, West Virginia, age 21.
McALEXANDER, James C. Company D, 51st Virginia Infantry. POW, Harrisonburg. September 25, 1864. Exchanged, March 17, 1865.
McALEXANDER, Jeremiah. Company D, 51st Virginia Infantry. PCDR, December 12, 1861 of fever in Mercer County, West Virginia.
McALEXANDER, Joel (September 7, 1839-March 29, 1865). Company K, 50th Virginia Infantry. Died at Richmond of scurvy.
McALEXANDER, John. Company D, 51st Virginia Infantry. Living 1909. BPC. CPA.
McALEXANDER, Peter. Company K, 10th Virginia Cavalry. Company H, 51st Virginia Infantry. Living in 1907.
McALEXANDER, Samuel. Company D, 51st Virginia Infantry. POW, Lee Town, August 25, 1864. Exchanged from Point Lookout Prison, Maryland, March 28, 1865.
McALEXANDER, William. Company H, 51st Virginia Infantry Company I, 5th Virginia Reserves. WIA, Fredericksburg. CDAR.
McALEXANDER, William. Company H, 58th Virginia Infantry. POW, Fredericksburg, May 3, 1863. Exchanged at Fort Delaware, May 23, 1863. Died of chronic rheumatism in Danville Hospital, December 26, 1864.
McCABE, Thomas. Company C, 10th Battalion Virginia Heavy Artillery.
McCANDLISH, Clarney. Company G, 21st Virginia Cavalry. POW, Harper's Ferry, July 8, 1864. Released from Elmira Prison, New York, July 19, 1865.
McCANDLISH (McCanless), Oscar William. Company G, 21st Virginia Cavalry. Paroled at Thomasville Hospital, North Carolina on May 1, 1865. CDAR. CPA.
McDONALD, Hiram F. Company D, 51st Virginia Infantry.
McGEE, Green M. Company D, 51st Virginia Infantry. POW, Waynesboro, March 2, 1865. Released from Fort Delaware Prison, June 20, 1865.
McGEE, John P. Company D, 51st Virginia Infantry. POW, Charlottesville, March 15, 1865. Released from Point Lookout Prison, Maryland, May 14, 1865. CPA.
McGEE, William. Company D, 51st Virginia Infantry. Musician. Living in 1907.
McHONE, E. Archibald. Company H, 51st Virginia Infantry.
McINTOSH, John H. Company H, 58th Virginia Infantry. POW, Fredericksburg on May 3, 1863. Exchanged at Fort Delaware, May 23, 1863. Discharged. Died January 1, 1865 at home.

McMILLAN, A. J. Company D, 12th Virginia Infantry. KIA, Battle of the Crater, Petersburg, Virginia on July 30, 1864.

McMILLAN, Edward W. Company K, 50th Virginia Infantry. Living in 1907.

McMILLAN, Ewell J. Company E, 29th Virginia Infantry. Living in Carroll County, 1870.

McMILLAN, Greenville P. Company E, 29th Virginia Infantry. WIA, Dinwiddie Court House, March 31, 1865. Died in 1895.

McMILLAN, Henry A. Company D, 12th Virginia Infantry. PCDR, measles at Norfolk, Virginia, May 1, 1862.

McMILLAN, James Lee. Captain, Company E, 29th Virginia Infantry. WIA, Drewry's Bluff. Died 1901.

McMILLAN, Joseph F. Company E, 29th Virginia Infantry. Medical discharge.

McMILLAN, Leftwich. Company E, 29th Virginia Infantry.

McMILLAN, Lorenzo Dow. Company E, 29th Virginia Infantry. POW, Drewry's Bluff, May 16, 1864. Imprisoned at Elmira Prison, New York and Point Lookout Prison, Maryland. Exchanged March 15, 1865. Living in 1909. CPA.

McMILLAN, William. Company E, 53rd Virginia Infantry. PCDR, Drewry's Bluff of erysipelas, November 16, 1862, age 20.

McPEAK, Bluford M. Company K, 50th Virginia Infantry. WIA. Living in 1909. BPC. UDC. CDAR. CPA.

MEADOR, William G. Company I, 58th Virginia Infantry.

MEREDITH, Bradley. Company D, 51st Virginia Infantry. CDAR.

MEREDITH, John. Company H, 51st Virginia Infantry.

MIDKIFF, Joseph W. Company C, 25th Virginia Infantry.

MILES, Andrew W. Company H, 51st Virginia Infantry. WIA, Gaines Mill. Died June 10, 1864 in Stuart Hospital, Richmond.

MILLS, James L. (July 30, 1846-June 25, 1931). Company I, 5th Battalion Virginia Reserves. BPC. UDC. CPA.

MILLS, William B. Company H, 58th Virginia Infantry. WIA, Williamsport, Maryland, July 6, 1863. KIA, April 3, 1865.

MITCHELL, John D. Lieutenant, Company I, 24th Virginia Infantry.

MITCHELL, Thomas J. Company D, 51st Virginia Infantry.

MITCHELL, William A. Company A, 2nd North Carolina Infantry. Lived at Laurel Hill.

MIZE, Lee. Company I, 5th Battalion Virginia Reserves.

MIZE, William Burrell (April 23, 1844-March 12, 1927). Company D, 51st Virginia Infantry. WIA, Gardner's Farm, May 31, 1864 and at Totopotomy Creek. POW, March 5, 1865. Released from Point Lookout Prison, Maryland, May 14, 1865. BPC. CDAR. CPA.

MONDAY, James J. Company K, 50th Virginia Infantry. Living in 1907.

MONTGOMERY, Floyd. Company E, 6th Virginia Infantry. POW in Maryland, 1864. Exchanged. Living in 1909. CDAR. CPA. 1910C. BPC.

MONTGOMERY, Madison T. Company E, 6th Virginia Infantry. POW twice. Exchanged and Released. Living in 1909. UDC. CDAR. CPA. 1910C.

MONTGOMERY, Richard. Company H, 6th Virginia Infantry. Mechanic and Blacksmith. WIA, Spotsylvania Court House 1864.

MOORE, Alfred Cleon (December 2, 1805-March 1, 1890). Brigadier General, Provisional Army of Virginia. Colonel, 29th Virginia Infantry. Born in Ararat, Virginia. Moved to North Carolina where he served in the State Legislature. Moved to Wythe County, Virginia. First Colonel of the 29th Infantry Regiment. Resigned because of advancing age and failing health in 1863. Died in Wythe County, Buried in McGavock Cemetery at Fort Chiswell, Virginia.

MOORE, Edward E. Company K, 50th Virginia Infantry. Left in Maryland, 1864. Died in Frederick County, 1913.

MOORE, Hardin F. Company H, 58th Virginia Infantry. POW, Sharpsburg, 1862.

MOORE, Hugh Lawson. Company E, 6th Virginia Infantry. WIA, Manassas. Killed, September 1864 by explosion of shell.

MOORE, Jacob S. Company D, 51st Virginia Infantry.

MOORE, William T. Company D, 51st Virginia Infantry. Company E, 6th Virginia Infantry. Died in Harrisonburg Hospital, June 9, 1864, of gunshot wound.

MORAN, Crawford (July 4, 1842-August 20, 1925). Company D, 51st Virginia Infantry. Buried in Salem. CDAR. CPA.

MORAN, George. Company I, 5th Battalion Virginia Reserves. Living in 1907.

MORAN, James. Company H, 51st Virginia Infantry. KIA, Lee Town. CPA.

MORAN, John J. Corporal, Company H, 51st Virginia Infantry. Died October 31, 1863. Buried in Edgehill Cemetery, Charleston, West Virginia. CPA.

MORRISON, David James (March 25, 1844-January 24, 1919). Company D, 51st Virginia Infantry. BPC. CPA.

MORRISON, Jarrett H. (February 29, 1838-November 14, 1912). Company H, 51st Virginia Infantry. Arm amputated. BPC. UDC. CDAR. CPA.

MORRISON, James Tyler. (June 6, 1844-May 20, 1913). Company D, 51st Virginia Infantry. POW, Waynesboro. Released from Fort Delaware, June 20, 1865. BPC. UDC. CPA.

MORRISON, John Tatum (1821-1911). Company D, 51st Virginia Infantry. WIA. POW, Waynesboro, 1865. Released from Fort Delaware, June 20, 1865. BPC. UDC. CPA.

MORRISON, M. .J. Died June 30, 1862 of fever.

MORRISON, Thomas C. (March 28, 1842-May 17, 1909). Company D, 51st Virginia Infantry. WIA in left knee, May 25, 1864. BPC. CPA.

MOSS, Jesse P. Company G, 51st Virginia Infantry. Buried in Mt. Jackson, Shenandoah County. CPA.

MOSS, Robert. Company H, 51st Virginia Infantry. POW, Waynesboro, March 2, 1865. Released from Fort Delaware, June 20, 1865. Served in Company I, 24th Virginia Infantry.

MOSS, Doctor M. Company I, 24th Virginia Infantry.

MOSS, William A. Company H, 23rd Virginia Cavalry. Living in 1909. UDC. CDAR. CPA. 1910C. BPC.

MURPHY, James Richard. Company H, 42nd Infantry. POW, May 12, 1864. Died at Point Lookout Prison, Maryland, August 27, 1864.

MURPHY, William F. Company H, 42nd Virginia Infantry. Teamster. Paroled at Appomattox. Died February 15, 1885.

MURPHY, William F. Company H, 42nd Virginia Infantry. Nurse. Died in hospital, June 29, 1863.

MURPHY, William Lee (1830-1862). Company H, 42nd Virginia Infantry. PCDR, wounds in Staunton Hospital, Virginia, June 8, 1862. BPC. CPA.

NAPIER, Joseph R. Company D, 12th Virginia Infantry. Medical discharge for tuberculosis, March 4, 1863.

NEWMAN, Hayman (Haman) (December 7, 1819-February 11, 1902). Company I, 5th Battalion Virginia Reserves. BPC. CPA.

NEWMAN, J. W. Company H, 51st Virginia Infantry. UDC.

NEWMAN, John W. (May 9, 1842-January 3, 1936). Company K, 50th Virginia Infantry. One of the last survivors of Civil War in County. BPC. CPA.

NEWMAN, Joseph. Company K, 50th Virginia Infantry. POW. Died at Point Lookout Prison, Maryland, September 21, Grave #191.

NEWMAN, Joseph. Company K, 50th Virginia Infantry. Company I, 5th Battalion Virginia Reserves. CPA.

NEWMAN, Robert. Company K, 50th Virginia Infantry. Killed, May 1864.

NOEL, Walker Timberlake (June 4, 1836-May 25, 1884). Lieutenant, Company K, 58th Virginia Infantry. POW, Fisher's Hill, September 22, 1864. POW, Fort Delaware. BPC.

NOLEN, Charles M. Company D, 51st Virginia Infantry. POW, Waynesboro, March 2, 1865. Released from Fort Delaware, June 20, 1865. BPC.

NOLEN, David. Company D, 51st Virginia Infantry.

NOLEN, Ephraim G. Company D, 51st Virginia Infantry. Died November 3, 1862 of diphtheria. BPC.

NOLEN, John A. Company D, 51st Virginia Infantry. CPA. BPC.

NOLEN (Nolan, Nowlin), Samuel J. Mountain and Orange Artillery. Conscripted 1862. NOONKESTER, Michael. Company E, 29th Virginia Infantry.

NORMAN, James C. Captain, Company E, 53rd North Carolina Infantry. UDC.

NOWLIN, Archibald S. Company H, 58th Virginia Infantry. WIA, Petersburg, April 1, 1865. Living in 1909. BPC. CPA.

NOWLIN (NOLEN), Isaac Alexander (September 11, 1840-February 21, 1923). Sergeant, Company D, 51st Virginia Infantry. Medical discharge. BPC. CPA.

NUNN, Andrew J. (1835-1904). Second Lieutenant, Company F, 21st North Carolina Infantry. Lost a leg in war.

NUNN, Edward (Edmund) L. Company I, 24th Virginia Infantry. CPA.

NUNN, Jesse. Hunley's Company, 64th Virginia Militia.

NUNN, Walter Frank. Company I, 24th Virginia Infantry. Died of disease in Richmond Hospital, January 12, 1862.

NUNN, William. Company H, 51st Virginia Infantry. Medical discharge, July 24, 1862. Company I, 24th Virginia Infantry. POW, Farmville, April 6, 1865. Released from Point Lookout Prison, Maryland, June 15, 1865. CPA.

OAKLEY, William M. Company I, 5th Battalion Virginia Reserves.

OLIVER, N. G. Sergeant, Company G, 1st Confederate Engineer Troops. CPA.

ORANDER, John. Company I, 5th Battalion Virginia Reserves. Living in 1907.

ORE, William Robert (January 1, 1834-March 6, 1916). Company H, 58th Virginia Infantry. WIA May 6, 1862 at McDowell. POW, Spotsylvania, June 12, 1864. Exchanged Fort Delaware, February 27, 1865. BPC. CPA.

OURY, Alfred. Courier for J. E. B. Stuart.

OVERBY, Thomas H. Company I, 24th Virginia Infantry. PCDR, pneumonia at Manassas, January 21, 1862.

OWENS, William F. Lieutenant, Company I, 37th Virginia Cavalry.

PACE, Ballard P. Company H, 24th Virginia Cavalry. 1910C. BPC. UDC. CPA.

PACK, James. Company K, 50th Virginia Infantry. KIA, Chancellorsville.

PACK, James. Company I, 24th Virginia Infantry. Died of disease, April 12, 1862, in Charlottesville Hospital. CPA.

PACK, John. Company K, 50th Virginia Infantry. KIA, Chancellorsville. CPA.

PACK, Jonathan. Company K, 50th Virginia Infantry. WIA, Chancellorsville. Died September 2, 1863 in Richmond.

PACK, Tyree. Captain, Company K, 50th Virginia Infantry. POW, Spotsylvania Court House, May 12, 1864. POW, Point Lookout, Maryland. Died August 11, 1864. CPA.

PADGETT, Andrew. Company K, 50th Virginia Infantry.

PADGETT, Campbell. Company K, 50th Virginia Infantry. Living in 1907. BPC.

PADGETT, William F. Company C, 29th Virginia Infantry. Served in 45th Virginia Infantry.

PALMER, Tiberious. Company K, 50th Virginia Infantry. Left in Maryland in 1864.

PANNILL, Joseph. Corporal, Company H, 58th Virginia Infantry. WIA, Gaines Mill.

PAUL, Micael (Micajah) J. Company H, 42nd Virginia Infantry. POW, May 12, 1864, Spotsylvania Court House. Released from Elmira Prison, New York, July 19, 1865.

PAUL, Vaden G. Company H, 42nd Virginia Infantry. Severe arm wound at Cedar Run, March 9, 1862. Detailed to enrolling duty.

PEARCE, Jacob. Company H, 23rd Battalion Virginia Infantry.

PEDIGO, Albert Gallatin (November 26, 1821-September 28, 1910). Company G, 21st Virginia Cavalry. Died Vinton.

PEDIGO, James Selden. Private. Company A, 28th North Carolina Infantry. Born in Elamsville, November 9, 1823. Married Louisa Lawless in 1860 and moved to Surry County, North Carolina. Enlisted at Dobson in May 1861 and served only until May 1, 1862 (was over age). Moved back to Patrick where he Died February 4, 1900.

PEDIGO, Joseph R. (July 19, 1842-June 19, 1921). Confederate Army Civil Engineer. 1910C.

PENDLETON, Abram C. Corporal, Company K, 50th Virginia Infantry. KIA, September 19,1864, at Winchester.

PENDLETON, Clairborne Green (February 25, 1843-September 16, 1917). Co H, 51st Virginia Infantry. WIA, Lee Town. BPC. CDAR. CPA.

PENDLETON, John (July 8, 1835-June 8, 1902). Company D, 51st Virginia Infantry. BPC. CDAR. CPA.

PENDLETON, George W. (April 14, 1847-November 17, 1897). Company I, 5th Battalion Virginia Reserves. BPC. CPA.

PENDLETON, Gilbert. Company I, 24th Virginia Infantry. WIA, May 16, 1864 at Drewry's Bluff. Died, June 8, 1864 at Chimborazo Hospital.

PENDLETON, (Josiah) Royal. Died October 25, 1861 of pneumonia. BPC.

PENDLETON, Valentine Hanson (1843-1917). Company D, 51st Virginia Infantry. POW, Waynesboro, March 2, 1865. Released from Fort Delaware, June 20, 1865.

PENDLETON, William B. General and Staff Assistant Adjutant General.
PENDLETON, Wilson T. Company D, 12th Virginia Infantry. WIA. POW. Exchanged. Died in Lynchburg General Hospital, May 28, 1864, from wounds received at the Battle of the Wilderness.
PENN, Abram C. Private, Company G, 10th Virginia Cavalry. Conscripted, Patrick Court House, July 27, 1864. LCA.
PENN, Edmund L. Capt, Company H, 42nd Virginia Infantry. WIA, Antietam. Assigned as recruiting officer. Died October 26, 1903.
PENN, Greenville R. Captain, Company H, 42nd Virginia Infantry. WIA, Cedar Run. WIA, Chancellorsville. POW, Fisher's Hill, September 22, 1864. Released from Fort Delaware, June 17, 1865.
PENN, James A. Company H, 58th Virginia Infantry. Wagon master. Discharged August 31, 1862.
PENN, James Gabriel (November 14, 1845-August 22, 1907). V.M.I. Cadet, Class of 1866. Enlisted September 27, 1862. Battle of New Market, Lieutenant in Tucker's Brigade. Bank President in Danville, Virginia and assisted in founding American Tobacco Company.
PENN, John Edmund. Lieutenant Colonel, Company H, 42nd Virginia Infantry. WIA, Antietam. Leg amputated. POW, Exchanged. Died 1895, Roanoke. CDAR.
PENN, John S. (December 4, 1842-October 27, 1861). Company H, 42nd Virginia Infantry. PCDR, hospital, Lewisburg, West Virginia, October 27, 1861 of typhoid and pneumonia. BPC.
PENN, Joseph G. Lieutenant, Company H, 42nd Virginia Infantry. POW, Exchanged at Point Lookout, 1865. BPC.
PENN, Peter P. (1811-1872). Family tradition states that he was active in militia early in war.
PENN, Peter Leath (1835-1901). Company K, 10th Virginia Cavalry.
PENN, Rufus G. Lieutenant, Company H, 42nd Virginia Infantry. Resigned in 1862 due to heart disease. Died 1898.
PENN, Samuel A, Company H, 42nd Virginia Infantry. Discharged after providing substitute. Company K, 10th Virginia Cavalry. PCDR, shot and died March 27, 1865. BPC.
PENN, Thomas Green (June 1838-1885). Company H, 42nd Virginia Infantry. Discharged after providing substitute in 1862. 10th Virginia Cavalry. BPC.
PENN, Thomas H. 1910C.
PENN, William A. Company H, 42nd Virginia Infantry. Discharged because of disability, September 18, 1861. Enlisted in Company E, 24th Virginia Infantry, October 11, 1864. BPC.
PENN, William L. Lieutenant, Company D, 12th Virginia Infantry. Replacing William E. Cameron, who later became governor of Virginia. Resigned commission in July of 1863.

PENN, William S. Captain, Company H, 58th Virginia Infantry. Died 1862.

PERKINS, C. T. Company K, 50th Virginia Infantry. KIA, Fort Donelson, Tennessee.

PERKINS, Jordan, Company I, 5th Battalion Virginia Reserves.

PERKINS, William H. Company K, 50th Virginia Infantry. KIA, February 15, 1862 at Fort Donelson, Tennessee.

PHILPOTT, Edward. Company B, 57th Virginia Infantry. Born in Patrick County. Died of typhoid at Chimborazo Hospital in Richmond on July 27, 1864.

PICKUREL (Pickeral), Richard (1845-1918). Company K, 50th Virginia Infantry. BPC. CPA. 1910C.

PICKUREL, Thomas. Company I, 5th Battalion Virginia Reserves. CPA.

PIGG, Beverly A. Company I, 5th Battalion Virginia Reserves. Living in 1907.

PIGG, George W. Company I, 5th Battalion Virginia Reserves. Living in 1907.

PIGG, Paul C. Company H, 51st Virginia Infantry. POW, Waynesboro, March 2, 1865. Released from Fort Delaware. June 7, 1865. UDC. CDAR. CPA.

PIGG, Thomas C. (October 20, 1837-April 6, 1905). Company H, 51st Virginia Infantry. POW, Waynesboro, March 3, 1865. Released, Fort Delaware, June 20, 1865. BPC. CPA.

PIKE, Henry A. Company D, 12th Virginia Infantry.

PIKE, Jacob. Company H, 58th Virginia Infantry.

PIKE, John. Company K, 50th Virginia Infantry. PCDR, Giles County on September 1, 1862, of erysipelas. CPA.

PILSON, John Richard (1840-1912). Lieutenant, 74th Regiment North Carolina Militia. Born on Sycamore Creek. Moved to Surry County, North Carolina in 1856.

PILSON, William (1820-1902). Company G, 21st Virginia Cavalry. BPC.

PLASTER, Thomas J. Company H, 51st Virginia Infantry.

PLASTERS, Creed W. Company E, 6th Virginia Infantry. WIA, Chancellorsville. POW, May 12, 1864, Spotsylvania Court House, Elmira, New York. Died Patrick County in 1920. UDC. CPA.

PLASTERS, Henry L. Company G, 29th Virginia Infantry. Moved to Russell County after war.

PLASTERS, Joseph W. Company D, 12th Virginia Infantry. PCDR, Richmond Hospital of measles, July 10, 1862.

PLASTERS, Mark. Company I, 24th Virginia Infantry. WIA, Seven Pines.

PLASTERS, Michael. Company I, 24th Virginia Infantry. PCDR, hospital, January 10, 1865, Newport News. Buried in Greenlawn Cemetery, Newport News. CPA.
PLASTERS, Thomas J. Company D, 12th Virginia Infantry Company H, 51st Virginia Infantry.
PLASTERS, William. Company D, 12th Virginia Infantry. Died August 25, 1862.
PLASTERS, William Conrad. Company I, 24th Virginia Infantry. WIA, Gettysburg. POW, Five Forks. Released from Point Lookout Prison, Maryland, June 16, 1865. Living in 1909. BPC. UDC.
POE, John T. Company K, 51st Virginia Infantry.
POORE, John. Company C, 58th Virginia Infantry.
PORTER, John A. Company H, 51st Virginia Infantry.
POWELL, Charles A. Company B (Ringgold), 13th Battalion Light Artillery. CPA.
PRATT, John H. Company D, 12th Virginia Infantry. WIA, Spotsylvania Court House May 12, 1864. POW, Burgess Mill, November 27, 1864. Released from Point Lookout, June 16, 1865.
PRICE, Bernard M. Company D, 51st Virginia Infantry. Schoolteacher.
PRICE, Francis M. Company B, 50th Virginia Infantry. POW, Spotsylvania Court House, May 12, 1864, Point Lookout, Maryland and Elmira, New York.
PRICE, William. Captain, Company D, 51st Virginia Infantry. Living in Oklahoma1913.
PRICE, William G. Captain, Company H, 51st Virginia Infantry. WIA, New Market, May 15, 1864. WIA. POW, March 27, 1865. Sent to Military Prison, Louisville, Kentucky. Released June 16, 1865.
PRICE, William J. Company H, 51st Virginia Infantry.
PRUITT, Isham. Company G, 53rd North Carolina Infantry. 1910C. CPA.
PUCKETT, Doctor Floyd. Company K, 50th Virginia Infantry. WIA. CPA.
PUCKETT, Elijah. Company K, 50th Virginia Infantry. Living in 1907.
PUCKETT, Ephram (February 2, 1846-December 24, 1917). Company K, 50th Virginia Infantry. BPC. CPA.
PUCKETT, Francis M. (September 25, 1847-August 29, 1905). Company C, 47th Virginia Cavalry. Company I, 26th Virginia Cavalry. BPC.
PUCKETT, C. Hosea (May 11, 1840-February 29, 1911). Company I, 24th Virginia Infantry. Company K, 21st Virginia Cavalry. BPC. CDAR.
PUCKETT, James M. Company G, 29th Virginia Infantry. POW, April 1, 1865. Released, June 20, 1865.
PUCKETT, John (June 9, 1838-March 30, 1912). Company K, 50th Virginia Infantry. BPC.

PUCKETT, John. Company H, 51st Virginia Infantry. Company E, 29th Virginia Infantry.
PUCKETT, Reed (March 31, 1839-May 8, 1908). Company K, 50th Virginia Infantry. WIA. BPC. CPA.
PUCKETT, Richard A. Company I, 37th Battalion Virginia Cavalry.
PUCKETT, Riley. Company E, 6th Virginia Infantry.
PUCKETT, Robert. Company K, 50th Virginia Infantry. Living in 1907.
PURDY, James Anderson (1841-1930). Company G, 42nd Virginia Infantry. Present at surrender. CPA. 1910C.
PURDY, John J. Company D, 6th Virginia Infantry. Died, October 31, 1862, in hospital in Richmond.
RADFORD, Abram Fulcher. Company F, 51st Virginia Infantry.
RADFORD, Robert F. Company I, 24th Virginia Infantry. WIA. POW, Seven Pines. Exchanged from Fort Delaware, August 5, 1862.
RAKES, Alexander (April 15, 1838-July 1, 1928). Company D, 51st Virginia Infantry. POW, Strasburg, June 19, 1864. Released from Point Lookout, June 7, 1865. Primitive Baptist preacher. BPC. CPA.
RAKES, Calvin C. Company B, 42nd Virginia Infantry. WIA, Wilderness, May 5, 1864.
RAKES, Charles Jackson. Company D, 51st Virginia Infantry. WIA. POW, Winchester, September 19, 1864. Paroled from General Hospital, Baltimore, Maryland. Living 1909. CDAR. CPA. BPC.
RAKES, Chesley B. Company K, 50th Virginia Infantry.
RAKES, Columbus C. Corporal, Company D, 51st Virginia Infantry. WIA. Living in 1907. BPC. CPA.
RAKES, David. Company D, 12th Virginia Infantry.
RAKES, David. Company H, 51st Virginia Infantry.
RAKES, David Cruise. Company D, 29th Virginia Infantry. POW, May 16, 1864, at Drewry's Bluff. Released June 21, 1865 from Elmira Prison, New York. Died in 1921 in Arkansas.
RAKES, John D. Company D, 51st Virginia Infantry. Died November 20, 1861 of typhoid.
RAKES, Richard R. (October 25, 1827-July 23, 1905). Company D, 51st Virginia Infantry. POW, Waynesboro, March 2, 1865. Released, Fort Delaware, June 21, 1865. BPC.
RAKES, Samuel J. (1831-1864). Company D, 51st Virginia Infantry. Died, April 16, 1864. Buried Emory and Henry College Cemetery, Washington County, Virginia. CPA.
RAKES, Sparrel. Company C, 51st Virginia Infantry.
RAKES, Thomas J. Family tradition states that he served in Civil War.
RAKES, Thomas Tennyson (November 6, 1844-January 3, 1939). Company H, 51st Virginia Infantry. Next to last Civil War survivor in Patrick County. BPC. CPA.

RANGELEY, James Henry (1843-1919). Lieutenant, Company K, 58th Virginia Infantry. Company K, 50 Virginia Infantry. BPC. UDC.

RANGELEY, John James. Lieutenant, Company G, 42nd Virginia Infantry. Died of typhoid fever, July 30, 1861 at Valley Mountain, Randolph County, West Virginia

RANGELEY, Joseph Ellis (1846-1928). Company C, Battery II, 10th Battalion Heavy Artillery. Survived typhoid. Company F, 5th Battalion Virginia Reserves. UDC. CPA. BPC.

RATLIFF (RATCLIFF), Columbus C. (February 5, 1828-July 20, 1898). Wagoner, Mountain and Orange Artillery. Paroled at Appomattox. BPC. CPA.

RATLIFF, Lewis G. Company D, 51st Virginia Infantry. Died of wounds, October 1, 1864, in Staunton General Hospital.

RATLIFF, Phillip. Company D, 51st Virginia Infantry. POW, Waynesboro, March 2, 1865. Released, Fort Delaware, June 2, 1865.

RAY, Abner. Company B, 57th Virginia Infantry.

RAY, John P. Company B, 57th Virginia Infantry. PCDR, January 14, 1865, Danville of pneumonia.

RAY, Joseph. Company D, 51st Virginia Infantry.

RAY, Pinkney. Company I, 5th Battalion Virginia Reserves.

RAY, Wilkins P. Company B, 54th Virginia Infantry.

REED, Flemon (Fleming). Company H, 51st Virginia Infantry. POW, Lee Town, August 16, 1864. Died at Camp Chase Prison, Ohio of pneumonia, December 3 or 12, 1864.

RESTON, J. M. Company D, 51st Virginia Infantry.

REYNOLDS, Abram David (August 13, 1847-September 23, 1925). Major, Company I, 5th Battalion Virginia Reserves. Brother of R. J. Reynolds, Founder of R. J. Reynolds Tobacco Company.

REYNOLDS, Abram Harden. Company H, 42nd Virginia Infantry. Died Staunton Hospital, April 1, 1863.

REYNOLDS, B. S. Patrick County Home Guard. Served two years per pension record.

REYNOLDS, Pleasant Callaway (January 30, 1847-April 8, 1932). Company I, 5th Battalion Virginia Reserves. BPC.

REYNOLDS, Cardwell. Company H, 5th Virginia State Line Troops. BPC.

REYNOLDS, George W. Company D, 51st Virginia Infantry. POW, Waynesboro, March 2, 1865. Released, Fort Delaware, June 21, 1865.

REYNOLDS, Henry C. Company I, 5th Battalion Virginia Reserves.

REYNOLDS, J. Dallas. Company K, 19th Virginia Infantry. BPC.

REYNOLDS, James. Company F, 42nd Virginia Infantry. BPC.

REYNOLDS, John J. Company K, 50th Virginia Infantry.

REYNOLDS, Joseph F. Company F, 5th Battalion Virginia Reserves.

REYNOLDS, P. C. Company I, 5th Battalion Virginia Reserves. BPC.

REYNOLDS, Powell Benton (1841-1914). Company K, 50th Virginia Infantry. Company D, 5th Kentucky Infantry. Company K, 15th Virginia Infantry. Living in 1907.

REYNOLDS, Shadrick B. (January 4, 1833-December 27, 1915). Company A, 12th Virginia Infantry. 1910C. UDC. CDAR. CPA. BPC.

REYNOLDS, Tilghman Dexter. Company C, 50th Virginia Infantry. Died April 30, 1862 of diphtheria. BPC.

REYNOLDS, William A. Company D, 51st Virginia Infantry. POW, Waynesboro, March 2, 1865. PCDR, Fort Delaware of measles, April 1, 1865.

RICHARDSON, Gabriel A. Company K, 50th Virginia Infantry. KIA, Chancellorsville.

RICHARDSON, Henry D. (September 18, 1835-January 9, 1919). Company K, 50th Virginia Infantry.

RICHARDSON, John Summerfield. Company H, 51st Virginia Infantry. KIA, Fayetteville, West Virginia, September 10, 1862.

RICHARDSON, Joseph. Company E, 53rd North Carolina Infantry. Regiment. Born Patrick County 1842. POW, July 11, 1864 and exchanged from Elmira Prison, New York October 29, 1864.

RICHARDSON, William Elcaney. Company K, 50th Virginia Infantry.

RICKMAN, Henry T. Company I, 5th Battalion Virginia Reserves.

ROBERSON, Abram. Company D, 51st Virginia Infantry. Living in 1909. BPC. CPA.

ROBERSON, Benjamin S. (1828-1887). Company C, 57th Virginia Infantry. CPA. BPC.

ROBERSON, James M. Company I, 24th Virginia Infantry.

ROBERSON, James Riley (1825-1913). In list of Civil War soldiers in Order Book #18. BPC.

ROBERSON, Landon (December 8, 1845-January 10, 1902). Company D, 51st Virginia Infantry. POW, March 2, 1865 at Waynesboro. Released from Fort Delaware, June 21, 1865. BPC.

ROBERSON, Samuel Turner (January 26, 1837-June 10, 1912). Company K, 10th Virginia Cavalry. BPC.

ROBERSON, Wilcher C. (1830-1878). Company G, 58th Virginia Infantry. CDAR.

ROBERSON, William H. (1822-1861). Company I, 24th Virginia Infantry. Died of disease in camp at Manassas, August 1, 1861.

ROBERTS, James. Company I, 21st Virginia Infantry.

ROBERTSON, Abram H. (1833-1889). Mountain and Orange Artillery. CDAR.

ROBERTSON, Daniel A. Company K, 10th Virginia Cavalry. Died July 12, 1865 of tuberculosis. BPC.

ROBERTSON, Edward F. Company E, 6th Virginia Infantry. Medical discharge.

ROBERTSON, Jackson. Company K, 50th Virginia Infantry. Living in 1907.

ROBERTSON, Joseph H. (June 18, 1827-November 1, 1913). Company E, 21st Virginia Infantry. BPC.

ROBERTSON, Nathaniel J. Company K, 50th Virginia Infantry.

ROGERS, Clement. (Clemmons) Company H, 48th Virginia Infantry. BPC.

ROGERS, George R. Company K, 50th Virginia Infantry and Company G, 21st Virginia Cavalry.

ROGERS, Hiram G. Company E, 42nd Virginia Infantry. Born in Patrick County Enlisted in Henry County. Died of gunshot wound at Lynchburg, September 6, 1862 at age 28.

ROGERS, James J. (1833-1923). Company F, 54th Virginia Infantry. 1910C.

ROGERS, John F. Company D, 12th Virginia Infantry. PCDR, April 7, 1862, Norfolk, Virginia, pneumonia.

ROGERS, John F. 24th Virginia Infantry. Died December 24, 1863 of pneumonia.

ROGERS, Sanders (Saunders) Witt (1839-1896). Company K, 50th Virginia Infantry. BPC.

RORRER, David C. Company G, 21st Virginia Cavalry. BPC.

RORRER, John W. Company H, 51st Virginia Infantry. PCDR, Fort Delaware Prison, September 23, 1865, of pneumonia. Buried at Finn's Point, New Jersey.

RORRER, Samuel G. Company H, 51st Virginia Infantry. Died from wounds. BPC.

RORRER, William Anderson (April 20, 1834-July 2, 1913). Mountain and Orange Artillery. BPC. CDAR. CPA.

RORRER, William Rudolph (November 13, 1836-January 5, 1928). Company D, 51st Virginia Infantry. BPC. CPA.

ROSE, Jacob. Company K, 50th Virginia Infantry.

ROSS, Charles Foster. 2nd Lt, Company D, 51st Virginia Infantry.

ROSS, Charles. Company G, 21st Virginia Cavalry.

ROSS, Charles P. Company D, 51st Virginia Infantry. Medical discharge, May 9, 1862, measles.

ROSS, David J. In list Confederate Veterans in Order Book #18.

ROSS, David Lee (November 8, 1831-July 16, 1927). Organized, Captain, Company C later Company D, 51st Virginia Infantry. Resigned and became Colonel of local militia. Re-entered army in Company G, 21st Virginia Cavalry. BPC. UDC. CPA.

ROSS, James W. Company D, 51st Virginia Infantry. PCDR, September 20, 1861 of measles, Bonsack, Virginia. BPC.

ROSS, Jefferson. Company I, 5th Battalion Virginia Reserves.

ROSS, John T. Corporal, Company D, 51st Virginia Infantry. POW December 19, 1863. Released from Fort Delaware, June 15, 1865.

ROSS, Joseph W. Company D, 51st Virginia Infantry. KIA, Totopotomy Creek, May 30, 1864.

ROSS, Lewis T. Company I, 24th Virginia Infantry. WIA, Drewry's Bluff.

ROSS, McDaniel. Company K, 6th Virginia Infantry. Lost leg in Battle of Wilderness. CPA. BPC.

ROSS, Samuel Anderson (December 9, 1818-August 12, 1903). Company D, 51st Virginia Infantry. Arm amputated. Company I, 5th Battalion Virginia Reserves. BPC. CPA.

ROSS, William. Company I, 5th Battalion Virginia Reserves. Living in 1907.

ROSS, William T. Company D, 51st Virginia Infantry. POW, Waynesboro, March 2, 1865. Released from Fort Delaware, June 21, 1865.

RUCKER, W. B. Company H, 51st Virginia Infantry.

RUCKER, Wooster B. (January 6, 1845-June 6, 1902). Lieutenant, Company H, 58th Virginia Infantry. WIA, Williamsport, Maryland on July 6, 1863. POW, Spotsylvania Court House, May 12, 1864. Released from Fort Delaware Prison June 16, 1865. UDC. CDAR.

RUTLEDGE, James. Company K, 50th Virginia Infantry. KIA, Gettysburg.

RUTLEDGE, James H. Company K, 50th Virginia Infantry. KIA, Chancellorsville.

SALMON, John. Company I, 5th Battalion Virginia Reserves. CPA.

SALMONS, John. Company D, 51st Virginia Infantry. POW, Winchester, September 19, 1864. Exchanged, March 15, 1865. CPA.

SALMONS, Jonathan (1820-1863). Company D, 51st Virginia Infantry. BPC.

SALMONS, Joseph Lafayette. Company H, 51st Virginia Infantry.

SANDERS, Witt Rodgers. Company K, 50th Virginia Infantry.

SANDIFER, Samuel T. (1839-1906). Born Patrick County. Died Surry County, North Carolina. 1st Sergeant, Company C, 21st North Carolina Infantry. WIA, Sharpsburg, September 17, 1862. POW, Gettysburg, Fort Delaware and Point Lookout. Paroled February 20, 1865.

SANDERSON, T. E. Company I, 5th Battalion Virginia Reserves. Died July 19, 1864 at Danville.

SAUNDERS, Adison T. Company H, 42nd Virginia Infantry. POW, May 12, 1864, Spotsylvania Court House. Exchanged from Point Lookout Prison, Maryland, November 15, 1864.

SAUNDERS, James F. Company H, 42nd Virginia Infantry. WIA, Antietam.

SAUNDERS, Philemon Jackson. Company H, 42nd Virginia Infantry. POW, Spotsylvania Court House, May 12, 1864, Elmira Prison, New York, and Point Lookout, Maryland. Exchanged March 2, 1865. Died at home in Patrick County, May 8, 1865 of disease. BPC.
SAUNDERS, Silas Green. Company H, 42nd Virginia Infantry. WIA, McDowell, West Virginia May 8, 1862. POW, Spotsylvania Court House, May 12, 1864, Elmira, New York, and Point Lookout, Maryland. Took oath and went to Kentucky.
SAUNDERS, Vincent. Company K, 50th Virginia Infantry. Died at Fort Donelson, Tennessee.
SAYERS (or SAWYERS), James, Jr. Company D, 12th Virginia Infantry. PCDR, July 17, 1862, Strasburg (or Petersburg), Virginia, of pneumonia. CPA.
SAYERS, Phillip W. Company K, 50th Virginia Infantry. KIA, near Richmond.
SAYERS, William. Company K, 50th Virginia Infantry.
SAYERS (SAWYERS), Thomas F. Company I, 24th Virginia Infantry. Died of disease at Chimborazo Hospital, Richmond, August 3, 1862.
SCALES, James R. (August 5, 1842-November 9, 1866). Company H, 42nd Virginia Infantry. Elected First Lieutenant. BPC.
SCALES, Joseph H. Captain, 54th Virginia Infantry. VMI student.
SCALES, Nathaniel M. Company H, 42nd Virginia Infantry. KIA, Kernstown, Virginia, March 23, 1862.
SCALES, Noah W. Company H, 42nd Virginia Infantry. Discharged September 29, 1862 for being under age. Possibly served later in 34th Battalion Virginia Cavalry.
SCOTT, Asa G. Lieutenant, Company K, 50th Virginia Infantry. BPC.
SCOTT, G. Boston. Commissary Sergeant, Company K, 50th Virginia Infantry. Died in General Hospital, POW Hospital in Washington D. C. on June 19, 1864.
SCOTT, Greenville B. Company K, 50th Virginia Infantry. Died September 9, 1861, of pneumonia. Death register says "typhoid fever" in North Carolina.
SCOTT, James G. Company I, 5th Battalion Virginia Reserves. Conscripted, June 1864. LCA.
SCOTT, Jehu. Company C, 54th Virginia Infantry. BPC.
SCOTT, Jesse P. Corporal, 42nd Virginia Infantry. BPC.
SCOTT, John W. Company H, 51st Virginia Infantry. POW, Waynesboro, March 2, 1865. Released from Fort Delaware, June 21, 1865.
SCOTT, Joseph. Company I, 5th Battalion Virginia Reserves. Living in 1907. BPC. CPA.

SCOTT, Samuel. Company D, 51st Virginia Infantry. POW, Waynesboro, March 2, 1865. Released from Fort Delaware, June 2, 1865.

SEMONES, J. H. Company H, 51st Virginia Infantry. POW, Fort Delaware. Buried Finn's Point, New Jersey.

SHARP, Thomas W. Company D. 12th Virginia Infantry. Substitute for William Barnard.

SHEFFIELD, L.C. Private, Company B, 24th Virginia Cavalry.

SHELOR, Albert Edwards. Company I, 5th Battalion Virginia Reserves.

SHELOR, G. B. Company K, 50th Virginia Infantry. Died at Fort Donelson, Tennessee, 1862.

SHELOR, Indiandozier Boganshield (John B.). Company K, 50th Virginia Infantry. Died in Elmira Prison, New York, February 15, 1865. Buried Woodlawn National Cemetery. CPA.

SHELOR, Isham Bernard (May 11, 1837-April 21, 1882). Captain, Company A, 24th Virginia Infantry. WIA, Five Forks in April 1865. POW, Point Lookout, Maryland. CDAR. CPA. BPC.

SHELOR, James F. Company H, 51st Virginia Infantry.

SHELOR, James T. Company D, 51st Virginia Infantry. Living in 1907.

SHELOR, John B. Company K, 50th Virginia Infantry. POW, Spotsylvania Courthouse, May 12, 1864.

SHELOR, Samuel Floyd. Sergeant, Company D, 51st Virginia Infantry. Died at Lee Camp Soldier's Home, June 22, 1913. BPC. LCA. CPA.

SHELOR, William F. Company I, 54th Virginia Infantry.

SHELTON, A. P. Company K, 24th Virginia Cavalry.

SHELTON, Anderson R. Company H, 42nd Virginia Infantry. Died of typhoid fever in West Virginia, November 4, 1861.

SHELTON, Archibald Critz (December 4, 1839-March 4, 1920). Company H, 58th Virginia Infantry. POW, Fredericksburg May 3, 1863. WIA, Spotsylvania Court House May 12, 1864. BPC. UDC. CDAR. CPA.

SHELTON, Charles Madison "Matt". Co H, 58th Virginia Infantry. Died after 1900.

SHELTON, Charles M. (son of Thomas Shelton). Company H, 58th Virginia Infantry. POW, Fredericksburg May 3, 1863. Exchanged from Fort Delaware May 23, 1863. POW, Winchester, September 19, 1864, Point Lookout, Maryland. Joined US Army. Died in Patrick County 1911.

SHELTON, Gabriel O. Company D, 12th Virginia Infantry. PCDR, measles at Marine Hospital, Portsmouth, Virginia, May 3, 1862.

SHELTON, George Franklin. Company H, 42nd Virginia Infantry. POW, Spotsylvania Court House, May 12, 1864, Elmira Prison, New York and at Point Lookout, Maryland. Exchanged, November 15, 1864. CDAR.

SHELTON, George J. Company D, 12th Virginia Infantry. Died of smallpox at Winchester Hospital, November 9, 1862.

SHELTON, Henderson. Lieutenant, Company H, 58th Virginia Infantry. Living in 1900.

SHELTON, Hiram Green. Company H, 42nd Virginia Infantry. Medical discharge, January 22, 1862. Re-enlisted. WIA, Chancellorsville, May 2, 1863. Disabled. 1910C. CDAR. CPA.

SHELTON, James P. (son of Thomas Shelton). Company I, 24th Virginia Infantry. PCDR, KIA, Williamsburg, May 5, 1862.

SHELTON, James W. Sergeant, Company H, 42nd Virginia Infantry.

SHELTON, Joseph A. (son of Thomas Shelton). Company I, 24th Virginia Infantry. PCDR, typhoid fever at Manassas, August 27 (or 29), 1861.

SHELTON, Joshua J. Company H, 42nd Virginia Infantry. POW twice. Exchanged. Released from Elmira Prison, New York, June 19, 1865. CDAR.

SHELTON, Josiah A. (son of Thomas Shelton) Company I, 24th Virginia Infantry.

SHELTON, Levi "Lee". Company H, 58th Virginia Infantry. Died of disease at Camp McCulloch, Highland County, November 1, 1861.

SHELTON, Peter M. Sergeant, Company H. 58th Virginia Infantry. WIA, Spotsylvania Court House on May 12, 1864. POW, Petersburg on April 2, 1865. Released from Point Lookout Prison, Maryland June 20, 1865. CDAR. CPA.

SHELTON, Peter Tobe (March 4, 1844-November 27, 1912) (son of Thomas Shelton). Company H, 42nd Virginia Infantry. WIA by bombshell at Chancellorsville, May 2, 1863. Great grandfather of Attorney General Mary Sue Terry. BPC. 1910C.

SHELTON, Robert Lee. Company D, 51st Virginia Infantry. Received medical discharge December 1861. Re-enlisted November 1862 in Giles County. Transferred August 21, 1863 to Captain. Frye's Light (Orange) Artillery. POW, Farmville April 6, 1865. Released from Newport News, July 1, 1865.

SHELTON, Thomas H. "Tobe" (1834-1912). Company H, 58th Virginia Infantry and Company A, 42nd Virginia Infantry. WIA, Winchester September 19, 1864.

SHELTON, William J. (son of Thomas Shelton) Company H, 58th Virginia Infantry. Died of wounds, September 19, 1864. POW Fredericksburg May 6, 1863. WIA, Winchester, September 14, 1864.

SHELTON, William A. Company D, 51st Virginia Infantry.

SHELTON, William C. Company H, 42nd Virginia Infantry.

SHELTON, William H. Company H, 58th Virginia Infantry. POW, September 19, 1864 at Winchester.

SHELTON, William Henderson. Company H, 42nd Virginia Infantry. POW, Spotsylvania Court House, May 12, 1864, Elmira, New York. Died of pneumonia January 27, 1865. Grave #1652. CPA.
SHEPPARD, Calvin L. Company D, 12th Virginia Infantry.
SHEPPARD, Joel J. PCDR, near New River on November 15, 1862 of ruptured bowels.
SHEPPARD, William R. Company D, 12th Virginia Infantry. Died of disease at Norfolk, Virginia, April 6, 1862.
SHIVELY, Daniel. Company C, 57th Virginia Infantry.
SHOCKLEY, William H. Company I, 24th Virginia Infantry. WIA twice. POW twice. Living in 1909. CPA.
SHOUGH, F. A. Company F, 42nd Virginia Infantry. POW. Took oath and went North.
SIMMS, James J. Company D, 12th Virginia Infantry. WIA twice.
SIMPSON, William Howard. Company I, 24th Virginia Infantry. Physician. Medical discharge, February 6, 1862. Died in Patrick County, November 8, 1891. BPC. CPA.
SLAUGHTER, John W. (1830-1862). Company D, 12th Virginia Infantry. PCDR, pneumonia at field hospital, Falling Creek, Chesterfield County, July 20, 1862.
SMART, William. Company K, 50th Virginia Infantry. PCDR, February 12, 1862 of diarrhea at Fort Donelson, Tennessee.
SMITH, Albert H. Company E, 29th Virginia Infantry. POW, Farmville on retreat to Appomattox, April 8, 1865. Released, Point Lookout, Maryland, June 2, 1865.
SMITH, Albert. Company K, 50th Virginia Infantry. Living 1907.
SMITH, Benjamin F. Company G, 21st Virginia Cavalry.
SMITH, Burwell. Company K, 50th Virginia Infantry.
SMITH, Byrd. Company H, 5th Battalion Virginia Reserves. BPC. CPA.
SMITH, Charles B. Company D, 51st Virginia Infantry. KIA.
SMITH, Daniel (December 17, 1817-February 20, 1900). Company K, 50th Virginia Infantry. Company I, 5th Battalion Virginia Reserves. BPC. CPA.
SMITH, Daniel (May 10, 1841-June 23, 1907). Company K, 50th Virginia Infantry. BPC.
SMITH, Eli. Company I, 54th Virginia Infantry.
SMITH, Ellis. Company K, 50th Virginia Infantry.
SMITH, Ewell. Company C, 26th Virginia Cavalry.
SMITH, Floyd. Company E. 53rd North Carolina Regiment Born in Patrick 1839. Enlisted in Surry County, North Carolina. POW, Gettysburg 1863. Died of diarrhea at Point Lookout, Maryland, December 22, 1863.
SMITH, George. Company D, 51st Virginia Infantry. POW, Waynesboro, March 2, 1865. Released, Fort Delaware, June 21, 1865.

SMITH, George (August 2, 1835-October 27, 1910). Company C, 63rd Virginia Infantry. BPC. CPA.
SMITH, George P. Company D, 12th Virginia Infantry. WIA, Chancellorsville and at Spotsylvania Court House. POW, Burgess Mill, October 27, 1864. Released from Point Lookout, June 19, 1865.
SMITH, Harden Moore (September 6, 1827-February 10, 1910). Company D, 12th Virginia Infantry. Received medical discharge. Re-enlisted Company E, 47th Battalion Virginia Cavalry. UDC. CPA. BPC.
SMITH, Isaac. Company K, 50th Virginia Infantry. Living in 1907.
SMITH, James Y. Company H, 42nd Virginia Infantry. Died February 28, 1862, cause unspecified.
SMITH, Jesse William. Lieutenant, Company E, 29th Virginia Infantry. POW, April 6, 1865 at Sailor's Creek. Released from Johnson's Island Prison, South Carolina, June 20, 1865.
SMITH, John W. Company C, 36th Virginia Infantry. UDC. CPA. BPC.
SMITH, Joseph Harrison (1845-1926). Company K, 50th Virginia Infantry. WIA twice. Moved to Missouri after war.
SMITH, Marshall (1831-1882). Quartermaster Sergeant, Company H, 58th Virginia Infantry. Quartermaster Sergeant, Teamster and Wagon Master. Surrendered at Appomattox. CPA.
SMITH, Munford (1823-1862). Company C, 47th Battalion Virginia Cavalry. Became 26th Virginia Cavalry. Died in prison at Fort Delaware. CPA.
SMITH, Octavius L. Company D, 12th Virginia Infantry. WIA, Weldon, North Carolina, August 19, 1864. POW, Burgess Mill, October 27, 1864. Released from Point Lookout Prison, Maryland, June 30, 1865. Died at home September 2, 1865.
SMITH, Samuel F. Company K, 50th Virginia Infantry. PCDR, wounds, Fort Donelson, Tennessee, March 12, 1862.
SMITH, Thomas. Company H, 42nd Virginia Infantry. WIA, Cedar Mountain, August 9, 1862. POW, while in hospital at Richmond, April 3, 1865. Released from prison at Newport News, July 1, 1865. BPC. CPA.
SMITH, Thomas. Company K, 50th Virginia Infantry. Living in 1907. CPA.
SMITH, William. Company K, 50th Virginia Infantry. PCDR, Blue Sulphur Springs, West Virginia of fever, October 22, 1861.
SMITH, William Burrell. Company G, 42nd Virginia Infantry. POW, May 12, 1864 at Spotsylvania Court House. Released from Elmira Prison, New York, June 27, 1865. Died 1910. BPC. CPA.
SMITH, William C. Company D, 12th Virginia Infantry.
SMITH, William Henry (1833-1906). Company D, 12th Virginia Infantry.
SNOW, Jordan H. Lieutenant, Company I, 28th North Carolina Regiment. Born in Patrick circa 1829. Moved to Surry County, North

Carolina, prior to war. Entered service 1862. WIA, Gettysburg. POW, July 1864, Point Lookout Prison, Maryland and Fort Delaware. Paroled June 17, 1865.

SOWDER, Emmanuel. Company D, 51st Virginia Infantry. Medical discharge, April 13, 1863. CPA.

SOWDER (Sawyers), Tazewell E. Company H, 51st Virginia Infantry. POW, Waynesboro, March 2, 1865. Released, Fort Delaware, June 2, 1865.

SOYARS, Dr. Joseph. Lieutenant, Company B, 2nd North Carolina Cavalry. POW, Roanoke Island 1862. Paroled. WIA, Gettysburg July 1863. Resigned from unit in July 1864 and joined 37th Regiment Virginia Cavalry. Born in Patrick County 1830. Practiced medicine in Dobson, North Carolina. Returned to Patrick after the war and practiced medicine in Ararat area. CPA.

SPAIN, James T. Company K, 50th Virginia Infantry. Company D, 12th Virginia Infantry. POW, Burgess Mill, October 27, 1864. Released from Point Lookout Prison, Maryland January 1, 1865.

SPANGLER, Coon. Company I, 5th Battalion Virginia Reserves.

SPANGLER, Fleming M. Company H or K, 50th Virginia Infantry. BPC. CDAR. CPA.

SPANGLER, George Washington. Company K, 50th Virginia Infantry. Living in 1909. CPA.

SPENCE, Drury. Company H, 29th Virginia Infantry. MIA.

SPENCE, Thomas Alderman. Company D, 54th Virginia Infantry.

SPENCER, Abram J. Possibly in Company A, 135th Virginia Militia. 1910C.

SPENCER, Benjamin. Company H, 42nd Virginia Infantry. PCDR, Edray, West Virginia, September 22, 1861 of measles.

SPENCER, Hardin. Company I, 24th Virginia Infantry. WIA. POW, Seven Pines. Exchanged. KIA, Drewry's Bluff. CPA.

SPENCER, Henry J. Company D, 12th Virginia Infantry. WIA, North Anna River, May 24, 1864. POW, Burgess Mill, October 27, 1864. Released from Point Lookout, June 1865.

SPENCER, James Jackson (1833-1865). Company H, 58th Virginia Infantry. Died of pneumonia in prison at Elmira Prison, New York, April 20, 1865. Buried at Woodlawn Cemetery. CPA.

SPENCER, James M. Company D, 51st Virginia Infantry. Medical discharge, June 14, 1862.

SPENCER, James W. Company G, 42nd Virginia Infantry.

SPENCER, John R. (or John W.). 24th Virginia Cavalry. Died of typhoid, February 15, 1865, Danville, Virginia

SPENCER, John R. Company I, 24th Virginia Infantry. (May be same as above).

SPENCER, John W. Company H, 42nd Virginia Infantry. PCDR, Valley Mountain, Pocahontas County, West Virginia, August 22, 1861 of typhoid fever.

SPENCER, Levi. Company D, 6th Virginia Infantry. Died Chimborazo Hospital No. 2, December 12, 1862. CPA.

SPENCER, Lewis Green. Company H, 42nd Virginia Infantry. Medical discharge. Died 1876.

SPENCER, Peter (April 6, 1822-March 17, 1902). Company G, 21st Virginia Cavalry. BPC. CPA.

SPENCER, Preston Toliver (June 17, 1846-October 9, 1935). Company I, 5th Battalion Virginia Reserves. Enlisted at age 17. Living 1907, Died Floyd County, Kentucky.

SPENCER, S. D. Possibly Corporal, Company B, 24th Virginia Cavalry. Died Sep. 21, 1862.

SPENCER, William Henry. Company I, 24th Virginia Infantry. PCDR, KIA, Seven Pines, May 31, 1862.

STANLEY, William W. PCDR, May 10, 1862 of measles.

STAPLES, Abram (1828-1911). Family tradition states he served, but no details available. BPC.

STAPLES, John. Company I, 24th Virginia Infantry. WIA, Williamsburg. BPC.

STAPLES, Martin (1839-1923). Company K, 50th Virginia Infantry. Lieutenant and /or Sergeant Major Co B, 24th Virginia Cavalry. BPC.

STAPLES, Samuel Granville (1821-1895). Born at Stonewall House in Taylorsville (Stuart). Lawyer and Deputy Clerk of County Court, House of Delegates. Served on staff of General J.E.B. Stuart as Volunteer Aide-de-camp April until July 1862 until injured in fall from horse. Post-war judge. Died and is buried in Roanoke. CDAR.

STEDMAN, Andrew Jackson (1822-1894). Sergeant, Company B, 49th North Carolina Infantry. CDAR. BPC.

STEPHENS, Elias R. (1843-1930). Corporal, Company A, 11th Virginia Infantry. POW, Fisher's Hill, Released April 14, 1865. BPC. UDC. CDAR. CPA.

STEVENS, J. T. Company D, 51st Virginia Infantry.

STONE, J. M. Company D, 51st Virginia Infantry.

STONE, James H. Company H, 42nd Virginia Infantry. Died 1911.

STONE, John C. Possibly in Company B, 57th Virginia Infantry. 1910C. CPA.

STONE, S. S. Company K, 36th Virginia Infantry.

STOOPS, John R. Corporal, Company K, 50th Virginia Infantry. WIA, June 3, 1864. Died, Richmond Hospital June 16, 1864. CPA.

STOOPS, William (1825-1904). Company G, 21st Virginia Cavalry. BPC.

STOVALL, George W. (1845-1902). Company H, 58th Virginia Infantry. WIA, Fredericksburg. BPC. LCA. CPA.
STOVALL, John P. Lt, Company I, 5th Battalion Virginia Reserves, Living in 1907.
STOVALL, Quincey A. Company D, 51st Virginia Infantry. POW in Loudon County. Released from Elmira Prison, New York, May 29, 1865.
STOWE, Edward. 1910C.
STOWE, James. Company G, 42nd Virginia Infantry. Died of unspecified cause, April 30, 1863.
STOWE, Thomas. Company G, 42nd Virginia Infantry. Born in Patrick County Moved to Henry County. WIA, Fisher's Hill. CDAR.
STOWE, William. 16th Regiment Virginia Cavalry.
STEWART, George M. 24th Virginia Cavalry. BPC. CPA.
STUART, James Ewell Brown (1833-1864). Major General See separate chapter.
STUART, John Dabney. Assistant Surgeon, 54th Virginia Infantry. Previously served as surgeon in 42nd Virginia Infantry. Born in Patrick County and brother of J. E. B. Stuart.
STUART, William. Company H, 42nd Virginia Infantry. Medical discharge, January 23, 1862.
SUMNER, Joshua H. Company A, 54th Virginia Infantry. In list of Confederate veterans in Order Book #18.
SUTLEFF (SETLIFF), Barnett. Company G, 37th Virginia Cavalry. BPC. CDAR.
TATE, James B. Company I, 5th Battalion Virginia Reserves. Company H, 58th Virginia Infantry.
TATUM, C. A. Company B, 54th Virginia Infantry.
TATUM, James E. (1847-1881). Company I, 5th Battalion Virginia Reserves. BPC.
TATUM, James M. BPC.
TATUM, John A. (1836-1862). 1st Lieutenant, Company H, 42nd Virginia Infantry. PCDR, KIA, Cedar Mountain, August 9, 1862. BPC.
TATUM, John Prior (1846-1928). 24th Virginia Cavalry. BPC. CPA. 1910C.
TATUM, Thomas Benton (1837-1903). Company C, 41st Virginia Infantry. CPA. BPC.
TATUM, Thomas G. 1910C.
TATUM, William F. Company H, 42nd Virginia Infantry. Died October 1861 at Greenbrier, White Sulphur Springs Hospital of fever.
TAYLOR, David Russell (June 25, 1842-November 28, 1924). Company D, 6th Virginia Infantry. WIA, Crampton's Gap, Maryland. BPC. 1910C.
TAYLOR, George S. Company I, 24th Virginia Infantry. Medical discharge, September 18, 1862. Re-enlisted June 3, 1864. POW, Farmville, April 5, 1865.

TAYLOR, George W. Company A, 42nd Virginia Infantry.
TAYLOR, Hannibal Hampson, Company I, 5th Battalion Virginia Reserves.
TAYLOR, James A. (January 8, 1829-February 17, 1897). Company I, 42nd Virginia Infantry. CPA.
TAYLOR, John A. Company K, 51st Virginia Infantry. PCDR, July 10, 1862 of diphtheria.
TAYLOR, Samuel C. Company G, 25thVirginia Cavalry. Obituary stated he was Civil War soldier. Died in April 1916.
TAYLOR, William A. (1831-1912). Company D, 12th Virginia Infantry. POW, Burgess Mill. Released, Point Lookout, June 20, 1865. UDC. CDAR. CPA.
TAYLOR, William Fountain Burrell. Physician, 51st Virginia Infantry.
TERRELL, John J. Possibly Assistant Surgeon with General Staff.
TERRY, Henry Clay. Company H, 51st Virginia Infantry. Died in Pearisburg General Hospital, May 2, 1863. BPC.
TERRY, John J. Company H, 51st Virginia Infantry. Died, January 20, 1880. BPC.
TERRY, Joseph Green. Company K, 50th Virginia Infantry. BPC. CPA.
TERRY, Nathan B. (1825-1911). Lieutenant, Company H, 51st Virginia Infantry. POW, Winchester, September 19, 1864. Released from Fort Delaware, June 17, 1865. UDC. CPA. BPC.
TERRY, Robert A. Company C, 10th Virginia Heavy Artillery. LCA.
TERRY, Reuben P. Company K, 50th Virginia Infantry. Company D, 12th Virginia Infantry. Living in 1907.
TERRY, Samuel Matt. Company H, 51st Virginia Infantry. WIA. POW, Fort Donelson, Tennessee, February 15, 1863. In Kentucky hospital, Returned to Patrick after war. CDAR. CPA.
TERRY, William. Company D, 12th Virginia Infantry. Died of disease at Falling Creek, Chesterfield County, August 12, 1862.
TERRY, William Anderson (1828-1913). Company H, 51st Virginia Infantry. POW, Lee Town, June 25, 1864. Released from Point Lookout, March 1 (or 4), 1865. CPA.
TERRY, William M. Company K, 50th Virginia Infantry. Died August 13, 1862, of meningitis.
THOMAS, Andrew Jackson. Mountain and Orange Artillery. WIA, Gettysburg. Died July 6, 1863.
THOMAS, Charles J. Company D, 51st Virginia Infantry. PCDR, Raleigh County, West Virginia of typhoid November 13, 1861.
THOMAS, David Crockett. Company E, 29th Virginia Infantry.
THOMAS, J. N. Mountain and Orange Artillery. Died January 5, 1863 in Caroline County.
THOMAS, James Marshall. Orange Artillery. Died January 5, 1863 of disease.

THOMAS, James W. Company H, 42nd Virginia Infantry. Transferred to Navy, April 4, 1864.

THOMAS, John. Company E, 29th Virginia Infantry. 1910C. Carroll County

THOMAS, J. R. Company D, 51st Virginia Infantry. Died in service.

THOMAS, Levi D, Company F, 29th Virginia Infantry. WIA, Drewry's Bluff. Died 1907 Carroll County

THOMAS, Lewis T. Company D, 51st Virginia Infantry. POW, Waynesboro, March 2, 1865. Released from Fort Delaware, June 2, 1865. Died 1890. CPA.

THOMAS, Nathaniel A. Company D, 51st Virginia Infantry. Died 1905.

THOMAS, Peter J. (May 15, 1828-December 18, 1912). Company D, 51st Virginia Infantry. BPC. CPA.

THOMAS, Pleasant C. Company D, 51st Virginia Infantry. Died in Patrick County, December 9, 1890.

THOMAS, Polk F. Sergeant, Company H, 4th Regiment Virginia Reserves.

THOMAS, Richard T. Mountain and Orange Artillery. Paroled at Appomattox. Living in 1907.

THOMAS, Robert. Company E, 29th Virginia Infantry. WIA, Cold Harbor. Died in Carroll County 1900.

THOMAS, Tazewell P. Company D, 51st Virginia Infantry. Mountain and Orange Artillery. POW, Strasburg, October 19, 1864. Released from Point Lookout, Maryland, June 21, 1865. Living in 1909. CPA.

THOMAS, Tyler L. Orange Artillery.

THOMAS, Walter Henry (April 29, 1829-May 8, 1919). Company D, 51st Virginia Infantry. BPC. CPA.

THOMAS, William E. Company E, 29th Virginia Infantry. WIA, Cold Harbor. Died in Carroll County circa 1911. CDAR.

THOMAS, William H. Company H, 24th Virginia Infantry. PCDR, fever in Richmond hospital on June 30, 1864 at age 21.

THOMAS, William Henry. Company E, 29th Virginia Infantry. WIA, Drewry's Bluff. Died 1881in Carroll County.

THOMPSON, Austin. Company H, 42nd Virginia Infantry.

THOMPSON, Creed F. Company G, 29th Virginia Infantry.

THOMPSON, Hiram. Company E, 3rd Virginia Reserves and Company B, 10th Virginia Reserves. 1910C. CDAR. CPA.

THOMPSON, Matthew S. Company H, 58th Virginia Infantry.

THOMPSON, Taylor. Company I, 5th Battalion Virginia Reserves.

THOMPSON, W. A. Company D, 51st Virginia Infantry.

THOMPSON, William H. PCDR, fever at Greenbrier River, December 22, 1861. Death register shows February 20, 1861.

THOMPSON, William M. Died March 5, 1862 of consumption.

THOMPSON, William Pleasant (December 25, 1836-June 9, 1910). 24th Virginia Infantry. WIA, Gettysburg and at Drewry's Bluff. Paroled at Appomattox. UDC. BPC.

THOMPSON, William Taylor (1847-1895). Company I, 55th Virginia Infantry. Born in Patrick. Died in Mt. Airy, North Carolina.

TIDMARSH, Charles. Company H, 51st Virginia Infantry.

TILLEY, Aaron Burwell. Company H, 42nd Virginia Infantry. Medical discharge. Died 1864 of diarrhea while home. CPA.

TILLEY, Ezekiel. 1910C.

TILLEY, James Elwood. Company K, 22nd North Carolina Infantry. POW, Chancellorsville, Old Capital Prison. Released, June 24, 1863. In list of Confederate soldiers in Order Book #18. BPC.

TILLEY, John H. Company H, 42nd Virginia Infantry. WIA, Cedar Mountain, August 9, 1862. Did not completely recover during war and was assigned hospital duty. CDAR.

TRENT, B. S. Patrick County Home Guard. Served two years per pension record.

TRENT, John (1847-1911). Company G, 21st Virginia Infantry. CPA. 1910C.

TRENT, Thomas. Company G, 21st Virginia Cavalry. WIA, December 2, 1864.

TRENT, William H. (1841-1910). Company G, 42nd Virginia Infantry. WIA, December 2, 1864. CPA.

TUCK, John. Company I, 5th Battalion Virginia Reserves.

TUGGLE, Thomas Anderson. Company I, 24th Virginia Infantry. PCDR, KIA, Second Manassas, July 10, 1862.

TUGGLE, Henry. Company I, 3rd Virginia Reserves. Patrick County Clerk of Court. Born November 26, 1818. Moved to Henry County after war and was sheriff there for twelve years.

TUGGLE, Nathaniel H. Company H, 42nd Virginia Infantry. POW, Spotsylvania Court House, May 12, 1864. Released from Elmira, New York, June 27, 1865. CPA.

TUGGLE, Tab (Tobe) Company I, 5th Battalion Virginia Reserves.

TUGGLE, William (1832-1877). Company H, 58th Virginia Infantry. Discharged, November 6, 1864.

TURNER, Bruce L. Company D, 51st Virginia Infantry. PCDR, pneumonia November 13, 1861, in Allegheny County, Virginia

TURNER, Creed O. Company D, 51st Virginia Infantry. Medical discharge, bladder problems, August 2, 1862. Living in 1907.

TURNER, Elkanah B. (January 6, 1823-August 17, 1886). Enlisted 1864, Company D, 51st Virginia Infantry. BPC.

TURNER, Fleming (1832-1892). Company I, 54th Virginia Infantry. Born in Patrick County served from Franklin County. CPA.

TURNER, George T. Company D, 51st Virginia Infantry. Took oath and went North.

TURNER, James Cornelius (1829-1862). Company A, 24th Virginia Infantry. Died of typhoid fever at Chimborazo Hospital, Richmond, August or June 21, 1862.

TURNER, James R. Company D, 51st Virginia Infantry. POW, Waynesboro, March 2, 1865. Released from Fort Delaware, June 21, 1865. Living in 1909. BPC. CPA.

TURNER, Jefferson (May 22, 1829-May 2, 1862). Company H, 54th Virginia Infantry.

TURNER, Meshach. Company E, 64th Virginia Militia. Company B, 57th Virginia Infantry.

TURNER, Rufus. Lieutenant, Company D, 12th Virginia Infantry. Died of diphtheria, September 19, 1862, while serving as Sheriff of Patrick County. BPC.

TURNER, Samuel Claiborne (March 24, 1833-April 20, 1916). Company D, 12th Virginia Infantry. POW, Chancellorsville, April 30, 1863. Exchanged. POW, Burgess Mill, October 27, 1864. Exchanged from Point Lookout, Maryland in March 1865. CPA.

TURNER, Tazewell A. Company H, 42nd Virginia Infantry. Also served in Company H, 51st Virginia Infantry. POW, Waynesboro, March 2, 1865. Released from Fort Delaware, June 2, 1865.

UNDERWOOD, Alfred (July 24, 1835-March 14, 1905). Company H, 51st Virginia Infantry. Went North. BPC.

UNDERWOOD, Isaac W. (May 23, 1835-September 23, 1902). Company D, 12th Virginia Infantry. Stayed in army, mostly in hospitals, until last 10 months. Went North from West Virginia. BPC.

UNDERWOOD, William Riley (December 24, 1837-July 21, 1934). Company K, 50th Virginia Infantry. One of last survivors of Civil War in Patrick County. BPC. CDAR.

VAUGHAN, Harden. Possibly served as Second Lieutenant in Company H, 37th Battalion Virginia Cavalry. Died June 26, 1917. In list of Confederate soldiers in Order Book #18.

VAUGHN, Columbus P. Company D, 51st Virginia Infantry. POW, Winchester, September 19, 1864. Exchanged from Point Lookout, March 15, 1865.

VAUGHN, D. S. Company I, 26th Virginia Infantry.

VAUGHN, Elijah D. Company D, 51st Virginia Infantry. POW, Winchester, September 9, 1864. Released from Point Lookout, Maryland, March 15, 1865.

VAUGHN, James P. Company D, 51st Virginia Infantry. Died in service.

VAUGHN, John J. Company D, 51st Virginia Infantry. KIA.

VAUGHN, John. Death register indicates he died Jun. 13, 1861. May be same as above.

VAUGHN, William R. (1840-1861). PCDR, pneumonia in Raleigh County, West Virginia on November 26, 1861.

VIA, Doctor Green (December 6, 1842-June 2, 1864). Company D, 51st Virginia Infantry. Died at home in Patrick County of typhoid on June 2, 1864. BPC.

VIA, Elijah DeHart. Lieutenant, Company H, 51st Virginia Infantry. POW, Waynesboro, March 2, 1865. Released, Fort Delaware, June 21, 1865.

VIA, James Ellyson (August 21, 1836-April 11, 1889). Company D, 51st Virginia Infantry.

VIA, James Fleming. Company H, 42nd Virginia Infantry. Medical discharge, December 5, 1861.

VIA, Isaac. Mountain and Orange Artillery.

VIA, James Robert (May 19, 1840-July 24, 1915). Company D, 51st Virginia Infantry. Medical discharge, June 8, 1862. BPC. UDC. CPA. 1910C.

VIA, Jesse T. Company D, 12th Virginia Infantry. Died of typhoid fever at Chimborazo Hospital, Richmond, June 24, 1862.

VIA, Reuben (August 29, 1833-May 3, 1863). 24th Virginia Cavalry. Mountain and Orange Artillery. KIA, Chancellorsville, May 3, 1863.

VIA, William. PCDR, May 26, 1861 of dyspepsia.

VIA, William B. (January 13, 1845-March 21, 1927). Company H, 42nd Virginia Infantry. POW, Front Royal Hospital. Exchanged. Discharged. BPC. CPA.

VIA, William C. Company D, 51st Virginia Infantry. PCDR, Mercer County, West Virginia on December 3, 1861 of camp fever. BPC.

VIA, William Dennis (September 12, 1838-March 6, 1915). Corporal, Company D, 51st Virginia Infantry. Became dentist after war. Served as member of first town council and as Mayor of Stuart. Chosen to represent the South at the fiftieth anniversary Battle of Gettysburg in 1913. UDC. CPA. 1910C. BPC.

VIPPERMAN, Emanuel Jackson. In list of Confederate soldiers in Order Book #18. BPC.

VIPPERMAN, George Washington. In list of Confederate soldiers in Order Book #18.

VIPPERMAN, Nicholas T. Company I, 24th Virginia Infantry. POW, Gettysburg. Died at Fort Delaware Prison, October 7, 1863.

VIPPERMAN, Thomas H. Company I, 24th Virginia Infantry. KIA, Drewry's Bluff.

WALLER, James C. Company I, 24th Virginia Infantry. PCDR, Danville Hospital August 15, 1862 or in Baltimore, Maryland, May 21, 1862.

WALLER, John. Company I, 24th Virginia Infantry. PCDR, typhoid at Liberty (Bedford County, Virginia), June 1, 1862.
WALLER, John C. Company I, 24th Virginia Infantry.
WALLER, William Peter. Company I, 24th Virginia Infantry.
WASHBURN, John T. Corporal, Company D, 51st Virginia Infantry. POW, Winchester, September 19, 1864. Exchanged from Point Lookout, Maryland, March 15, 1865.
WASHBURN, William H. Company H, 42nd Virginia Infantry. Died of typhoid fever at Greenbrier Bridge, West Virginia, November 15, 1861.
WASHINGTON, David. Company D, 51st Virginia Infantry. Blacksmith. Living in 1907.
WEAVER, Jesse. Company A, 24th Virginia Infantry.
WEBB, Henry (April 26, 1827-February 6, 1896). Company K, 50th Virginia Infantry. BPC.
WERTH, William H. Lieutenant Colonel, 45th Virginia Infantry. Sent to iron works on Goblintown Creek (now Fairy Stone Park area) to aid in delivering iron for Confederacy. Died February 10, 1872. BPC at Patrick Springs Hotel.
WEST, James G. Company K, 50th Virginia Infantry. Died August 1863.
WEST, Wilson J. (1829-1904). Company K, 50th Virginia Infantry. CPA. BPC.
WHALING, James L. Company D, 51st Virginia Infantry. Medical discharge, April 19, 1863.
WHITE, George E. 1910C.
WHITLOCK, Thomas H. Company E, 17th Virginia Cavalry. POW.
WHITLOCK, William B. Company I, 34th Virginia Infantry.
WICKHAM, Joseph R. Company A, 54th Virginia Infantry. Living in 1909. BPC. CPA.
WIGGINGTON, Andrew Jackson. Company I, 24th Virginia Infantry. WIA, Gettysburg and Cold Harbor. BPC. UDC. CPA.
WIGGINGTON, Callahill Menis. Company I, 24th Virginia Infantry. WIA, Gettysburg. CPA.
WIGGINGTON, Thomas H. Company I, 24th Virginia Infantry. WIA, Williamsburg, 1862. KIA, Drewry's Bluff.
WIGGINGTON, William Jefferson (February 11, 1833-February 13, 1917). Company I, 24th Virginia Infantry. WIA, June 19, 1864. POW, Five Forks. Released from Point Lookout, June 22, 1865. UDC. CDAR.
WILLARD, Allen Jackson. Company H, 51st Virginia Infantry. 1910C. CPA. BPC.
WILLARD, Isaac Hezekiah. Company I, 24th Virginia Infantry. Died of typhoid at Chimborazo Hospital, Richmond, December 10, 1861.
WILLARD, Jackson. Company H, 51st Virginia Infantry.
WILLARD, James. Company D, 51st Virginia Infantry. CPA.
WILLIAMS, A. J. Company H, 51st Virginia Infantry. Living in 1909.

WILLIAMS, Francis M. Company I, 24th Virginia Infantry.
WILLIAMS, George W. PCDR, pneumonia at Manassas, January 4, 1862 at age 23.
WILLIAMS, Henry. Company I, 5th Battalion Virginia Reserves. Also Company H, 58th Virginia Infantry.
WILLIAMS, Jacob W. (1839-1919). Company B, 6th Virginia Infantry.
WILLIAMS, James. Company H, 51st Virginia Infantry.
WILLIAMS, John D. Company I, 24th Virginia Infantry. Scout. POW, Frayser's Farm. Exchanged. WIA, Gettysburg. POW, Cherry Grove, March 30, 1864. Exchanged from Point Lookout, March 1865.
WILLIAMS, Marshall. Company E, 6th Virginia Infantry. Died 1902. CPA.
WILLIAMS, Robert B. Sergeant, Company H, 51st Virginia Infantry. Living 1907.
WILLIAMS, Robert S. Company D, 6th Virginia Infantry. Living in 1909. CPA.
WILLIAMS, Samuel. Company H, 58th Virginia Infantry. POW, Cedar Creek, October 19, 1864. Released from Point Lookout Prison, Maryland, June 6, 1865.
WILLIAMS, William C. Company H, 42nd Virginia Infantry. PCDR, pneumonia and measles, Lynchburg Hospital, May 3, 1862. Buried in Lynchburg.
WILLIS, John. Company D, 12th Virginia Infantry. WIA, Spotsylvania Court House May 12, 1864. POW, Burgess Mill, October 29, 1864. Released from Point Lookout, May 14, 1865.
WIMBISH, James Lee. Company I, 5th Battalion Virginia Reserves. PCDR, "brain fever" at Danville, November 28, 1864.
WIMBISH, John Lee. Company I, 24th Virginia Infantry. KIA, Drewry's Bluff.
WIMBISH, John W. Company I, 24th Virginia Infantry.
WIMBISH, Peter H. Company I, 24th Virginia Infantry. POW, Sharpsburg. Died of wounds, October 22, 1862 in Frederick, Maryland hospital. Buried at Mt. Olivet Cemetery, Frederick, Maryland.
WIMBISH, William. 24th Virginia Infantry.
WINGFIELD, Henry Wyatt (1829-1902). Captain, Company H, 58th Virginia Infantry. Enlisted Patrick Court House. WIA, Fredericksburg May 6, 1863. Commanded regiment July 1864. POW, Winchester, September 15, 1864. Released Fort Delaware, June 17, 1865.
WOLFE, Harry. Company I, 24th Virginia Infantry. POW, Five Forks, April 2, 1865.
WOOD, Alexander. Company E, 23rd Battalion Virginia Infantry. BPC.
WOOD, Alexander A. Mountain and Orange Artillery. Company D, 6th Virginia Infantry. PCDR, Liberty (Bedford County) Hospital of tuberculosis.

WOOD, Elijah (March 17, 1833-April 8, 1911). Orange Artillery. Also in Company H, 51st Virginia Infantry. BPC.
WOOD, German (1840-1871). Company D, 51st Virginia Infantry. POW, Winchester, September 19, 1864. Released, Point Lookout, Maryland, March 15, 1865. BPC.
WOOD, James. Company H, 51st Virginia Infantry.
WOOD, James M. Company D, 6th Virginia Infantry.
WOOD, James Madison. Company D, 51st Virginia Infantry. POW. Took oath and went North.
WOOD, Jeremiah. Mountain and Orange Artillery.
WOOD, John. Company D, 51st Virginia Infantry. CPA.
WOOD, John Alexander Company D, 6th Virginia Infantry. PCDR, Liberty (Bedford County) Hospital of diphtheria.
WOOD, John B. (1839-1907). Company H, 51st Virginia Infantry.
WOOD, John W. Company K, 50th Virginia Infantry. KIA, Gettysburg.
WOOD, Levi. Company D, 51st Virginia Infantry.
WOOD, Richard Johnson (October 27, 1828-December 7, 1917). Company D, 51st Virginia Infantry. Medical discharge for heart disease, July 23, 1862.
WOOD, Stephen H. (September 22, 1822-April 11, 1890). Company K, 50th Virginia Infantry. CDAR. CPA.
WOODALL, James. Company H, 42nd Virginia Infantry. CPA.
WOODALL, Samuel. Company H, 42nd Virginia Infantry. POW, May 12, 1864, Spotsylvania Court House. Died of chronic diarrhea at Elmira Prison, New York, November 26, 1864. Buried there in Grave #944.
WOODALL, William H. Company H, 58th Virginia Infantry. POW, Fredericksburg. Exchanged at Fort Delaware, June 23, 1863.
WOODS, Sparrel (1847-1937). Company I, 4th Virginia Reserves. CPA.
WOODS, W. Green. Company H, 51st Virginia Infantry.
WOOLWINE, Rufus James (October 20, 1840-December 14, 1903). Captain, Company D, 51st Virginia Infantry. POW, Waynesboro, March 2, 1865. Released from Fort Delaware Prison, March 12, 1865. Sheriff of Patrick County. CDAR. CPA. BPC.
WORF, Romulus S. Company H, 58th Virginia Infantry. Discharged for illness/age, October 9, 1862.
WRIGHT, A. J. Orange Artillery.
WRIGHT, Columbus J. (June 8, 1835-June 1, 1879). Company D, 51st Virginia Infantry. BPC.
WRIGHT, General Jackson (July 23, 1838-April 30, 1906). Mountain and Orange Artillery. CPA.
WRIGHT, Jefferson N. Mountain and Orange Artillery. Patrick County Home Guard per pension record. CPA. BPC.
WRIGHT, James Patterson (December 29, 1835-August 24, 1889). Company H, 23rd Virginia Infantry.

WRIGHT, Josiah. Company I, 5th Battalion Virginia Reserves. CPA. BPC.

WRIGHT, Labourn P. Company I, 24th Virginia Infantry. Sent to hospital, June 7, 1862.

WRIGHT, Nash Jefferson (May 17, 1840-December 29, 1920). Orange Artillery. Paroled at Appomattox.

WRIGHT, Samuel Connor. Company H, 51st Virginia Infantry.

WRIGHT, Squire Green (July 23, 1838-March 20, 1904). Mountain and Orange Artillery. POW, Spotsylvania Court House, May 12, 1864. CPA.

WRIGHT, Washington. Orange Artillery.

YATES, Henry (C. A.) Patrick County Home Guard per pension record.

YEATTS, George W. (November 7, 1838-May 27, 1922). Company K, 50th Virginia Infantry. CDAR. CPA. 1910C. BPC.

YEATTS, Richard D. Company K, 50th Virginia Infantry. Living in 1907. CDAR. CPA.

YOUNG, Andrew J. Company I, 24th Virginia Infantry. Died in Richmond Hospital.

YOUNG, C. Company D, 51st Virginia Infantry.

YOUNG, Charles Henry. Sergeant, Company B, 24th Virginia Cavalry.

YOUNG, T. (J) P. Company D, 51st Virginia Infantry.

YOUNG, Jefferson (1836-1862). Company H, 58th Virginia Infantry. Died of typhoid near Richmond, December 29, 1862.

YOUNG, Pleasant. Company D, 51st Virginia Infantry. KIA.

YOUNG, William. Company I, 51st Virginia Infantry. Died of wounds.

ZENTMEYER, David F. Company D, 51st Virginia Infantry.

ZEIGLER (ZIGLAR), Leonard. Corporal. Company H, 58th Virginia Infantry. POW, Fredericksburg, May 3, 1863. Exchanged. WIA and arm amputated, October 19, 1864 at Cedar Creek. Sent to "Invalid Corps." CDAR. BPC.

ZIGLAR, John. Company D, 12th Virginia Infantry. WIA, Second Manassas. CDAR. CPA. BPC.

ZIGLAR, William. Company I, 24th Virginia Infantry. Company I, 5th Battalion Virginia Reserves. Company C, 10th Virginia Cavalry. Living in 1909. UDC. CPA. BPC.

Roster of Union Soldiers From Patrick County

BANKS, William H. S. Captain 120th Michigan Infantry, 1861-63. Lived at Johnson Creek Post Office.

BRANCH, Joshua. Company K, 140th Indiana Infantry. Buried Pedigo Cemetery at Ararat, Virginia near Laurel Hill, Birthplace of J. E. B. Stuart.

EPPERSON, John H. Company C, 6th U. S. Volunteers, March 18, 1865-October 15, 1866. Lived at Carter's Mill Post Office.

FLEMING, Samuel M. Company K, 138th Ohio Volunteer Infantry, May 1863-September 1863. Lived at Lone Cedar Post Office. (May have been in U. S. Colored Troops. Three listed)

GOIN, Morgan S. Company F, 11th Pennsylvania Infantry, January 4, 1864-August 19, 1865. Lived at Stuart Post Office.

GRAY, George. Company H, 119th U. S. Colored Infantry (Kentucky Infantry), April 14, 1865-April 27, 1866. Widow, Lavina, applied for pension. Lived at Colesville Post Office.

GRAY, Peter. Company K, 119th U. S. Colored Infantry (Kentucky Infantry), April 14, 1865-April 27, 1866. Lived at Consent Post Office.

HYLTON, Edmond (Edward). Company H, 119th U. S. Colored Infantry (Kentucky Infantry), April 14, 1865-April 27, 1866. Lived at Consent Post Office.

PUCKETT, Lewis B. Company B, 175th Ohio Infantry. Moved to Ohio in 1850.

REYNOLDS, Jacob. Company K, 119th U. S. Colored Infantry. Widow, Letty, applied for pension. Lived at Patrick Springs Post Office.

REYNOLDS, Miles. Company H, 119th U. S. Colored Infantry. Widow, Rhoda, applied for pension. Lived at Patrick Springs Post Office.

SHELTON, Charles, Jr. Company D, 4th U. S. Infantry, October 16, 1864-June 20, 1866. Lived at Shuff Post Office.

SHELTON, Charles M. Company D 4th U. S. Infantry, September 1864-July 20, 1866. Lived at Dobyns Post Office.

TATUM, Samuel. Company H, 119th U. S. Colored Infantry (Kentucky Infantry), April 14, 1865-April 27, 1866. Lived at Dobyns Post Office.

Civil War Pension Applications From Patrick County
1888

Adams, J. T.
Ayers, William
Blackard, Aaron
Bowling, Wm. W.
Bowman, Martha
Brim, R. D.
Campbell, Cena
Clark, Mattie
Craig, Lucinda
Dickerson, Lucinda
Duncan, Gilly
Edwards, Ruth
Epperson, Elizabeth J.
Gilbert, America E.
Going, Leroy
Gunter, B. L.
Gwinn, Sarah
Hall, Jane
Hardy, Joseph H.
Hatcher, W. H.
Helms, G. M.
Hughes, Delilah
Hylton, B. P.
Ingrum, Elizabeth A.
Kasy, Florentine
Lawrence, William R.
Lewis, Ruth
Loyd, Martha
Martin, Louisa M.
Mays, A. F.
McMillion, L. D.
Morrison, Jarrett H.
Pack, Luisa
Pack, Susan
Plastens, William C.
Rakes, Ruth A.
Reynolds, S. B.
Ross, McD.
Shelton, H. G.
Shiveley, Sallie

Adams, William
Beasley, R. M.
Blackard, America
Bowman, C. G.
Bowman, Rurall
Brock, Mary E.
Carter, Robt
Cockram, Ruth
Cruise, Mary A.
Dillon, H. H.
Durham, Caleb C.
Edwards, W. H.
Foley, Nancy J.
Gilbert, Elizabeth Jane
Griggs, Sarah D.
Gunter, Wm
Haley, Samuel Henry
Harbour, A. J.
Harris, G. L.
Haynes, Ferdnand
Hooker, Samuel
Hundley, Lucinda
Hylton, Emeline
Joyce, Sarah
Keaton, Sarah A.
Lawson, C. T.
Light, Henry C.
Martin, A. W.
Martin, Martha
McAlexander, John
Moran, Crawford
Moss, Easter
Pack, Martha A.
Pendleton, John
Pucket, Elizabeth
Ray, Abner
Right, Sarah
Sawyers, Sarah
Shelton, Mary E.
Smith, Catharine

Atkinson, J. E.
Belcher, Cosley
Blackard, S.
Bowman, Linda
Bowman, S. G.
Brown, Francis
Chapman, W.H.
Cockram, T.
Dehart, A. P.
Dalton, Sarah
Edwards, J. W.
Elizabeth, G.
Fulcher, Sarah
Gilly, Martha
Griggs, Wm. J.
Guslen, E.
Hall, Henry
Harbour, R. H.
Harris, S. G.
Hazlewood, E.
Hubbard, J. C.
Hyatt, Polly
Hylton, W. B.
Joyce, Wm. G.
Lawrence, E. F.
Lee, Hardin
Lovins, Mina
Martin, James
Martin, Mary
McCanless, W.
Morrison, J. T.
Murphy, Susan
Pack, Penah
Pike, Matilda
Pucket, Reed
Ray, Phoebe
Rorrer, Wm. R.
Shelor, E. A.
Shelton, Susan
Soyars, Sarah J.

325

Spangley, Geo. W.
Spencer, Peter
Tilley, Elizabeth
Wiggenton, C. M.
Woodes, Jensey
Ziglar, John

Spencer, Nancy S.
Taylor, Martha A.
Tuggle, Francis
Willard, James
Wright, Sarah

Spencer, N.
Terry, S. M.
Wiggenton, A.
Wood, Martha
Yeatts, R. D.

1900

Adams, J. J
Adams, Sarah J.
Akers, Isaac N.
Ayers, W. H
Beach, Jas. T
Boaz, J. R.
Bowman, T. Frank
Boyd, Nancy
Brown, J. H.,
Carter, James F.
Clark, John H.
Clifton, Malinda
Coleman, Samuel
Collins, Jesse
Compton, J. R.
Cooper, Mary A.
Craddock, J. T.
Craig, Peter D.
Cunningham, J. J.
Dalton, Samuel P.
Dehart, A. Pleasent
Dehart, Thomas
Dunkley, William
Ferrell, J. M.
Foster, A. P.
Gilbert, Bettie
Giles, P. H.
Gray, John F.
Griggs, Sallie F.
Haden, Wm. H.
Hall, Jasper R.
Harbour, M. J.
Hiatt, William
Hooker, Nancy
Howell, Mary

Adams, John H
Agee, Eliza J.
Akers, W. T.
Baker, James H.
Belcher, Causley
Bowman, Anderson
Boyd, Caleb
Brammer, Sallie
Bryant, John W.
Cassell, B. W.
Clark, Martha B.
Cockran, Sarah Jane
Collins, Delila
Collins, Levi P.
Conner, Esconia J
Corbin, Benjamin
Craddock, Peter J.
Creasy, J. H.
Dalton, Frederick
Davis, Mary E.
Dehart, Eli
Dehart, William
Fain, J. W.
Foley, Peyton
Foster, P. M.
Gilbert, L. D.
Gilley, Wm.
Gregory, C. C.
Grogan, James A.
Hall, E. H.
Hall, N. R.
Haymore, D. H.
Hooker, James M.
Hopkins, John
Hylton, James

Adams, Ruth H
Aistrope, H. C.
Arrington, S. G.
Barbour, Susan E
Belcher, Peter
Bowman, Gailen
Boyd, Jacob
Brown, J. H
Burge, D. C.
Clark, Geo. W.
Clark, Wm. A.
Cockran, Alexander
Collins, Jack
Collins, R. S.
Conner, S. A.
Cox, Cynthia
Craddock, Wm. J.
Critz, Haman B.
Dalton, Isham
Deatherage, W. A
Dehart, S. H.
Dillion, A. M.
Fain, Louisa J.
Foley, Reed
Fulcher, Mary S.
Gilbert, Robert
Goard, Wm. M.
Griffin, S. J.
Gunter, Elizabeth F.
Hall, James F.
Hancock, John H.
Hazlewood, R. F.
Hooker, Lucinda
Houchins, Abram W.
Jennings, Luther

Joyce, Parthenia
Keaton, Jamimy W.
Lawless, G. W.
Martin, A. W.
Martin, S. I.
Massey, John A.
Mize, W. B.
Morrison, John T.
Nowlin, Archer S.
Ore, Wm. R.
Pickerel, Richard
Puckett, Matilda
Ratcliff, Emily Ann
Rorrer, W. A.
Shelton, Peter M.
Smith, John W.
Smith, W. B.
Spangler, Geo. W.
Stovall, Geo. W. F.
Thomas, Amanda A.
Tuggle, Nat H.
Vaughn, D. S.
Whitlock, T. H.
Wigginton, W. J.
Williams, Robert S.
Wright, J. N.
Zeigler, Wm

Joyce, Sarah A.
King, George
Lawrence, Mary E.
Martin, E. Noah
Martin, W. A.
McGee, Green T.
Montgomery, Floyd
Morrison, T. C.
Nunn, Jesse
Pace, B. P.
Pigg, Paul C.
Purdy, James A.
Roberson, Abram
Ross, Samuel A.
Shockley, W. H.
Smith, Mary A.
Sowder, Exony
Spencer, James W.
Terry, N. B.
Thomas, Tazewell
Turner, James R.
Via, Wm. B.
Whitlow, Alice
Willard, Ruth
Witt, Charles R.
Wright, S. G.

Keton, James M.
King, Rebecca Matilda
Lawson, Malinda
Martin, James
Martin, W. G.
McPeak, B. M.
Montgomery, Madison
Moss, W. A.
Nunn, William
Pickerel, Margaret
Pigg, Thos. C.
Rakes, Chas. J.
Rodgers, Ruth
Shelor, S. F.
Smith, Ewell
Smith, Thomas
Sowder, Honey
Stewart, Geo. M.
Terry, William A.
Trent, Wm. H.
Turner, Samuel C.
West, Wilson J.
Wickham, Joseph R.
Williams, Marshall
Wright, G. J.
Yeatts, Geo. W.

1902

Ables, Joseph
Adams, Malinda
Agee, Ruth L.
Anglin, James P.
Arrington, W. H.
Barnard, Susan R.
Belton, Fosie
Bishop, A. J.
Bolt, Lucy F.
Bowman, Leona K.
Boyd, Elizabeth
Boyd, Mary M.
Brim, Martha A.
Campbell, Elizabeth

Adams, Betsy A. P.
Adams, Martha
Akers, N. C.
Anglin, Lillie C.
Barnard, Jas. W.
Barnard, Virginia A.
Belton, Hampton
Blackard, Aaron
Boswell, Julia A.
Bowman, Lourainah
Boyd, Elmira
Boyd, Nancy A.
Brown, Lena F.
Cassell, Martha J.

Adams, Elizabeth
Agee, John T.
Akers, S. R.
Arander, Jamima F.
Barnard, John
Belcher, Nancy
Biggs, Kate
Boaz, Tirpheny T.
Bowman, Jane
Bowman, Nannie
Boyd, H. H.
Bray, R. F.
Burkhart, E. W.
Chaney, Margarett

Chaney, Stephen B.
Clement, A. E.
Clifton, Mary E.
Cockram, German
Cockram, Mary J.
Coleman, Frances
Collins, Tempa
Conner, Onie J.
Crawford, W. E.
Croaff, Henry F.
Dalton, Lucy A.
Dalton, Willis
Dehart, Eli H.
Dehart, Mahala
Dehart, Wm. T.
Doss, Rachel A.
Dunkley, Samuel H.
Emberson, W. A.
Epperson, Wm
Fry, Celia
Fulcher, Catharine
Gilbert, Martha J.
Going, Ewell
Goode, Julia A.
Griffin, S. J.
Gunter, Mary
Hagood, W. R.
Hall, Francis
Hall, Mary Judy
Hall, W. L.
Hancock, Esther E.
Handy, Serrena
Harbour, Nancy A.
Harris, Isreal
Harrold, Manervia
Hatcher, Martha J.
Haynes, Bettie E.
Hill, W. D.
Houchins, Malinda
Hutchens, Martha A.
Hylton, Levi
Jarrell, Albert H.
Jefferson, M. P.
Jessup, E. S.

Chappell, Alexander
Clement, J. T. W.
Cock, Joel H.
Cockram, Isham
Cockram, Sarah E.
Collins, J. H.
Compton, Frances
Conner, R. W.
Creasey, Jas. D.
Cruise, Rosa
Dalton, Martha
Dehart, Belle
Dehart, Ellen
Dehart, Mary J.
Dent, McH.
Droughn, W.
Durham, Fannie
Epperson, H. T.
Foley, Mahala
Fry, John
Fulcher, Edmond
Gilbert, Wm. P.
Going, Priscilla
Gray, Mary A.
Griggs, Mary C.
Gusler, Page S.
Haley, Louvenia
Hall, Jas. P.
Hall, W. C.
Hall, Waller
Handy, J. R.
Harbour, A. J.
Harbour, Nancy L.
Harris, Nancy P.
Harrold, Mary J.
Hatcher, Mary B.
Hazlewood, America
Hines, James H.
Hubbard, Sarah E.
Hylton, Charity
Hylton, Nancy
Jarrell, Jane J.
Jefferson, W. J.
Johnston, David

Clark, Lizzie A.
Clifton, James
Cock, Ruth
Cockram, Mahala
Cockran, Peter
Collins, Mary
Conner, John
Craddock, Elizabeth
Crews, W. B.
Cruise, Zina
Dalton, Mary J.
Dehart, Eleasure
Dehart, Green W.
Dehart, Thos. T.
Dison, John
Dunkley, Eliza J.
Durham, John
Epperson, Margie
Freeman, A. J.
Fry, Mary A.
George, John W.
Gilley, Martha W.
Going, Rosa A.
Griffin, Lucinda
Grogan, Mary Jane
Haden, Seaten
Hall, Emaline
Hall, John R.
Hall, W. H.
Hanby, Susan N.
Handy, Nancy L.
Harbour, Martha A.
Harrell, Adline
Harrold, D. K.
Harrold, T. M.
Hayden, Tildy
Hendricks, R. D.
Hines, Rachel D.
Hundley, Bettie
Hylton, Jas. J.
Ingram, Geo. W.
Jefferson, Louvenia
Jessup, Deliah
Joyce, Mary

327

Joyce, Sarah
Joyce, Susan
Kendrick, John H.
Kendrick, Lizzie
Koger, Joseph H.
Koger, Mary A.
Lankford, James
Lankford, Mary A.
Lawson, James W.
Lawson, Ruth
Lawson, W. T.
Lawson, Wm S.
Lee, John
Lewis, Wm.
Light, Bettie
Mabe, Susan A.
Mabe, W. C.
Madden, Charles
Marshall, Elizah
Marshall, Martha A.
Martin, A. J.
Martin, C. J.
Martin, Fannie E.
Martin, C. T.
Martin, Harriett E.
Martin, John K.
Martin, Josephine
Martin, Lucinda
Martin, Mary Ann
Martin, Ruth
Martin, Sarah E.
Martin, W. F.
Martin, W. G.
Martin, Mary E.
Massey, Wilmouth O.
Massey, Elizabeth
Mays, Elizabeth D.
Mcalexander, David
Mccabe, Rachel A.
McMillion, Bethaniah
Mills, Fannie
Mills, J. L.
Mitchell, Lucy C.
Montgomery, Luetsy
Moran, Xonie
Morrison, Adaline
Morrison, David J.
Morrison, Nannie A.
Morrison, Susan M.
Newman, Jno. W.
Newman, Ruth
Newman, Sarah A. R.
Nolen, Isaac A.
Nolen, Jane
Nolen, John A.
Nolen, Judie A. E.
Nunn, America N.
Oliver, Martha
Owens, Edna
Pace, Mary E.
Padgett, Elizabeth
Pearce, Jacob
Pendleton, C. G.
Pendleton, Martha J.
Pendleton, Mary B.
Pendleton, Mary J.
Pigg, Susan J.
Plasters, Creed W.
Plasters, Ruhama
Powell, Lucy
Pratt, Pollie M.
Pruitt, Frances
Pruitt, Isham
Puckett, Emillie
Puckett, Ephraim
Radford, Lucinda J.
Rakes, Alexander
Rakes, Priscilla
Rakes, T. T.
Rakes, C. C.
Rangeley, Mary
Rangeley, J. E.
Reynolds, Joseph F.
Reynolds, P. C.
Reynolds, Sarah
Roberson, Sarah E.
Rorrer, Catharine
Rorrer, Ruth
Rorrer, W. R.
Ross, D. Lee
Ross, Esther J.
Salmons, J. L.
Salmons, Johnathan
Salmons, Luthina B.
Salmons, Nancy
Salmons, John
Scott, J. G.
Shelor, Mahala
Shelor, Sarah H.
Shelor, Susannah A.
Shelton, A. C.
Shelton, Mary A.
Shelton, Augusta
Simpson, Eliza A.
Smith, Amanda E.
Smith, Daniel
Smith, Byrd
Smith, Elizabeth
Smith, George
Smith, H. M.
Smith, Eli
Soyers, Nancy J.
Spangler, Mary E.
Spangler, S. A.
Spence, Sarah
Stephens, E. R.
Stone, Cassey A.
Stone, J. C.
Tatum, C. A.
Tatum, John P.
Tatum, Ruth S.
Tatum, Martha
Taylor, P. A.
Taylor, Satira E.
Taylor, W. A.
Taylor, Adaline
Terry, Mary A.
Terry, Rosa E.
Terry, J. G.
Thomas, Juda Va
Thomas, Peter J.
Thomas, Walter H.

Thomas, Mary	Thompson, Hiram	Trent, John
Tuggle, N. H.	Turner, Sabrina	Turner, Nancy E.
Via, James R.	Via, M. C.	Via, Minnie
Weaver, Mentoria	West, Susan A.	Whitlock, Allie P.
Wigginton, Sarah E.	Wigginton, Nancy J.	Willard, A. J.
Willard, Mary	Williams, Amanda	Wood, Lucinda A.
Wood, Sparrel	Wood, S. H.	Woodall, Mary A.
Woolwine, Sarah R.	Wright, Mary	Wright, Susan S.
Wright, Mary S.	Yeatts, Mary J.	Yeatts, C. A.
Young, C. Henry		

Confederate Disability Applications From Patrick County

1882

Adams, John S.	Adams, J. T.	Adams, Thomas S.
Baker, C. J.	Beamer, W. H.	Bowman, C. G.
Brain, R. O.	Brian, Rice O.	Cales, Solomon R.
Cates, Solomon R.	Caty, Joe R.	Chapman, Williams
Chatman, W. H.	Cockran, William H.	Dalton, Frederick
Dehart, A. P.	Dehart, Robert	Dillen, W. B.
Edwards, William H.	Foster, Peyton M.	Gilbert, L. D.
Harbour, Richard H.	Harris, George S.	Hatcher, Daniel G.
Hatcher, James W.	Hubbard, John C.	Hylton, James
Hylton, William B.	King, John	Light, Henry C.
Martin, Samuel I.	McAlexander, David	Merideth, Bradley
Midkiff, Joseph W.	Morrison, J.T.	Parr, E.
Pendleton, John	Pigg, Thomas	Poore, John
Rakes, C. J.	Reynolds, Shadrack B.	Roberts, Patrick H.
Robertson, Wilcher	Smith, John J.	Smith, Thomas
Staples, Samuel G.	Taylor, William A.	Thomas, Tyler,
Underwood, Riley	Woolwine, R. J.	Yates, Richard D.

1883

Agee, E. H.	Agee, Jarrett	Ayres, William
Belcher, Costly	Belcher, Peter	Bowling, J. T.
Bowling, William W.	Carter, Robert	Clark, C. C.
Conway B. D.	Cooper, William H.	Craddock, Joshua T.
Edwards, William H.	Gunter, B. L.	Haley, Samuel H.
Harrell, David K.	Hearboun, Ahiarah	Hooker, Samuel
King, George R.	Lawless, George W.	Lawrence, William R.
Lawson, W. T.	Lee, Hardin	Lewis, A. J.
McGrath, Patrick Mize,	Moss, William B.	Moss, William A.
Pendleton, C. G.	Plasters, Conrad	Rucker, W. B.

1884

Adam, John S.	Agee, A. G.	Agee, Garrett
Ayers, E. H.	Beasley, Robert M.	Blackard, Aaron
Bryant, Patrick H.	Childress, James H.	Childress, Robert
Clement, James L. W.	Collins, Andrew J.	Compton, James R.
Compton, William A.	Conner, John	Craddock, Peter J.
Danner, J. T.	Dehart, Eli	Dehart, Mariah E.
Edwards, W. H.	Edwards, William	Folen, Peyton

Foley, Reed
Glenn, Patrick T.
Griffin, Samuel J.
Hagood, William
Handy, Peter
Hayden, Site
Helms, Adam
King, John
Lawrence, William R.
Mabe, William C.
Mays, Abram F.
McGrath, Patrick
Montgomery, Madison
Pigg, Paul C.
Pucket, Hosea
Reynolds, S. B.
Robertson, Abram H.
Rorrer, Willaim A.
Rosser, W. R.
Shelton A. C.
Shelton, H. G.
Smith, Thomas
Stephens, E. R.
Terry, Samuel M.
Wood, Stephen H.
Zigler, John H.

Foley, William L.
Glidewell, James A.
Griffith, James H.
Haley, Samuel
Harbour, R. H.
Haymore, David H.
Jefferson, Peyton G.
Larrance, W. R.
Lee, Harden
Martin, David N.
McAlexander, David
McPeak, Bluford
Moran, Crawford
Pinn, John E.
Rakes, C. J.
Roberts, James
Robertson, Wilcher
Roser, W. R.
Shelor, J. B.
Shelton, A. P.
Shelton, Joshua
Spangler, F. M.
Stow, Thomas
Thompson, Hiram
Yates, George W.

Gleason, Patrick H.
Gregory, C. C.
Gunter, William W.
Hall, Henry
Hatcher, D. E.
Haynes, Ferdinand
Keaton, Hansford
Lawson, C. T.
Lyon, Silas T.
Martin, Samuel J.
McCanless, Oscar
Mitchell, W. A.
Padgett, Andrew C.
Poe, John
Ray, Abner
Roberts, Patrick H.
Rogers, Clement
Rosser, W. A.
Shelten, Hiram G.
Shelton, George F.
Shelton, Peter M.
Staples, Samuel G.
Sutliff, Barne B.
Tilly, John H.
Zigler, John

1886-1887

Adams, William
Bowman, Kheuel
Martin, James
Morrison, J. H.

Anglin, James P.
Boyd, James
McAlexander, William
Wiggenton, William J.

Blackburn, Thomas J.
Goode, Jonas
McPeak, Bluford
Ziglar, Leonard

Patrick County, Virginia, and Confederate Officials

Gentleman Justices 1861-65

Adams, John S.
Baxter, William D.
Brown, Nicholas
Cassell, Austin J.
Cloud, Martin
Corn, Jesse
Davis, Charles E.
Epperson, Hillary T.
Floyd, William P.
Gates, John W.
Harbour, Marion J.
Houchins, Issac C.
Joyce, James
Martin, William
Nolen, Issac A.
Robertson, James R.
Smith, Thomas
Spencer, Joshua T.
Taylor, James A.
Waller, Edmund
Wood, Asa
Young, Charles H.
Ziglar, Richard M.

Ashworth, Granville H.
Brammer, John W.
Carter, Banes
Clark, Robert M.
Cobb, John R.
Critz, James P.
Davis, Samuel
Epperly, Jesse P.
Frans, Joseph
Giles, Jesse H.
Herd, Claiborne
Hylton, Moses
Joyce, Perrin G.
Noel, John F.
Robertson, David J.
Shelor, Randolph T.
Spencer, Howard D.
Tatum, John G.
Terry, Henry B.
Williams, Sparrell D.
Wood, Richard J.
Ziglar, Reuben

County Officials

Clerk of Circuit Court	Abram Staples	1852 to 1869
Clerk of County Court	Henry Tuggle	1852 to 1869
Commonwealth Attorney	John W. Shelton	1860 to 1864
	Daniel Robertson	1865
	John E. Penn	1865 to 1869
Sheriff	Murray Turner	1860 to 1866
	Rufus Turner	1862

Virginia Officials

Governor	John Letcher	1860 to 1864
	William Smith	1864 to 1865
Virginia State Senators	Christopher Y. Thomas	1859 to 1862
	Peter Saunders Jr.	1863-1864
	Jefferson T. Lawson	1865 to 1868
Virginia House of Delegates	John Staples	1860-1865
Virginia Secession Convention	Samuel G. Staples	1861

Confederate Officials

Confederate Congress (6th District)	John Goode	1861-65
Confederate Senate	Allen T. Caperton	1861-65
	Robert M. T. Hunter	1861-65

Patrick County People in the Southern Claims Commission

In 1871 the United States Congress authorized a commission to "receive, examine and consider the claims of those citizens who remained loyal". Listed below are those persons from Patrick County who applied for one of these claims. Only two were accepted of the thirteen listed. These records are located in the National Archives in Washington, D. C.

Name of Claimant	Commission #	Office Report #		Year	Decision
Creasy, William O.	40909	783	7	1877	D
Cruise, David	2034				B
Dillon, William	17668	724	6	1876	D
Edwards, Joseph H.	7606				B
Hines, Rachel	6449	269	10	1880	D
Light, James	8901		8	1878	A
Nowlen, Christopher C.	1717				B
Rosser, Thomas D.	15180	848	7	1877	D
Sanford, George T.	5703	1288	3	1873	D
Scott, Daniel S.	12536				B
Shelton, Thomas	12917		8	1878	A
Staples, William C.	1701	281	10	1880	D
Stoops, William	6448	862	7	1877	D

Key
D = Disallowed
B = Barred (Submitted after the deadline)
A = Allowed

Robert E. Lee Camp Soldier Home Applications for Admission

BIGGS, Robert T. Company H, 23rd Battalion Virginia Infantry. Enlisted at Patrick County on July 27, 1863. Applied to admission to Lee Home of February 22, 1899 at age 55. Application signed by D. K. Smith and T. G. Tatum. Discharged at his request August 15, 1907.

HEFFLEFINGER, Henry A. Company K, 50th Virginia Infantry. POW, Snickers Gap July 18, 1864. POW, Washington D. C. and Elmira, New York. R. E. Lee Camp Soldier's Home, September 2, 1919. Died, February 9, 1922. Buried Hollywood Cemetery, Richmond.

HUBBARD, Thomas M. Company D, 51st Virginia Infantry. Enlisted in Giles County, but resided in Woolwine, Patrick County, Virginia. POW, Waynesboro, March 2, 1865. Released from Fort Delaware Prison, June 20, 1865 Applied for admission to Lee Home on May 9, 1895 and approved on July 11, 1895.

PENN, Abram C. Company G, 10th Virginia Cavalry. Conscripted from Stella, Patrick County, Virginia, July 27, 1864. WIA, Amelia Court House in April 1865. Applied for admission to Lee Home on February 12, 1914. Discharged at his request September 17, 1914. Reapplied on May 5, 1916, but was rejected.

SCOTT, James G. Company I, 5th Battalion Virginia Reserves. Conscripted at Patrick Court House in June 1864. Born in Patrick County on April 27, 1847. Applied for admission to Lee Home on April 6, 1927. Application signed by J. C. Justice. Discharge at his request on June 14, 1928. Died and buried in Tazewell County, Virginia, on February 8, 1932.

SHELOR, Samuel F. Company C, 51st Virginia Infantry. Applied to Lee Home on August 24, 1909 and entered on November 27, 1912. Application signed by W. T. Akers and Isaac N. Akers. Died on furlough in Roanoke on June 22, 1913.

STOVALL, George W. F. (1845-1902). Company H, 58th Virginia Infantry. Enlisted at Patrick Court House on September 5, 1861. WIA, Fredericksburg, December 13, 1862. Applied for admission to Lee Home on February 15, 1902 due to indigence, age 54.

TERRY, Robert A. Company C, 10th Virginia Heavy Artillery. Enlisted at Jamestown in March 1862. Applied to Lee Home on July 25, 1889, due to Kidney disease, age 69.

United Daughters of the Confederacy Applications

Akers, W. T.
Bowman, W. W.
Coleman, Sam
Craddock, William I.
Dillon, A. M.
Fulcher, Edd
Haden, William
Harman, Essais
Johnson, David
Light, H. C.
Martin, James
Martin, William
Mills, J. L.
Morrison, J. H.
Newman, J. W.
Pigg, P. C.
Rangely, J. E.
Ross, D. Lee
Smith, H. M.
Taylor, W. A.
Via, James R.
Zeigler, William

Ayers, William
Campbell, James P. E.
Collins, Levi P.
Dalton, Isham
Dunkley, S. H.
Gilbert, L. D.
Haden, Seaton
Haymore, D. H.
King, S. B.
Martin, A. W.
Martin, John K.
Mays, A. F.
Montgomery, Mat
Morrison, J. T.
Norman, James C.
Plasters, C. W.
Rangely, J. H.
Rucker, W. B.
Smith, John W.
Terry, N. B.
Via, W. D.

Beasley, R. M.
Clark, Jefferson T.
Craddock, Peter J.
Dehart, Green W.
Fain, Jacob W.
Goard, W.M.
Hall, N. R.
Hundley, William F.
Lawson, W. S.
Martin, D. H.
Martin, W. G.
McPeak, Bell
Montgomery, Floyd
Moss, W. A.
Pace, B. P.
Plasters, William C.
Reynolds, S. B.
Shelton, Arch
Stephens, E. R.
Thompson, William P.
Wiggington, W. J.

Roster of Patrick County Patrol Members

Adams, Isaac
Alley, Zach
Arnold, Moses
Barnes, Shadrach
Bowling, Henry T.
Brammer, John W.
Cabel, Peter
Cannaday, Pleasant
Clark, Joseph M.
Cobb, John R.
Corn, Jess
Critz, Gabriel
Crtiz, William G.
Dalton, John
Deatherage, Frank
Dehart, J. E.
Ferguson, Lafayette
Francis, William
Frans, Joseph
Giles, Jesee
Hanby, D. S.
Harris, James
Hooker, John W.
Hatcher, Rush
Howell, Fountain
Hutts, Owen
Hylton, V.
Joyce, Richard
King, B. S.
Lawson, M. T.
Light, James
Mabe, Mathew
Martin, John H.
Mills, Richard
Moore, H. J.
Nail, John
Newman, Joseph
Nowlin, C. P.
Padgett, Campbell
Penn, Jackson
Penn, Thomas
Plenty, James

Adams, Joshua T.
Anderson, Ben
Ashworth, G. H.
Blackard, Willoughby
Boyd, A.
Brown, Nicholas
Campbell, L. S.
Carter, Banes
Clark, Thomas J.
Conner, Grenville
Corn, Peter
Critz, Harman
Critz, William Jr.
Dalton, Nicholas
Deatherage, John
Doss, Joel A.
Ferguson, B.
Franklin, S. H.
Furney, William
Good, Jess
Hancock, Green
Hatcher, J. W.
Hopkins, William
Hooker, John
Hadnell, Richard
Hylton, Gabriel
Joyce, James
Joyce, Samuel G.
King, George
Lawson, William
McArthur, Perry
Martin, C. J. Jr.
Martin, William
Moir, W. W.
Moore, N. S.
Napier, William A.
Newman, S.
Nowlin, S. F.
Pannill, Joseph
Penn, James A.
Penn, William H.
Powell, William

Allen, A. J.
Andrews, B.
Barnard, William
Bowling, H. L.
Bradley, M. W.
Burnett, Jacob J.
Cannaday, M.
Carter, Madison
Cloud, Martin
Conner, William
Corn, R.
Critz, James
Dalton, James Jr.
Davis, Charles E.
Dehart, Charles
Dunkley, M. R.
Foster, Abram
Frans, George
Gilbert, John
Griffin, William
Hancock, John
Hines, James H.
Hatcher, Burwell
Houchins, J. C.
Hull, Hardin
Hylton, Moses
Joyce, Perrin
Kennerly, Joseph
Koger, William
Lee, William
McCauley, C.
Martin, John
Miles, John
Moore, Hardin F.
Murphy, William
Newman, A. W.
Noel, John F.
Padgit, A. C.
Penn George
Penn, Peter
Penn, Willie
Purdy, Braxton

338

Rangeley, James
Reynolds, H. W.
Richardson, James W.
Robertson, James R.
Ross, H. D.
Rucker, Larkin G.
Shelor, I. B.
Shelton, Thomas
Simpson, W. H.
Smith, Marshall S.
Spencer, James
Spencer, M. S.
Steward, David
Studwall, Rick
Tatum, Thomas B.
Taylor, James
Thomas, Wellington. H.
Tudor, John
Turner, Samuel H.
Vaden, R. W.
Washburn, Thompson
Wood, Asa
Woodall, Lafayette
Ziglar, Leonard

Ratcliff, C. C.
Reynolds, Peter
Robertson, D.A.
Robertson S.T.
Ross, Lee
Satterfield, Anthony
Shelor, R. T. (J)
Shelton, William H.
Smith, Charles
Sneed, Samuel
Spencer, L. D.
Spencer, S. D.
Stoops, William W.
Tatum, James
Tatum, Thomas G.
Taylor, William B.
Thompson, John
Tuggle, Henry
Turner, Samuel G.
Via, Elijah D.
Wellington, Thomas
Wood, John
Wright, Martin
Ziglar, Rueben

Reynolds, A. D.
Richardson, G. A.
Robertson, David
Ross, Charles
Ross, P. R.
Scales, Nathaniel
Shelton, Herbert
Shepherd, Joel
Smith, M. L.
Snow, Samuel
Spencer, Lewis
Spencer, Samuel
Stovall, Joseph
Tatum, John G.
Tatum, William
Terry, R. A.
Trent, Abram
Turner, Rufus
Turner, Stephen
Via, Doctor
Wills, Reed
Wood, Richard J.
Young, C. H.

Free Negroes Conscripted into Confederate Service

Beaver, James (Jarvus)
Fenly, Alice
Givny, Josephus
Johnson, Soloman
Loggin, Edward
Loggin, Jackson
Nelson, Samuel
Phillips, Governor
Rickman, Peter
Steward, Harrison
Steward, Henry
Stuart, Salie
Stuart, Granville
Travis, William H. H.
Vaughan, John

Slave Requisitions by Virginia and Confederate

Name of Owner	1862	1863	1865
Adams, Joshua	1		
Anthony, Mrs. Ben		1	
Auggker, Phillip		1	
Ayres, Martha		1	
Barnard, Isham		1	
Brim, Jospeh		1	
Burwell, William		1	
Carnaday, William		1	
Carter, Madison	1		
Clark, James H.	1	1	
Clark, Jane		1	1
Clark, Robert M.			1
Clark, Thomas M.		1	1
Cobb, John		2	1
Cochram, Edward		1	1
Conner, William		1	
Critz, Gabe		1	
Critz, James P.	1	1	1
Critz, William		1	
Davis, B. A.		1	1
DeHart, Charles	1		
Foster, Abram	5	1	
Frans, Joseph	1		
Gray, David(Daniel)		1	
Hairston, Samuel		3	
Hubbard, Mrs. E.			1
Hubbard, Mrs. John		1	
Hylton, Gabe		1	
Hylton, George	1	1	
Hylton, Valentine			1
Joyce, John		1	
Kennerly, Joseph		2	
King, Ben S.		1	
Langhorn, James S.		1	1
McCabe, Mrs. Mary	1		
Moir, James		1	1
Morrison, Thomas		1	
Murphy, Mrs.		1	
Nelson, Charles	1		
Nowlin, Spencer F.		1	
Parker, John		1	
Penn, George	1		

Penn, Jackson	3	1	1
Penn, James A.	1	1	
Penn, Jane		1	
Penn, Mary		1	1
Penn, Mrs.		1	
Penn, Mrs. James		1	
Penn, Mrs. Gabriel		1	
Penn, Peter		1	
Penn, Polly		1	
Slave Requisitions			
Penn, Thomas	5	1	1
Rangeley, James			1
Reynolds, Hardin W.	5	1	1
Sayars (Sawyers), James			1
Scales, Farmer	1	1	
Spencer, William B.		1	
Staples, Mary	1		
Staples, Mrs. C.	1		
Staples, Samuel G.		1	1
Shelton, Lewis		1	
Smith, Alexander			1
Stovall, Barksdale		4	
Tatum, Edward		1	
Tatum, Pryor		1	1
Tatum, William F.		1	
Thomas, Mrs. Richard	1		
Tuggle, Henry	1	1	1
Turner, E. B.	1		
Via, Alexander C.		2	1
Wilson, Samuel	6	1	2
Ziglar, C.		2	
Zentmeyer, John N.		1	
Total	63	48	19

130 Total Persons

"Brothers in Arms"
Acknowledgments

You could not escape "Jeb" Stuart growing up next door to Zeb Stuart Scales and his son, Stuart, in Ararat, Patrick County, Virginia. The county seat bears his name. His silhouetted image adorned the only bank in Ararat as a logo. Burke Davis brought him to life for me in J. E. B. Stuart, The Last Cavalier at a young age. It was only natural that my love of history, proximity to his birthplace (two miles down the road), and the gifts of many great teachers would lead to this book.

Great teachers bring their subject to life. They do not hoard or guard their knowledge. They share it. Thanks to my teachers at Blue Ridge Elementary School: Inez Cooke, Peggy Marshall, Katie Hiatt, Jeanne Currier, Mattie Young, Maxine Smith, Maybelle Smith, Edward Nester, Librarian Evelyn Powell, teachers I did not have Toni Wray and Ann Radford, Principal Charles Cooke, staff including Philgene Montgomery and the late Margie Hall, who always encouraged me. Thanks to my teachers at Patrick County High School: Fern Agee, Janice Axelson, Ann Belcher, Grandy Biggs, Fred Brim, Phil Dieckhoff, Phyllis Eastridge, Laura Flippin, Marvin Foley, Conrad "Mac" George, Homer Hall, Evelyn Hazelwood, Doug Kapfer, Phyllis Kodenski, Connie Martin, Danny Martin, Glenda Martin, Nelson McConnell, Mike McHone, Mary Lee Mitchell, Tim Parker, Judy Pollard, George Rigney, Peggy Rorrer, Brenda Scott, Paul T. Swails and Rachel Williamson under the leadership of Principal James K. Hiatt.

My first college professor, the late Conrad C. Holcomb, challenged me like none had before. I enjoyed talking history with him, James Hutchens, Carlos Surratt and Marion Venable at Surry Community College. In addition, Pat Barfield, Minnie Hyler, Bill McCachren, Charles Strickland, and John VanHorn deserve mention. Dr. James I. Robertson, Jr. and Dr. Crandall Shifflett of Virginia Tech opened a young man's mind to the history of the Civil War, the South and Appalachia over twenty years ago. George G. Shackelford, a relative of Thomas Jefferson, left his mark then as William C. Davis does today. It is my hope that as Virginia Tech's motto "Ut Prosim" states that I may serve by bringing this history to the reader.

Thanks to C. W. Anglin, Margaret Blackard, Marie T. Bowman, K. D. Cecil, Bobbi Clement, Elizabeth Ann Cruise, Betty A. Earles, Benjamin W. Fulcher, Jr., Ermigene Fulcher, Elizabeth Gillispie, Mildred Hill, Tangie Holcomb, Veril G. Jones, Jim Nowlin, Wilma Padgett, Louise S. Rogers, William S. Rodgers, Jim Spencer, Catheryn S. Vaughn, Cynthia Wilson, Jim Wood, Coy Yeatts and Gentry Zentmeyer for sharing their information.

The letters in the chapter on the 50th Virginia Infantry relating to G. Boston Scott are courtesy of Jerry and Marianne Bayer of Harper's Ferry, West Virginia. Lois Barnard Harris transcribed the letters of the Barnard brothers. They are courtesy of Helen Frazier and Mr. and Mrs. Blaine Barnard. The letters of the Smith brothers are courtesy of Marie T. Bowman. The letter of Tilghman Reynolds is courtesy of Virginia Reynolds Hopkins. The photo of Samuel Dunkley is courtesy of Rick Hudson.

Virginia born, Christopher James Hartley, author of Stuart's Tarheels, and Patricia Walenista, the authority on Turner Ashby, read the entire manuscript twice and continued their friendship through good and bad times. John Cail of the Surry County Civil War Round Table continued his support just like his ancestor in the 54th Virginia Infantry did beside mine in the 17th Tennessee at Chickamauga in 1864.

The staff of the Blue Ridge Regional Library's Bassett Historical Center, the best local history library, led by Patricia Ross with Anne Copeland, Pamela Hollandsworth and Sam Eanes came through every time.

The Lovely Ladies of the Patrick County Clerk's Office, Susan Gasperini along with Tiffany Gregory, Sherri Robertson, Vickie Williams and others have for years shown patience and the best service you could ask for. The Surry and Patrick County Genealogical Societies have supported this project especially Esther Johnson, Kenney Kirkman and David Sheley. Thanks to Marianne and Jerry Bayer, John Chapla, Dr. Peter Carmichael of West Virginia University, The Honorable Martin F. Clark, Jr., Deborah Coalson Goodrich and Miss Deborah Hall of the Martinsville-Henry County Historical Society, offered many positive suggestions. Chris Washburn and members of the Stuart-Wharton Camp Sons of Confederate Veterans read the draft and offered insights that improved this book.

Thanks to the staffs of the Library of Virginia, the Museum of the Confederacy especially John and Ruth Ann Coski, the Virginia Historical Society especially Frances Pollard, Toni Carter and Ham Dozier and the Carol M. Newman Library at Virginia Tech especially Joyce Nester. Dr. James A. Davis, President of Shenandoah University, offered encouragement and his multiple writings on the 51st Virginia Infantry.

Dr. Gary W. Gallagher of the University of Virginia along with National Park Service Historians Robert K. and Robert E. L. Krick assisted in more ways than they will ever know and have for years guided me across every eastern battlefield for the Civil War Education Association. Thanks to Robert Maher and Catherine Boyers at CWEA. I sit with the "feckless awe of a neophyte" in all their presence.

Over the years, the late Charles Baughan shared his knowledge and encouragement. The research especially on the roster and regimental histories of the late Ophus Eugene Pilson along with the mentoring he gave the author made this book possible. His greatness lives in the many people that he shared his time, knowledge and passion for history.

Amy Elizabeth DeBone read this manuscript multiple times, researched pensions online and to quote Thomas Wolfe, "She has more human greatness in her than any woman I've have ever known." Special thanks to the Misses Allyson Nicole Snyder, and Lee Ann Riekehof, along with Adam Christopher Snyder his wife, Lauren Eloise, the parents of Mr. E. C. Snyder and Andrew "Jackson" Snyder and for accepting me in their lives. I view them all favorably.

Growing up under the shadow of the blue-misted mountains, swimming in a river named Ararat on the land of George Guynn was the ideal youth. Thanks to his children Lola, Theodore, Gray, daughters-in-law, Bertie and Louise, my second mothers, all of them are descendants of the first soldier of the Civil War I ever heard of, Private Levi Guynn, Company E, 29th Virginia Infantry.

I first came to Patrick County to live one hundred years after the Presidential Election of 1860. My parents brought me to the same community that J. E. B. Stuart's family lived. Betty Jane Hobbs Perry instilled a love of history in their only child that has only grown over the years. This book, nor the preservation of Laurel Hill, would have occurred without their support. My father, Erie Meredith Perry, the first member of his family to graduate college, spent nearly thirty years educating the youth of Patrick County "The Free State Of Patrick." I dedicate this book to him.

About Thomas D. Perry

J. E. B. Stuart's biographer Emory Thomas describes Tom Perry as "a fine and generous gentleman who grew up near Laurel Hill, where Stuart grew up, has founded J. E. B. Stuart Birthplace and attracted considerable interest in the preservation of Laurel Hill. He has started a symposium series about aspects of Stuart's life to sustain interest in Stuart beyond Ararat, Virginia." Perry graduated Patrick County High School in 1979 and Virginia Tech in 1983 with a Bachelor's Degree in history.

Tom started the J. E. B. Stuart Birthplace in 1990. The non-profit organization has preserved 75 acres of the Stuart property including the house site where J. E. B. Stuart was born on February 6, 1833. Perry wrote the eight interpretive signs about Laurel Hill's history along with the Virginia Civil War Trails sign and the new Virginia Historical Highway Marker in 2002. He spent many years researching traveling all over the nation to find Stuart materials. He continues his work to preserve Stuart's Birthplace producing the Laurel Hill Teacher's Guide for educators and the Laurel Hill Reference Guide for groups.

Tom can be seen on Virginia Public Television's Forgotten Battlefields: The Civil War in Southwest Virginia with his mentor noted Civil War Historian Dr. James I. Robertson, Jr. Perry has begun a collection of papers relating to Stuart and Patrick County history in the Special Collections Department of the Carol M. Newman Library at Virginia Tech under the auspices of the Virginia Center For Civil War Studies.

He is the author of Ascent to Glory, The Genealogy of J. E. B. Stuart, The Free State of Patrick: Patrick County Virginia in the Civil War, J. E. B. Stuart's Birthplace: The History of the Stuart Family and the Laurel Hill Farm, Images of America: Patrick County Virginia and Notes From The Free State Of Patrick.

In 2004, Perry began the Free State Of Patrick Internet History Group, which has become the largest historical organization in the area with over 500 members. It covers Patrick County Virginia and regional history. Tom produces a monthly email newsletter about regional history entitled Notes From The Free State of Patrick that goes from his website **www.freestateofpatrick.com.**

Bibliography

Manuscripts and Original Records

Bassett Historical Center, Blue Ridge Regional Library, Bassett, Virginia
    The O. E. Pilson Collection
    Patrick Countians in the Civil War
    Nettie S. Clifton Roster
    Patrick County Virginia Civil War Pensioners
    Tombstone Inscriptions of Confederate Veterans in Patrick County
    Potential Veterans Buried and Reasons
    Tombstone less Soldiers Believed to be from Patrick County
    Civil War Soldiers Buried in Patrick County
    All Soldiers From Patrick County
    Reunion of Patrick County Soldiers
    Miscellaneous Papers
    Vertical Files
    Civil War File
    Ross Family
    Stoneman's Raid File
    J. E. B. Stuart File
    Publications
    Civil War Pensioners from Henry, Pittsylvania, Franklin and Patrick
    Family Records Complied by William T. Ross. Roanoke, 1973

Duke University
    Green W. Penn Papers.

The Museum of the Confederacy
    Partial Roster and Account Book, Blackhawk Company, Company F 51st Virginia Infantry, 1861.
    Diary of John Hunter, Jr., 1861, Sergeant, 51st Virginia Infantry.
    Speech of August Forsberg to Garland Rodes Camp, UCV, Lynchburg, Virginia 1900.

National Archives and Records Administration
M87 Records of the Commissioners of Claims (Southern Claims Commission).
M324 Compiled Service Records of Confederate Soldiers Who Served in Organizations from the State of Virginia.
M346 Confederate Papers Relating to Citizens or Business Firms.
M1407 Barred and Disallowed Case Files of the Southern Claims Commission.
P2257 Records of the U. S. House of Representatives: Southern Claims Commission.
RG109 Register of Free Negroes Enrolled and Detailed May 1864-January 1865 Chapter 1 Volume 241.

Patrick County Court House
    Order Books 8, 9, 13 and 18
    Supervisor's Order Book 2
    Death Register
    Will Books
    Land Tax Books

Patrick County Historical Society
    Civil War Files
    J. E. B. Stuart Files
    U. D. C. Application File

Surry County Historical Society
    Ruth Minnick Papers

Virginia Historical Society
> William Guerrant Papers
> J. E. B. Stuart Papers
> W. A. Stuart Papers
> Rufus Woolwine Papers
> Early Family Papers

Virginia Polytechnic Institute and State University (Virginia Tech)
> Becker, Gertrude. "Patrick County Virginia in the Civil War." MA, 1990.
> Thomas David Perry Collection.

Library of Virginia (Formerly Virginia State Library)
Accession 36787, Governor John Letcher Executive Papers, Box 29, Folders 1, 2, 3.
Accession 20006, Confederate States of America. War Department. Adjutant and Inspector General's Office
> 51st Virginia Infantry 8-May-1862 – 11-September-1862.

Accession 21700 Confederate States of America.
> 50th Virginia Infantry Regiment

Accession 27684, Virginia Department of Confederate Military Records.
Series II: Unit Records.
Subseries III: Infantry.
Company I, 24th Virginia Infantry . (Box 23, Folder 20).
> > Company E, 29th Virginia Infantry . (Box 24, Folder 17).
> > Company H, 42nd Virginia Infantry . (Box 25, Folder 62).
> > Company K, 50th Virginia Infantry . (Box 27, Folder 9).

Company D, 51st Virginia Infantry . (Box 27, Folder 14).
Company H, 51st Virginia Infantry . (Box 27, Folder 18).
> Subseries V: Reserves.

5th Battalion, Company I Reynolds Company (Box 32, Folder 65).
> > Subseries VI: Home Guard

Patrick County (Box 33, Folder 15).
Series IV: Confederate Rosters 1861-1865.
> Shelf Volume 5 44th-52nd Infantry.

Accession 25307, Rosters, 1861-1865.
24th Virginia Infantry Roster 1861-1865.
51st Virginia Infantry Roster 1861-1865.
50th Virginia Infantry Roster 1861-1865.
Accession 38183 James B. Smart Papers 1862.
Accession 40508 Timberlak Walker Letter of June 2, 1863.
Proceedings of the Virginia State Convention of 1861.
Acts of the Virginia General Assembly 1861-1862.
Index to Virginia Confederate Rosters.
http://ajax.lva.lib.va.us/F/?func=file&file_name=find-b-clas31&local_base=CLAS31
Confederate Disability Applications and Receipts (Artificial Limbs).
http://ajax.lva.lib.va.us/F/?func=file&file_name=find-b-clas11&local_base=CLAS11
Index to Confederate Pension Applications.
http://ajax.lva.lib.va.us/F/?func=file&file_name=find-b-clas10&local_base=CLAS10
Confederate Pension Rolls, Veterans and Widows.
http://lvaimage.lib.va.us/collections/CW.html
Robert E. Lee Camp Confederate Soldiers' Home Applications for Admission
http://ajax.lva.lib.va.us/F/?func=file&file_name=find-b-clas16&local_base=clas16

West Virginia University Library, Archives and Manuscripts Section, West Virginia Collection
> Powell B. Reynolds Papers

Newspapers
The Bull Mountain Bugle [Stuart, Va.]
The Danville Appeal
The Enterprise [Stuart, Va.]
The Martinsville Bulletin [Va.]
The Richmond Dispatch, 1861-1865
The New York Times, 1913

Periodicals
Confederate Veteran, 1892-1932.
Southern Historical Society Papers, 1876-1952.

Articles and Books
Alderman, John P. The 29th Virginia Infantry. Lynchburg, Va.: H. E. Howard, 1989.
Armstrong, Richard L. The 19th and 20th Virginia Cavalry. Lynchburg, Va.: H. E. Howard, 1994.
Armstrong, Richard L. The 26th Virginia Cavalry. Lynchburg, Va.: H. E. Howard, 1994.
Balfour, Daniel T. The 13th Virginia Cavalry. Lynchburg, Va.: H. E. Howard, 1986.
Blackford, W. W. War Years with Jeb Stuart. Baton Rouge, La: LSU, 1993.
Bliss, Aaron T. Record of the Service of Michigan Volunteers in the Civil War 1861-1865. Kalamazoo, Michigan, 1902.
Burnham, W. Dean. Presidential Ballots. New York, 1976.
Burton, Lawrence. Tales of Old Patrick. Stuart, 1999.
Cavanaugh, Michael A. The 6th Virginia Infantry. Lynchburg, Va.: H. E. Howard, 1990.
Chapla, John D. The 42nd Virginia Infantry. Lynchburg, Va.: H. E. Howard, 1983.
Chapla, John D. The 48th Virginia Infantry. Lynchburg, Va.: H. E. Howard, 1989.
Chapla, John D. The 50th Virginia Infantry. Lynchburg, Va.: H. E. Howard, 1997.
Couper, William. The V. M. I. New Market Cadets. Charlottesville, Va.: Michie, 1933.
Current, Richard N., ed. Encyclopedia of the Confederacy. New York: Simon and Schuster, 1993.
Davis, Burke. J.E.B Stuart, The Last Cavalier, New York, 1957.
Davis, James A. "The 51st Regiment, Virginia Volunteers, 1861-1865" West Virginia History 29(3)(April 1968) pp.178-202.
Davis, James A. "The 51st Virginia Infantry, farmers turned soldiers." Journal of the Roanoke Historical Society, v. 8, n. 1, p: 6-11 (Winter 1972). Roanoke, Va.
Davis, James A. "The Footsoldier's Story: Virginia Volunteers in the Civil War from Franklin, Henry and Patrick Counties." Franklin County in the Civil War. Rocky Mount, Va., 1976.
Davis, James A. The 51st Virginia Infantry. Lynchburg, Va.: H. E. Howard, 1984.
Driver, Robert J. Jr. The 10th Virginia Cavalry. Lynchburg, Va.: H. E. Howard, 1992.
Driver, Robert J. Jr. The 24th Virginia Cavalry. Lynchburg, Va.: H. E. Howard, 1995.
Driver, Robert J. Jr. The 52nd Virginia Infantry. Lynchburg, Va.: H. E. Howard, 1986.
Driver, Robert J. Jr. The 58th Virginia Infantry. Lynchburg, Va.: H. E. Howard, 1990.
Edwards, Richard Statistical Gazetteer of Virginia. Richmond, 1855.
Fields, Frank E. Jr. The 28th Virginia Infantry. Lynchburg, Va.: H. E. Howard, 1985.
Frazier, Helen B. and Harris, Lois B. Confederate Soldiers' Letters. Meadows of Dan, Va.: 1989.
Gaines, William H. Biographical Register of Members Virginia State Convention of 1861. Richmond, VA: Virginia State Library, 1969.
Gladstone, William A. United States Colored Troops 1863-1867. Gettysburg Pa.: Thomas Publishing, 1990.
Gregory, G. Howard. The 38th Virginia Infantry. Lynchburg, Va.: H. E. Howard, 1988.

Gunn, Ralph W. The 24th Virginia Infantry . Lynchburg , Va.: H. E. Howard, 1987.
Hadden, Sally E. Slave Patrols: Law and Violence in Virginia and the Carolinas. Cambridge, Ma.: Harvard University Press, 2001.
Hairston , Peter W. ed. "J. E. B. Stuart 's Letters to His Hairston Kin 1850-1855."North Carolina Historical Review 51(3)(July 1974) pp.261-333.
Harris , Nelson. The 17th Virginia Cavalry. Lynchburg , Va.: H. E. Howard, 1994.
Henderson, William D., The 12th Virginia Infantry . Lynchburg , Va.: H. E. Howard, 1984.
Henderson, William D. The 41st Virginia Infantry. Lynchburg , Va.: H. E. Howard, 1986.
Hewett, Janet B. The Roster of Confederate Soldiers 1861-1865. 16 vols. Wilmington, Nc.: Broadfoot, 1995.
Hewett, Janet B. The Roster of Union Soldiers 1861-1865. Wilmington, Nc.: Broadfoot, 1996.
Howard, Oliver Otis. The Autobiography. New York, 1908.
Hunt, Roger D. and Brown , Jack R. Brevet Brigadier Generals in Blue. Gaithersburg, Md.: Olde Soldier Books, 1990.
Hylton , Ora Mae Pilson , comp. Poems by "Bradley" Honorable Daniel Hillsman Wood . Collinsville, 1988.
Ingram , E. Renee. In View of the Great Want of Labor. Westminster MD: Willow Bend Books, 1999.
Jackson , Harry L. First Regiment Engineer Troops PACS. Louisa, Va.: 1998.
James, Anne. Patrick County, Virginia Death Register 1853-1870. Signal Mountain, Tn.: 1991.
Jones , Richard H. Virginia Obsolete Paper Money. Annandale, Va.: 1992.
Jordan, Ervin L. Jr. Black Confederates and Afro-Yankees in Civil War Virginia. Charlottesville , Va.:
University of Virginia Press, 1995.
Jordan, Weymouth T. Jr. and Manarin , Louis H. North Carolina Troops 1861-1865 A Roster. Volumes
15 vols. Raleigh, NC: 1966.
Joslyn, Mauriel. The Biographical Roster of the Immortal 600.Shippensburg, Pa.: White Mane, 1992.
Joslyn, Mauriel. Immortal Captives. Shippensburg, Pa.: White Mane, 1996.
Kirk, Charles H. History of the Fifteenth Pennsylvania Volunteer Cavalry. Philadelphia, 1906.
Kleese, Richard B. The 23rd Virginia Cavalry. Lynchburg , Va.: H. E. Howard, 1996.
Klingbert, Frank W. The Southern Claims Commission. Berkley, Ca.: University of California Press, 1955.
Krick , Robert E. L. Staff Officers in Gray. Chapel Hill, NC: UNC Press, 2003.
Krick , Robert K. Lee 's Colonels. Dayton, OH: Morningside, 1979.
Krick , Robert K. The Smoothbore Volley That Doomed the Confederacy. Baton Rouge: LSU, 2002.
Krick , Robert K. The Gettysburg Death Roster. Dayton, Oh. Morningside, 1981.
Lambert, Dobbie E. The 25th Virginia Cavalry. Lynchburg , Va.: H. E. Howard, 1994.
Leonard, Cynthia M. The General Assembly of Virginia: A Bicentennial Register of Members. Richmond , 1978.
Lowry, Terry D. The 22nd Virginia Infantry. Lynchburg , Va.: H. E. Howard, 1988.
Lowry, Jerry. The 26th Battalion Virginia Infantry . Lynchburg , Va.: H. E. Howard, 1991.
McKinney, Tim. West Virginia Civil War Almanac. Charleston 1998.
McClellan , Henry B. I Rode With J. E. B. Stuart . New York: Da Capo Press, 1994.
Macaluso, Gregory J. Morris , Orange, and King William Artillery. Lynchburg , Va.: H. E. Howard, 1991.

Manarin, Louis H. "The Civil War Diary of Rufus J. Woolwine." The Virginia Magazine of History and Biography, Volume 71, (4) October 1963:416-448.
Martin, Joseph. A New and Comprehensive Gazetteer of Virginia. Richmond, 1835.
Mauriel, Joslyn. The Biographical Roster of the Immortal 600. Shippensburg Pa: White Mane, 1992.
Millhouse, Barbara B. Recollections of Major A. D. Reynolds. Winston-Salem, NC: Reynolda House, 1978.
Mills, Gary B. Civil War Claims in the South An Index. Laguna Hills CA, 1980
Mills, Gary B. Southern Loyalists in the Civil War. Baltimore, 1994
Mitchell, Adele H. The Letters of Major General James E. B. Stuart. 1990.
Moore, Albert B. Conscription and Conflict in the Confederacy. Columbia, 1996.
Murray, J. Ogden. The Immortal Six Hundred. Little Rock Ar.: Eagle Press, 1986.
Musick, Michael P. The 6th Virginia Cavalry. Lynchburg, Va.: H. E. Howard, 1990.
Olson, John E. The 21st Virginia Cavalry. Lynchburg, Va.: H. E. Howard, 1989.
Osborne, Randall and Weaver, Jeffrey C. The Virginia State Rangers and State Line. Lynchburg, Va.: H. E. Howard, 1994.
Patrick County Genealogical Society. Patrick County Heritage Book. Stuart, Va.: 1999.
Patrick County Historical Society. History of Patrick County. Stuart, Va.: 1999
Pedigo, Virginia G. and Lewis G. History of Patrick and Henry Counties Virginia. Baltimore, 1977.
Pilson, Betty A. Confederate Soldiers From Virginia Who Died at Elmira Prison Camp. 1997.
Pilson, Betty and Baughan, Barbara. Alphabetical List of Lands Taxed in Patrick County Virginia.
Pilson and Baughan. Selected Excerpts From Patrick County Virginia Order Books 1&2.
Pilson and Baughan. Miscellaneous and Notes Taken from the Clerk of the Courts Personal Minute Book.
Pilson, O. E. Tombstone Inscriptions of Patrick County, Virginia. Ridgeway, Virginia 1984.
Quarstein, John V. C. S. S. Virginia: Mistress of Hampton Roads. Lynchburg, Va.: H. E. Howard, 2000.
Rankin, Thomas M. The 23rd Virginia Infantry. Lynchburg, Va.: H. E. Howard, 1985.
Rankin, Thomas M. The 37th Virginia Infantry. Lynchburg, Va.: H. E. Howard, 1987.
Reese, George H. ed. Proceedings of the Virginia State Convention of 1861, February 13-May 1.4 vols. Richmond, VA: Virginia State Library, 1965.
Robertson, James I. Jr. Tenting Tonight:The Soldier's Life. Alexandria, Va.:Time-Life, 1984.
Robertson, James I. Jr. Soldiers Blue and Gray. Columbia, SC: University of South Carolina, 1988.
Robertson, James I. Jr. Stonewall Jackson :The Man, The Soldier, The Legend. New York: Simon and Schuster MacMillan, 1997.
Robertson, Rhonda. Patrick County, Virginia muster roll, 1861-1865. Clintwood, Va., 1986.
Rodgers, Mark E. Tracing the Civil War Veteran Pension System in the State of Virginia Entitlement of
Privilege. Lewiston NY: Edwin Mellen Press.
Riggs, Susan A. The 21st Virginia Infantry. Lynchburg, Va.: H. E. Howard, 1991.
Ringold, May S. The Role of the State Legislatures in the Confederacy. Athens, Ga.: University of Georgia, 1966.
Schwab, John C. The Confederate States of America, A Financial and Industrial History of the South During the Civil War. New York: Charles Scribner's and Sons, 1904.
Scott, J. L. The 23rd Battalion Virginia Infantry. Lynchburg, Va.: H. E. Howard, 1991.
Scott, J. L The 34th Virginia Infantry. Lynchburg, Va.: H. E. Howard, 1999.

Scott, J. L. The 36th and 37th Battalions Virginia Cavalry. Lynchburg, Va.: H. E. Howard, 1986.
Scott, J. L. The 36th Virginia Infantry. Lynchburg, Va.: H. E. Howard, 1987.
Scott, J. L. The 45th Virginia Infantry. Lynchburg, Va.: H. E. Howard, 1989.
Scott, J. L. The 60th Virginia Infantry. Lynchburg, Va.: H. E. Howard, 1997.
Scott, Johnny Lee. The 23rd Battalion Virginia Infantry. Lynchburg, Va.: H. E. Howard, 1991.
Scott, Samuel W. and Angel, Samuel P. History of the Thirteenth Regiment Tennessee Volunteer Cavalry. Philadelphia, 1903.
Sherwood, G. L. and Weaver, Jeffrey C. The 54th Virginia Infantry. Lynchburg, Va.: H. E. Howard, 1993.
Simon, John Y. and Stevens, Michael E. New Perspectives on the Civil War: Myths and Realities of the National Conflict. Madison Wi: Madison House, 2000.
Spencer, Cornelia P. The Last Ninety Days of the War in North Carolina. Wilmington NC: Broadfoot, 1993.
Sublett, Charles W. The 57th Virginia Infantry. Lynchburg, Va.: H. E. Howard, 1985.
Taff, Cecil W. and Hartley, Romona T. The Descendants of John "Bennett" Gilbert of Patrick County,
Virginia. 2000.
Thomas, Emory M. Bold Dragoon: The Life of J. E. B. Stuart. New York: Harper and Row, 1986.
Thomason, John W. JEB Stuart. New York, 1930.
Tilley, Nannie M. Reynolds Homestead. Richmond, VA: Robert Kline, 1970.
Trout, Robert J. They Followed the Plume. Mechanicsburg, PA: Stackpole, 1993.
Trowbridge, L. S. "The Stoneman Raid of 1865." Military Order of the Loyal Legion of the United States, 1 (1893).
Turner, Ronald R. Virginia Union Veterans, Eleventh Census of the United States. Manassas, 1994.
Underwood, Willie B. Isaac W. Underwood His Ancestors and Descendants. Baltimore, 1988.
U. S. Government. Congressional Record: Containing the Proceedings and Debates of the 54th Congress, First Session. Vol. 28. Washington, 1896.
U. S. Government. Ninth Census of the United States Statistical of Population. Washington, 1872.
U. S. Government. Eleventh Census of the United States. Schedule of Union Veterans. Washington, 1890.
U. S. Government. Thirteenth Census of the United States Statistical of Population. Washington, 1910.
U. S. War Department. The War of the Rebellion: A Compilation of the Official Records of the Union and
Confederate Armies 128 vols. Washington D. C.: Government Printing Office, 1880-1901.
[Stoneman's Raid, OR, I, 49:pt. 1:323-339. OR, I 47:pt. 3:750]
Van Noppen, Ina W. Stoneman's Last Raid, Raleigh, 1961
Wallace, Lee A. A Guide to Virginia Military Organizations 1861-1865. Lynchburg, Va.: H. E. Howard, 1986.
Wallace, Lee A. Jr. The 3rd Virginia Infantry. Lynchburg, Va.: H. E. Howard, 1986.
Wallace, Lee A. Jr. The 5th Virginia Infantry. Lynchburg, Va.: H. E. Howard, 1988.
Wallace, Lee A. Jr. The 17th Virginia Infantry. Lynchburg, Va.: H. E. Howard, 1990.
Warner, Ezra J. General is Gray. Baton Rouge: LSU, 1959.
Warner, Ezra J. Generals in Blue. Baton Rouge: LSU, 1964.
Warner, Ezra and Yearns, W. Buck. Biographical Register of the Confederate Congress. Baton Rouge, 1975

Weaver , Jeffrey C. Goochland Light, Goochland Turner and Mountain Artillery. Lynchburg, Va.: H. E. Howard, 1994.
Weaver , Jeffrey C. The Virginia Home Guards . Lynchburg , Va.: H. E. Howard, 1996
Weaver , Jeffrey C. The 10th and 19th Battalions of Heavy Artillery. Lynchburg , Va.: H. E. Howard, 1996.
Weaver , Jeffrey C. and Chernault, Tracy. The 18th and 20th Battalions of Virginia Heavy Artillery. Lynchburg , Va.: H. E. Howard, 1995.
Weaver , Jeffrey C. and Patti O. The Reserves. Lynchburg , Va.: H. E. Howard, 2002.
Wiatt, Alex L. The 26th Virginia Infantry. Lynchburg , Va.: H. E. Howard, 1984.
Wiley , Bell Irvin. The Life of Johnny Reb:The Common Soldier of the Union. Baton Rouge, La: LSU, 1980.
Wiley , Bell Irvin. The Life of Billy Yank: The Common Solider of the Confederacy. Baton Rouge, La: LSU, 1981.
Williamson , John P. Fayerdale Industries. Bassett, Va: 1999.
Wilson , Cynthia A. Registration of Free Black People of Colour in Patrick County Virginia. 1998.
Wilson , Cynthia A. Some African American Families of Patrick County Virginia. 1998
Wood , Jim. The Wood Family of Patrick Spring, Virginia, and Their Kinsmen. Beckley, WV: 2001.
Young , William A. Jr. and Patricia C. The 56th Virginia Infantry. Lynchburg , Va.: H. E. Howard, 1990.

Index

1

10th Battalion Virginia Heavy Artillery, 247, 252, 292
10th Virginia Cavalry, 24, 26, 213, 221, 226, 228, 248, 251, 253, 262, 268, 282, 284, 292, 298, 303, 322, 335
119th United States Colored Troops, 168
12th Virginia Infantry, 31, 236, 250, 251, 252, 253, 254, 255, 256, 259, 261, 263, 264, 265, 268, 269, 270, 271, 272, 273, 276, 277, 279, 280, 281, 282, 283, 286, 287, 288, 289, 290, 293, 295, 298, 299, 300, 301, 303, 304, 306, 307, 308, 309, 310, 311, 314, 317, 318, 320, 322
13th Tennessee Cavalry, 162
140th Indiana, 32, 255, 323
15th Pennsylvania, 147, 164
16th North Carolina Infantry, 197, 202, 257
1st Tennessee, 117
1st Tennessee Light Artillery, 162

2

21st North Carolina Infantry, 250, 284, 296, 305
21st Virginia Cavalry, 27, 39, 239, 248, 250, 251, 254, 256, 257, 261, 267, 271, 273, 274, 276, 278, 279, 280, 281, 284, 286, 287, 291, 292, 297, 299, 300, 304, 309, 312, 316
24th Virginia Cavalry, 239, 248, 249, 252, 255, 256, 260, 266, 269, 270, 282, 284, 286, 296, 307, 311, 312, 313, 318, 322
24th Virginia Infantry, 24, 29, 34, 180, 181, 184, 185, 186, 187, 189, 190, 191, 192, 195, 196, 198, 207, 223, 229, 239, 241, 248, 249, 250, 251, 252, 253, 256, 257, 258, 259, 260, 261, 262, 263, 264, 265, 266, 267, 268, 269, 271, 272, 273, 274, 276, 277, 279, 280, 282, 283, 284, 285, 286, 287, 288, 289, 290, 291, 293, 295, 296, 297, 298, 299, 300, 301, 303, 304, 305, 306, 307, 308, 309, 311, 312, 313, 315, 316, 317, 318, 319, 320, 322
24th Virginia Infantry Regiment, 190, 240, 241
25th Virginia Infantry, 263, 293
26th Battalion Virginia Infantry, 247
26th Virginia Cavalry, 254, 258, 260, 263, 300, 309, 310
28th Virginia Infantry, 266
29th Virginia Infantry, 29, 30, 33, 79, 242, 249, 250, 254, 255, 256, 257, 258, 260, 261, 264, 267, 273, 276, 277, 278, 279, 284, 288, 289, 291, 293, 294, 296, 297, 299, 300, 301, 309, 310, 311, 314, 315, 345
2nd Battalion North Carolina Infantry, 255, 261, 270
2nd Cavalry Regiment, 27
2nd Virginia Cavalry, 252

3

30th Battalion, 41, 45, 46, 105, 263
36th Virginia Infantry, 206, 208, 210, 211, 213, 215, 262, 269, 310, 312
3rd Confederate Engineer Troops, 263
3rd Virginia, 119, 201, 288, 315, 316

4

42nd Virginia Infantry, 23, 27, 29, 31, 111, 121, 124, 128, 133, 134, 135, 247, 248, 249, 250, 252, 255, 256, 258, 259, 260, 261, 262, 263, 264, 266, 268, 269, 270, 271, 272, 273, 275, 276, 277, 278, 279, 282, 283, 284, 285, 286, 288, 291, 295, 297, 298, 301, 302, 304, 305, 306, 307, 308, 309, 310, 311, 312, 313, 314, 315, 316, 317, 318, 319, 320, 321
45th Virginia, 14, 45, 59, 184, 253, 256, 267, 268, 283, 297, 319
48th Virginia, 83, 102, 105, 117, 124, 304
49th North Carolina Infantry, 32, 312

5

50th Virginia, 18, 29, 40, 53, 56, 57, 59, 60, 65, 66, 71, 72, 74, 78, 79, 81, 84, 92, 95, 99, 101, 104, 105, 106, 107, 108, 109, 129, 131, 244, 249, 250, 251, 252, 253, 254, 257, 258, 259, 260, 262, 263, 264, 266, 267, 268, 270, 272, 273, 275, 276, 277,

278, 279, 280,訓281, 283, 285, 286, 287, 288, 289, 291, 292, 293, 294, 295, 296, 297, 299, 300, 301, 302, 303, 304, 305, 306, 307, 309, 310, 311, 312, 314, 317, 319, 321, 322, 335, 344
50th Virginia Infantry, 18, 29, 53, 56, 57, 59, 74, 105, 108, 131, 244, 249, 250, 251, 252, 253, 254, 257, 258, 259, 260, 262, 263, 264, 266, 267, 268, 270, 272, 273, 275, 276, 277, 278, 279, 280, 281, 283, 285, 286, 287, 288, 289, 291, 292, 293, 294, 295, 296, 297, 299, 300, 301, 302, 303, 304, 305, 306, 307, 309, 310, 311, 312, 314, 317, 319, 321, 322, 335, 344
51st Virginia, 11, 22, 25, 27, 29, 32, 33, 35, 36, 38, 46, 47, 48, 50, 59, 65, 66, 71, 105, 108, 177, 188, 193, 194, 210, 211, 247, 248, 249, 250, 251, 252, 253, 254, 255, 256, 257, 258, 259, 260, 261, 262, 263, 264, 265, 266, 267, 268, 269, 270, 271, 272, 273, 274, 275, 276, 277, 278, 279, 280, 281, 282, 283, 284, 285, 286, 287, 288, 289, 290, 291, 292, 293, 294, 295, 296, 297, 299, 300, 301, 302, 303, 304, 305, 306, 307, 308, 309, 311, 312, 313, 314, 315, 316, 317, 318, 319, 320, 321, 322, 335, 344
51st Virginia Infantry, 11, 22, 25, 27, 29, 32, 33, 35, 36, 47, 48, 50, 59, 105, 108, 177, 188, 193, 194, 210, 211, 247, 248, 249, 250, 251, 252, 253, 254, 255, 256, 257, 258, 259, 260, 261, 262, 263, 264, 265, 266, 267, 268, 269, 270, 271, 272, 273, 274, 275, 276, 277, 278, 279, 280, 281, 282, 283, 284, 285, 286, 287, 288, 289, 290, 291, 292, 293, 294, 295, 296, 297, 299, 300, 301, 302, 303, 304, 305, 306, 307, 308, 309, 311, 312, 313, 314, 315, 316, 317, 318, 319, 320, 321, 322, 335, 344
51st Virginia Regiment, 29, 71
53rd Infantry Regiment, 27
53rd North Carolina Infantry, 248, 261, 263, 265, 273, 275, 282, 296, 300, 303
54th Virginia, 28, 79, 244, 252, 254, 273, 274, 278, 279, 285, 288, 289, 302, 304, 306, 307, 309, 311, 313, 316, 317, 319, 344
54th Virginia Infantry., 28, 252, 254, 273, 274, 278, 279, 285, 288, 289, 302, 304, 306, 307, 309, 311, 313, 316, 317, 319
57th Virginia Infantry, 255, 263, 286, 299, 302, 303, 309, 312, 317
58 Virginia Infantry, 255
58th Virginia, 24, 26, 27, 30, 125, 244, 249, 250, 251, 252, 254, 255, 257, 258, 259, 262, 263, 264, 265, 266, 268, 269, 270, 272, 273, 274, 277, 278, 279, 282, 283, 284, 285, 288, 289, 290, 291, 292, 293, 294, 295, 296, 297, 298, 299, 300, 302, 303, 305, 307, 308, 310, 311, 313, 315, 316, 320, 321, 322, 335
58th Virginia Infantry, 24, 26, 27, 30, 244, 247, 249, 250, 251, 252, 254, 255, 257, 258, 259, 262, 263, 264, 265, 266, 268, 269, 270, 272, 273, 274, 277, 278, 279, 282, 283, 284, 285, 288, 289, 290, 291, 292, 293, 294, 295, 296, 297, 298, 299, 300, 302, 303, 305, 307, 308, 310, 311, 313, 315, 316, 320, 321, 322, 335
5th Kentucky, 96, 303

6

61st Virginia Infantry, 247
63rd Virginia, 78, 79, 81, 310
64th Virginia Regiment, 183
65th Virginia Infantry, 254
6th Virginia Cavalry, 32, 250, 259
6th Virginia Infantry, 21, 27, 235, 236, 247, 248, 254, 258, 267, 268, 270, 272, 273, 275, 276, 280, 283, 284, 288, 290, 291, 294, 299, 301, 303, 305, 312, 313, 320, 321

8

83rd Pennsylvania, 127, 128
8th Tennessee, 161
8th Virginia, 179

9

93rd New York, 133
9th Tennessee, 162

A

Abell, 247
Ables, 326
Ables, 247
Adam, 330
Adams, 17, 18, 20, 33, 35, 46, 112, 177, 193, 248, 324, 325, 326, 330, 331, 332, 337, 340
Adams, 247, 248
Agee, 29, 46, 122, 177, 325, 326, 330, 343
Agee, 248
Aistrip, 248
Aistrop, 195, 207
Aistrop, 248
Aistrope, 325
Akers, 18, 22, 29, 35, 37, 39, 42, 44, 45, 46, 194, 208, 209, 210, 325, 326, 335, 336
Akers, 248, 249
Albright, 8, 13, 17
Allen, 46
Allen, 249
Alley, 337
Alley, 249
Ames, 107
Anderson, 134, 189, 195, 240, 249, 253, 258, 279, 301, 304, 305, 307, 314, 316, 325, 337
Andersonville, 158
Andrews, 225, 337
Anglin, 10, 19, 21, 193, 326, 331, 343
Anglin, 249
Anthony, 46, 340
Anthony, 249
Antietam, 14, 28, 87, 121, 128, 129, 130, 134, 135, 151, 236, 237, 240, 255, 264, 271, 288, 298, 305
Appomattox, 27, 32, 34, 134, 135, 166, 236, 239, 241, 244, 246, 248, 250, 251, 252, 261, 264, 267, 272, 277, 282, 295, 302, 309, 310, 315, 316, 322
Arander, 326
Ararat, 27, 31, 32, 56, 111, 137, 138, 140, 163, 278, 294, 311, 323, 343, 345, 346
Army Of Northern Virginia, 14, 30, 32, 40, 41, 42, 47, 48, 83, 87, 92, 130, 150, 152, 163, 166, 196, 221, 222, 228, 246
Arnold, 337
Arnold, 249

Arrington, 58, 325, 326
Arrington, 249
Ashby, 32, 125, 147, 344
Ashworth, 15, 332, 337
Atkins, 249
Atkinson, 324
Atkinson, 249
Auggker, 340
Augusta, Georgia, 50, 244, 260
Averell, 40
Averett, 141
Ayers, 324, 325, 330, 336
Ayers, 249, 250
Ayres, 330, 340

B

Baker, 44, 160, 325, 330
Baker, 250
Baliles, 239, 250
Baliles, 250
Banks, 323
Barbour, 250
Barfield, 343, 344
Barksdale, 14, 19, 35, 49, 341
Barnard, 57, 58, 60, 61, 63, 65, 66, 67, 68, 69, 70, 71, 72, 77, 79, 80, 81, 82, 83, 84, 85, 86, 87, 88, 89, 93, 94, 96, 97, 98, 99, 100, 101, 102, 105, 106, 107, 108, 181, 184, 185, 186, 187, 212, 307, 326, 337, 340, 344
Barnard, 250, 251, 252
Barnes, 15, 337
Barnett, 194, 313
Barrett, 251
Barrow, 207, 217
Bartlett, 56, 67, 168
Baughan, 26, 345
Baxter, 332
Bayer, 344
Beach, 325
Beamer, 330
Beasley, 324, 330, 336
Beauregard, 148, 163, 169, 179
Beaver, 11, 138, 142, 144, 340
Becker, 22
Belcher, 324, 325, 326, 330, 343
Belcher, 251
Bell, 9
Belton, 326
Belton, 251
Bennett, 183, 185, 193
Bennett, 251

Benton, 56, 76, 92, 93, 96, 100, 108, 303, 313
Bernard, 252
Biggs, 326, 343
Biggs, 252, 335
Bishop, 171, 326
Bishop, 252
Blackard, 186, 240, 324, 326, 330, 337, 343
Blackard, 252
Blackburn, 331
Blackburn, 252
Blancet, 252
Boaz, 325, 326
Boaz, 252
Bococks, 226
Boling, 64
Bolt, 71, 79, 86, 326
Bolt, 252
Booker, 29, 119, 244, 249
Booker, 252
Boone, North Carolina, 162, 165
Borcke, 149, 152, 197, 202
Boswell, 57, 62, 66, 107, 108, 191, 326
Boswell, 252
Bowers, 252
Bowie, 146
Bowles, 252
Bowling, 18, 38, 46, 71, 72, 194, 213, 324, 330, 337
Bowling, 252, 253
Bowman, 56, 58, 79, 84, 175, 206, 213, 215, 253, 324, 325, 326, 330, 331, 336, 343, 344
Bowman, 253, 254
Boyd, 79, 95, 100, 172, 186, 325, 326, 331, 337
Boyd, 254
Boyers, 344
Boyles, 254
Bradley, 337
Bradley, 254
Brain, 330
Brammer, 15, 208, 325, 332, 337
Brammer, 254, 255
Branch, 12, 21, 32
Branch, 255, 323
Brandy Station, 16, 152, 158
Branson, 255
Bray, 255
Breckenridge, 173, 209
Breckinridge, 9, 29, 41, 42, 43, 74, 208, 209
Brewer, 196, 202

356

Brian, 330
Bridgeman, 255
Brim, 324, 326, 340, 343
Brim, 255
Bristoe Station, 92, 131
Brock, 324
Brock, 255
Broome, 255
Brown, 23, 27, 34, 44, 49, 77, 132, 137, 139, 140, 141, 145, 146, 154, 155, 156, 160, 161, 164, 210, 313, 324, 325, 326, 332, 337
Brown, 255, 256
Bryant, 16, 207, 325, 330
Bryant, 256
Buchanan, 12, 43, 44, 60, 155
Buckner, 40
Bull Run, 148
Burge, 325
Burge, 256
Burgess, 214, 226, 228, 259, 264, 271, 277, 286, 287, 300, 310, 311, 314, 317, 320
Burkhart, 326
Burkhart, 256
Burks, 111, 117, 124
Burnett, 256, 257
Burnside, 41, 151, 152
Burroughs, 46
Burroughs, 257
Burwell, 340
Byrd, 127, 309, 328

C

C. S. S. Virginia, 13
Cabel, 337
Cabell, 19
Cahill, 182
Cail, 344
Calahan, 202
Cales, 330
Callahan, 197
Callahan, 257
Camp Jackson, 36, 57, 58, 59, 64, 66, 74, 75, 76, 77, 105
Camp Nelson, 168
Campbell, 8, 12, 13, 17, 18, 93, 111, 124, 139, 297, 324, 326, 336, 337
Canady, 177
Cannaday, 46, 337
Caperton, 333
Cardinal, 121
Carmichael, 344

357

Carnifex Ferry, 65, 66
Carter, 14, 15, 16, 18, 155, 161, 165, 177, 218, 230, 258, 323, 324, 325, 330, 332, 337, 340, 344
Carter, 257, 258
Cassaday, 258
Cassell, 75, 207, 325, 326, 332
Cassell, 258
Cates, 258
Caty, 330
Cecil, 343
Cedar Creek, 45, 105, 246, 255, 279, 288, 320, 322
Cedar Creek., 45, 255, 288, 322
Cemise, 48
Chambersburg, 44, 87, 90, 239
Chancellorsville, 16, 85, 92, 96, 98, 102, 108, 131, 143, 152, 158, 194, 236, 237, 243, 245, 249, 256, 258, 266, 285, 296, 298, 299, 303, 305, 308, 310, 316, 317, 318
Chandler, 258
Chaney, 326, 327
Chaney, 258
Chapla, 129, 344
Chapman, 78, 252, 276, 324, 330
Chapman, 258
Chappell, 327
Chappell, 258
Charlottesville, 31, 112, 116, 141, 198, 210, 220, 269, 271, 272, 276, 278, 282, 284, 285, 292, 296
Chatman, 330
Chattanooga, 38, 39, 40, 74, 160, 244, 267
Cheat Mountain, 67, 114
Cheeley, 258, 259
Cheely, 46, 175, 193
Chickamauga, 16, 158, 244, 274, 344
Childress, 330
Childress, 259
Chimborazo, 220
Christiansburg, 10, 19, 35, 36, 47, 57, 64, 107, 164, 178, 184, 252
Clark, 10, 14, 19, 20, 24, 46, 92, 100, 155, 171, 186, 188, 189, 230, 324, 325, 327, 330, 332, 336, 337, 340, 344
Clark, 259
Clay, 42, 141, 288, 314
Clement, 304, 327, 330, 331, 343
Clement, 259
Cleveland, 30, 166
Clifton, 171, 189, 287, 325, 327

Clifton, 259, 260
Cloud, 56, 74, 332, 337
Cloud, 260
Coalson, 344
Coan, 226
Cobb, 232, 332, 337, 340
Cobb, 260
Cochram, 340
Cock, 327
Cock, 260
Cockram, 102, 324, 327
Cockram, 260, 261
Cockran, 325, 327, 330
Cole, 228
Coleman, 171, 189, 253, 264, 325, 327, 336
Coleman, 261
College Of William And Mary, 32, 156
Collier, 239
Collins, 325, 327, 330, 336
Collins, 261
Colston, 79, 83, 85, 131
Combs, 261
Compton, 325, 327, 330
Compton, 261
Congressional Medal Of Honor, 101, 160
Conner, 20, 29, 35, 46, 177, 209, 210, 325, 327, 330, 337, 340
Conner, 261, 262
Conners, 118, 177
Conway, 262
Cooke, 145, 149, 150, 155, 201, 202, 343
Cooleemee, 144, 168
Cooper, 180, 325, 330
Cooper, 262
Copeland, 344
Corbin, 130, 325
Corbin, 262
Corey, 202
Corn, 14, 332, 337
Corn, 262
Cornwallis, 138
Coski, 344
Cox, 12, 206, 208, 210, 211, 213, 215, 325
Cox, 262
Craddock, 325, 327, 330, 336
Craddock, 262, 263
Craig, 119, 263, 324, 325
Craig, 263
Crampton's Gap, 236, 291, 313

358

Crampton's Gap, 237, 270, 277, 280, 283
Cranford, 263
Crater, 236, 276, 291, 293
Crawford, 15, 155, 165, 215, 263, 275, 289, 294, 324, 327, 331
Creasey, 21, 327
Creasey, 263
Creasy, 325, 334
Critz, 18, 29, 111, 127, 190, 210, 239, 255, 256, 263, 264, 284, 307, 325, 332, 337, 340
Critz, 263
Croaf, 263
Croaff, 327
Crockett, 140, 239, 253, 314
Croley, 188
Cruise, 10, 35, 46, 177, 301, 324, 327, 334, 343
Cruise, 263
Culpepper, 89, 100
Cummings, 263
Cunningham, 325
Cunningham, 263
Currier, 343
Curtis, 263
Custer, 46, 107, 134, 152, 153

D

Dalton, 31, 127, 171, 191, 207, 240, 324, 325, 327, 330, 336, 337
Dalton, 263, 264
Dan River, 17, 108, 173
Danbury, 164, 165, 166, 168, 170, 171
Danner, 330
Danville, 16, 31, 134, 155, 156, 166, 188, 205, 218, 224, 229, 230, 233, 235, 242, 250, 292, 298, 302, 305, 311, 318, 320
Davis, 7, 10, 11, 17, 19, 20, 29, 35, 46, 48, 50, 57, 59, 68, 106, 141, 145, 166, 167, 169, 235, 255, 266, 280, 325, 332, 337, 340, 343, 344
Davis, 264
Dean, 264
Dearthridge, 83
Deatherage, 325, 337
Deatherage, 264
Debone, 345
Dehart, 33, 324, 325, 327, 330, 336, 337
Dehart, 21, 36, 46, 71, 318, 340
Dehart, 265, 266

Dellenback, 156
Dent, 327
Dent, 266
Dickerson, 33, 57, 79, 102, 324
Dickerson, 266
Dickey, 37
Dieckhoff, 343
Dillard, 37, 214, 259
Dillen, 330
Dillion, 325
Dillon, 230, 324, 334, 336
Dillon, 266
Dison, 327
Dison, 266
Dobson, 163, 170, 297, 311
Dobyns, 48, 239, 323
Dodson, 266
Donathan, 266
Dorman, 206
Doss, 327, 337
Doss, 266
Dowell, 195, 206
Dozier, 90, 92, 103, 344
Draughn, 267
Drewry's Bluff, 198, 236, 265, 271, 285, 286, 297, 311, 315, 316, 318, 319, 320
Droughn, 327
Duggins, 267
Duncan, 84, 324
Duncan, 267
Dungan, 102
Dunkley, 33, 57, 101, 102, 106, 108, 175, 325, 327, 336, 337, 344
Dunkley, 267
Dunn, 59
Durham, 324, 327
Durham, 267

E

Eanes, 344
Earles, 343
Early, 13, 15, 29, 40, 41, 43, 44, 45, 46, 49, 89, 102, 105, 133, 134, 148, 165, 166, 176, 179, 209, 240, 245, 246
East, 267
Easter, 267
Eastridge, 343
Echols, 40, 42, 43, 78, 79, 107, 163
Edens, 267
Edwards, 307, 324, 330, 334
Edwards, 267, 268
Elamsville, 14, 20, 27, 29, 39, 157, 297

Elgin, 268
Elkin, 162
Elliot, 76
Elmira, 34, 47, 101, 106, 107, 108, 248, 250, 251, 253, 263, 264, 265, 268, 270, 275, 278, 279, 285, 287, 288, 289, 290, 291, 292, 293, 297, 299, 300, 301, 303, 306, 307, 308, 309, 310, 311, 313, 316, 321, 326, 335
Emancipation Proclamation, 15
Emberson, 327
Emberson, 268
Emory And Henry College, 39, 75, 141, 259, 262, 281, 282, 289, 301
Epperson, 94, 185, 324, 327, 332
Epperson, 268, 323
Estill, 37
Ewell, 14, 27, 35, 87, 131, 137, 139, 140, 141, 145, 146, 154, 156, 177, 253, 272, 289, 293, 309, 313, 326, 327

F

Fain, 10, 325, 336
Fain, 268
Farley, 149
Farley, 268
Fayerdale, 14
Feagans, 268
Fenly, 11, 340
Ferguson, 239, 337
Ferguson, 268
Ferrell, 325
Ferrell, 268
Ficklen, 205
Fisher, 268
Fisher's Hill, 45, 105, 133, 209, 210, 239, 295
Fitzpatrick, 60
Five Forks, 24, 34, 241, 244, 256, 288, 300, 307, 319, 320
Fleming, 268, 323
Flippin, 343
Flippin, 268
Floyd, 10, 15, 17, 20, 28, 37, 38, 57, 59, 61, 64, 65, 66, 68, 69, 70, 71, 72, 73, 74, 75, 102, 111, 112, 118, 119, 120, 155, 164, 165, 177, 178, 189, 239, 244, 256, 266, 272, 277, 294, 300, 307, 309, 312, 326, 332, 336
Floyd, 268
Folen, 330
Foley, 20, 46, 324, 325, 327, 331, 343

Foley, 269
Ford, 149
Forest, 269
Forsberg, 35, 36, 40, 46, 50, 105, 106, 209
Fort Delaware, 31, 47, 133, 248, 249, 252, 257, 258, 259, 262, 263, 264, 265, 266, 269, 270, 274, 275, 277, 278, 280, 281, 283, 285, 287, 288, 289, 290, 292, 294, 295, 296, 297, 298, 299, 301, 302, 303, 304, 305, 306, 307, 309, 310, 311, 314, 315, 317, 318, 320, 321, 335
Fort Donelson, 11, 34, 38, 49, 53, 72, 73, 108, 109, 253, 257, 274, 275, 299, 306, 307, 309, 310, 314
Fort Fisher, 32
Fort Henry, 38, 72
Fort Leavenworth, 145, 157
Fort Riley, 145, 147
Fort Wise, 9, 147
Foster, 304, 325, 330, 337, 340
Foster, 269
Francis, 337
Francis, 269
Franklin, 269
Frans, 332, 337, 340
Frashure, 22, 245
Frazier, 344
Frazier, 269, 270
Fredericksburg, 42, 80, 83, 84, 86, 89, 130, 151, 152, 158, 237, 240, 245, 259, 270, 271, 272, 274, 279, 282, 285, 292, 307, 308, 313, 320, 321, 322, 335
Freeman, 270
French, 270
Fry, 67, 195, 246, 327
Fry, 270
Fulcher, 245, 301, 324, 325, 327, 336, 343
Fulcher, 270
Furney, 337

G

Gaines Mill, 127, 245, 254, 277, 293, 297
Gallagher, 344
Galloway, 156
Garfield, 30, 242, 244
Garnet, 189
Gates, 32, 63, 332
Gates, 270

360

Gauley Bridge, 66, 68, 69
George, 343
George, 270
Gettysburg, 16, 34, 40, 50, 87, 90, 108, 131, 152, 158, 190, 193, 236, 238, 241, 243, 245, 251, 253, 255, 256, 257, 263, 265, 267, 270, 271, 272, 274, 275, 277, 278, 286, 288, 300, 305, 309, 311, 314, 316, 318, 319, 320, 321
Gilbert, 175, 189, 190, 191, 192, 193, 195, 196, 206, 211, 283, 297, 324, 325, 327, 330, 336, 337
Gilbert, 270, 271
Giles, 20, 39, 74, 79, 137, 213, 235, 247, 254, 255, 290, 299, 308, 325, 332, 335, 337
Giles, 271
Gillem, 159, 160, 162, 164, 165, 169, 170
Gilley, 325, 327
Gilley, 271
Gillispie, 343
Gilly, 324
Gilpin, 271
Givny, 11, 340
Glade Spring, 39, 194
Gleason, 331
Glidewell, 331
Glidewell, 271
Goad, 272
Goard, 325, 336
Goin, 272, 323
Going, 10, 39, 324, 327
Goings, 272
Goins, 272
Gone With The Wind, 7
Good, 337
Goode, 214, 327, 331, 333
Goode, 272
Gordon, 29, 43, 47, 102, 104, 162, 270
Gracie, 143
Grady, 324
Grady, 272
Graham, 272
Grant, 11, 36, 38, 42, 72, 98, 99, 100, 103, 104, 133, 134, 135, 153, 158, 159, 166, 168, 170, 204, 214, 238, 243
Gray, 325, 340
Gray, 272, 323
Greenwood, 272
Gregory, 325, 331, 344
Grehsam, 212

Griffin, 325, 327, 331, 337
Griffin, 272
Griffith, 28, 163, 244, 331
Griffith, 272, 273
Griggs, 193, 324, 325, 327
Griggs, 273
Grogan, 32, 325, 327
Grogan, 273
Guerrant, 184
Guinea Station, 84, 191, 195
Gunnell, 273
Gunter, 173, 207, 324, 325, 327, 330, 331
Gunter, 273
Guslen, 324
Gusler, 327
Gusler, 273
Guynn, 33, 345
Guynn, 273
Gwinn, 324
Gwyn, 163

H

Haden, 325, 327, 336
Haden, 273
Hadnell, 337
Hagerstown, 89, 90, 91, 198
Hagood, 327, 331
Hagood, 273
Hairston, 14, 24, 114, 138, 140, 142, 144, 168, 214, 217, 227, 341
Hairston, 273, 274
Hale, 22
Hale, 274
Haley, 189, 207, 324, 327, 330, 331
Haley, 274
Hall, 46, 63, 324, 325, 327, 331, 336, 343, 344
Hall, 274
Hanby, 14, 102, 327, 337
Hanby, 275
Hancock, 14, 19, 46, 283, 325, 327, 337
Hancock, 275
Handy, 46, 106, 327, 331
Handy, 275
Hanks, 276
Hannah, 59
Hansford, 284, 331
Harbor, 20, 42, 43, 104, 236, 245, 250, 264, 277, 289, 315, 319
Harbour, 35, 194, 209, 290, 324, 325, 327, 330, 331, 332

Harbour, 276
Harden, 57, 267, 268, 272, 274, 282, 288, 302, 310, 317, 331
Hardy, 182, 202, 324
Hardy, 276
Harmon, 276
Harper's Ferry, 47, 89, 90, 129, 146, 209, 344
Harper's Ferry, 47, 146, 147, 245, 292
Harrell, 60, 102, 108, 327, 330
Harrell, 276
Harris, 11, 46, 63, 109, 203, 284, 324, 327, 330, 337, 344
Harris, 276, 277
Harrison, 11, 160, 217, 259, 275, 276, 310, 340
Harrold, 327
Harrold, 277
Hartley, 344
Hatcher, 10, 16, 46, 67, 106, 179, 186, 188, 239, 245, 249, 250, 273, 324, 327, 330, 331, 337
Hatcher, 277, 278
Hawks, 278
Hayden, 273, 327, 331
Hayes, 39, 170
Haymore, 325, 331, 336
Haymore, 278
Haynes, 29, 231, 242, 243, 324, 327, 331
Haynes, 278
Hazelwood, 279
Hazlewood, 324, 325, 327
Headen, 279
Hearboun, 330
Heard, 279
Hefflefinger, 59, 87, 106, 108
Hefflefinger, 279, 335
Helms, 324, 331
Helms, 279
Hendricks, 279
Henry Court House, 203, 205, 224, 226
Hensley, 279
Herd, 332
Heth, 65, 66
Hiatt, 325, 343
Hiatt, 279
Hickman, 11
Higginbotham, 101
High, 279
Highley, 37
Hill, 32, 327, 343
Hill, 279
Hill, A. P., 157

Hines, 327, 334, 337
Hines, 280
Hodges, 37
Hodges, 280
Hogan, 280
Holcomb, 343
Holland, 280
Hollandsworth, 344
Hollandsworth, 280
Holley, 280
Hollingsworth, 280
Holmes, 31
Holt, 68
Holt, 280
Home Guard, 20, 22, 33, 162, 164, 260, 273, 278, 302, 316, 321, 322
Home Guards, 17, 158
Hood, 158, 244
Hooker, 20, 68, 152, 158, 180, 194, 237, 280, 324, 325, 330, 337
Hooker, 280
Hopkins, 21, 46, 325, 337, 344
Hopkins, 280, 281
Horsley, 281
Houchins, 325, 327, 332, 337
Houchins, 281
Houston, 30, 141, 244
Howard, 143
Howell, 21, 46, 102, 195, 325, 337
Howell, 281
Hubbard, 41, 46, 79, 132, 193, 255, 260, 265, 324, 327, 330, 341
Hubbard, 281, 335
Hudnall, 282
Huff, 282
Hughes, 21, 137, 259, 324
Hughes, 282
Hull, 337
Hundley, 324, 327, 336
Hundley, 282
Hungate, 282
Hunley, 282
Hunter, 32, 42, 43, 44, 124, 126, 133, 228, 239, 333
Hurd, 279, 282
Hutchens, 327, 343
Hutcherson, 132
Hutchins, 282
Hutts, 337
Hutts, 282
Hyatt, 324
Hyler, 343

Hylton, 11, 23, 24, 26, 168, 226, 232, 245, 324, 325, 327, 330, 332, 337, 341
Hylton, 282, 283, 323

I

Ingram, 19, 80, 86, 327
Ingram, 283
Ingrum, 324
Ivie, 283

J

J. E. B. Stuart Birthplace, 346
J. E. B. Stuart Birthplace Preservation Trust, 156
Jackson, 11, 16, 32, 33, 67, 85, 96, 116, 123, 124, 126, 127, 129, 130, 131, 134, 147, 148, 151, 152, 157, 158, 160, 179, 188, 194, 225, 237, 239, 245, 250, 256, 259, 261, 262, 272, 274, 278, 280, 286, 289, 295, 301, 304, 306, 311, 312, 314, 318, 319, 321, 337, 340, 341, 345
Jackson, 283
Jacksonville,, 50, 164
James, 283
Janney, 283
Jarrell, 327
Jarrell, 283
Jefferson, 46, 327, 331, 343
Jefferson, 283
Jefferson, Thomas, 43, 267, 286
Jenkins, 283
Jennings, 185, 325
Jennings, 283
Jessup, 327
Jessup, 283
Johnson, 10, 11, 87, 92, 99, 102, 131, 132, 160, 162, 170, 177, 233, 239, 248, 277, 310, 321, 323, 336, 340, 344
Johnson, 283
Johnston, 38, 63, 64, 68, 147, 148, 169, 176, 237, 244, 327
Jones, 7, 16, 40, 41, 83, 92, 101, 102, 127, 129, 130, 131, 133, 182, 201, 206, 343
Jones, 284
Joyce, 10, 15, 172, 324, 326, 327, 328, 332, 337, 341, 344
Joyce, 284
Justice, 284

K

Kasey, 284
Kasy, 324
Keaton, 324, 326, 331
Keaton, 284, 285
Keesling, 285
Keister, 285
Kemper, 34, 240
Kendrick, 328
Kendrick, 285
Kennelly, 285
Kennerly, 111, 112, 337, 341
Kennerlys, 126
Kenyon, 164
Kernstown, 31, 105, 124, 134, 209, 256, 263, 269, 271, 277, 278, 306
Keton, 326
Key, 47
Kibler Valley, 108
Kimball, 285
King, 23, 79, 198, 207, 285, 326, 330, 331, 336, 337, 341
King, 285
Kirkman, 344
Knowles, 46
Knowles,, 285
Koger, 126, 135, 225, 328, 337
Koger, 285, 286
Krick, 344

L

Lac, 11
Lackey, 286
Lacy, 11
Lamb, 286
Lambert, 286
Lancaster, 286
Lane, 85, 115, 124, 126
Langhorn, 341
Langhorne, 117, 124, 126, 196, 231
Lankford, 328
Lankford, 286
Larrance, 331
Latane, 150
Laurel Fork, 17
Laurel Hill, 32, 138, 139, 140, 141, 142, 144, 153, 155, 156, 293, 323, 345, 346
Law, 286
Lawless, 19, 189, 297, 326, 330
Lawless, 286
Lawrence, 324, 326, 330, 331
Lawrence, 286

Lawson, 15, 17, 18, 29, 46, 56, 57, 58, 66, 68, 69, 71, 76, 86, 97, 118, 173, 179, 287, 294, 324, 326, 328, 330, 331, 332, 336, 337
Lawson, 287
Layman, 287
Leak, 287
Leary, 288
Lee, 8, 12, 14, 15, 16, 20, 22, 28, 29, 30, 34, 35, 37, 39, 40, 41, 42, 45, 47, 48, 59, 65, 66, 68, 75, 83, 85, 87, 99, 101, 104, 107, 108, 111, 114, 115, 117, 118, 129, 130, 131, 133, 134, 138, 142, 143, 146, 150, 151, 152, 153, 156, 159, 163, 164, 166, 169,뭐170, 177, 196, 204, 209, 213, 221, 228, 229, 231, 233, 236, 237, 238, 239, 240, 243, 247, 250, 254, 260, 266, 269, 270, 272, 274, 275, 281, 282, 284, 286, 289, 292, 293, 294, 295, 297, 302, 304, 307, 308, 314, 320, 324, 328, 330, 331, 335, 336, 337, 338, 343
Lee, 288
Leigh, 7, 130
Letcher, 9, 14, 15, 17, 18, 137, 138, 139, 150, 156, 245, 332
Lewis, 64, 324, 328, 330
Lewis, 288
Light, 21, 324, 328, 330, 334, 336
Light, 288
Lincoln, 7, 9, 15, 55, 151, 152, 162, 166, 172, 174
Lincoln, Abraham, 215, 227
Lindsey, 288
Logan, 59, 78, 92
Loggin, 11, 340
Lomax, 145
Longstreet, 32, 41, 100, 103, 132, 145, 148, 150, 236, 240, 243
Loring, 39, 40, 68, 78, 114
Lovell, 288
Lovins, 324
Lovyns, 189
Loyd, 324
Loyd, 288
Lusk, 288
Lybrook, 29, 33, 173, 187, 239, 240
Lybrook, 288
Lynchburg, 31, 43, 47, 49, 50, 88, 93, 103, 105, 107, 111, 112, 114, 116, 117, 120, 133, 141, 164, 173, 181, 196, 239, 240, 257, 259, 260, 269, 282, 286, 298, 304, 320, 353

Lyon, 331
Lyon, 288

M

Mabe, 328, 331, 337
Mabe, 288, 289
Madison, James, 87, 131, 261, 321
Maher, 344
Mahone, 236, 237
Mallaby, 162, 165
Malvern Hill, 32, 127, 237, 247
Manarin, 35
Manassas, 14, 59, 61, 64, 91, 93, 112, 121, 129, 134, 148, 151, 176, 189, 236, 237, 240, 245, 263, 267, 269, 273, 284, 291, 294, 296, 303, 308, 316, 320, 322
Mankins, 70, 79, 83, 94
Mankins, 289
Manon, 289
Mansfield, 30
Marsh, 289
Marshall, 343
Marshall, 289
Martin, 19, 33, 46, 56, 61, 74, 114, 124, 126, 188, 214, 221, 233, 254, 259, 263, 267, 312, 324, 326, 328, 330, 331, 332, 336, 337, 338, 343, 344
Martin, 289, 290, 291
Martinsville, 164, 230, 344
Mason, 291
Massey, 326, 328
Massey, 291
Massie, 38
May, 291
Mayo Forge, 111, 135
Mays, 70, 102, 214, 217, 220, 225, 324, 328, 331, 336
Mays, 291
Mcalexander, 328
Mcalexander, 178, 285, 324, 330, 331
Mcalexander, 249, 291, 292
Mcarthur, 337
Mccabe, 328
Mccabe, 341
Mccabe, 292
Mccachren, 343
Mccandlish, 292
Mccausland, 44, 72, 239
Mcclellan, 124, 127, 129, 139, 150, 151, 157, 158, 236, 237, 240
Mcconnell, 343
Mcdonald, 59, 203

Mcdonald, 292
Mcgavoc, 30
Mcgee, 46, 326
Mcgee, 292
Mcgrath, 330, 331
Mchone, 343
Mchone, 292
Mcintosh, 195
Mcintosh, 292
Mckinley, 49
Mcmillan, 293
Mcmillion, 324, 328
Mcpeak, 67, 326, 331, 336
Mcpeak, 293
Meade, 152, 153, 238, 243
Meador, 293
Meadows, 213
Meadows Of Dan, 173, 287
Meredith, 293
Merideth, 330
Middle Creek., 30
Middleburg, 90, 196, 197
Midkiff, 293
Miles, 293
Mill Springs, 38
Miller, 161, 164, 205
Mills, 127, 328, 336, 337
Mills, 293
Mine Run, 92
Minick, 170
Mitchell, 156, 229, 230, 240, 328, 331, 343
Mitchell, 293
Mize, 326, 330
Mize, 293
Moir, 16, 18, 19, 186, 337, 341
Monday, 293
Monocacy, 43, 105
Montgomery, 9, 20, 32, 40, 85, 88, 213, 326, 328, 331, 336, 343
Montgomery, 294
Moomau, 178
Moore, 11, 15, 16, 18, 19, 30, 76, 93, 242, 243, 310, 337
Moore, 294
Moran, 33, 324, 328, 331
Moran, 294
Morgan, 160, 239, 272, 323
Morris, 31, 119, 121
Morrison, 46, 324, 326, 328, 330, 331, 336, 341
Morrison, 294, 295
Morton's Ford, 92, 93, 101, 201
Mosby, 149, 201

Moss, 33, 46, 83, 130, 324, 326, 330, 336
Moss, 295
Mount Airy, North Carolina, 232, 233, 316
Mowbrey Gap, 165
Mundy, 71
Murfreesboro, 32, 72, 73, 74, 244
Murphy, 117, 233, 324, 337, 341
Murphy, 295

N

Napier, 337
Napier, 295
Nelson, 340, 341
Nester, 343, 344
New Market, 31, 33, 42, 43, 45, 49, 105, 215, 298, 300
Newberry, 37
Newman, 84, 102, 277, 328, 336, 337, 344, 346
Newman, 295
Noel, 56, 61, 96, 332, 337
Noel, 295
Nolen, 46, 177, 208, 328, 332
Nolen, 295, 296
Noppen, 169
Norman, 172, 336
Norman, 296
Nowlen, 334
Nowlin, 16, 19, 127, 296, 326, 337, 341, 343
Nowlin, 296
Nunn, 137, 326, 328
Nunn, 296

O

O'hara, 7, 121
Oakley, 296
Oliver, 328
Oliver, 296
Orander, 296
Orange Artillery, 27, 195, 246, 248, 251, 255, 256, 266, 268, 269, 272, 273, 274, 276, 279, 280, 281, 283, 289, 290, 296, 302, 303, 304, 314, 315, 318, 320, 321, 322
Orange Court House, 89, 92, 93, 94, 96, 97, 98, 100, 101, 132, 181
Ord, 149
Ore, 326
Ore, 296
Otey, 29

Oury, 296
Overby, 296
Owens, 328
Owens, 296

P

Pace, 182, 183, 326, 328, 336
Pace, 296
Pack, 324
Pack, 296
Padgett, 328, 331, 337, 343
Padgett, 297
Padgit, 337
Palmer, 160, 162, 163, 164, 169, 170
Palmer, 297
Pannill, 138, 139, 337
Pannill, 297
Parker, 341, 343
Parr, 330
Parsons, 161
Patrick County Notes, 8, 13, 17, 19
Patterson, 12, 94, 148, 162, 251, 261, 272, 321
Patton, 161
Paul, 297
Pearce, 328
Pearce, 297
Pedigo, 297
Pegram, 142
Pelham, 145, 151
Pender, 143
Pendleton, 46, 70, 87, 88, 208, 271, 324, 328, 330
Pendleton, 297, 298
Penn, 10, 14, 16, 19, 23, 24, 29, 31, 111, 112, 113, 115, 116, 117, 119, 120, 121, 122, 123, 124, 125, 126, 127, 129, 130, 131, 132, 133, 135, 172, 203, 204, 214, 217, 221, 223, 224, 225, 227, 228, 229, 232, 233, 245, 269, 332, 337, 341
Penn, 298, 299, 335
Perkins, 14, 59, 67, 105, 137, 144
Perkins, 299
Perry, 3, 255, 273, 337, 345, 346
Peters, 171, 193, 239
Petersburg, 22, 30, 31, 34, 79, 80, 133, 134, 137, 159, 163, 187, 193, 212, 214, 216, 221, 222, 230, 231, 236, 239, 240, 241, 243, 246, 250, 261, 264, 269, 276, 282, 293, 296, 306, 308
Phillips, 11, 340

Philpott, 299
Pickeral, 299
Pickerel, 326
Pickett, 34, 116, 152, 157, 238, 241, 243
Pickurel, 299
Pigg, 46, 326, 328, 330, 331, 336
Pigg, 299
Pike, 324
Pike, 299
Pilson, 8, 247, 345
Pilson, 299
Pinn, 331
Plastens, 324
Plaster, 299
Plasters, 186, 328, 330, 336
Plasters, 299, 300
Pleasanton, 158
Plenty, 182, 193, 337
Poage, 60, 78, 81
Poe, 331
Poe, 300
Point Lookout, 24, 101, 105, 106, 108, 130, 248, 249, 250, 251, 253, 256, 257, 258, 259, 261, 262, 263, 264, 265, 266, 267, 268, 269, 270, 271, 273, 275, 276, 277, 278, 279, 280, 281, 282, 283, 284, 285, 286, 287, 289, 291, 292, 293, 295, 296, 297, 298, 300, 301, 305, 306, 307, 308, 309, 310, 311, 314, 315, 317, 319, 320, 321
Pointer, 104, 105, 147
Pollard, 343, 344
Poole, 11
Poore, 300
Port Republic, 125, 245
Porter, 300
Powell, 56, 92, 96, 100, 108, 165, 282, 303, 328, 337, 343
Powell, 300
Pratt, 328
Pratt, 300
Price, 17, 35, 118
Price, 300
Pruitt, 328
Pruitt, 300
Pryor, 81, 175, 341
Pucket, 63, 69, 324, 331
Puckett, 56, 64, 70, 84, 102, 130, 326, 328
Puckett, 300, 301, 323
Purdy, 120, 134, 135, 326, 337
Purdy, 301

R

Radford, 47, 189, 328, 343
Radford, 301
Rakes, 46, 210, 324, 326, 328, 330, 331
Rakes, 301
Randolph Macon, 111
Randolph-Macon, 30, 32, 244
Rangeley, 11, 74, 328, 338, 341
Rangeley, 302
Rangely, 336
Rangley, 80, 82, 102
Rapidan, 92, 101, 131, 132, 238
Rappahannock, 83, 130, 194, 238
Ratcliff, 326, 338
Ratliff, 216
Ratliff, 302
Ray, 121, 324, 331
Ray, 302
Red Hill, Alabama, 160
Reed, 302
Regan, 162
Reston, 302
Reynolds, 10, 12, 15, 18, 19, 22, 23, 24, 46, 49, 56, 57, 59, 69, 70, 73, 74, 92, 93, 96, 100, 103, 108, 140, 167, 168, 235, 302, 324, 328, 330, 331, 336, 338, 341, 344
Reynolds, 302, 303, 323
Reynolds Homestead, 12, 352
Richardson, 63, 106, 338
Richardson, 303
Richmond, 9, 17, 18, 21, 23, 27, 31, 34, 42, 45, 48, 49, 59, 62, 72, 76, 78, 79, 80, 98, 100, 102, 104, 105, 116, 124, 133, 134, 137, 138, 144, 146, 150, 153, 154, 155, 158, 160, 163, 174, 180, 181, 185, 186, 187, 188, 191, 197, 201, 204, 205, 206, 214, 216, 218, 219, 220, 229, 230, 233, 236, 237, 238, 240, 241, 243, 245, 251, 252, 253, 254, 255, 256, 266, 268, 270, 271, 272, 275, 277, 278, 279, 280, 281, 286, 290, 292, 293, 296, 299, 301, 306, 310, 312, 315, 317, 318, 319, 322, 335
Rickman, 11, 340
Rickman, 303
Riekehof, 345
Right, 324
Rigney, 343
Roberson, 46, 326, 328
Roberson, 303
Roberts, 70, 194, 330, 331
Roberts, 303
Robertson, 19, 38, 93, 96, 330, 331, 332, 338, 343, 344, 346
Robertson, 303, 304
Rock Spring, 12, 24, 167
Rodes, 50, 99, 100
Rogers, 19, 21, 188, 331, 343
Rogers, 304
Rorrer, 16, 21, 46, 194, 195, 197, 202, 208, 324, 326, 328, 331, 343
Rorrer, 304
Rose,, 304
Roser, 331
Ross, 11, 14, 19, 20, 29, 35, 36, 37, 39, 46, 50, 118, 176, 177, 178, 192, 193, 194, 210, 211, 249, 324, 326, 328, 336, 338, 344
Ross, 304, 305
Rosser, 113, 202, 331, 334
Rucker, 16, 19, 155, 330, 336, 338
Rucker, 305
Rutledge, 305

S

Salisbury, 158, 159, 163, 168, 169, 170
Salmon, 305
Salmons, 46, 328
Salmons, 305
Saltville, 12, 17, 20, 39, 40, 155, 156, 158, 258
Salyer, 59, 78, 87, 92
Sanders, 305
Sanderson, 305
Sandifer, 305
Sanford, 334
Satterfield, 338
Saunders, 175, 304, 332
Saunders, 305, 306
Sawyers, 10, 311, 324, 341
Sawyers, 306
Sayers, 306
Scales, 197, 244, 338, 341, 343
Scales, 306
Schoepf, 47
Schofield, 158, 201, 214
Scoles, 203
Scott, 21, 23, 24, 39, 46, 47, 57, 61, 64, 65, 67, 68, 69, 70, 71, 74, 88, 93, 97, 101, 104, 142, 143, 201, 328, 334, 343, 344
Scott, 306, 307, 335
Seddon, 19, 20
Sedgwick, 145

Semones, 307
Setliff, 313
Seven Days, 14, 134, 158, 245
Seven Pines, 237, 240, 256, 259, 266, 287, 288, 299, 301, 311, 312
Shackelford, 343
Sharp, 307
Sheffield, 307
Sheley, 344
Shelor, 74, 76, 77, 106, 324, 326, 328, 331, 332, 338
Shelor, 307, 335
Shelton, 10, 12, 16, 21, 112, 307, 308, 324, 326, 328, 331, 332, 334, 336, 338, 341
Shelton, 307, 308, 309, 323
Shepherd, 338
Sheppard, 309
Sheridan, 32, 44, 45, 46, 133, 143, 153, 154, 246
Sherman, 158, 159, 169, 176, 227, 231, 233
Shiveley, 324
Shively, 309
Shockley, 326
Shough, 309
Shriver, 101
Simms, 309
Simonson, 144
Simpson, 328, 338
Simpson,, 309
Slaughter, 309
Slaves, 9, 10, 11, 12, 14, 15, 19, 22, 31, 137, 139, 140, 162, 168, 204, 219
Smart, 11
Smart, 309
Smith, 14, 18, 28, 29, 30, 35, 56, 57, 58, 67, 69, 70, 78, 79, 80, 81, 83, 84, 85, 86, 89, 97, 108, 124, 126, 133, 146, 160, 171, 175, 208, 209, 233, 238, 271, 324, 326, 328, 330, 331, 332, 335, 336, 338, 341, 343, 344
Smith, 309, 310
Smiths, 233
Smyth, 59, 60, 242
Sneed, 338
Snow, 338
Snow, 310
Snyder, 345
Sowder, 326
Sowder, 311
Soyar, 106
Soyars, 10, 324
Soyars, 311

Soyers, 328
Spain, 311
Spangler, 57, 63, 67, 68, 69, 78, 104, 108, 326, 328, 331
Spangler, 311
Spangley, 325
Spence, 328
Spence, 311
Spencer, 127, 189, 260, 270, 325, 326, 332, 338, 341, 343
Spencer, 311, 312
Spotsylvania, 31, 53, 101, 102, 103, 105, 108, 133, 153, 238, 245, 249, 250, 257, 258, 263, 264, 266, 267, 270, 277, 278, 279, 281, 285, 287, 289, 294, 296, 297, 299, 300, 305, 306, 307, 308, 309, 310, 316, 320, 321, 322
Stanley, 312
Staples, 9, 13, 16, 17, 19, 20, 22, 32, 56, 61, 74, 100, 140, 167, 203, 212, 214, 218, 233, 330, 331, 332, 333, 334, 341
Staples, 312
Staunton, Virginia, 40, 41, 43, 44, 47, 111, 112, 123, 125, 126, 127, 145, 155, 206, 210, 216, 244, 249, 250, 262, 263, 272, 282, 283, 284, 288, 295, 302
Stedman, 32, 47, 49, 112
Stedman, 312
Stephens, 328, 331, 336
Stephens, 312
Stephenson's Depot, 44
Sterling, 8, 13, 17, 242
Stevens, 312
Steward, 11, 202, 338, 340
Stewart, 11, 102, 145, 255, 326
Stewart, 313
Stone, 14, 183, 319, 328
Stone,, 312
Stoneman, 8, 14, 21, 24, 33, 107, 157, 158, 159, 160, 162, 163, 164, 165, 166, 168, 169, 170
Stoops, 21, 334, 338
Stoops, 312
Stovall, 14, 18, 19, 21, 124, 193, 211, 235, 326, 338, 341
Stovall, 313, 335
Stow, 331
Stowe, 313
Strickland, 343
Stringfellow, 149

Stuart, 9, 11, 12, 16, 27, 30, 32, 33, 35, 42, 49, 50, 85, 102, 103, 112, 129, 131, 137, 138, 139, 140, 141, 142, 143, 144, 145, 146, 147, 148, 149, 150, 151, 152, 153, 154, 155, 156, 158, 162, 164, 165, 197, 201, 202, 226, 237, 245, 247, 273, 274, 277, 293, 296, 312, 313, 318, 323, 340, 343, 344, 345, 346
Stuart, 313
Stuart, Flora, 158, 196
Stuart, J. E. B., 8, 9, 12, 14, 140, 143, 148, 154, 155, 156, 343, 346
Stuart, William A., 12, 140, 153, 155, 202
Studwall, 338
Sumner, 145
Sumner, 313
Surratt, 343
Sutleff, 313
Swails, 343
Swanson, 165, 166

T

Taliaferro, 130, 205, 206
Tate, 313
Tatum, 19, 46, 115, 122, 168, 171, 173, 233, 294, 328, 332, 335, 338, 341
Tatum, 313, 323
Taylor, 20, 141, 157, 182, 207, 270, 287, 291, 315, 316, 325, 328, 330, 332, 336, 338
Taylor, 313, 314
Taylorsville, 9, 10, 18, 29, 140, 156, 164, 165, 169, 203, 204, 259, 312
Terrell, 30, 112, 113
Terrell, 314
Terry, 11, 14, 18, 35, 58, 82, 86, 94, 102, 105, 178, 193, 240, 308, 325, 326, 328, 331, 332, 336, 338
Terry,, 314, 335
Thomas, 46, 125, 326, 328, 332, 338, 341, 346
Thomas, 314, 315
Thompson, 23, 56, 60, 76, 122, 248, 287, 329, 331, 336, 338
Thompson, 315, 316
Tidmarsh, 316
Tilghman, 63, 69, 74, 303, 344
Tilley, 325
Tilley, 316
Travis, 11, 340
Trent, 326, 329, 338

368

Trent, 316
Tuck, 316
Tudor, 20, 338
Tuggle, 10, 19, 36, 37, 189, 193, 325, 326, 329, 332, 338, 342
Tuggle, 316
Tullahoma, 160
Turner, 10, 15, 16, 19, 23, 28, 46, 147, 155, 165, 176, 183, 191, 215, 239, 303, 326, 329, 332, 338, 342
Turner, 316, 317
Twiggs, 56

U

Underwood, 20, 31, 63, 330
Underwood, 317
University Of Virginia, 32, 111, 141, 344
Upperville, 197
Upton, 102

V

Vaden, 297, 338
Vandeventer, 59, 78, 83
Vanhorn, 343
Vaughan, 11, 340
Vaughan, 317
Vaughn, 10, 37, 74, 193, 326, 343
Venable, 343
Via, 8, 37, 46, 49, 50, 112, 194, 326, 329, 336, 338, 342
Via, 318
Vipperman, 318
Virginia Military Institute, 15, 18, 31, 36, 42, 43, 111, 147, 155
Virginia Reserves, 18, 27, 211, 235, 248, 249, 250, 251, 253, 254, 257, 258, 259, 261, 262, 264, 265, 266, 267, 268, 269, 270, 271, 273, 274, 275, 278, 280, 281, 283, 284, 285, 286, 289, 290, 291, 292, 293, 294, 295, 296, 297, 299, 302, 303, 304, 305, 306, 307, 309, 311, 312, 313, 314, 315, 316, 320, 321, 322, 335
Virginia Tech, 22, 47, 135, 145, 343, 344, 346

W

Wade, 57
Walker, 24, 102, 258, 295
Waller, 218, 252, 275, 327, 332
Waller, 318, 319

War Between The States, 7
Washburn, 23, 37, 122, 210, 338, 344
Washburn, 319
Washington, 319
Washington, D. C., 33, 104, 334
Waynesboro, 46, 47, 107, 134, 206, 210, 248, 249, 252, 257, 259, 262, 263, 264, 265, 266, 269, 274, 275, 277, 280, 281, 283, 285, 287, 289, 290, 292, 294, 295, 297, 299, 301, 302, 303, 305, 306, 307, 309, 311, 315, 317, 318, 321, 335
Weaver, 33, 168, 329
Weaver, 319
Webb, 319
Webster, 141
Wells, 31
Werth, 14, 184
Werth, 319
West, 326, 329
West, 319
Whaling, 319
Wharton, 29, 33, 37, 38, 39, 40, 41, 43, 45, 46, 47, 105, 209, 344
White, 319
White Sulphur Springs, 39, 66, 67, 68, 69, 70, 71, 286, 287, 313
Whitlock, 210, 326, 329
Whitlock, 319
Wickham, 326
Wickham, 319
Wiggenton, 325, 331
Wiggington, 207, 336
Wiggington, 319
Wigginton, 189, 326, 329
Wilcox, 32
Wilderness, 42, 101, 103, 108, 133, 153, 236, 238, 245, 251, 260, 272, 273, 275, 276, 284, 298, 301, 305
Wiley, 253
Willard, 325, 326, 329
Willard, 319
Williams, 46, 79, 144, 326, 329, 330, 332, 344
Williams, 319, 320
Williamsburg, 31, 144, 240, 259, 271, 286, 288, 289, 308, 312, 319
Williamson, 343
Williamsport, 91, 293, 305
Willis, 320
Willis Church, 127
Wilson, 14, 50, 59, 93, 140, 166, 287, 298, 319, 326, 342, 343
Wimbish, 320

Wimbush, 33
Winchester, 40, 43, 44, 45, 47, 89, 90, 91, 105, 123, 124, 126, 148, 190, 207, 208, 209, 210, 237, 239, 246, 248, 250, 251, 256, 257, 258, 259, 261, 264, 268, 270, 274, 281, 282, 283, 286, 290, 291, 297, 301, 305, 307, 308, 314, 317, 319, 320, 321
Wingfield, 119, 245
Winginton, 189
Wise, 140
Witcher, 101
Withers, 125, 129, 131, 133
Witt, 137, 304, 305, 326
Wolfe, 37, 41, 42, 44, 345
Wolfe, 320
Wood, 10, 15, 18, 109, 187, 188, 254, 325, 329, 331, 332, 338, 343
Wood, 320, 321
Woodall, 329, 338
Woodall, 321
Woodes, 325
Woods, 321
Woolwine, 8, 18, 25, 29, 33, 34, 35, 36, 37, 38, 39, 40, 41, 42, 43, 44, 45, 46, 47, 48, 49, 50, 51, 52, 193, 210, 329, 330, 335
Woolwine, 321
Wooton, 183, 214
Worf, 321
Wray, 343
Wright, 180, 325, 326, 329, 338
Wright, 321, 322
Wytheville, 35, 36, 57, 58, 59, 60, 61, 63, 64, 69, 70, 74, 75, 105, 140, 155, 164, 194, 239, 243, 254, 274, 291

Y

Yadkin River, 162, 217
Yankee, 29, 32, 59, 68, 73, 84, 89, 98, 99, 103, 150, 158, 162, 163, 168, 169, 176, 182, 188, 196, 197, 201, 204, 209, 217, 219
Yankees, 24, 59, 61, 62, 65, 66, 67, 68, 69, 70, 76, 84, 91, 93, 94, 95, 101, 102, 103, 107, 115, 130, 132, 148, 149, 163, 168, 173, 176, 179, 182, 186, 187, 188, 189, 194, 208, 209, 210, 213, 217, 221, 226, 228, 232, 350
Yankeys, 119, 126, 128
Yates, 330, 331
Yates, 322

Yeatts, 63, 93, 108, 325, 326, 329, 343
Yeatts, 322
Yellow Tavern, 32, 153, 259
Young, 12, 36, 37, 140, 158, 217, 230, 329, 332, 338, 343
Young, 322

Z

Zeigler, 326, 336
Zeigler, 322
Zentmeyer, 120, 121, 122, 218, 224, 226, 229, 230, 342, 343
Zentmeyer, 322
Ziglar, 15, 325, 331, 332, 338, 342
Ziglar, 322
Zigler, 331
Zollicoffer, 38, 279

Made in the USA
Columbia, SC
14 November 2018